HOW THE INDIANS LOST THEIR LAND

HOW THE INDIANS

⇒ LOST ⇐

THEIR LAND

*Law and Power
on the Frontier*

STUART BANNER

THE BELKNAP PRESS OF
HARVARD UNIVERSITY PRESS
Cambridge, Massachusetts
London, England
2005

Copyright © 2005 by the President and Fellows of Harvard College
All rights reserved
Printed in the United States of America

Library of Congress Cataloging-in-Publication Data

Banner, Stuart, 1963–
How the Indians lost their land :
law and power on the frontier / Stuart Banner.
p. cm.
Includes bibliographical references and index.
ISBN 0-674-01871-0 (alk. paper)
1. Indians of North America—Land tenure.
2. Indians of North America—Legal status, laws, etc.
3. Indians of North America—Government relations.
4. Indian land transfers—United States—History.
5. Property—United States.
6. Land tenure—Law and legislation—United States.
7. Land tenure—Government policy—United States.
8. United States—Politics and government.
9. United states—Race relations.   I. Title.
E98.L3B36 2005
333.2—dc22   2005043617

Designed by Gwen Nefsky Frankfeldt

CONTENTS

How the Indians Lost Their Land

INTRODUCTION

BETWEEN the early seventeenth century and the early twentieth century, almost all the land in the present-day United States was transferred from American Indians to non-Indians. But how did that happen? Did the Indians sell it? Was it taken from them by conquest? Or does the truth lie somewhere in the middle? And where exactly *is* the middle? The answers to these questions are not simple. Even to say *why* they are not simple requires some explanation.

Several years ago a student asked me whether the Indians sold their land or had it taken from them, and I responded with the offhand answer I suspect many would give. There were transactions called "treaties," I explained, but of course they weren't genuine contracts, because the Indians didn't *consent* to sell their land. Indians had different conceptions of property than European settlers had, I said, so they couldn't have understood what the settlers meant by a sale. The Indians were really conquered by force, I told the student, but Americans and their British colonial predecessors papered over their conquest with these documents to make the process look proper and legal.

The student seemed satisfied with my answer, but it bothered me even as I was giving it. For one thing, my explanation was internally inconsistent. Were the Indians *tricked* into selling their land? Or were they *forced* into selling it? Either way, moreover, my answer seemed to require implausibly pliable Indians. Was it true that the Indians didn't know what the settlers meant by a sale? Many land transactions occurred in places where there had already been considerable contact between Indians and settlers. Shouldn't the Indians have been able to figure out the consequences of a land sale, especially if it was not the first sale in the area? If so, why would the Indians keep on signing? What was the relationship between violence and land transfer?

When I tried to imagine myself as an Indian or a settler, I only became more confused. If I had lots of land, and I wanted to obtain useful things like guns or tools, why *wouldn't* I sell some land? What else could I sell? Was I too quick to assume that the Indians could not have consented to sell their land? If the transactions were unfair to the Indians, might that unfairness have been manifested, not in whether or not land was sold, but rather in the quantities that were sold or the prices the sellers received? And if I were a settler planning to seize the Indians' land, why would I go to the trouble of tricking or forcing them into signing a piece of paper? What kind of conqueror takes such care to keep up the appearance that no conquest is taking place? Indeed, if land was cheap and conquest dangerous, wouldn't I prefer paying a little money to risking my life? Could Anglo-Americans really have been so much bolder or more miserly in the past? If settlers purchased land from the Indians because that was easier than seizing it, was there still something inauthentic about the transactions? Or was I being too quick to assume that they could not have genuinely intended to buy the Indians' land?

I was also bothered by the timeless and regionless quality of my response. I was implicitly lumping transactions from the 1600s and the 1900s together in a single category, as if nothing had changed in more than three hundred years, and as if events in Rhode Island and Georgia, Minnesota and Arizona, all happened in the same way. Did methods of land transfer change over time? Did they vary between parts of the country? Similarly, I was lumping all "Indians" and all "settlers" together as character types rather than seeing them as diverse groups of people with a wide range of interests and motivations. American historiography was once populated by noble settlers and savage Indians; now, more often than not, it is populated by noble Indians and savage settlers. I wondered whether there might be a more intelligible story to be told in which whites disagreed among themselves over whether and how to acquire land, and in which Indians disagreed among themselves over whether and how to sell it.

The more I read, the more inconsistencies I discovered in what has been written on the subject. Histories of British colonial Indian policy, for instance, often describe a world in which settlers believed they had a right to take land away from Indians by force. Some of these very same histories, however, include accounts of land purchases, transactions that at first sight are hard to square with a belief in a right of conquest. The law of the past as recounted in court opinions, to pick another example, sometimes looks very different from the way it has been described by historians. I found myself wishing for a book that would synthesize all this material into a comprehensible whole.

These inconsistencies arise, I think, because much of what has been written on Indian land acquisition implicitly assumes that conquest and sale are mutually exclusive alternatives that exhaust the possible methods of land transfer. Most often this assumption takes the form of straightforward descriptions of the acquisition of land by one method or the other, either as a simple conquest, with no suggestion that the transaction involved any free will on the part of the Indians, or as a simple purchase, with no suggestion that any element of compulsion was involved. It can also take the form of an implicit claim that by rejecting one method the author has proven the other. Sometimes an author suggests that because a given transaction or set of transactions involved no force on the part of the buyers, the land was purchased fair and square. Sometimes an author points out that a given transaction included egregious fraud on the part of the purchasers, or the presence of armed men within the sight of the sellers, and concludes that the Indians must have sold the land against their will. These styles of argument all rest on the mistaken assumption that land transfers can be categorized dichotomously as either voluntary or involuntary, as instances of either contract or conquest.

As analysts of the legal system have pointed out for some time, however, there is no sharp distinction between voluntariness and involuntariness. The difference between them is one of degree, not kind. All human activity is performed under constraints. These may vary in their strength, but there is no point at which one can say that constraints have become so confining as to tip an action from one category into the other. In deciding whether to enter into employment contracts, for instance, workers are constrained by their need to earn money to obtain food, by the range of jobs within commuting distance of their homes, by the educational opportunities they had when they were young, by the state of the economy, and so on. Their decision to sign the contract is voluntary in some senses and involuntary in others. We can say the same thing about transactions in Indian land. Any given decision on the part of Indians to sell land, like any decision made by anyone about any subject, may be more or less voluntary, along a continuum that lacks any dividing line between categories. There is a large middle ground between conquest and contract.

This idea of a spectrum bounded by poles of conquest and contract is helpful, I think, in understanding how the Indians lost their land. At most times, and in most places, the Indians were not exactly conquered, but they did not exactly choose to sell their land either. The truth was somewhere in the middle. The interesting question about Indian land sales is not whether they were voluntary or involuntary, but where they were located within that middle ground at any given time or place.

To put the matter in perhaps a more useful way, every land transfer of any form included elements of *law* and elements of *power.* No non-Indian acquiring Indian land thought himself unconstrained by Anglo-American law. Whites always acquired Indian land within a legal framework of their own construction. Law was always present, but so was power. The more powerful whites became relative to Indians, the more they were able to mold the legal system to produce outcomes in their favor—more sales, of larger tracts, at lower prices than would have existed had power relationships been more equal.

From the Indians' perspective, the overarching story from the early seventeenth to the early twentieth century is thus one of decline. In the seventeenth century, when Indians and whites were close to equally powerful, transactions in Indian land often increased the well-being of both sides. These early land sales were as close to the "contract" end of the continuum as they would ever be. As time went on, the power relationship between the two sides became more and more lopsided, and transactions moved ever closer to the "conquest" end. By the late nineteenth century, there was little pretense that land cessions were voluntary in any meaningful sense of the word, even as they retained the form of negotiated treaties.

Even then, however, the law was not meaningless. As the legal system came to express non-Indians' power over Indians, it nevertheless continued to constrain the way non-Indians acquired Indian land. Settlers on the frontier and the local governments accountable to them often pressed against the limits of that framework (and sometimes passed over them) in their eagerness to get the Indians' land, but at all times there were influential people, first in London and then in Washington, who were genuinely interested in protecting the Indians from settlers. There has always been a tension between the capital and the frontier, between the center and the periphery. Even in the darkest period of set-tler–Indian relations, the formal law has had some bearing on events. And today, when Indians are sometimes able to win redress for the misdeeds of the past, the law of the past is still relevant—in some cases even more relevant than it was at the time—because it is still the standard by which the actions of the past are measured within the legal system. Thus there are two parallel stories to tell: one about how the Indians actually lost their land, and another about the law that in principle governed how the Indians were to lose their land. Neither story can be understood without the other.

Formal law and actual practice could diverge, sometimes quite markedly, because policies conceived in the capital have always needed to be implemented on the frontier by local officials with the capacity to subvert the intentions of easterners. The Indian land policy in effect at any given time was determined only in part by the balance of power between whites and Indians. It was also largely determined by the balance of power between eastern whites and western whites, and by the communication and transportation technologies through which officials in the capital could (or could not) constrain their agents in the field. At almost every step of this story we will find government officials unsuccessfully trying to keep far-off settlers from antagonizing the Indians, even if only to avoid incurring the cost of war.

What it means to "protect" the Indians, of course, is itself a contested question. For most of American history, whites interested in helping the Indians believed and said things that are no longer considered as helpful as they once were. The humanitarians of the seventeenth through the early twentieth centuries did not think that Indian ways of life were as good as their own. Most of them were not interested in preserving traditional Indian forms of politics, or culture, or land tenure. To be a humanitarian was to believe that with proper training Indians were capable of becoming as "civilized" as whites, and that the compassionate thing to do was to offer that kind of training—in Christianity, in European-style agriculture, in literacy, and in all the other characteristics of civilized life. To the progressive thinkers of the era, to allow the Indians to go on living as they always had was to consign them to misery, both in this life and in the next. The intellectual descendants of such thinkers now believe precisely the opposite. That transformation in thought took place in the twentieth century. One of its effects has been to obscure the variety of opinion among whites in the preceding three centuries, because from today's perspective *all* shades of white opinion are susceptible to criticism. That diversity of opinion, however, was once much more visible.

Conflict between eastern white humanitarians and western white land-grabbers was a constant, but each major twist in Indian land policy required the support of both groups. Removal in the early nineteenth century, reservations in the middle and late nineteenth century, allotment in the late nineteenth and early twentieth centuries—all were supported simultaneously by pro-Indian reformers and by anti-Indian expansionists. The road to Indian land loss has always been paved with both good and bad intentions. These coalitions explain the cycle of optimism and disappointment that has always characterized Indian land policy, particularly in the century and a half after the Revolution. Reformers have consistently launched new programs with high hopes, only to see those hopes dashed in practice, after policies devised by well-intentioned easterners have been implemented in the field by less well-intentioned westerners.

Whites were never a single bloc with uniform interests, and neither were Indians. At all times there have been Indians with good reasons to sell land and others with good reasons not to sell. Many Indians opposed policies like removal and allotment, but many others supported them as the least bad of the available options, and those were not unreasonable positions at the time. Indians were no more monolithic in their views than whites.

In the end, the story of the colonization of the United States is still a story of power, but it was a more subtle and complex kind of power than we conventionally recognize. It was the power to establish the legal institutions and the rules by which land transactions would be enforced. The threat of physical force would always be present, but most of the time it could be kept out of view because it was not needed. Anglo-Americans could sincerely believe, for most of American history, that they were *not* conquerors, because they believed they were buying land from the Indians in the same way they bought land from each other. What kind of conqueror takes such care to draft contracts to keep up the appearance that no conquest is taking place? A conqueror that genuinely does not think of itself as one.

Before beginning, a few points may require some explanation.

This book is about the acquisition of *property* in land, not the acquisition of *sovereignty* over territory. Property means ownership; sovereignty means the right to govern. The United States and California both have sovereignty over the land on which my house sits, but they don't have property rights in it. We often say colloquially that a particular zone of land "belongs" to this or that country without specifying whether we mean to speak of property or sovereignty, but one has to be more precise when discussing the relationship between whites and Indians, because the history of the acquisition of the Indians' property is very different from the history of the acquisition of sovereignty over the areas where the Indians lived.[1]

From the seventeenth century through the twentieth century, Anglo-Americans consistently asserted sovereignty over American Indians without the Indians' consent. They believed that this sovereignty followed from the British discovery and settlement of the part of North America that is now the United States. The boundaries of the entity called "New York," just to pick one example, encompassed large tracts of land inhabited by Indians who had never agreed to be included. After the Revolution, the boundaries of "the United States" likewise encircled all sorts of people who had been given no say in the matter. These claims of sovereignty often far outreached the actual capacity of Anglo-Americans to govern particular areas—indeed, at many times and places, Indians could have lived to old age without ever discovering that they were located within the nominal sovereignty of an Anglo-American jurisdiction. This continual assertion of sovereignty was based on an assumption of white superiority that was uncontroversial among whites at the time.

To be sure, American law has always treated tribes as sovereigns in their own right, in the sense that tribes have always exercised powers of self-governance, powers that have fluctuated in their extent over time. But that treatment has never been inconsistent with the broader assertion of white sovereignty over Indians. White Americans routinely distinguished, for example, between "American" Indians, "British" Indians, "French" Indians, and so on, based on which nation claimed sovereignty over the territory where the Indians lived, even while Indian tribes were sovereign within their own domains.

The assertion of sovereignty over a given area occupied by Indians normally preceded, sometimes by quite a long time, the acquisition of the Indians' property rights in that area. The founding of colonial Massachusetts, for instance, long predated the acquisition of Indian property rights in the western parts of the colony. The Louisiana Purchase preceded by several decades some of the treaties by which Indian tribes located within the Purchase's boundaries ceded their property rights. To say that the Indians were subject to the sovereignty of the United States did not mean that their land was owned by the United States. Property and sovereignty are separate issues, and they were treated as separate issues as far back as the seventeenth century.

Acquisitions of territory from Indians, therefore, were in a different category from acquisitions of territory from European nations. When the United States (or Britain, before the Revolution) acquired territory in North America from a European country, it was acquiring sovereignty over that territory. Purchases from Indian tribes, by contrast, were primarily transfers of property. The two concepts could be intermingled in practice, in the sense that the acquisition of territory sometimes took place at a time when the *actual* governance of that territory shifted from Indians to whites. At such times, Anglo-Americans sometimes spoke of the transactions as transfers of effective sovereignty as well as conveyances of property. Even then, however, Anglo-American governments were not acquiring any new *claims* to sovereignty. They were merely beginning to exercise in practice a sovereignty they had asserted in principle all along.

In telling this story, I use the word *Indian* (rather than *Native American* or any similar alternative) because that is the term most often used in historical and legal scholarship today, by Indians and non-Indians alike. What it means to be an "Indian," legally and culturally, is and always has been a complicated question, but it is a question I do not address here.

There is unfortunately no good word for non-Indians. Sometimes I speak of non-Indians as "whites," but of course not all of them were white. Sometimes I call them "Anglo-Americans" or (in the colonial period) "Britons," but not all of them traced their ancestry to England or even Britain. Sometimes I call them "Euro-Americans," but they were not all from Europe. Sometimes I call them "settlers," sometimes "colonists," and sometimes I just call them "non-Indians." I use all these terms as synonyms, even though I realize they are not, because it feels awkward to say "non-Indians" over and over again. All these terms harbor the same complications as *Indian*. What it means to be "white," for instance, or to be a "colonist," is not a simple matter, but again these are questions I do not address.

I use the word *property* to describe the way both Indians and non-Indians organized rights to use land, but I certainly do not mean to imply all the connotations that sometimes go along with the word. To the extent that the idea of property rights implies enforcement by a central state, for example, or a market for their transfer, the word *property* is no doubt misleading as applied to precontact Indian life. Nor do I mean, by speaking of Indian property rights, to imply that the Indians' conception of the relationship between land and people was the same as the non-Indians' conception. I use the word *property* in its most culturally neutral sense, to mean only the intellectual apparatus by which a group of people organizes who will get to use which resources located on which land. On this definition, every known society in the history of the world has had property. As we will see, the Indians had property just as much as the settlers did; they just organized it differently.

Finally, when I began this book I expected to include a series of maps, showing snapshots of the extent to which land had been transferred from Indians to non-Indians at various points in time. I soon realized, however, that the creation of such maps would require taking sides in a very large number of past and present disputes. There are many zones within the United States that were never acquired by contract or treaty, there are others that were obtained in treaties that were never ratified by the Senate, and there are still others acquired in ratified treaties the legitimacy of which was bitterly contested; indeed, some are still bitterly contested by the descendants of the ostensible sellers. How could such areas be drawn on a map?[2] One would need (1) a complete knowledge of the facts surrounding all acts of land acquisition in the entire country and the opinions of all the parties thereto, and (2) a set of rules for distinguishing valid from invalid claims. If anyone possesses the former, it isn't me. As for the latter, the way such rules have changed over time, on paper and in practice, is the very subject of this book. The rules themselves have always been contested and in flux. Better to include no maps, I decided, than to publish maps that would inevitably convey a false sense of certainty.

NATIVE PROPRIETORS

THE English colonists who arrived in North America saw a vast amount of land. They met many people who lived on the land. Wherever they went, they had a decision to make: Did the Indians *own* the land? Were the English bound to purchase it, or could they simply take it?

The issue was a controversial one in the earliest years of colonization, eliciting a variety of theories on both sides. By the late seventeenth century, however, English government officials settled on an answer. In principle, if not always in practice, the English recognized the Indians as the owners of North America. If the English wanted Indian land, they would have to buy it.

The point deserves some emphasis, because the dominant view among historians of the colonization of North America is that the English did *not* recognize Indian property rights. The leading environmental history of the colonies depicts English colonists who "rationalized their conquest of New England . . . by refusing to extend the rights of property to the Indians." The best study of the intellectual underpinnings of early English colonization relates that in colonial North America "the argument from vacancy *(vacuum domicilium)* or absence of ownership *(terra nullius)* became a standard foundation for English and, later, British dispossession of indigenous peoples." Essays specifically about colonial English conceptions of Indian property rights have titles that accurately describe their contents: one is called "The Moral and Legal Justifications for Dispossessing the Indians," another "The Puritans' Justification for Taking the Land."[1]

The most thorough study of the legal beliefs underlying the English colonization of North America, Robert Williams's *The American Indian in Western Legal Thought*, reaches the same conclusion. Williams traces European "discourses of conquest" back to the Crusades, to demonstrate that the earliest English settlers considered themselves justified in seizing the Indians' land. English colonists believed that the Indians "possessed no rights that civilized English monarchs or subjects were bound to recognize," Williams argues. As a result, the "Indians could be dispossessed of the lands they claimed by a race of cultivators destined by Providence to plant the seeds of a superior civilization in the New World." And this belief that the Indians lacked any property rights in their land, Williams concludes, lasted throughout the colonial period, providing "a firm and self-assured foundation for pursuit of the English will to empire in the New World through the American Revolutionary era."[2]

This view is shared by the other occupational group with an interest in the issue—lawyers. In *Johnson v. M'Intosh* (1823), Chief Justice John Marshall explained that "all the nations of Europe, who have acquired territory on this continent, have asserted in themselves, and have recognised in others, the exclusive right of the discoverer to appropriate the lands occupied by the Indians." Because the English had not treated the Indians as property owners, the Supreme Court held, neither must the United States.[3]

In the nearly two centuries since, lawyers and judges have always treated *Johnson v. M'Intosh*—"the great case of *Johnson v. McIntosh*," the Supreme Court called it in the 1950s—as one of the cornerstones of American law. *Johnson*'s continuing prominence is reinforced every year in law schools, where it is the very first case most beginning students read in their required course in Property. The best-selling Property casebook calls *Johnson* "the genesis of our subject" because it lays "the foundations of landownership in the United States." Given current sympathies for the Indians, the outcome of the case has come to be viewed with disapproval in law school. *Johnson* has joined *Dred Scott v. Sandford* and a few others to form a small canon (or maybe an anti-canon) of famous cases law students are taught to criticize. The leading casebook describes the philosophy underlying *Johnson* as "discomfiting," and quotes with approval the recent view of a law professor that Marshall's opinion "was rooted in a Eurocentric view of the inferiority of the

Indian people."[4] *Johnson*, though, might be the only member of this anti-canon that remains the law, and that is still cited as authority by lower courts several times a year.

I will argue against this near-consensus among historians and lawyers, but a few words of caution may first be necessary. The principle of Indian landownership was never recognized with unanimity. There were always some English colonists, and sometimes even some colonial governments, willing to take land from the Indians without paying for it. All laws are violated sometimes, and this one was probably violated more than most. As the English population of the colonies grew, so did the English demand for Indian land, and incidents of trespassing grew more frequent. But if one is interested in overall English colonial land policy, in how the English treated Indian land as a general matter, the answer is that they treated the Indians as owners of their land.

That the English normally recognized Indian property rights does not imply that the English were as concerned with the Indians' welfare as they were with their own, or that they considered the Indians their equals.[5] The English had several reasons to buy the Indians' land, none of which depended on liking the Indians or wishing them well. By recognizing the Indians as owners of their land, the English were helping *themselves*, not the Indians.

Finally, that the English normally purchased Indian land says nothing about whether, from the Indians' point of view, the transactions were voluntary in any meaningful sense, or whether the Indians interpreted the sales the same way the English did, or whether the Indians were sometimes defrauded by individual settlers or even by colonial governments, or whether the prices were fair, or whether large-scale land purchasing would turn out to have devastating effects on Indian life. Such issues will be taken up in Chapter 2. The purpose of the present chapter is to demonstrate a single point: that after some controversy in the early years, the English normally acknowledged that Indian land had to be obtained by contract, not by force.

Intricasy, Perplexity, and Replication

Soon after the Virginia Company's ships had safely arrived at Jamestown, the Company turned to the next pressing matter—public relations. Members recognized that colonization was controversial, in part because of doubts as to whether the English could legally settle on a continent everyone knew to be already inhabited. One member accordingly proposed "that some forme of writinge in way of Justification of our plantation might be conceived, and pass, (though not by publique authorytye) into many handes." But after some debate the Company decided against the proposal. Publishing a defense of the project, the Company reasoned, was likely only to provoke criticism. The firm's "pen-adversaries . . . will wright agaynst the lawfulnes of plantation" in America to such an extent that the issue "must necessarily grow to disputation of so much intricasy, perplexity, and replication, as shall conduce unto theyr end of slackening us" from continuing to settle Virginia. The Company was well aware that this precise debate over the legality of obtaining land in America had taken place in Spain in the previous century, a debate that in the Company's view had only delayed Spanish colonization.[6] It would not be long, the Company realized, before issues of sovereignty and property would become hot topics in England as well. "We shalbe putt to defend our title, not yet publiquely quarreled, not only comparatively to be as good as the Spaniards," a question of which European nation had sovereignty over Virginia, "but absolutely to be good agaynst the Naturall people," the Indians. The latter question was one of property: Did the Virginia Company have any right to occupy the Indians' land? In the end, "some thought it better to abstayne from this unnessisary way of provication, and reserve ourselves to the defensive part, when they shall offer any thing agaynst us."[7] The Company would lie low for the time being.

But the issue would not go away. Even the ministers who preached sermons to the Virginia Company spoke of it. In his sermon delivered in February 1609, William Crashaw observed that the "first and fundamentall" objection to the new colony in Virginia "is the *doubt of lawfulnes of the action.*" Was it right to take land from the Indians? Crashaw insisted that it was *not* right. "A Christian may take nothing from a Heathen against his will, but in faire and lawfull bargaine," Crashaw explained. He cited precedent to support his argument. "*Abraham* wanted a place to burie in, and liked a peece of land," Crashaw recalled, "and being a great man, and therefore *feared*, a just and meek man, and therefore *loved* of the heathen, they bad him *chuse where hee would, and take it.*" But Abraham would not. "No, saith *Abraham*, but *I will buie it*, and so he paide the price of it: so must all the children of *Abraham* doe." The lesson, Crashaw concluded, was that the Virginia colonists must "take nothing from the *Savages* by power nor pillage, by craft nor violence, neither goods, lands nor libertie." How then was the colony to acquire the land it would need? Crashaw had an answer. "We will *exchange* with them for that which *they may spare*, and we doe neede," he asserted, "and they shall have that which we may spare, and they doe much more need." Fortunately the Indians had plenty of land to spare, "in so much as a great part of it lieth wild & inhabited of none but the beasts of the fielde, and the trees." Nevertheless, Crashaw affirmed, the colonists would have to buy it.[8]

A few weeks later the Virginia Company heard from a different minister, William Symonds, who sermonized on the same theme. "There is one scruple, which some, that thinke themselves to be very wise, do cast in our way," Symonds noted. "The countrey, they say, is possessed by owners, that rule, and governe it in their owne right: then with what conscience, and equitie can we offer to thrust them, by violence, out of their inheritances?" Symonds posed the same question Crashaw had raised, but he had a very different answer. The critics' mistake, Symonds concluded, was to suppose that "it is not lawfull to invade the territories of other princes, by force of sword," when in fact human history was largely a catalogue of invasions and wars, with the winners taking the land of the losers.[9] The English had every right to seize Virginia by force.

Two ministers, two theories of property. Even on Sundays the Virginia Company could not escape argument over whether Indian land could be seized or had to be purchased. The ministers were representative of the wider culture. In the early seventeenth century, settlement posed an unsettled question.

The difficulty concerned *property*, the question of who owned the land in North America, not *sovereignty*, the question of who had the power to govern in North America. To be sure, the line between the two concepts was not drawn as sharply in the seventeenth century as it is today. Vestiges of feudal tenure still lingered in England, where land had once been held of the Crown rather than owned outright. In the colonies, however, sovereignty and property were usually understood as distinct issues, because each pitted the English against a different opponent. Sovereignty involved the competing claims of England and other European nations, while property involved the competing claims of England and the Indians.[10] Sovereignty, the English agreed, belonged to the English Crown, by virtue of the English "discovery" and settlement of North America. Indian tribes might retain powers of self-government within the territories they occupied, but those territories were located within larger zones of sovereignty allocated to European nations on the basis of discovery. "This Right arising from the first discovery," affirmed Harman Verelst, one of the promoters of the colony of Georgia, "is the first and fundamental Right of all European Nations, as to their Claim of Lands in America." The Indians were not recognized to have any legal capacity to withstand an assertion of sovereignty by a European government. As settlers performed the ritual acts they understood to confer sovereignty on their monarchs, the Indians watched from the side, without any role to play.[11] Among the English, there was nothing controversial about their power to govern in North America.[12] The hard question was one of property. Who owned the land?

The English government embarked on colonization with the optimistic view that land in North America was unowned and available for the taking. The charters by which the Crown granted rights to establish colonies in North America almost uniformly purported to convey property rights to their recipients, without any hesitation over the possibility that Indians might already possess property rights in the same land. The first charter of Virginia granted to four men "all the Lands, Tenements, and Hereditaments," to be found in Virginia, a formula drafted to mimic conveyances of property in England. If the drafters of this clause had any model in mind it would have been Ireland, where English colonization was already well under way, and where the English were taking land by force rather than purchasing it. Most of the subsequent charters included similar clauses. They were generally written before any permanent settlements had been attempted in the colony in question, so little was known in England about who would be there to greet them when the first settlers arrived. Only in Providence, settled by Roger Williams and his followers *before* they sought official recognition from the government, did the charter acknowledge that there was more to the issue than could be seen from London. The Providence charter recognized that the settlers had moved beyond the bounds of earlier charters, and "have also purchased, and are purchasing of and amongst the said Natives, some other Places, which may be convenient both for Plantations, and also for building of Ships, Supply of Pipe Staves and other Merchandize."[13] But Providence was unusual. Most of the charters granted property rights as if the charters' recipients were to be the first human beings in the area.

In this view the government was hardly alone. Many early theorists of colonization assumed likewise that a patent from the Crown was all that was necessary for an English settler to claim property in North America. There were a few theories in circulation in the early seventeenth century justifying the right of settlers to occupy Indian land without purchasing it.

Some early writers asserted that Christians had the right to take land from non-Christians. Because Virginia was "voide of Christian inhabitants," William Strachey asked, "may it not then be lawfull nowe to attempt the possession of such lands?" Such was the view of the directors of the Virginia Company, who were no closer to Virginia than was the English government. In 1622 the Company refused to recognize a land purchase made from the Algonquian chief Opechancanough because to do so would require acknowledging the property rights of "that heathen Infidell." Robert Gray, one of Virginia's early propagandists, proclaimed that "all Polititians doe with one consent, holde and maintaine, that a Christian king may lawfullie make warre uppon barbarous and Savage people." The point could be made more benignly. One of the commonly professed reasons for venturing to North America was to introduce the Indians to Christianity. Surely that was a benefit the Indians would find to be well worth some land, a benefit that might justify taking land even before the Indians realized how good a bargain they were getting.[14]

But the notion that the heathen lacked property rights was controversial, even in the earliest years of colonization. "Neither yet is it lawfull for Christians, to usurpe the goods and lands of Heathens," insisted Samuel Purchas, an ardent supporter of colonization; "for they are villains not to us; but to our and their Lorde." The treatise-writer Hugo Grotius found it "shameless . . . to claim for oneself by right of discovery what is held by another, even though the occupant . . . may hold wrong views about God." As time went on, and the English settled more of North America, the religious justification for acquiring land virtually disappeared. Cotton Mather thought the Indians "infinitely barbarous," but he nevertheless insisted that "the *Indians* had not by their Paganism so forfeited all Right unto any of their Possessions" that the English could simply take their land. No Indian land could be settled, Mather explained, "without a fair Purchase and Consent from the Natives." By 1691 the Massachusetts minister John Higginson mocked "the Popish Principle, that Christians have a right to the Lands of Heathen," a principle that might suit Catholics but one "disowned by all Protestants." "That we have any Claim upon the Foot that we were *Christians*, and they *Heathen,*" Jeremiah Dummer scoffed in 1721, was something that "no Body will say." The assertion that Christians had the right to take the property of non-Christians can scarcely be found in Britain or British America after the early seventeenth century.[15]

Other early writers claimed a more general right of conquest, arising not out of Christianity but from sheer power. One advocate of colonizing Virginia had no trouble explaining "how we can warrant a supplantation of those Indians, or an insuasion into their rights and possessions." The answer: "Honourable I graunt is just Conquest by sword." "Where can witt and worth be more truely exprest," asked Robert Wintour, one of the original promoters of Maryland, than "in conquering nations[?]" In 1614, when the Virginia Company's lawyer was called before the House of Commons to defend the Company's activities, he explained that the Company was in the midst of a just conquest.[16]

Proponents of conquest could draw on a common fund of knowledge of human history, which was full of episodes in which groups had planted colonies on the land of others. "The *Hebrewes,* and *Lacadae-monians,* the *Goths,* the *Grecians,* the *Romanes,* and the rest, what was it they would not undertake to enlarge their Territories[?]" John Smith pointedly asked. "And what have ever beene the workes of the greatest Princes of the earth, but planting of countries, and civilizing barbarous and inhumane Nations, to civilitie and humanitie?" The conquest of weaker people had a long and honorable history. It could hardly be wrong to do something that had brought so much glory to the Greeks and the Romans. And of course everyone knew of examples right at home—the Norman Conquest, in which an invading army had taken much of the country's land, and the Anglo-Saxon conquest before that. "Some have a sly whispering slighting way of Reflecting upon those that Transplant themselves and Interest into *America,* as men of unsetled brains," complained William Loddington in the late seventeenth century. "Let such consider, what a Country *England* it self had now been, if their Ancestors had not had Plantation Principles. If their brains had not been thus unsetled, these grave men had not had such pleasant and profitable Setlements as they have. . . . England was once as rough and rugged as *America,* and the Inhabitants as blind and barbarous as the *Indians.*"[17]

But this asserted general right of conquest was no less controversial than the supposed right of Christians to take the land of heathens. International law already distinguished between just and unjust conquests, and it was understood that the simple desire to obtain the territory of another nation did not furnish a just cause for war. In 1684, when George Talbot, surveyor-general of Maryland, justified the colony's seizure of the Susquehanna's hunting grounds "by right of Conquest," he was immediately rebuked by William Penn for this reason. "I will justifie that the Conquest of the Susquehannes was noe just Conquest," Penn insisted, "for noe cause of warr was given by them." Penn was hardly defending an abstract principle, for every acre not yet taken by Maryland was one more available for Pennsylvania. But every assertion that might makes right could be countered with the distinction between just and unjust conquests. "No colony hath any just right to dispose of any lands conquered from the natives," a royal commission advised the government of Massachusetts in 1665, unless "the cause of the conquest be just." As a result, the claim to property rights by conquest virtually died out among the English after the seventeenth century. The claim "scarcely merits a serious reflection or refutation," scoffed one writer by the 1770s. Like the claimed right of Christians to take the land of the heathen, the supposed right of conquest flourished only briefly, in the period before colonial settlement had become routine enough for English thought on the subject to crystallize.[18]

A third theory in circulation in the early seventeenth century justifying the right of settlers to occupy Indian land was that the Indians themselves did not claim any property rights. Some of the early colonists thought of the Indians not as humans capable of dividing their land but rather as features of the land itself. Maine, one early settler reported, was "but a desert Wildernesse replete onely with a kind of *Savage* People, and overgrowne trees." Some claimed that the Indians were "a wild people," a people that "have no Lawes" to govern themselves, a people lacking any conception of property. "They hold all things, except their Wives, in common," declared John Lederer, of the Indians inhabiting Piedmont Virginia. Such statements were nonsense, often springing from the imaginations of armchair travelers seeking to sell sensational books, who were drawing not on their own observation but upon the long tradition of depicting wild, primitive people inhabiting distant parts of the earth. Indians, like all other peoples, recognized property rights in food, clothing, houses, tools, and the like. The details of property systems vary greatly across cultures, and the differences between the English system and Indian systems could be large.[19] But it was clear to anyone with firsthand knowledge of Indians that they possessed property.

The claim that the Indians themselves had no notion of property rights was also made in a more limited form, as an assertion that the Indians were nomadic and did not stay long enough in any given location to conceive of property rights *in land*. "This savage people ruleth over many lands without title or property," John Winthrop assumed in 1629, "for they enclose no ground, neither have they any cattel to maintayne it, but remove their dwellings as they have occasion."[20] In 1632, when the Dutch government complained of English interference with Dutch settlers in Manhattan, which the Dutch claimed by virtue of the famous purchase a few years before, the English government disputed the Dutch claim on the ground that the Indians were not "*possessores bonae fidei* of those countries, so as to be able to dispose of them either by sale or donation, their residences being unsettled and uncertain, and only being in common."[21] If the Indians were constantly in motion, the argument was, they could not claim an attachment to any particular area of land sufficient to give rise to property rights.

But assertions like these were quickly contradicted by experience. The early European explorers and settlers of North America all reported that the Indians were agriculturalists, not nomads. Verrazano found plots "carefully cultivated" in Newport harbor in 1524. Thomas Hariot left a detailed description of the Indian farming techniques he saw at Roanoke in the 1580s. On Cape Cod in 1603, Martin Pring observed "sowne Tobacco, Pompions, Cowcumbers and such like." And of course even schoolchildren know how the Indians saved the earliest English colonists at Jamestown and Plymouth from starvation by bringing them corn and teaching them how to plant. Up and down the continent, the Indians were farmers.[22] Theories of property that required nonfarming Indians could not survive long in the face of so many facts to the contrary.

Nor was it long before colonists' accounts confirmed that the Indians in fact *did* allocate property rights in land. "Each household knoweth their owne lands & gardens," John Smith reported of the Indians near Jamestown. "They all know their severall landes, and habitations, and limits, to fish, fowle, or hunt in." The Virginia minister Alexander Whitaker affirmed that the Indians "observe the limits of their owne possessions, and incroach not upon their neighbours dwellings." From

Plymouth, Edward Winslow reported that every tribe knew its territory, and within that zone, when individuals wished to plant, the sachem "giveth them as much as they can use, and sets them their bounds." In Pennsylvania, William Penn found the Indians "exact Observers of Property." John Lawson noticed that the Indians in North Carolina "have no Fence to part one anothers Lots in their Corn-Fields; but every Man knows his own, and it scarce ever happens, that they rob one another of so much as an Ear of Corn."[23] The English found a preexisting system of property rights everywhere they went. It was different in one important respect from the English system. When the soil in one area became depleted, the village would move to a new area, and the village chiefs would have to allot new fields to individuals and families. The English lacked sufficient land to be as mobile. But if the Indian property system was not exactly like the English system, it clearly *was* a property system. The fact that villages did move from time to time would prove to be important to the question of *which* Indian property rights would be recognized by the English, but after the early seventeenth century it was not used as an excuse to deny property rights to Indians completely. Everyone acknowledged that the Indians had property too.

Acknowledged and Right Owners

The early writers seeking to justify the acquisition of land in North America often resorted to lawyer-like lists, setting out arguments in the alternative. When the Virginia Company finally decided to go public with a statement of why "it is not unlawfull, that wee possesse part of their land," the Company combined variants of the argument from Christianity and the right of conquest. Settlement in Virginia was legal, the Company affirmed,

> Partlie, because there is no other, moderate, and mixt course, to bring them to conversion, but by dailie conversation, where they may see the life, and learne the language each of other.
> Partlie, because there is no trust to the fidelitie of human beasts, except a man will make a league, with Lions, Beares, and Crocodiles.
> Partlie, because there is roome sufficient in the land . . . for them, and us: the extent of an hundred miles, being scarce peopled with 2000 inhabitants.
> Partlie, because they have violated the lawe of nations, and used our

Ambassadors as *Ammon* did the servants of *David:* If in him it were a just cause to warre against the Ammonites, it is lawfull, in us, to secure our selves, against the infidels.

But these were all subsidiary arguments, the Company admitted. The main reason the English could settle on Indian land had nothing to do with Christianity or conquest. In fact, these arguments did not make the slightest bit of difference.

But chieflie because *Paspehay,* one of their Kings, sold unto us for copper, land to inherit and inhabite.[24]

For all the Company's theorizing about its rights to take the land, in the end the Company purchased it from the Indians.

The other lists drawn up by seventeenth-century defenders of settlers' property rights were internally inconsistent in the same way. They began with claims that did not depend on the consent of the Indians, but by the end they relied on a purchase or a gift from the Indians. The most detailed justification of the colony at Plymouth was published shortly after the colony was founded, written by Robert Cushman, who had three distinct answers to the question he knew others would pose: "what right have I to go live in the heathens' country?" The first was Christianity. Englishmen ought to convert the Indians, but conversion was impossible "unless we go to them or they come to us; to us they cannot come, our land is full; to them we may go, their land is empty." The task of Christianizing the Indians thus required settling on their land. Cushman's discussion of relative population densities brought him to his second reason the English could occupy North America: "their land is spacious and void." The Indians did not use all the land available to them. "They are not industrious," Cushman explained, "neither have art, science, skill or faculty to use either the land or the commodities of it, but all spoils, rots, and is marred for want of manuring, gathering, ordering, etc." Cushman could invoke the familiar Biblical precedent for the migration of peoples: "As the ancient patriarchs therefore removed from straiter places into more roomy, where land lay idle and waste, and none used it, though there dwelt inhabitants by them, . . . so is it lawful now to take a land which none useth, and make use of it."

But after twice justifying a simple seizure of the Indians' land, Cushman reversed course. The English would not have to seize the land after all, because "we have it by common consent, composition and agreement." It turned out that the chief Massasoit had *given* the English the land. Massasoit "hath promised and appointed us to live at peace where we will in all his dominions, taking what place we will, and as much land as we will." Cushman assured readers that this fortunate transaction had not "been accomplished by threats and blows, or shaking of sword and sound of trumpet." The Plymouth settlers were a small group far from home, in no position to take land by force. Cushman admitted that "our faculty that way is small, and our strength less." The land was a genuine gift from the Indians, given because Massasoit "found us just, honest, kind and peaceable, and so loves our company."[25] Cushman's theorizing as to the English right of conquest, like the Virginia Company's similar theorizing a decade earlier, was irrelevant in practice. In Plymouth as in Jamestown, the English settled land with the Indians' consent.

English colonists would make such lists into the early eighteenth century. Daniel Gookin declared in 1674 that a patent from the king was enough for an Englishman to claim property rights in North America, but he recognized that it made no difference, because "the English had the grant of most of the land within this jurisdiction, either by purchase or donation from the Indian sachems and sagamores, which were actually in possession, when the English first came over." The New Hampshire Assembly insisted in 1707 that the Indians had no property rights when the English first arrived because the lands "were not onely then Vacuum Domicilium but a miserable desert," but then immediately conceded that the land had in fact been inhabited by Indians, "from whose Sachims, our Ancestors all along informed and assured us the said Lands were honestly and justly purchased."[26] In these lists of arguments the theories justifying conquest were merely prefaces to the empirical fact that the colonists had not conquered any land at all. They had bought it.

By the late seventeenth century, discussions of land and Indians tended to jettison the theory and stick to the facts. The English "settled by the Indians consent and good liking, and bought the Land of them, that we settle on, which they conveyed to us by Deed under their Hands and Seals," Thomas Budd explained in 1685. Robert Morden's \Geography Rectified (1693) described how the residents of New England "purchased their Lands of the *Sachems*, which were the heads; and the eldest of the *Indian* Families, the Antient Proprietors" of the land. Nathaniel Crouch reported the same of New Jersey: "The *English* that are setled here buy the Lands of the Natives, and give them real satisfaction for the same." By 1728 Daniel Dulany was incredulous when he "heard it asserted, that Maryland is a Conquered Country," an assertion "which, by the By, is false."[27] Maryland, he implied, like the other colonies of British North America, was a *purchased* country.

Indian land had to be purchased, many English and American writers explained, because the Indians *owned* it. In Connecticut, explained Lord Saye, one of the colony's original patentees, settlers "purchased the land from the natives," because the Indians were "the acknowledged and right owners thereof." Many, like Increase Mather and William Penn, referred to the Indians as the "Native Proprietors" or the "Owners" of North America. The early Maine settler Christopher Levett arrived in 1623 with the belief that the Indians owned Maine by "a natural right of inheritance, as they are the sons of Noah." An early governor of New Haven declared that the Indians "were the true proprietours of the land (for we found it not a vacuum)." No matter how weak or impoverished the Indians seemed, the Scottish writer Robert Ferguson insisted, they nevertheless held "Title unto, and Property in what was anciently and originally theirs," because "the point of Right and Property is the same in the Poor that it is in the Rich, and in the Weak that it is in the Strong." Even James Glen, the expansionist governor of South Carolina in the mid-eighteenth century, was adamant that the Indians were the "Original possessors and Proprietors of the Lands and Countries they Inhabit."[28]

Some of these writers were hardly disinterested in the matter. Ferguson, for instance, was defending the right of Scottish colonists to obtain land in present-day Panama, land already claimed by Spain. Even if some of their motives were impure, however, they were stating a legal proposition that had come to command most Americans' assent. The uncertainty of the early seventeenth century about whether the Indians owned their land had gradually disappeared, until by the eighteenth century Anglo-Americans had settled on an answer. The Indians owned their land just as much as the English did. If the English wanted Indians' land, they would have to buy it, just like they bought land owned by other English people.

This view of Indian property rights was never unanimous. One can find, all through the colonial period, occasional expressions to the contrary, including some by people powerful enough to put their opinions into practice. In 1739, for example, when South Carolina required government approval of land purchases from the Indians, the measure was intended only in part to protect the Indians from being defrauded. The other problem with private land purchases, the legislature explained, was that the Indians did not really own the land they were selling. The land was instead owned by the Crown. Sales by the Indians "tend to the manifest prejudice of his Majesty's just right and title to the soil of this Province." But even this example shows the dominance of the view that the Indians were property owners. If South Carolinians believed the land was owned by the Crown rather than the Indians, the legislature ought to have banned purchases from the Indians altogether, rather than merely requiring the government's license.[29]

Practice had crystallized long before theory. Purchasing land from the Indians became common almost from the beginning of English settlement. In Virginia the early governor Thomas Dale bought land from the Indians. The earliest settlers of Massachusetts carried instructions that "if any of the savages pretend right of inheritance to all or any part of the lands granted in our pattent, wee pray you endeavor to purchase their tytle, that wee may avoyde the least scruple of intrusion." Early seventeenth-century Massachusetts towns were typically founded by purchases from the Indians. In 1663 the proprietors of the new colony of Carolina assumed that the first settlers would buy land from local Indians. The same year in New York, when the Dutch government tried to prevent three English settlers from purchasing Indian land, the settlers proudly declared "that wee would purchase the land as wee are Englishmen."[30] It did not take long for the recognition of Indian ownership to become the norm.

The quick emergence of that norm can be seen most clearly by tracing land policy in a single colony, New York. England took control of New York in 1664, and the following year the colony's first English governor informed the Duke of York that "upon this tract of land several new purchases are made from the Indians since my coming." By 1669 an anonymous New York writer could explain that while the "Tenure of Lands is derived from his R[oyal] H[ighnes]s, who gives and graunts lands to Planters as their freehold forever," a grant from the Crown was not enough to put a colonist in possession of land. It merely gave the colonist the right to buy land from the Indians: "the Planters themselves are purchasers from the Indyans." New York was so free, the writer exclaimed, that "the Governour gives liberty to Planters to find out and buy lands from the Indians where it pleaseth best the Planters." In 1674 the Duke of York instructed the colony's lieutenant governor that "when opportunities shall offer themselfes (as I am informed they frequently doe) for purchaseing great tracts of land for Me from the Indians, for small sumes," he should seize the chance to do so. Such instructions then became standard, repeated to new governors and lieutenant governors when they took office. Colonial officials in New York thought of themselves not as conquerors but as bargain shoppers, waiting for the Indians to put their land on sale.[31]

By 1698, when the Earl of Bellomont, New York's new governor, asked the colony's attorney general, James Graham, about "the Methods of making grants of Land since the settlement of the Government under the Crown of England," Graham had no trouble providing an answer. The land first had to be purchased from the Indians. "If the lands were not purchased of the Indians then a petition was made to the Governor and Councill for a License to purchase the same. Then there was an order for a purchase in the presence of the Magistrates of the County where the land lay, and in such a time, and if that method not followed then the License and purchase void, then if regularly purchased should usually preferr a petition to the Governor and Councill for a Grant of the same." The colonial government could grant licenses to purchase, and it could ratify purchases already made, but it could not dispense with the requirement of a purchase from the Indians. Prospective purchasers seeking licenses were careful to specify that the land they wished to buy was "yet unpurchased of the Natives." By the middle of the eighteenth century, New York required that lands purchased from Indians be first surveyed, by a government surveyor, in the company of Indians from the selling nation, to avoid subsequent disputes.[32] Land purchasing had become a routine matter.

Purchasing quickly became the norm in the other colonies as well. In 1687 the Proprietors of East New Jersey bitterly complained that having already purchased their patent from the Crown, they were "notwithstanding forced to buy every Acre over again at a considerable rate from the Indians, who daily raise the price of land as they understand our want of it." William Penn reported in 1685 that "I have made seven Purchases" of land from the Indians in Pennsylvania, "and in Pay and Presents they have received at least *twelve hundred pounds* of me." James Glen, the governor of South Carolina between 1738 and 1756, proudly recalled how he had "made a considerable Purchase from that *Indian* Nation," the Cherokees, "of some of those hunting Grounds." Glen "had the Deeds of Conveyance formally executed in their own Country, by their head Men, in the Name of the whole People, and with their universal Approbation and good Will." Throughout the south, the Creek leader Alexander McGillivray declared at the end of the colonial period, "no title has ever been or pretended to be made by his Britannic Majesty to our lands except what was obtained by free Gift or by purchase for good and valuable Considerations." William Johnson, superintendent of Indian affairs through the 1750s and 1760s, summarized matters the same way. It was a "well judg'd Policy," he concluded, that the English government "have always made an Indian Purchase the Basis or Foundation of all Grants."[33] From Maine to Georgia, the ordinary way to acquire Indian land was to buy it.

There were many wars between colonists and Indians, of course, and when the English won they took some of their adversaries' land. The English did not conceive of any of these wars, however, as wars of conquest, undertaken for the purpose of obtaining land. Rightly or wrongly, they perceived each of the wars as provoked by the Indians, and the land taken as just compensation for their trouble. The amount of land acquired by war was in any event a small percentage of the colonies' surface area. Much more land was obtained by purchase than by conquest.

Any assessment of the relative amounts of land acquired by different methods requires qualification. It would be an enormous and perhaps impossible task to count the number of acres in North America that the English purchased, conquered, or simply occupied without either permission or violent contest. The purchase of land resulted in the creation of a document, but the occupation of land by other means did not, so even a complete assessment of the documentary record would be likely to overestimate the percentage of land purchased. But there are three indications suggesting that the purchase of land was, at the very least, extremely common.

The first is the sheer number of surviving deeds by which Indians sold their land to English colonists. In every colony, many of the earliest property transactions for which there is still a record involve Indian sellers and English buyers.[34] Some of the surviving Indian deeds, particularly in the later colonial period, cover enormous areas. There are so many surviving Indian deeds, ranging from sales of small parcels to individuals right up to sales of huge territories to colonial governments, that the English purchase of Indian lands must have been a common event. "Every Man that pretended to Propriety, had gotten his Right by Purchase from the *Natives*," a group of New Jersey colonists recalled in

1747; "without which purchase, the People there would *hiss* at the person pretending Property."[35]

A second suggestion that purchase was the ordinary method of acquiring Indian land is the ubiquity of colonial statutes regulating the purchasing process. These laws required private purchasers to obtain permission from the colonial government before buying Indian land. The first was enacted in Massachusetts in 1634. Most of the other colonies followed suit.[36] There were several reasons to require land purchasers to obtain the government's consent. The government might be able to ascertain whether the land in question had already been purchased by someone else, and thereby prevent disputes from arising between competing English purchasers. The government might promote the colony's security, by seeing that far-flung land was not acquired before land closer in was settled, or by preventing the acquisition of land in a location that might provoke opposition from another tribe. The government might also police fraud against the Indians, by denying permission to unscrupulous frontier characters or to others whose proposed transactions seemed dubious for one reason or another (although this motive must not have been uppermost in a few of the colonies, where the penalty for an unauthorized purchase was that the land would pass to the colonial government rather than being returned to the sellers). But these laws were not intended to discourage purchasing, or to promote land acquisition by some other method. To the contrary, their purpose was to *facilitate* purchasing, like the laws regulating any other market. The fact that every colony had such laws again suggests that the norm was to purchase land from the Indians.

A third indication that purchasing was the norm, and that the English recognized Indian property rights in land, is that colonial officials often enforced Indian property rights against the competing claims of colonists. New England court records are full of property disputes, many involving Indian property owners, and the Indians were treated the same as English litigants. When colonists or their livestock trespassed on Indian land, for example, Indian plaintiffs prevailed in court. In 1710, when a group of Mohawks refused to permit New York officials to survey land the Mohawks claimed not to have sold, Governor Robert Hunter returned to Albany, checked the property records, discovered the Mohawks were right, and called off the survey. In 1733, when the Mohawks persuaded Governor William Cosby that a purported sale of

their land had been fraudulently procured, Cosby invalidated the transaction.[37] Colonial officials would hardly have protected Indian property
rights if they believed the Indians had none. To be sure, they sometimes did less than the law required. The officials charged with enforcing British land policy were often big land speculators themselves, because many drew little or no salary and needed a source of outside
income, and the resulting conflict of interest could lead officials to ignore Indian property rights when they became inconvenient. But if
Indian property rights were not always enforced, they were enforced
enough to suggest that colonial officials recognized that purchase was
the normal and proper way of obtaining them.

It bears emphasizing that Indian property rights in land in the colonial
period were full property rights, not the limited "right of occupancy"
discussed by John Marshall in *Johnson v. M'Intosh* and by later writers.
Colonial writers used the same words to denote Indian and English
property holdings—the Indians, like the English, were described as
"owners" or "proprietors" of their land. The Indians, like the English,
had the legal right to refuse an offer to buy their land. Transactions between Indian sellers and English buyers were, in legal contemplation,
identical to transactions between English sellers and English buyers.
Land was "bought from the natives," related one mid-eighteenth-
century pamphleteer, "in the same manner as is practised among ourselves." The deeds by which Indians sold land were typically worded
the same as the deeds by which English colonists sold land. They conveyed the same kind of ownership enjoyed by the English. "I make
no doubt," affirmed the minister Christopher Toppan, that the Indians
"have as full, and firm a Right, to their Lands as any white men have to
theirs."[38]

Toppan was wrong in one respect. For most of the colonial period, the
Indians could legally sell land only to the government or to a purchaser
who had been (or would later be) licensed by the government. This
was one limit on Indian sellers that did not apply to English sellers.
Throughout the colonial period, however, this restriction was not a serious impediment to Indian land sales. Colonial governments wanted to
encourage settlers to buy Indian land. The requirement of a license most
likely reduced prices, as we will see in the next chapter, but it does not
appear to have prevented many sales. The Indians were not shy about
making their land-related grievances known, but there is little or no record of thwarted sellers objecting to the license requirement.

Because licenses to buy Indian land were so easy to obtain, the license requirement did not cause the English to think of Indian land title as a lesser form of ownership than English title. All landowners, then as now, faced a variety of restrictions on what they could do with their land. An English owner of land might be denied permission to build a mill or a tannery on it, but his neighbors and their lawyers still considered him the owner of his property. The same was true of the Indians: their ability to choose among competing purchase offers might be limited, but they were still proprietors of their land. One can find no claims in the colonial period of an Indian "right of occupancy" midway between full ownership and no rights at all. Some, especially in the early seventeenth century when the issue was still unsettled, asserted that the Indians had no property rights. From the late seventeenth century on, most believed that the Indians were full owners of their land. But no one was in the middle, so far as one can discern today. The right of occupancy described in *Johnson v. M'Intosh* did not yet exist.

Uncultivated Country

To acknowledge the Indians as property owners, however, only raised another question—whether the Indians owned all of North America, or some lesser amount.

North America was so big and the Indian population so small, many of the early English writers on colonization reasoned, that there would be room enough for everyone. "The Land affords void ground to receive more people than this State can spare," exclaimed the anonymous author of *The Planters Plea* in 1630. "The *Indians*," agreed Francis Higginson in the same year, "are not able to make use of the one fourth part of the Land." The apparent sparseness of the Indian population was in part a product of colonization itself, as Europeans unwittingly brought along microorganisms to which Indians had never been exposed, producing diseases that killed Indians in very large numbers. Much of the "void ground," remarked the author of *The Planters Plea*, "comes to passe by the desolation hapning through a three yeeres Plague" in the 1610s, "which swept away most of the Inhabitants all along the Sea coast, and in some places utterly consumed man, woman & childe, so that there is no person left to lay claime to the soyle which they possessed." Massachusett and Patuxet societies numbering around twenty-five thousand in 1600 had been reduced to fewer than three hundred survivors by 1700. The southern Indian population, approximately two hundred thousand in 1685, had been reduced to a quarter of that by 1760. The English were as baffled as the Indians as to why these repeated epidemics killed only Indians. Many, like Daniel Denton, saw "a Divine Hand" making way for English settlement, "by removing or cutting off the *Indians*."[39] But even without the devastation of disease, the English would have found in most of North America a population density much lower than that to which they were accustomed. There seemed to be plenty of space.

England, meanwhile, seemed to be overflowing with people. The population density of England was low by modern standards, but it was the highest contemporaries had ever known. England seemed dangerously full of the poor and the criminal. There was simply not enough land. North America, by contrast, seemed a "howling desart Land," full of "paths untrod by man and beast," a place "where lands lye wast and free."[40] There was no doubt some prejudice in comments like these, a willingness to overlook the Indians who walked the paths supposedly untrod by man, but there was more to it than just contempt for the Indians. Emptiness can be a relative concept.

If the Indians had more land than they could use, and England had extra people, one could easily construct a legal argument justifying English settlers in occupying surplus North American land. The lawyer Thomas More anticipated the argument in the early sixteenth century. When his Utopians found their island too crowded, they sent out colonists to settle on the nearby mainland, "wherever the natives have plenty of unoccupied and uncultivated land." The Utopians forced out natives who resisted, More explained, because "the Utopians say it's perfectly justifiable to make war on people who leave their land idle and waste yet forbid the use and possession of it to others who, by the law of nature, ought to be supported from it."[41] More wrote nearly a century before the argument could be put to practical use in North America, but when the argument became useful it was quickly sharpened. Lawyers in England and throughout Europe agreed that settlers had a legal right to occupy uninhabited land.[42] But what about land that was inhabited very sparsely? Was there no limit to the quantity of land a single person or a small group might claim?

The question was quite relevant to Walter Raleigh's plans for colonization when Raleigh raised it in the late sixteenth century. "Should one family, or one thousand, hold possession of all the southern undiscovered continent, because they had seated themselves in Nova Guiana, or about the straits of Magellan?" asked Raleigh. "Why might not then the like be done in Afric, in Europe, and in Asia?" The idea's absurdity implied that a people could not legitimately claim property rights in too big an area. The Indians, Raleigh reasoned, were not the owners of all of North America. Part of the continent was open for English settlement. "If the inhabitants doe not in some measure fill the Land," preached John Donne to the Virginia Company, the inhabitants had no right to exclude the English, "for as a man does not become proprietary of the Sea, because he hath two or three Boats, fishing in it, so neither does a man become Lord of a maine Continent, because he hath two or three Cottages in the Skirts thereof."[43]

Many concluded that the only place to draw the line was at actual occupation: The Indians were the owners of the land upon which they were physically present, but the rest was open for settlement. "If any Countrey be not possessed by other men," Samuel Purchas argued in 1625, "every man by Law of Nature and Humanitie hath right of Plantation." And the same principle applied to a land that was *partially* possessed, as he understood North America to be. "If a country be inhabited in parts thereof, other parts remaining unpeopled, the same reason giveth liberty to other men which want convenient habitation to seat themselves, where (without wrong to others) they may provide for themselves." The Massachusetts minister John Cotton affirmed that "God makes room for a People" when "he makes a Countrey, though not altogether void of Inhabitants, yet void in that place where they reside. Where there is a vacant place, there is liberty for the Son of *Adam* or *Noah* to come and inhabit, though they neither buy it, nor ask their leaves." Massachusetts, he hardly needed to say, included such vacant places. Even William Penn, who was scrupulous about purchasing Indian land, declared that the Indians lacked any claim to "Waste, or uncultivated Country."[44] For a great many colonists, the association of property with physical occupation was the only conceivable way of striking a balance somewhere between two unacceptable polar positions— that the Indians possessed *no* property rights in their land, or that a relatively small number of Indians could possess all of North America.

The earliest settlements in some of the colonies appear to have proceeded on this principle. In Virginia, contemporary accounts suggest that the English simply fenced in land that did not seem to be in use. George Percy recalled that although "the Savages murmured at our planting in the Countrie," the initial English occupation did not bother Powhatan, who remarked "very wisely of a Savage, Why should you bee offended with them as long as they hurt you not, nor take any thing away by force, they take but a little waste ground, which doth you nor any of us any good." For some time thereafter colonial officials continued making grants of land they perceived to be "empty." An account of the first settlement in Georgia likewise begins with the construction of a fence in a place that seemed to be uninhabited, without any mention of the possibility that the Indians might own the land beneath.[45] In parts of New England, the Indians were so decimated by disease that colonists could get right to work on land the previous farmers of which were all dead. The English could, as John Winthrop did, concede to the Indians "a natural right to so much land as they had or could improve," but leave the rest of the continent "open to any that could and would improve it."[46]

The language used by the seventeenth-century writers bears close examination, because one can detect in it an ambiguity in thought that would poison relations between settlers and Indians for a long time to come. Penn equated "waste" with "uncultivated country." Winthrop rested property ownership not on physical presence but on the capacity to "improve" land. It was easy for the English to slide between three concepts—the *occupation* of land, the *use* of land, and the *cultivation* of land—that were much closer in England than they were for the Indians. Because the population density of England was so much higher than in North America, the English used their land more intensively. A far greater percentage of the land was in cultivation. Agricultural land was farmed year in and year out. In North America, the greater ratio of land to people allowed Indians to set aside large areas as hunting grounds— zones that were *occupied* and *used*, but not *cultivated*. Some tribes inhabited cultivated areas only during the agricultural cycle, and moved elsewhere for the winter. Others had enough land to warrant shifting the areas under cultivation every few years, to allow the soil in any given place to be naturally replenished with nutrients before it was planted again. Cultivated land abandoned for the winter, and land intentionally kept out of cultivation for a period of years, was being *used*, but it was not being *occupied*, and it was specifically not being *cultivated*.[47] The ambiguity as to which activity was the relevant one for determining property rights had very important practical consequences. Did the Indians own their hunting grounds? Did they own the land they had once cultivated but were not currently cultivating? These categories of land amounted to a majority of the land in North America. Did the English have to buy it, or could they simply take it?

The dilemma would persist throughout the colonial period.[48] On the one hand, to recognize Indian property rights in uncultivated land was nearly tantamount to recognizing the Indians as owners of the whole continent, a land area that to many seemed disproportionately large to the Indians' small numbers. "Where they have subdued, replenished, & are actually improving," one early eighteenth-century writer conceded, "that is their Property; and to take that from them, is to Rob them." But he found it "unaccountable, that the *Natives* or *Indians* should be invested with the Property of all this vast unsubdued, unreplenished, unimproved, unknown, and greatest part of this Creation, exclusive of all others."[49] On the other hand, cultivation was not a prerequisite for property ownership in England. Everyone knew that land could still be owned even if it was not being farmed, and indeed even if it was not being used or occupied at all. Why should land in North America be any different?

The proponents of limiting Indian property rights to cultivated land had an answer. All people, they argued, had a natural right to the property they were actually occupying and using. But a society has to leave the state of nature and reach a certain stage of civilization before it develops institutions of government capable of recognizing and enforcing property rights in uncultivated land. The English had such institutions, the argument went, but the Indians did not. The Indians were limited to what they could claim by natural law. The argument that property can exist only where there is a government, at least as advanced during the period in which the English colonized North America, is today most associated with Hobbes, who stated it in highly abstract terms without any reference to current events. In North America, however, the point was not at all abstract. For some American writers it was crucial to know whether the Indians "were a People in the *State* of *Nature*, and so had only what the *Law of Nature* gave them, or had quitted that State, entred into *Communities*, and . . . had fixed *the Bounds* of each *Community* respectively and Settled or Determin'd the matter of Property in Land." The law of nature, explained the Connecticut minister John Bulkley, "makes and allows the Land a *Man Tills & Subdues* to be his *Peculiar Property*," but no more. The Indians had none of the "Essentials of a state of *Civil Policy*," Bulkley concluded, so they lacked property rights in their un-cultivated land.[50]

But not everyone agreed that the Indians were in a state of nature. Close observers frequently remarked on institutions of tribal govern-ment. Maryland colonist George Alsop found Susquehanna government "so various and intricate a Laborynth, that the speculativ'st Artist in the whole World, with his artificial and natural Opticks, cannot see into the rule or sway of these *Indians*, to distinguish what name of Government to call them by." The name was uncertain, but they had a government. And not everyone agreed that natural law conferred property rights only on the cultivator. John Cowell's 1651 treatise affirmed that *any* occupa-tion of land, including hunting, fishing, and fowling, gave rise to prop-erty rights under the law of nature. Even the sea, claimed John Selden the following year, might be subject to property rights derived from oc-cupation.[51] On the level of theory, the argument was fought to a stand-still.

The controversy persisted as a matter of practice as well. After some uncertainty in the early years, imperial and colonial officials normally recognized the Indians as owners of their entire territories, including hunting grounds and other uncultivated areas. By 1644 even John Win-throp, who earlier had recognized Indian property rights only in cul-tivated land, purchased from two men, named Webomscom and Nodowahunt, an enormous tract (more than three hundred square miles) near the Massachusetts–Connecticut border, apparently without inquiring into how much of the land was in cultivation. In 1665 a visiting royal commission reminded the Massachusetts General Court that "no doubt the country is theirs till they give or sell it, though it be not im-proved." In New York, Governor William Cosby authorized the pur-chase from "the Native Indian proprietors" of "fifteen thousand acres of Vacant Land," and there are ample surviving records of English pur-chases so much bigger that they had to have included vast uncultivated areas, like the one New York lieutenant governor John Nanfan proudly reported to the Board of Trade in 1701, "a tract of land 800 miles long and 400 miles broad" he had bought from the Five Nations. The Earl of Egremont, secretary of state, emphasized in 1763 the importance of "guarding against any Invasion or Occupation of their Hunting Lands, the Possession of which is to be acquired by fair Purchase only."[52] As a matter of official policy, the Indians were acknowledged as the owners of North America—not just of their farmland, but of the entire continent.

As the English population grew, however, and as the demand among colonists for land increased, this policy became more difficult to enforce. Settlers bordering on uncultivated Indian land were often unconvinced of the legitimacy of Indian property rights. As time went on, more English colonists simply took over uncultivated Indian land, without permission from either the Indians or the colonial government, and often over the vigorous but ineffectual opposition of the colonial government. In some instances, colonial governments began granting uncultivated Indian land to colonists even without a prior purchase from the Indians. Actual practice on the frontier increasingly began to diverge from the law as stated in England.

The effect was an odd reversal. At the start of the colonial period, the imperial government had (in the colonial charters) assumed that the Indians' land could simply be taken, but the actual colonists found themselves often purchasing it. By the end of the colonial period, the imperial government was insisting that Indian land—even land upon which no Indians were physically present—had to be purchased. But the colonists now were much more powerful relative to the Indians than their predecessors had been a century and a half before, and many saw things differently. Much of the Indians' uncultivated land was being illegally appropriated—"illegally" not just under the Indians' law but under the colonizers' law as well.

Too Much like the Indians

There were several reasons why an English colonist would have naturally assumed that the Indians owned their land. To begin with, the English were heirs to an ancient strand of thought associating the development of property rights with a society's passage through specific stages of civilization. Greek and Roman writers were unanimous in holding that property was a man-made institution. "There is," Cicero declared, "no such thing as private ownership established by nature." They agreed that there had once been a time, long ago, when property was unknown—when, as Seneca put it, "the bounties of nature lay open to all, for men's indiscriminate use." They knew of far-off primitive peoples, like the Scythians, who lacked property even while the Greek and Roman civilizations were at their peak. And they agreed that it was the invention of agriculture that gave rise to property rights in land. The reason the Scythians and other primitive tribes did not divide up the land they occupied, the classical writers believed, was that they were nomads who had never learned to cultivate the land. The Scythians "have no fixed boundaries," observed the second-century writer Justin, because "they do not engage in agriculture. . . . Instead they pasture their cattle and sheep throughout the year, and live a nomadic life in the desolate wilds." It was only when "Ceres first taught men to plough the land," Virgil explained, that land was first divided. When there were "no ploughshares to break up the landscape," Ovid agreed, there were "no surveyors pegging out the boundaries of estates."[53] Humans had once been wanderers, without property in land, but when they settled down and began farming, they simultaneously established property rights.

The classical association of agriculture and property in land persisted through the medieval and early modern eras. The link was familiar to seventeenth-century theorists like Locke, Grotius, and Pufendorf, who endorsed it. By the time the English were colonizing North America, many writers had used the connection between agriculture and property to develop a framework for understanding the development of societies. As Adam Smith (among others) explained, societies progressed through four stages: "hunting, pasturage, farming, and commerce." Each stage corresponded to a particular set of political and economic institutions, including the institution of property. Hunters knew no property. Pastoralists needed, and thus developed, property in their animals. Farmers developed property in their land. And a commercial people like the English invented more complex property arrangements, to suit their needs. In the mind of an educated Englishman, property in land went along with agriculture. As William Blackstone noted in his ubiquitous legal treatise, "the art of agriculture . . . introduced and established the idea of a more permanent property in the soil."[54]

When the English reached North America, they tended to understand the Indians within this structure of anthropological thought. They often analogized the Indians to the ancient peoples that had once inhabited Britain, and to other ancient societies about which they had read. The Virginian Hugh Jones found that he had "a much truer and clearer notion of the Canaanites, Hebrews, etc., since I have seen the Indians."[55] North America lacked indigenous domesticated mammals, which required some modification in the standard march from hunter to pastoralist to farmer, but otherwise English colonists could assume that the Indians, like other peoples the world over, followed the same progression, with the same attendant institutional developments. If they were farmers, they had to have property in land.

That was why the repeated observation of Indian agriculture was so important. For an educated Englishman it was unthinkable that a society of farmers would not own the land they cultivated. The Indians may have lacked fences (because they had no domesticated animals to eat the crops), and written deeds, and all the other devices by which the English manifested their property rights in land. But none of that mattered, so long as they cultivated the land.

English colonists carried a second kind of intellectual heritage that likewise predisposed them to recognize the Indians as property owners. One of the most controversial social issues in seventeenth- and eighteenth-century England involved the enclosure of common fields. Enclosure meant the conversion of an ancient system of property rights, in which individuals and groups often possessed rights to use particular resources scattered in various places, into the familiar modern property system, in which individuals possess *all* the resources within a given area of land. Supporters of enclosure emphasized the efficiency of exclusive property rights; opponents stressed the harm to the poor from the loss of their traditional means of subsistence. But everyone on both sides of the debate had to be well aware that property rights could come in multiple forms. They knew that landownership could consist of the right to *use* resources as well as the exclusive control of geographic space. Indeed, in some colonies the earliest settlers must have preferred to allocate some property by use rights, because they replicated the common fields they remembered from home.[56]

Indian property arrangements were similar in some respects to the English common fields. Villages exercised control over large land areas. Village chiefs allocated plots for farming to families, based on their size and food needs. Unallocated lands were available to all village members for berry picking, wood gathering, and so on. The combination of individual planting rights in particular plots of land and group resource-gathering rights in the remainder would have reminded many English colonists of property systems back home. Even the way some Indian villages divided the cultivated areas would have been familiar to the English. As one observer of Indian agriculture explained, "the whole town plant in one vast field together; but yet the part or share of every individual family or habitation, is separated from the next adjoining, by a narrow strip,

A late sixteenth-century depiction of an Indian village in what is today North Carolina, showing extensive planted fields. Colonists observed Indian agriculture throughout eastern North America. Knowledge that the Indians were farmers contributed to the recognition of Indian property rights in land. Engraving by Theodor de Bry, from a drawing by John White.

or verge of grass." This was exactly how common fields were sometimes divided in England. English critics of the common fields sometimes explicitly made the analogy between England and America. The Quaker reformer John Bellers complained that common fields "make the Poor that are upon them too much like the *Indians*." John Locke referred to "the wild *Indian*, who knows no Inclosure, and is still a Tenant in common."[57]

The resemblances between Indian and pre-enclosure English property systems most likely inclined English settlers to recognize the Indians as property owners. Even if they perceived Indian property arrangements as inferior to the emerging English norm of exclusive rights to all the resources within a given physical space, they would have had to acknowledge that such a norm was not a prerequisite to property. The Indians' relationship to their land would have been instantly recognizable as a form of property.

Apart from these intellectual influences, there were three immediate material circumstances that impelled the English to recognize the Indians as landowners. First was the simple matter of power. In the earliest years of colonization, the English lacked the military superiority that would have been necessary to implement a policy of conquest. Even after the English population increased to the point where conquest would have been feasible, taking the Indians' land by force would have required sacrificing the lives of thousands of English colonists at the very least, in what would have been a protracted war. "Let now any soldier or politician consider the enormous endless expence of all this conduct," reasoned Thomas Pownall in his treatise on colonial administration, "and then answer to what profitable purpose such measure leads." It was far cheaper in money and in lives to maintain cordial relationships with the Indians, by purchasing land rather than seizing it. The "principle Care" of colonial policy was "to cultivate and maintain a good Understanding with all the Indians," the *Pennsylvania Gazette* declared in 1736. To that end, "nothing hath contributed more than the Practice . . . of purchasing their Claims to Lands."[58]

The need to maintain good relationships with the Indians was made even stronger by the fact that for almost the entire colonial period the English were competing with the French for control of North America. Both sides often needed the Indians as allies. It "is apparent to the meanest Capacity," noted Archibald Kennedy in 1751, that "the *French*, our natural Enemies and Competitors in every Corner of the World

where we have any Concern, are indefatigable in cultivating the Friendship of their own *Indians,* and by all Means and Arts in their Power, . . .
endeavouring to seduce those in the *British* Interest." At many times, in
many places, the English could not afford to do anything that would too
greatly offend the Indians. Seizing land was one such thing. For reasons
of security, it was ordinarily preferable to purchase Indian land, especially where the French were trying to purchase it too. As one Boston
correspondent reported in 1684, "sundry inland Indians that inhabit
about 60 miles from Hadley . . . came to Hadley or Northhampton and
informed the French had sent to them to purchase the Lands, but that if
the English would buy them the French should have [none] and that
the English to whom this information & tender was made, answered the
Indians they would recommend the matter to the General Court in October, but the Indians being impatient of so long a delay, and uncertain
in the end of the result, then presently struck up with the French." William Johnson experienced the same kind of pressure. In 1751, when the
Onondaga offered to sell some far-off land, Johnson promptly bought it,
even though it was too remote for settlement in the foreseeable future,
"to prevent the said Lands from falling into the Hands of the French of
Canada."[59] In this kind of climate, refusing to acknowledge Indian property rights would have been perilous.

The danger posed by the French, if the English insufficiently respected Indian property rights, came to the fore in the middle of the
eighteenth century, when the illegal encroachments of English settlers
on Indian land drove many tribes to ally with France. As the Board of
Trade explained toward the end of the French and Indian War, "the primary cause" of many tribes' decision to switch their alliance from England to France "was the Cruelty and Injustice with which they had been
treated with respect to their Hunting Grounds, in open Violation of
those solemn Compacts by which they had yielded to us the Dominion
but not the Property of their Lands."[60] Until the 1760s, when France
ceased to be a competitor, the struggle with France was a factor pressing
strongly for the recognition of Indian property rights.

A second material factor was equally important. Land was abundant,
and it was usually cheap. Whether to buy an asset or simply seize it, in
any context, is in large part an economic calculation, involving a comparison of the costs of each method. The less expensive the Indians' land,
the more likely the English were to buy it. In 1697 two New Yorkers
found "Lands to be procured at easy prices from the Indians." The Indi-

ans were often eager sellers. Roger Pederick happily informed his wife in 1676 that he had found a place for them in New Jersey, because "the Natives were as willing to sell as we were to Buy; and there is Land enough bought." Robert Wade, another New Jersey colonist, agreed that the Indians "are very willing to sell their land to the *English*." The Scottish settler Gavin Laury reported that the Indians "do not refuse to sell Land."[61]

Land seemed inexpensive to the English because the population density along the frontier was minuscule relative to that back home. In many areas the Indian population had been reduced drastically by disease, and the survivors had much more land than they needed. Even without disease, the sparseness of the frontier population, both Indian and English, yielded real estate prices much lower than those in more thickly settled areas. Low prices made purchasing land an attractive option.

Finally, once the English began purchasing land from the Indians, it became very difficult as a political matter to refuse to recognize the Indians as property owners, because much of the English population derived title to their land from the Indians. Many colonists had bought land either from the Indians directly or at the end of a chain of title that originated with the Indians. To suggest that the Indians were not property owners would have been to upset the settled expectations of a large number of *English* property owners, who would suddenly have found their land titles open to question. David Dunbar reported from Maine in 1730, for example, that the inhabitants all traced their ownership back to Indian deeds from the previous century. Landowners whose title was dependent on Indian property rights were a latent but powerful political force, capable of defeating any effort to declare the Indians non-owners of land.[62]

That power can be seen in an episode that occurred in the late 1680s, when the imperial government briefly united the northern colonies into the Dominion of New England. As part of the reorganization of colonial administration, the Dominion's governor, Edmund Andros, determined to resolve inconsistent land claims by invalidating all titles that could not be traced back to a government grant. Andros rejected land claims based on what he called "pretended Purchases from Indians," on the ground that "from the Indians noe title cann be Derived." The sudden change in policy aroused a storm of protest from New Englanders. If purchase from the Indians could not serve as the root of a valid land title, declared a group of prominent Bostonians, then *"no Man was owner of a Foot of Land in all the Colony."* One minister insisted that he and his parishioners had acquired their land "by a right of purchase from the Indians, who were Native Inhabitants, and had possession of the Land before the English came hither." The Glorious Revolution put an end to the Dominion of New England, so Andros was never able to pursue his intended reform. The incident nevertheless demonstrated that Indian property rights had an entrenched and constantly growing group of supporters, made up of all the settlers who traced their titles back to the Indians. The policy of treating the Indians as property owners was self-replicating. Once it started, it was extraordinarily difficult to stop.[63]

In light of the changes that would come after the American Revolution, it is worth emphasizing that the policy of respecting Indian property rights in the colonial period did *not* rest on English respect for the Indians themselves, or on any sense among the English that they and the Indians were equals. Indian property rights under English law could coexist easily with English prejudice toward the Indians, and with unequal treatment in other areas of the law.

That the English were advancing their *own* interests rather than the Indians' interests by recognizing Indian property rights did not imply that the English were merely pretending to treat the Indians as landowners. We can, in principle, distinguish between two English states of mind—one in which the Indians were believed to be property owners in some pure moral sense, and another in which the Indians were treated *as if* they were property owners because treating them that way was most advantageous to the English. In 1674, for example, New York's Council insisted that although it was "the usuall practice" for New Yorkers acquiring land "to give their Indians some recompence for their land & so [the landowner] seems to purchase it of them, yet that is not done for want of sufficient title from the King," the king being the land's true owner. Paying the Indians was a matter of "prudence & christian charity lest otherwise the Indians might have destroyed the first planters," not a recognition that the Indians owned the land.[64] But the two states of mind were indistinguishable in actual practice, because both produced the same real-world consequences—the perceived need to buy the Indians' land rather than seize it. There is no actual difference between respecting others' property rights and treating them as if one is respecting their property rights. That's what a property right *is*—the knowledge that one will be treated as a property owner.

The mix of culture and self-interested calculation that created English colonial land policy was unstable, however, and in this sense it would make an enormous difference, in later years, that the English respected Indian property rights for their own benefit rather than the Indians'. Each of the factors that gave rise to Indian property rights was subject to change. Some were already changing in the colonial period. The balance of power between settlers and Indians was constantly in flux, and over the long run it was tipping inexorably in favor of the settlers. Land was growing more expensive with each new wave of European immigration. In later years, other factors would change as well. Settlers would begin encountering Indians farther west who lacked agriculture. Memories of the English common fields would grow dim with the passage of time. Eventually the percentage of American landowners who traced their titles back to a purchase from the Indians would begin to decline. The respect paid to Indian property rights during the colonial period was far from perfect; but after the Revolution, Indian property rights would never again be as strong, because white residents of the United States would face a very different set of circumstances.

Roger Williams and John Locke

Roger Williams and John Locke are the two men most frequently quoted by historians in connection with British colonial land policy. Williams, the early seventeenth-century religious leader and founder of Rhode Island, is conventionally assumed to have been a rare English defender of Indian property rights who was drummed out of Massachusetts for holding unorthodox views like this one. Wilcomb Washburn, for instance, cites Williams as "one of the few Englishmen who dared to dismiss European claims to American soil as unjustified and illegal if the prior right of the Indian were not recognized." Locke, the late seventeenth-century philosopher and government official, is typically read as a representative and influential exponent of the view that the Indians lacked property rights, as a writer who "captured the essence of his age in his treatment of the relation of property, colonial expansion, and good government."[65] The two most well known colonial commentators on Indians and land were unrepresentative figures, however, and in some respects provided misleading observations of the world around them.

Roger Williams was no doubt a staunch defender of Indian property rights. "The *Natives* are very exact and punctuall in the bounds of their

Lands," he observed. "And I have knowne them make bargaine and sale amongst themselves for a small piece, or quantity of ground." Williams believed that his English colonial colleagues disagreed with him. He claimed to find "a sinfull opinion amongst many that Christians have right to *Heathens* Lands."[66] Williams accused "not a few" of the English settlers of thinking that "*Christian Kings* (so calld) are invested with Right by virtue of their *Christianitie*, to take and give away the *Lands* and *Countries* of other men."[67] Historians have tended to take such assertions at face value, as evidence not just of Williams's opinion but of the views of the other English colonists.

As we have seen, however, colonial opinion as to Indian property rights was not nearly as anti-Indian as Williams claimed. In the early seventeenth century there were indeed some who believed that Christians had the right to take the land of non-Christians, but there were many who believed they did not have that right, and as time went on, belief in a Christian right of conquest dwindled away. In 1634, a decade *before* Williams published his criticism of his ostensibly conquest-minded neighbors, Massachusetts passed a statute declaring that "what lands any of the Indians in this jurisdiction have possessed and improved, by subduing the same, they have just right unto." As was common in New England in the early years of colonization, the statute cited scripture in support of its declaration—Genesis 1:28 and 9:1 (God's double command to "replenish the earth"), and Psalm 115:16 ("The heaven, even the heavens, are the Lord's: but the earth hath he given to the children of men"). Far from a Christian right of conquest, this was a Christian recognition that the Indians owned their land. The statute went on to protect Indian property rights by two methods. First, if any English person "shall offer injuriously to put any of the Indians from their planting grounds, or fishing places," the Indians "shall have relief in any of the Courts of Justice amongst the English, as the English have." Second, the statute authorized English settlers to purchase land from the Indians, provided they had license from the General Court.[68] Colonial land policy hardly embodied a supposed right to seize the land of the heathen.

An exasperated John Cotton replied to Williams's charges by emphasizing their inaccuracy. "It was answered to him," Cotton explained, that "it was neither the Kings intendment, nor the *English* Planters to take possession of the Countrey by murther of the Natives, or by robbery." The English did not conceive of themselves as conquerors, as Williams claimed. Instead, they would acquire land by two means. Either they would "take possession of the voyd places of the Countrey by the Law of Nature, . . . or if we tooke any Lands from the Natives, it was by way of purchase, and free consent." There would be disagreement for some time yet over whether uncultivated ground could be occupied as vacant, but at the very least the English would purchase the Indians' farmland. "This answer did not satsfie Mr. *Williams*," Cotton recalled, "who pleaded, the Natives, though they did not, nor could subdue the Countrey, . . . yet they hunted all the Countrey over, and for the expedition of their hunting voyages, they burnt up all the underwoods in the Countrey." In the debate over whether hunting grounds had to be purchased, Williams was taking the pro-Indian side, a view that was apparently a minority view in early Massachusetts but would soon prevail. Cotton responded with the standard argument on the other side: "We did not conceive that it is a just Title to so vast a Continent, to make no other improvement of millions of Acres in it, but onely to burne it up for pastime."[69] There had to be some limit to the territory a small society could claim, or else a single person might own a continent. Like many early theorists of colonization, Cotton drew the line at cultivation. Today that view may seem insufficiently sensitive to differences in food production between the two peoples, and indeed the English began routinely purchasing hunting grounds not long after Williams and Cotton had their dispute. But Cotton's side of the argument was hardly a defense of a Christian right of conquest. Williams's fellow colonists simply did not believe what Williams claimed they did.

From the perspective of the men governing Massachusetts, the problem with Williams was not that he defended Indian property rights—most other colonists did too—but that he denied the right of the Crown to grant patents authorizing the settlement of particular areas of land, and thus denied the Crown's right to limit settlement to particular places. Williams seems to have envisioned a free-for-all, in which any English person could go anywhere in North America and buy land from the Indians. The Massachusetts authorities would have disagreed not with the concept of purchasing but with that of unconstrained settlement, because it would have made governing the colony and defending it from external attack much more difficult. The colony was far easier to govern and defend if the colonists could be kept close together, and the only way to do that was to prevent them from settling too far away. Roger Williams was thus not a lone defender of Indian property rights in a society that refused to recognize them. Williams was an unorthodox thinker in many respects, but on the question of whether the Indians owned their land he was well within the mainstream of English opinion.

A different kind of misunderstanding persists with respect to the work of John Locke. Locke's *Two Treatises of Government,* published in a few editions in the 1690s, is well known for, among other things, Locke's assertion that property rights arise from labor. "Though the Earth, and all inferior Creatures be common to all Men, yet every Man has a *Property* in his own *Person,*" Locke asserted. "The *Labour* of his Body, and the *Work* of his Hands, we may say, are properly his." From that premise, Locke concluded that "whatsoever then he removes out of the State that Nature hath provided, and left it in, he hath mixed his *Labour* with, and joyned to it something that is his own, and thereby makes it his *Property.*" As applied to land, Locke's labor theory provided a clear rule: "*As much Land* as a Man Tills, Plants, Improves, Cultivates, and can use the Product of, so much is his *Property.*" This was a rule that was obviously helpful in figuring out which land the Indians owned and which they did not, and we have seen it put to use, before Locke was even born, by English writers limiting Indian property rights to cultivated land.

To illustrate the importance of agriculture in giving value to land, Locke contrasted the English, who cultivated their land and thus enjoyed property rights in it, with the Indians, who Locke asserted did not cultivate their land and thus lacked property rights. He compared the cultivated land of England with "the wild woods and uncultivated wast of America left to nature, without any improvement, tillage or husbandry." It was this supposed failure of the Indians to practice agriculture that made them so poor. The Indians "are rich in Land, and poor in all the Comforts of Life," Locke reasoned, "for want of improving it by labour." America provided Locke a window onto the distant past of England and the rest of the civilized world, a glimpse of a time when land had not yet been appropriated as property. "Thus in the beginning," Locke concluded, in perhaps the most often quoted passage from the *Two Treatises,* "all the World was *America.*"[70]

By the time Locke wrote these words, however, every English colonist knew very well that the Indians were farmers and that they had a system of property. Locke's account of the Indians is completely at odds with virtually all other accounts of the period, many of which included detailed observations of Indian agricultural techniques and property ownership. What makes Locke's error all the more remarkable is that Locke must have *known* he was providing inaccurate information about the Indians.

John Locke was not just a philosopher. He was also an administrator of the American colonies, first as an aide to the Earl of Shaftesbury, one of the original proprietors of Carolina, and then in the 1670s as secretary to the Board of Trade, the part of the English government with responsibility for colonial administration. Locke had a big library, including many accounts of travel in North America. He could hardly have avoided reading descriptions of Indian agriculture. As part of his work, Locke consistently wrote and received correspondence relating to North America that contained accounts of Indian property rights. In 1672, for instance, Locke wrote for Shaftesbury's benefit an abstract of several recent letters from the colonists in Carolina, one of which Locke summarized as "Desire Commoditys for Indian trade to purchase land." On Shaftesbury's behalf Locke wrote a letter to one colonial governor urging "that you suffer not your people out of greedinesse to molest . . . any of the neighbour Indians in their quiet possessions." Locke endorsed a letter to Shaftesbury from one of the early Carolina colonists reporting that "wee found very great Assistans from the Indians who showed themselves very kind [and] sould us provisions att very reasonable rates."[71] Locke had to have known that the Indians were farmers and that colonists were purchasing land from the Indians. But he did not make use of this knowledge in the *Two Treatises.*

It is hard to understand why Locke would have knowingly painted such a misleading picture of the Indians. Locke probably wrote the *Two Treatises* at a time when he was out of office, and indeed out of England, so he does not seem to have been trying to influence colonial policy. Perhaps he succumbed to the temptation to provide vivid examples in support of his theory of property. Maybe he felt constrained to be consistent with the view he had expressed in 1669, as the author of Carolina's first constitution, perhaps before he had acquired much knowledge of the Indians. Locke's "Fundamental Constitutions of Carolina" was an exercise in high theory, bearing little relation to actual conditions in Carolina. It envisioned, among other things, a hereditary nobility of "Landgraves" and "Casiques," each with a defined number of "baronies" subject to elaborate rules of inheritance. Toward the end of this scheme, in article 112, Locke declared that land could not be obtained from the Indians: "No person whatever, shall hold or claim any land in

Carolina, by purchase or gift, or otherwise, from the natives or any other whatsoever; but merely from and under the Lords Proprietors."[72] Carolina settlers paid no more attention to this provision than to the part about the Landgraves and Casiques. They had already been buying land from the Indians, and they kept right on buying it.

Whatever the reason for Locke's error, there is no evidence that the *Two Treatises* caused anyone in colonial North America to cease respecting Indian property rights or to stop purchasing land from the Indians. It would be a further error to take Locke's writings as being representative of English thought about land and Indians in the late seventeenth century, or as having influenced colonial land policy in the eighteenth century.[73] Anyone in a position to affect land policy would have known Locke was wrong.

A combination of ideological and material circumstances impelled the English to recognize the Indians as the "Native Proprietors" of North America, as owners from whom land would have to be purchased. But of course we know what happened. Repeated land sales only drove the Indians farther and farther west, and deeper into poverty. This outcome would be easy to understand if it had been produced by outright conquest, but how could it have resulted from a series of transactions? That is the subject of the next chapter.

2

Manhattan for Twenty-four Dollars

By the end of the colonial period, the easternmost tribes had scarcely any land left. Some tribes, reduced in numbers by disease and poverty, remained in the east. Others found themselves forced to migrate west, past the frontier of English settlement. By the early 1760s, when the Board of Trade inquired into the colonies' relations with the Indians, the governors of Virginia and Massachusetts reported that the Indians were almost gone. "The number of Indians residing in the known parts of this Colony, is very small," explained Virginia governor Francis Fauquier. When the Board of Trade circulated proposed regulations for the purchase of Indian land, Governor Francis Bernard of Massachusetts replied that "there is no occasion for them here."[1] The Indians had lost nearly all their land. But they had little to show for it. After selling much of eastern North America, the Indians were poorer than when they began.

In this chapter we will look again at Indian land sales in the colonial period, but this time from the Indians' point of view. What were these transactions like? How could the Indians have sold so much land and ended up so poor?

Were the Sales Voluntary?

One possibility is that the sales were not voluntary transactions at all, that instead the Indians were forced to accept them. On this view, the ostensible deeds or treaties memorializing the sales were nothing but shams, legal fictions that covered up exercises of brute force. Such was the private opinion of one early historian, Thomas Jefferson. In the pub-lished version of *Notes on the State of Virginia*, Jefferson explained that the extensive documentary record of Indian land sales demonstrated that Virginia had been taken from the Indians not by conquest but rather "by purchases made in the most unexceptionable form." In Jefferson's origi-nal manuscript, however, he added a qualification that removed most of the force from this statement. "It is true," he noted there, "that these purchases were sometimes made with the price in one hand and the sword in the other." Jefferson, Virginia's governor at the time, could not afford to antagonize landowners by casting doubt on the validity of their titles. He crossed this comment out before publication. Some recent his-torians have similarly described the process of land purchasing as "inva-sion" or "dispossession," papered over with what Francis Jennings calls "the deed game," an array of tricks to put a legal face on what was really theft.[2] This is a view with considerable plausibility today, because many of the treaties by which Indian tribes ceded land to the United States in the nineteenth century were signed by the tribes under the threat of force. But we must be careful not to use our knowledge of the nine-teenth century to interpret colonial transactions. That tribes were com-pelled to sign treaties in the nineteenth century does not mean they were also compelled to sell land two hundred years earlier.

The difference between voluntariness and involuntariness is one of degree, not of kind.[3] Like any other decision, the decision to enter into a contract may be more or less voluntary, along a spectrum that lacks any dividing line between categories. The best one can say is that there are some choices so far toward one extreme or the other that there would be a consensus as to whether to call those choices voluntary or involuntary. When an armed robber offers to take "your money or your life," we would most likely call the ensuing decision involuntary, despite the for-mal choice involved. When a millionaire decides what kind of car to buy, we would most likely call the choice voluntary, even if circumstances narrow his range of options. Many decisions are not so easily labeled, however, because they are not so close to one end of the spectrum. Our question is thus not whether to call conveyances of Indian land "volun-tary" or "involuntary," but rather how close any given transaction was to one or the other extreme.

Freedom of activity is largely a function of one's power relative to oth-ers. In the early years of English colonization, when the English were not powerful enough to force the Indians to sell their land, sales by Indians seem to have been close to the "voluntary" end of the spectrum. English purchasers sometimes complained about having to buy land from the Indians, a complaint that would make no sense if the purchasers were forcing the sellers to sell. Land purchasers sometimes had to bide their time and wait for the Indians to offer land at prices low enough to warrant the purchase, a practice that would likewise be incomprehensible if the English could force sales at times and prices of their choosing.[4] The Indians often complained about the transactions afterward, but the complaint was usually that they had been defrauded by English misdescription of the land being sold, or that they had been tricked into signing a deed while drunk. The Indians' complaint was *not* that they had been compelled to sell land by the threat of force.

Indians had two reasons to sell land. First, and most obviously, land could be exchanged for all the useful things the English brought. The precontact population density of North America was very low by European standards, and it only grew lower when the Indians were ravaged by European diseases. The Indians had lots of land. The English, meanwhile, were well stocked with clothing, axes, hoes, knives, fish hooks, kettles, guns, and the like, goods the Indians could put to immediate use in procuring food. The English also had a surplus of nonutilitarian commodities like glass beads, which the Indians valued because they could be incorporated into traditional ceremonies, along with familiar objects like shells and crystals.[5] The English, who had plenty of goods, wanted Indian land, while the Indians, who had plenty of land, wanted English goods. There were enormous gains to be had from trade. It would have been remarkable if the Indians *hadn't* traded land for other things. If creatures from another planet were to arrive on earth bearing astonishing labor-saving devices of which we had never conceived, and offered them to us in exchange for some commodity we possessed in abundance, we would make the same trade today.

In retrospect, to be sure, the new availability to the Indians of English products can look less like a marvelous expansion of the possibilities of life and more like the insidious fostering of colonial dependence. "By the Habitual necessity those Indians acquire of European Assistance, and the Supply of European Goods," one English settler could write as early as the middle of the eighteenth century, "by Degrees they become insensibly altogether dependant on the European Nation that settles among them."[6] The introduction of alcohol soon became widely recognized as an instance of this phenomenon. In some areas, the English introduction of guns set off arms races, in which tribes rushed to acquire guns to defend themselves against neighboring tribes doing the same thing. But if trading land for English products looks like a bad deal today, there was no way to know that at the time. Land was the Indians' primary asset. If they wanted to obtain English products, they had to sell it.

The Indians' second reason to sell land was to cement political alliances between Indian and English communities. Tribes were sporadically at war with one another all through the seventeenth and eighteenth centuries. As Samuel Wilson explained of late seventeenth-century Carolina, "the *Indians* have been always so ingaged in Wars one Town or Village against another." Nearby English allies were very useful for defense. The mere presence of a nearby English settlement could be enough to deter an attack from an enemy tribe. In New England, John Winthrop reported, the Pequots offered the English land to settle near them, "because they were now in war with the Naragansetts" and needed help.[7] Less powerful tribes in the Connecticut River Valley, meanwhile, were offering land to English settlers in the hope that a powerful ally would help extricate them from the domination of the Pequots. The earliest colonists in Carolina observed that the local tribes "seem to be very well pleased att our Settling here expecting protection under us which we have promised them against another sort of Indians . . . called Westoes."[8] Trading land for military protection against other tribes was clearly not in the interest of Indians collectively, but it *was* in the interest of individual tribes. The Indians were more politically fragmented than the English, and this would not be the only respect in which they would suffer for it.

From the onset of colonization, the Indians thus had ample reason to sell land to the English. In the early years, it was still possible for tribes to sell the tracts they used least intensively but retain the rest. The combined effects of English immigration and disease among the Indians had not yet tipped the population balance decisively in favor of the English. Under those circumstances, selective land sales could allow the Indians to mix old and new ways on their own terms, by using land to acquire the best of what the English brought without giving up the best aspects of traditional life. After selling some of their land, one late seventeenth-century English writer concluded, "the poor creatures are never the worse but much better, as [they] themselves confess, being now supplyed by way of Trade with all they want or stand in need of, [and] hunting and fishing as they did before."[9] This view seems absurdly optimistic today, but that is only because we know what eventually happened. At the time, it would not have been irrational for Indians to have thought the same. In the earliest years of English settlement in many parts of North America, the Indians could reasonably have anticipated peacefully coexisting with the settlers.

As time went on, the constraints pushing Indians to sell land grew stronger. In any given area, a mounting English population posed a latent military threat to tribes unwilling to accede to requests to sell land, even when no violence actually occurred, because the incidents when violence did occur must have been widely known. In such circumstances it was prudent for tribes to sell land they might have preferred to retain. On Long Island, for example, the Matinecock leader Suscaneman appears to have pursued this strategy, by selling small tracts to appease settlers in the hope of forestalling demands for larger ones, and sometimes even by deliberately selling ambiguously defined adjacent tracts to competing groups, in order to take advantage of the delay caused by the ensuing litigation.[10]

Even worse from the Indian point of view, English population pressure often caused individual settlers, and sometimes even colonial governments, to ignore boundary lines and occupy Indian land. Illegal settlement was a constant source of complaint among the Indians. John Stuart, sent by the English government to smooth relationships with the southern tribes, was "greatly mortified" upon arriving in South Carolina to learn that the Cherokees "were much distressed by the encroachments of the Neighbouring Provinces who granted their hunting Grounds" to English settlers, "by which means their Game were drove away." More often the trespasses were committed by individual settlers who knew they were beyond the effective control of colonial officials. "Some of our own inhabitants," complained Virginia governor Francis Fauquier to the Board of Trade, have "gone and seated themselves on [Indian land] near the Ohio, not only without right to do so, but even against orders of council and advertisements posted to prevent this practise."[11]

The imperial government and the colonial governments often sided with the Indians in such disputes, but there was little they could do. The imperial government was too far away to exert much control over the frontier. Colonial governors had the formal power to stop illegal settlement, but governors tended to be weak in practice, hemmed in by the practical need to keep the support of the locally powerful, some of whom were occupying Indian land themselves. And given the technology of the seventeenth and eighteenth centuries, even colonial governors were far from the frontier. In 1755 New York governor Charles Hardy received instructions from London to do something about the "great Complaints" the government was receiving from the Five Nations, "that Settlements have been made upon their Lands by Persons claiming the same under Pretended Deeds of Sale or Conveyance from the said Indians." Hardy was ordered to "forthwith make the most strict and Impartial Enquiry into the Cause of their Complaints" to "take the most speedy and Effectual methods, which the Law in such Cases will allow, to redress their Grievances," and to use his "utmost Endeavours to quiet the uneasiness and Discontent which have of late appeared amongst them."[12] Whatever action Hardy took did little good.

Sometimes the only way colonial governments could prevent trespassing was to keep up with the settlers, by buying the Indians' land as quickly as colonists could snatch it, in a desperate effort to legalize the inevitable. A "great point which must without any loss of time be resolved on," James Logan warned William Penn's sons, the heirs to Pennsylvania, "is to make new Purchases of the Indians, without which we may expect a war that would run this Province into the extreamest confusion."[13] But such a policy was doomed to fail, because it was effectively an invitation to settle on Indian land. Once the westernmost settlers learned to anticipate that a colony would retroactively authorize their trespasses, trespassing would only grow more common.

Repeated encroachment must have tipped Indians toward selling land they would not have otherwise sold, as a means of obtaining some recompense for a state of affairs they had great trouble preventing. Even before any encroachment, the buildup of English settlement in an area would have made local tribes more prone to sell land in anticipation of future trespasses. Every increase in the English population gave the Indians more reason to sell their land.

Even when settlers respected Indian boundaries, large-scale English settlement often produced dramatic ecological changes that could be devastating to traditional Indian life. English hunters thinned the population of deer that the Indians had always hunted. English cows and pigs ate Indian crops, as well as the grass that had once supported deer and other indigenous animals. English demand for fur drove the beaver and similar animals close to extinction. English mill dams threatened

Indian fishing. As traditional ecosystems gradually vanished, land became less valuable to the Indians than it had formerly been. "His land was spoiled," the Catawbas' chief complained to colonial officials in 1763. The English had simply settled nearby, but in so doing "they have spoiled him 100 Miles every way."[14] The less the Indians' land was able to support traditional ways of life, the more the Indians would have been willing to sell it. Ecological change could thus be an indirect catalyst for land sales that would not have otherwise occurred.

The Indians' engagement with the English colonial economy could also indirectly cause land to be sold. Colonial North America was chronically short of specie or anything else that could serve as payment for goods. As on other frontiers in other times and places, colonial merchants normally sold goods on credit, to other settlers and to the Indians. As Indians entered into this economy, by obtaining goods on the promise of later payment, they placed their assets at risk. Most Indians had only one significant asset, and that was land. If they could not pay off their debts in any other currency, their only recourse was to pay in land. In the Connecticut River Valley, for example, English traders would sell goods to the Indians on credit, to be paid for in beaver pelts at the conclusion of the following year's hunt. As beaver became hunted close to extinction in the 1660s, Indians found it increasingly difficult to pay their debts. The English acquired many parcels of land by foreclosing on loans in the 1660s and 1670s. In Natick, Massachusetts, most Indian land sales were prompted by the need to pay off debts. In the southern colonies, settlers obtained land by selling goods to the Indians on credit and later agreeing to cancel the Indians' debt in exchange for land cessions, a practice that became so common that by the late colonial period land acquisition was the primary reason to enter the Indian trade in the first place. William Stith, the mid-eighteenth-century historian of Virginia, had effusive praise for the early governor Thomas Dale, because of Dale's foresight in lending hundreds of bushels of corn to local tribes. "The next year," Stith marveled, "he took a Mortgage of their whole Countries."[15]

Were all these pressures enough for us to call the later land sales involuntary? Perhaps, although again there is no magic tipping point at which pressure to sell turns a voluntary transaction into the opposite. Some of the constraints under which the Indians sold land, such as the need to pay off debts, are often experienced by sellers today, and although we recognize an element of compulsion in sales under these circumstances, we don't normally think of them as less than voluntary. Some of the constraints faced by the Indians, on the other hand, were much closer to the involuntary end of the spectrum. Real estate sales prompted by environmental degradation are hardly unknown today, of course, but the arrival of Europeans in North America caused ecological change of a magnitude that dwarfs just about any comparable event today. Transactions entered into because of a thinly veiled threat of expropriation—sell your land or else I'll forcibly take it—are even closer to the robber's ultimatum of your money or your life. In the colonial land economy, however, the threat of expropriation was more likely to remain implicit than to be voiced; and the Indians probably had a stronger perception of implicit threat than the English, many of whom no doubt did not consider themselves to be at all threatening. Even when the threat of expropriation was explicit, there was no neutral arbiter to whom disputes as to the voluntariness of a land sale could be referred. If the English perceived a transaction as voluntary and the Indians did not, enforcement of the transaction was a function of the relative power of the two groups, a balance that increasingly favored the English.

On the whole, then, while it is an overstatement to think of colonial land purchasing as a sham, as a legalistic way of papering over what was really an invasion premised on brute force, the allegation is not completely hollow. From the English point of view, these were genuine contracts, in the sense that both sellers and purchasers had the freedom to sign them or walk away. But Indians' perceptions were most likely mixed. In the early years of colonization in any given place, the Indians appear to have been as free to sell or not sell as the English were to buy or not buy. Over time, however, the force of a mounting English population, often combined with a dwindling Indian population, strengthened the constraints pressuring the Indians to sell. In the colonial period this pressure was often not explicit or direct. But it did not have to be. The net result was most likely sales that would not have otherwise occurred, and sales at prices lower than they would otherwise have been.

Did the Indians and the English Understand the Transactions in the Same Way?

A second explanation of how the Indians could have sold so much land and yet ended up so poor might be that the Indians did not realize what they were giving up until too late, because their understanding of the transactions was different from the English understanding. "No early seventeenth-century Wabanaki sagamore," suggests one anthropologist, "could have been as aware then as he later might have become of the key European value/attitude/assumption of exclusive monopoly take-over." The point has been made for some time, with varying degrees of respect for the Indians' ability to catch on.[16] If the Indians thought they were merely agreeing to share resources with English purchasers, and found out only afterward that the English believed they had acquired sole possession of the purchased land, the Indians would have "sold" much more land than they intended to, at prices far too low to compensate them for what they were giving up. Could such misunderstandings have accounted for a significant number of transactions?

The Indians did not sell land before the English arrived. Within the area controlled by a tribe, individuals and families had exclusive rights to cultivate particular tracts, rights that were allocated by tribal leaders. The population density was low enough that a tribe member desiring farmland could presumably obtain some from the tribe without having to purchase the rights already allocated to someone else. Nor was there any occasion for a member of one tribe to buy land from a member of another. The control that a tribe exercised over its territory was closely akin to the European concept of sovereignty; a member of one tribe could no more convey land to a member of another than a resident of England could place his property under the sovereignty of France. The lack of land sales was also due to the fact that rights to land were not perpetual. They would come to an end when the owner stopped farming the land, and probably more frequently when the tribe as a whole moved to another location within its territory. When local resources— whether the soil, game, or firewood—became depleted, the tribe would move on, and might not return to the first site for generations. Iroquois towns, for example, shifted every decade or two. Other tribes, especially to the north where the land was less fertile, moved more often.[17] Upon arriving at a new location, the tribe would clear fields for farming and tribal leaders would allocate new exclusive rights within the fields. Indian property rights in land were thus inherently temporary. There was little reason for one tribe member to purchase them from another, even if farmland in one location was scarce, because at any given time the existing distribution of land was soon to end.

Precontact Indian economies afforded little opportunity for the accumulation of material wealth, so even if there had been a reason to buy land there would have been little with which to buy it. In a society that never stayed in one place for more than a few years, without institutions like banks to convert physical assets into portable, intangible ones, material possessions could be unwanted encumbrances. The English tended to interpret the Indian way of life as poverty. Locke, to pick the most famous example, found the Indians "rich in Land, and poor in all the Comforts of Life," in that they "have not one hundredth part of the Conveniences we enjoy." The dissident Massachusetts settler Thomas Morton probably came closer to the Indians' perception of the matter when he suggested that "they may be rather accompted to live richly, wanting nothing that is needefull; and to be commended for leading a contented life."[18] But whether one sees their way of life as bountiful or wanting, the Indians had no reason to buy and sell land among themselves, and the concept of a land sale did not exist in North America before the English arrived.

The English, by contrast, had been buying and selling land for centuries, so it would be surprising if the two cultures had the same interpretation of the earliest English offers to purchase Indian land. The very first transactions were most likely understood by the Indians not as real estate sales in the English sense but rather as devices for incorporating English settlers within traditional Indian social and political networks. The English, that is, would receive the right to use the natural resources within the "purchased" location, just like members of the tribe. The benefit the Indians sought to obtain was not just the purchase price but also the expectation that the settlers would become long-term trading partners and military allies. Such an understanding would permit the "sale" of the same land many times over, for the purpose of creating a denser network of mutual interdependence between a tribe and various groups of settlers. In early colonial Maine, for example, tribes repeatedly sold the same tracts to multiple English purchasers, apparently on the assumption that they were conveying nonexclusive rights to use resources, not "ownership" in the English sense. One Plymouth colonist complained that a local parcel had been "several times sold by the *Indian* Sachems and people to the *English*." In many cases Indians continued to inhabit land even after "selling" it to the English, which again suggests that the Indians did not intend to convey exclusive rights.[19]

When the English thought they had purchased land, and the Indians thought they had merely formalized an alliance, the result could be enduring ill will on both sides. In 1755, South Carolina governor James

Glen convened a meeting with the Cherokees at Saluda, for the purpose—as colonial officials understood it—of acquiring a large tract of
Cherokee land. More than five hundred settlers attended, joined by
more than five hundred Cherokees. The two peoples exchanged all
sorts of gifts, including some "furniture laced with gold" presented by
Glen to the Cherokee leaders. Participants enjoyed a meal served on silver bowls and cups. A Cherokee speaker declared (at least as his words
were translated into English) that the tribe wished to give "all their
Lands to the King of Great Britain . . . for they acknowledge him to be
the owner of all their Lands and Waters." Both sides left the conference
pleased with the outcome. But Glen and his colleagues might have suspected that the Cherokees' understanding of what had taken place did
not match their own, for the Cherokees had refused to accept payment
for the land. To be polite, they relented and took a token sum only when
Glen insisted that they do so, hardly the behavior to be expected from a
seller of land. The Cherokees most likely believed that the point of the
conference was to make a symbolic statement of the alliance between
South Carolina and the Cherokees, an alliance useful to both parties because both had to fight sporadic wars against nearby enemies. The ac-
knowledgment of the king of England as owner of the Cherokees' land
must have been a metaphor, like the frequent reference to the king (and
later the president of the United States) as a "great father." The mutual
misunderstanding of the "sale" was one of the causes of the war between South Carolina and the Cherokees that began a few years later.[20]

These differences in the way members of the two cultures understood land transactions were most likely exacerbated by differences in
how they understood the significance of writing.[21] The English practice
had long been to memorialize an agreement in writing, and to think of
the writing as the best evidence of what the parties had agreed to. The
Indians lacked writing. Theirs was an oral culture, in which events were
often remembered in the form of stories. In the early transactions the
Indians would have had no reason to suppose that in the event of a future dispute the English would privilege the written contract over the
memories of the participants, or that oral promises on the part of the
English were less likely to be fulfilled than written promises. Many of
the early English settlers could not read or write either, to be sure, but
they at least had a sense of the way their own culture treated written
documents. This difference may have added to the mismatch between
English and Indian interpretations of early sales.

But if the earliest transactions were subject to multiple misunderstandings, the Indians seem to have learned very quickly what the English meant by a sale.[22] Some of the earliest surviving deeds include explicit reservations of the Indians' rights to use resources on the land they sold, clauses that would have made no sense had the Indians believed they were selling only nonexclusive rights. In 1636, for example, when William Pynchon and two other settlers purchased from the Indians of Agawam the area that became Springfield, Massachusetts, the sellers were careful to reserve all the "ground that is now planted," as well as the "liberty to take Fish & Deer, ground nuts, walnuts akornes & sasachiminesh or a kind of pease" throughout the land sold. This language most likely reflected the preferences of the Indians rather than the English, because it is hard to see why the English would have wanted to preserve such rights for the Indians. The Indians must have known that without these reservations the English would believe that they were acquiring the right to evict the Indians from the land. The same could be said of many of the early transactions, such as the 1644 sale by "Bucksham Chief Sachem and Right owner of Tantiusques" of a large parcel near the Connecticut River, in which Bucksham expressly reserved "for my self and people liberty of fishing and Hunting and Convenient planting in the said Grounds and ponds and Rivers." The town of Mendon, Massachusetts, was founded in 1662 by a purchase from four Indians, by a deed including an addendum specifying that the sellers, "together with their heirs forever, have liberty to fish fowl & hunt" on the land.[23] Presumably the English purchasers were not the ones insisting that the Indians keep them company. Many of these early deeds bear witness, not to Indian ignorance of the English concept of property, but to the fact that the Indians understood it all too well.

Indeed, one might reasonably suspect that a single misunderstood transaction would have been enough to drive the point home, not just for the tribe caught by surprise but also for other tribes even at a great distance. The news of what the English meant by a sale most likely reached many areas in advance of the English themselves. In the earliest purchases in any location the Indians were probably victims of cross-cultural misunderstanding, but it is unlikely that the tribes in any given area could have been misled repeatedly. The size of the initial purchase from any tribe may thus have been very important. If it was of a small tract, like many of the early colonial purchases, the sellers could learn from experience and still have most of their land left. If their initial sale was of a significant percentage of their land, however, as would increasingly become the case in later years, especially in the west in the nineteenth century, a single misunderstanding could be much more costly.

The Indians' recognition of the English concept of property would have been facilitated by an important aspect of the relationship between the two cultures. Indian and English societies were not sealed off from one another. Relations were mediated by individuals who were members of both cultures, people who had lived in both Indian and English villages and who spoke both languages, people who had married someone from the other society or whose parents had intermarried.[24] These intermediaries smoothed relationships by explaining each culture to the other. One way they did so was by assisting at negotiations for land sales, and sometimes by conducting land sales themselves.

The Reverend Thomas Bosomworth, for example, arrived in Georgia in 1743 as a missionary to the Creeks. In 1747 he married a woman known as Mary to the English and Coosaponakeesa to the Creeks. Mary/Coosaponakeesa's mother was Creek, her father English. After the marriage Thomas Bosomworth deserted his ministry, and the Bosomworths began living among the Creeks. In the years following, the Bosomworths were often mediators between the English and the Creeks, and they seem to have moved easily in both societies. In the late 1740s they purchased from the Creeks three islands near Savannah, as well as another tract on the mainland near Savannah, all land that had been within the Creek hunting grounds. The government of Georgia learned of the sale only several years later, when the colony tried to buy the same land from the Creeks. The result was a dispute that lasted several years between Georgia and the Bosomworths over the validity of the Bosomworths' purchases, a dispute that turned on whether the Bosomworths had secured the consent of the appropriate members of the tribe, a question over which the Creeks themselves were divided. A compromise was reached in the end, according to which Georgia gave the Bosomworths one of the islands plus some compensation for the rest of the land.[25] This set of events took place very early in the colonization of Georgia, but it was not an encounter between two cultures standing wholly apart.

In some places, repeated contact between the English and the Indians brought Indian property practices closer to English practices. Missionaries spread literacy along with Christianity. By the early eighteenth century the percentage of literate speakers of the Massachusett language may have been higher than the percentage of settlers who could read or write English. Indians in the area around Boston began conveying land *to one another* with written contracts. Written records began as confirmations of earlier oral agreements, but they seem eventually to have been executed at the same time as oral agreements to convey land, just like written contracts among the English. The Nantucket Indians began writing their own deeds in the 1660s. For decades they operated their own deed-based land title system, separate from the English system.[26] Rising Indian literacy, and changing Indian norms regarding land sales, would have reduced cross-cultural misunderstandings of transactions between Indians and English settlers.

Despite some clear instances of misunderstanding, then, particularly in the early years of contact between the two cultures, the Indians most likely lost less land than is commonly supposed due to their unfamiliarity with the English concept of a sale.

Were the Indians Defrauded?

In 1717, Sir Bibye Lake petitioned the Crown for a grant to a ten-mile tract along the Kennebec River in Maine, a parcel of land that Lake's grandfather had purchased from the Indians in a series of transactions between 1639 and 1654. His grandfather had settled the land, Lake explained, but had been driven out by the Indians in 1684. War with France had prevented Lake and his family from returning to the land until after the 1713 Treaty of Utrecht brought peace. He asked that his ownership of the tract be confirmed, as he was "well inform'd that a purchase of the Natives and an occupation of the land has always been adjudged a good Title in those parts and what most of the Estates there are held by."

Lake's petition drew quick opposition from Thomas Coram, who probably had his eye on the same land. The purchases made by Lake's grandfather, Coram argued, "cannot be of any value," because "Indians, when drunk would for a bottle of strong Liquor sign any paper presented to them." As Coram explained in opposing a group of similar petitions for land purchased from Indians in Maine, the transactions were frauds from the start. The settlers "practised so with the Indian Natives," Coram alleged, "that debauching them with strong Liquors, they drew in the Indians to execute Deeds for Large Quantities of Land, whether their own or his Majesty's, without any valuable consideration for the same." Another English resident of Maine in the early eighteenth century recalled the "old Indian grants when a span of land was got for a Gallon of Rum." How much land was a *span?* "Extend your hand as open as possible, then bring the hand close to the eye looking upon the Horizon and so far as the little finger and thumb extend from each other from the top of them, on that Horizon is called a span which perhaps is 20 miles."[27]

Could the Indians have been systematically defrauded by the English? If, in enough cases, the English tricked the Indians into signing contracts, or failed to fulfill the promises they made in exchange for land, or wrote deeds that intentionally described the land in question ambiguously or incorrectly, they might have obtained North America without paying adequate compensation. Could the Indians' poverty have been the result of pervasive deceit on the part of the English?

There was certainly no shortage of deceit. The unscrupulous frontier purchaser plying Indian landowners with liquor appears so frequently in colonial discourse, mentioned by both the Indians and the English, that he must have had a substantial basis in fact. The Oneida sachem Conochquiesie despaired that one notorious purchaser "is a Devil and has stole our Lands, he takes Indians slyly by the Blanket one at a time, and when they are drunk, puts some money in their Bosoms, and perswades them to sign deeds for our lands." In Massachusetts the Mashpees complained that the English "bate [us] with Strong Licker" to secure signatures on deeds. Cotton Mather concluded that the Indians "will *Sell* and *Pawn* all they have in the world for *Strong Drink.*" Some unknowable but probably large quantity of land was acquired by what the Indian agent Peter Wraxall called "this scandalous & irregular Method of purchasing Lands from Young Indians by making them drunk." The occasional efforts by colonial governments to crack down on the practice were ineffectual. In New York in 1762, George Klock "did bribe, and make drunk a few Indians, and perswaded them to sign a Deed, which they knew not the purport of, without a Magistrate or Interpreter present." When the ostensible sellers learned what they had signed, "they were ready to hang themselves, and exclaimed greatly against Klock." The colonial government returned the land to the Indians and prosecuted Klock for fraud, but Klock was acquitted, apparently because the government was unable to prove to the satisfaction of the settler jury that the Indians were drunk.[28] The result could not have been a powerful deterrent for other settlers planning to use the same technique.

Fraud could take many shapes. In several cases English purchasers told the Indians they wished to buy parcels of a given size but then, without alerting the Indians, inserted in the deeds descriptions of parcels much larger. As one duped seller complained, "when a Small parcel of Land is bought of us a Large Quantity is taken instead." Cadwallader Colden, surveyor general of New York in the 1730s (and later governor), reported that such deception was possible because "the Indians have been perswaded to sign these Deeds without having them interpreted by persons sufficiently Skill'd in the English and Indian languages." Devious purchasers could also slip misdescriptions of the land past Indian sellers, Colden explained, by drafting deeds to express boundaries not in terms of natural landmarks but "by points or Degrees of the Compass & by English Measures which are absolutely unknown to the Indians." By the middle of the eighteenth century, as a result of this pattern of fraud, New York and Virginia (and perhaps other colonies as well) required that land purchased from Indians be first surveyed by a government surveyor in the presence of the selling tribe.[29] But some unknown quantity of land had already slipped fraudulently out of the Indians' possession.

In other instances, settlers purchased a given quantity of land from the Indians but then, in obtaining patents from colonial governments, claimed they had purchased much more. Such was the case with the infamous Kayaderosseras Patent in New York, granting title to hundreds of thousands of acres near Albany, on the basis of a purchase decades earlier from the Mohawks of a parcel large enough only for a few farms. After more than a decade of arguing their case before colonial officials, the Mohawks reached a settlement greatly reducing the size of the patent, but not down to the boundaries upon which they had originally agreed.[30]

Although this kind of fraud was perpetrated on colonial governments as well as on the Indians, it could not have been difficult to persuade the colonial officials responsible for overseeing the land market to go in on the scheme, because they were often land purchasers themselves. Colonial officials were typically paid very small salaries, and were given insufficient resources to cover their expenses. Many accordingly resorted to land speculation for an income. Some received kickbacks of shares in the parcels they granted.[31] The result was a dismal set of incentives.

John Tabor Kempe, for example, was the last royal attorney general of New York. Despite a trivial salary, and despite having virtually no assets when he took office in 1759, by the start of the Revolution Kempe was one of the richest people in New York. He made most of the money in land, accumulating 163,000 acres within a decade, much of which was purchased from Indians. Indians in New York could not have been confident that Kempe would enforce their property rights in a dispute against English purchasers. Indeed, at the height of the Kayaderosseras controversy, Kempe expressed the opinion, as attorney general, that the patent was valid even if the land had been fraudulently obtained from the Indians. Ignoring a century of precedent, Kempe declared that the colonies possessed the power to grant land to settlers whether or not the land had ever been purchased from the Indians. Kempe conceded that the Crown had consistently instructed colonial governors *not* to grant land that had not been purchased from the Indians, but he nevertheless argued that this order did not invalidate a grant of unpurchased land. "And tho if a Governor should act contrary to his Instructions it would justly expose him to the Kings Displeasure," Kempe concluded, "yet perhaps his Acts might be nevertheless binding, and a Grant contrary to the Instructions good." Kempe was promptly rebuked by William Johnson, superintendent of Indian affairs, for taking a view of the law so contrary to that which had prevailed in the colonies for a century. "I never found that the Government claimed the right of Soil," Johnson insisted, "beyond what had been Legally pattented by Virtue of Grants from the Native Proprietors . . . our rights of Soil Extend no farther than they are actually purchased by Consent of the Natives."[32] But if Kempe's opinion on the Kayaderosseras Patent was hard to understand as a legal matter, it was all too easy to understand in financial terms. Kempe, like other colonial officials responsible for policing the market in Indian land, had a stake in confirming even fraudulent purchases from the Indians. The point should not be overstated—William Johnson was also heavily involved in purchasing land from the Indians, and yet he was a consistent defender of Indian property rights, and there were other colonial officials about whom the same could be said. But with the right people in office it was possible to defraud the Indians and the colonial government simultaneously.

To get a sense of the difficulties tribes faced when they tried to complain about fraud, consider a petition the Montauk Indians sent in 1763 to Cadwallader Colden, by then New York's lieutenant governor. They had once been "a numerous Tribe," they explained, but now the Montauks were reduced to thirty families, living on the east end of Long Island, near the colonial town of Easthampton. They "suffer great Inconveniences from the Contempt shewn to the Indian Tribes by their English Neighbors," they told Colden, because residents of Easthampton "continually encroach upon their Occupations, by fencing in more and more of the Indians' Lands, under Pretence of Sales made by their Ancestors." They conceded that they could not prove the land was theirs to the satisfaction of the colonial legal system, because they lacked any written records that might distinguish the land they had sold from the land they had not. They accordingly asked Colden to bring a lawsuit against the trespassers on their behalf, to require the trespassers to prove which land the Indians had sold, and to confirm the Montauks' title to the rest. Colden ordered the state's attorney general to do exactly that.

But New York's attorney general was John Tabor Kempe. For a year Kempe did nothing. At the end of the year, he sent a letter to Colden giving three disingenuous reasons for his inactivity. First, he insisted, "I am not possessed of sufficient materials to judge of the Validity of their Claim," and he could not procure such materials from the Indians, "who are so extremely ignorant that after many Endeavours for that Purpose I cannot make understand what I want." He could not commence a suit on the Indians' behalf, he reasoned, without knowing what land to ask for. (Of course, as Kempe no doubt realized, the Montauks did not know either; that was why they had asked the colony to file the suit in the first place.) Second, in any event, he had been informed that the land the Indians claimed had been occupied by settlers for sixty years or more. Surely, he suggested, the statute of limitations would long since have run on any Indian claim to be put back in possession, and the settlers would have acquired title by the legal doctrine of adverse possession. And finally, Kempe asserted, the Indians had as much right as any New Yorker to bring a lawsuit in court. Not only would it smack of favoritism for the attorney general to be involved on one side of an ostensibly private lawsuit, but it might even subject Kempe to punishment for intervening. The Montauks, he concluded, should bring their own suit. Colden and the rest of New York's Council acquiesced. The Council advised Colden to recommend to the Montauks that they sue as paupers in chancery court.[33]

What were the Montauks to do? They lacked the power to budge the colonial government to stop settlers from trespassing on the basis of claimed purchases they believed to be fraudulent. The colony's lieutenant governor was apparently sympathetic to their plea, but not sympathetic enough to override an attorney general who was determined to stall and who was himself a major speculator in Indian land. They knew they couldn't win in court; in 1764 they learned they couldn't appeal to the executive branch of colonial government either.

On occasion fraud could reach spectacular heights, as in the case of the celebrated Walking Purchase. In 1735 the government of Pennsylvania showed the Lenape Indians a copy of a deed dated 1686 by which they had sold to William Penn a large tract along the west bank of the Delaware River. The deed may have been authentic or it may have been forged; the English produced several witnesses who claimed to have seen the Lenape sign it, but the Lenape themselves were surprised to learn of the deed's existence. The land conveyed in the deed extended along the Delaware for a distance defined as a day and a half's walk. The Lenape assumed, reasonably enough, that the walk would be through the woods, at a conventional pace, resulting in a distance of approximately twenty miles. After some negotiation, the Lenape agreed to the sale in 1737. James Logan, the chief justice of the Pennsylvania Supreme Court and the colony's intermediary with the Lenape, promptly had a route surveyed and cleared, and hired the three fastest men he could find. The walkers were unencumbered, because they were accompanied by horses carrying provisions. In a day and a half they covered fifty-five miles, or nearly three times the distance the Lenape intended the boundary to run, which caused the total area covered by the purchase to be several hundred square miles greater than the Lenape had anticipated.

Deceit on such a flagrant scale may have been unusual, but the concept was well enough known to give rise to Indian tales of colonial trickery. One was the story of the settlers who asked for a parcel of land merely the size of a cow's hide, but who then, once the Indians agreed, cut the hide into a long thin continuous strip to measure out an enormous tract. In another version, land purchasers uncaned the seat of a chair for the same purpose.[34]

There is no way to know what percentage of Indian land was obtained through fraudulent means. Even if there were, there would be no way to know how that percentage compared with the fraction of other kinds of assets purchased fraudulently, which is the relevant question if we are seeking to understand how the market in Indian land compared with other markets. The best that can be said is that many of the purchases were made deceitfully.

Did the Sellers Have Authority to Sell?

The Indians sold some land under the pressure of English population increase and encroachment. They may have sold some under the misapprehension that they were merely selling the right to share natural resources. They were defrauded out of some. But the largest share of Indian losses from land sales may have been attributable to a different kind of problem. There was no clear answer to a question that in most markets is easily answered: Who had the right to sell?

The Indians did not sell land before the English arrived, so they had no reason to develop rules or customs governing exactly who had the authority to enter into a land sale. Suddenly confronted with offers to purchase land, the Indians had to improvise such principles on the fly. Did an individual have the authority to sell the parcel he had the exclusive right to cultivate? Did he need the permission of the tribe before selling his parcel? Could the leader of a tribe sell his tribe's land? Did he need the permission of the tribe as a whole? the permission of all the individual tribe members whose property rights would be affected? The prospect of selling land gave rise to some urgent questions of internal tribal organization, questions that had never come up before.

There was considerable disagreement within individual tribes as to exactly who had the authority to sell. "Some lands have been bought by the proprietor or his agents from Indians who had not a right to sell," the Delaware chief Teedyuscung told Pennsylvania governor William Denny in 1757. Teedyuscung's complaint was a common one—that individual Indians had sold tribal land without the consent of the tribe. William Johnson knew of several occasions on which "a few Indians have signed a Deed for Lands which they had no right to convey, and therefore kept their transactions private, to prevent the resentment of the rest."[35] Indian tribes faced a formidable collective action problem. It could be in the interest of individual tribe members to sell land and pocket the proceeds, even when the tribe's collective interest was not to sell. It could accordingly be very difficult, sometimes impossible, for the tribe as a whole to prevent its members from selling land.

Much land appears to have been purchased by settlers deliberately exploiting the collective action problem, by offering to pay individual Indians for their signatures on deeds to land the settlers knew was owned by many people other than the sellers.[36] As with other species of fraud, the Indians complained loudly and often to colonial officials, who sometimes attempted to undo the transactions but probably more often did nothing.

What made the problem even worse than simple fraud, from the Indians' perspective, was that many of the purchases from Indians with dubious authority to sell were undertaken by settlers or colonial governments acting in good faith. From the purchaser's perspective, negotiating with every Indian with use rights in a particular parcel was time-consuming and expensive. Without an intimate knowledge of the local residents and their culture, a purchaser could never be sure if he had obtained the consent of everyone with standing to object, or whether other tribe members with rights in the parcel might surface later to demand compensation. English purchasers tended to adopt shortcuts. They often negotiated with village sachems, on the assumption that the sachems had the authority to sell land on behalf of the tribe. The result in many cases was to expand the power of the sachems, who had never been authorized to sell tribal land.[37]

In southeastern Pennsylvania, for example, much of the land was owned by the Delawares. When settlers or the colonial government wanted to buy land, it came naturally to them to analogize the Delawares to a European state, and to try to identify a tribal leadership who could act as an agent for the sellers. To purchase land efficiently, the purchasers needed to buy from someone who, by signing a deed, could prevent other tribe members from coming forward later with claims to the land. But the Delawares were not organized like a European state. There was no tribe member or group of tribe members with the authority to speak for the tribe as a whole, or even for a significant part of the tribe. (Indeed, our continued use of the term *tribe*, for what might be better described as an association of self-governing villages, is itself a vestige of this analogy to a European state.) Delaware political power was less centralized than power in Europe or colonial America. Delaware signatures that created binding contracts in the eyes of Pennsylvania purchasers were meaningless to most Delawares themselves, who did not recognize the authority of the signers to sell land they did not personally own.[38]

The practice of purchasing a tribe's land from individuals raised an issue that would have been familiar to English lawyers if it had been conceptualized as a legal question. There was already an English common law of agency, consisting of doctrines governing the authority of one person to engage in commercial transactions on behalf of another. The law of property already included rules pertaining to land owned by many people simultaneously, and the effect that a sale by one owner would have on the others. Had these disputes involved tracts owned collectively by large numbers of *Englishmen* but ostensibly sold by a few, the nonselling owners would have proceeded straight to court, and the court would have confirmed that the nonsellers lost no property rights in the sale. Something close to this outcome evolved on the island of Martha's Vineyard in Massachusetts, where colonial courts ruled that purchasers of land from sachems took the land subject to the use rights of the Indians who farmed it, an outcome that prevented ostensible sellers of land from forcing the ouster of the people who actually occupied it.[39]

But Martha's Vineyard was an unusual place, where settlers and Indians lived peacefully in close proximity long enough for Indians to feel comfortable litigating in colonial courts. In most places the Indians took their complaints to colonial governors or legislatures, not to the courts, and colonial officials tended to conceive of the complaints as raising questions of diplomacy rather than law. As the English grew more powerful relative to the Indians, they often became unwilling to look behind the form of a deed to ensure that it bore the names of the proper members of the tribe according to the tribe's own internal method of allocating authority. The English were no more inclined to inquire into the authority of a sachem to sell land than they would have been to second-guess the prerogative of the king of France to enter into a treaty. A tribe was instead usually held responsible for the acts of its members.[40]

Indian tribes were thus caught in a tragedy of the commons. An individual tribe member, confronted with an offer to purchase land, might have had a personal incentive to sell even where the good of the tribe would not be advanced by selling. Had the Indians been able to prevent unauthorized land sales, tribes could have held out for higher prices. Instead, individual tribe members, knowing that their authority to sell land might be called into question by the tribe, and aware that fellow tribe members might simultaneously be trying to sell the very same land, had every incentive to accept purchase offers quickly, and were thus more likely than tribes as a whole to sell at low prices.

Although it is impossible to quantify the losses the Indians suffered from this problem, a simple model of the purchasing process suggests that the losses could easily have amounted to a significant part of the value of the land sold. Assume a tribe of five hundred people that owns a parcel of land it could sell to the English for five hundred pounds, and assume that after the sale the tribe would distribute the proceeds evenly, one pound per person. Assume a single tribe member who has a pressing need to obtain money, perhaps to pay a debt, or perhaps to feed an addiction to alcohol. How much would an English purchaser have to offer in order to obtain his signature on a contract purporting to sell the entire tract? The would-be seller knows that in the event of a collective tribal sale he would earn only one pound, so any purchase price greater than a pound is a gain from his perspective. He knows he will suffer the disapproval of others in his tribe, and maybe even ostracism from the tribe, so that has to be reckoned as a cost of selling. But if the cost of ostracism to the seller is less than the value of everyone else's share of the land, he will sell the parcel for less than five hundred pounds. How much less will depend on how strongly the seller needs the money and how much he cares about the esteem of others in his tribe. He might even sell it for less than one pound, if the alternative to a private sale is not a collective sale but instead either no sale at all or a sale by a different self-interested tribe member.

The collective action problem was most tragic when sachems were willing to accept payment for land the rest of the tribe did not wish to sell, because in such circumstances a tribe's ordinary internal political checks on unauthorized sales were at their weakest. As an exasperated delegation of Mohegans explained during the course of their prolonged litigation against Connecticut over the validity of grants made by successive Mohegan sachems, "they had of late years been much dissatisfied & disgusted with their Sachems; for that they had betrayed the Tribe & sold or endeavoured to sell all their Lands to the Government and they were determined to have no Sachem at all."[41] In some cases, it appears that tribal elders were willing to sell the tribe's land in order to distribute the proceeds among tribe members to solidify their own position within the tribe, a position that depended in part on the ability to give gifts to younger men. In other cases, the elders' motives were more directly economic. Some "Elderly or Chief Men among the Indians," one English observer pointed out, seemed willing to sell their tribes' land when offered "great Sums of Money or Presents." The Narragansetts repeatedly petitioned the Rhode Island legislature to ban their sachem from selling any more of the tribe's land to pay off his personal debts. If he "goes on selling Land," they despaired, "the Tribe will soon have none left." But the legislature did nothing, most likely because among the sachem's creditors were some legislators.[42] The interests of a tribe and its leadership were not always in alignment. The result was to drive land prices down.

In addition to collective action problems *within* tribes, land sales also presented collective action problems *between* tribes. Boundaries between tribal areas were sometimes imprecisely defined, particularly when the areas concerned were hunting grounds or other uncultivated lands. Before colonization, when the population density of North America was still very low, there was no reason to draw boundary lines any more clearly. But the arrival of English land purchasers created an insoluble intertribal collective action problem. When more than one tribe had a claim to an area, the incentive facing each of the tribes was to sell the land to the English before any other tribe did. The English were not slow to recognize the opportunity. The problem could have been solved if tribes had been able to coordinate with one another, to reach collective decisions on whether to sell land that was subject to overlapping tribal claims. They tried. In the late colonial period, the Creeks and the Cherokees worked toward developing a mutual land sale policy. They discussed the issue with representatives of several other tribes as well. But these agreements among tribes tended not to last very long. Within a few years, the Cherokees initiated negotiations with Georgia to sell land claimed by the Creeks.[43] This kind of political fragmentation among the Indians also drove land prices down.

Unlike the Indians, who were divided into multiple nations, the English were subjects of a single government and conceived of themselves as a single people. Within a short time after the beginning of settlement in each colony, they were able to coordinate land purchasing by requiring prospective English purchasers to obtain the permission of the colonial government. The result was to dampen competition among purchasers. Without the requirement of a license from the colonial government, competing purchasers might have bid up the price for a given tract of Indian land, and the selling tribe might have been the beneficiary. Instead, the purchaser who reached the colonial government first was granted the exclusive right to transact with the Indians. Indian land was sold not to the highest bidder but to the first person to apply for a license. A tribe wishing to sell land but unsatisfied with the purchaser's offer had no ability to turn to another purchaser; it had to accept the price tendered or refuse to sell land at all. When there were other settlers willing to pay more, the beneficiary was the license holder, not the Indians. When the need to sell was particularly pressing—when a sale was necessary to pay off debts, for example—purchasers with a license had sellers over a barrel.

An even greater restraint on competition among purchasers was the fact that the government itself was a major land purchaser.[44] Until 1763, when private land purchasing was outlawed, the colonial government was in principle just one purchaser among many. But the government also had the power to grant or deny private purchasers the right to buy land from the Indians. When the government had its eye on a tract of Indian land, prospective private purchasers were unlikely to obtain the government's permission to buy the very same land. The government, in its dual capacity as regulator of and participant in the Indian land market, had the power to exclude competing purchasers.

This lack of competition among purchasers forced land prices down in a direct sense. It also most likely reduced prices indirectly, by exacerbating whatever informational advantages the English had over the Indians. Especially in the earliest years of contact, the English had more experience of colonization than the Indians. They had a better sense of how the settler population was likely to increase in the future, and of how that increase was likely to affect the price of land. Whenever the Indians were less able than the English to forecast the inevitable rise in land values, whenever the Indians misunderstood what the English meant by a sale, and whenever the Indians were less experienced at negotiation than the English, an English purchaser with no competitors was able to capture the full disparity between what the land was worth and what the Indians thought it was worth. That disparity might have been reduced somewhat in a competitive market, because competing English purchasers would have bid the price up, even if both would-be purchasers had more information than the Indian sellers. In a market with multiple lawful noncolluding purchasers, even a seller who is ignorant of the value of what he is selling will receive that value, so long as the purchasers know what the value is. Where there is only one lawful purchaser, however, he can profit from the seller's ignorance. To some unmeasurable extent, that happened to the Indians.

The English could engineer these results only because they enjoyed a higher degree of political organization than the Indians. Had North America been colonized by citizens of hundreds of tiny European nations, there would not have been any political entity capable of channeling land purchases through a single point. Had the Indians been organized as a single nation, with a single government, they would have been able to counter the English license requirement with one of their own, a requirement that *sellers* obtain the permission of the single Indian sovereign before selling. But the English were a polity much larger than any Indian tribe. Two societies converged in a marketplace, and the better organized took wealth from the poorly organized.

Were Prices Unfair?

A variety of forces, then, pushed the Indians to sell more land to the English, and to sell it faster, than they would have otherwise. To what extent did those pressures reduce the prices at which the Indians sold their land?

There are several obstacles in the way of any attempt to assess the adequacy of colonial land prices. Land values have risen so much in the past few centuries that all colonial prices look ridiculously low today, even those at which the English sold land to one another. The problem is not just, or even mostly, one of across-the-board inflation; it primarily involves the relative scarcity of land and other assets. We're accustomed to a world in which land is scarce and money and manufactured goods are plentiful, but in the colonies the relationship was the opposite. Money and goods were in chronically short supply, while land was all around. Land was accordingly worth far less, relative to goods, than it is today. An additional complication is introduced by the fact that in many of the colonial Indian land sales with surviving price evidence, the price is expressed as a bundle of goods rather than in monetary terms. To assess the fairness of a sale of land for blankets, coats, needles, and the like, we would need to know the value of those items—and not just their value in general but their value at the place where they were provided, a figure that must include the high cost of transportation. A kettle in the wilderness, several days' journey from any English settlement, must have been worth much more than a kettle in Philadelphia, which in turn must have been worth more than a kettle in England.

Some account must be taken, as well, of the absence of any institutional framework that would have allowed the Indians to invest the proceeds of a land sale. The Indians (and indeed most of the colonists) lacked realistic access to banks and similar institutions. To be useful, money had to be spent; and there was nothing to spend it on that was nearly as durable as the land itself. In such circumstances *any* price was likely to appear too low in retrospect, when the goods acquired with the proceeds were long gone but the land had increased in value. The Mohawk sachem Hendrick was painfully aware, while assenting to the sale of much of the tribe's land in 1754, that "After We have sold our Land We in a little time have nothing to Shew for it; but it is not so with You, Your Grandchildren will get something from it as long as the World stands; our Grandchildren will have no advantage from it; They will say We were Fools for selling so much Land for so small a matter, and curse Us."[45] Today's descendants of English colonists who sold land rather than holding it might utter the same curse. Each generation has a plausible claim of intergenerational injustice—a claim that its predecessors dissipated wealth that should have been kept within the family. As Hendrick realized, however, land prices are not easily translated from one era into another, and the pressing needs of the day are likely to appear less pressing the farther they recede into the past.

Consider the most famous land transaction of all, the 1626 sale of Manhattan to the Dutch for goods supposedly worth twenty-four dollars. Even to begin thinking about the adequacy of the price requires clearing away a few complications. There was no such currency as the American dollar in 1626. The Dutch believed they had purchased Manhattan in exchange for goods—there is no surviving evidence of what they were—worth a total of sixty guilders. The legendary figure of twenty-four dollars was most likely the creation of nineteenth-century American historians, who may have used then-current exchange rates between the guilder and the American dollar, or who may have converted guilders into *thalers*, a coin then in use in the Low Countries, and simply substituted *dollar* for *thaler*.[46] But the conversion to dollars doesn't matter much. At any exchange rate, sixty guilders was a small sum. The ship bearing the letter reporting the purchase of Manhattan was also carrying assorted cargo, mostly crops and beaver skins, collectively worth more than forty-five thousand guilders. We don't know what the sellers thought of the transaction. They don't seem to have vacated the island afterward, so it is doubtful that they intended to convey exclusive rights to the Dutch.[47] The Dutch had no reason to want the sellers to leave, because the Indians were useful trading partners and there was still plenty of room on the island for the small combined population, so we can assume that the Dutch had no occasion to instruct the Indians as to the European meaning of a sale. Because it was the first time the Indians had ever sold land, and because they were not likely to have heard about any previous land sales by other tribes in places already inhabited by Europeans, they probably anticipated that the Dutch would be sharing Manhattan's resources with them. But suppose that the Indians genuinely intended to sell Manhattan in the European sense of a sale and that the price was sixty guilders or twenty-four dollars. Was it enough?

None of the conceivable ways of converting that sum into a current figure yields a satisfying answer. In 1626, sixty guilders was worth approximately five pounds eight shillings in English money, which, adjusted for inflation and converted into American dollars, would have had about the purchasing power of $888 in 2001 dollars.[48] Maybe sixty guilders was too low a price. But this is not helpful, because only a negligible part of the increase in the value of land in Manhattan over the past 375 years is attributable to inflation. Land is fixed in quantity but the quantity of everything else has skyrocketed, so the price of land has risen much faster than the prices of the commodities used to construct price indexes. We might alternatively ask how much $24 would be worth today if the Indians could have invested it. The answer is quite sensitive to assumptions about interest rates. Twenty-four dollars invested at 5 percent would have yielded $2 billion by 2001; at 7 percent the sum would have been $2.5 trillion; and at 10 percent the Indians would have enjoyed nearly $80 quadrillion, a figure that far exceeds the total wealth in the United States.[49] Maybe $24 was too much. But those numbers aren't useful either, because the Indians hardly had access to a securities market or anything like it in the seventeenth century. Even if the Indians had perfect foresight as to land prices, they could not have invested money at interest. We might finally observe that Manhattan today is worth more than $24 or even $888, and conclude that the Indians would have been better off holding on to the island, or perhaps leasing it rather than selling it. But that's not a realistic view of the matter either. Had the Indians not sold Manhattan to the Dutch, the inevitable rise in the English population in the area later in the seventeenth century, driven by the advantages of New York as a harbor, would have put steadily mounting pressure on the Indians to sell. There would have been repeated incidents of colonists trespassing on Indian land. Given the increasingly lopsided power relationship between the English and the Indians, the Indians could not have held on to Manhattan very long into the eighteenth century.

Rather than try to convert colonial prices into modern prices, we might instead try to compare the prices at which the Indians sold land to the English with the prices at which the English sold land to one another. If the prices at which the Indians sold land to the English were similar to the prices at which the English sold land to the English, we might conclude that the Indians were receiving a fair return; if those prices were significantly lower, we might conclude otherwise. But this is an imperfect measure as well. All commercial intermediaries, even those taking few risks, expect to be compensated for their time and effort in the form of a resale price higher than the original purchase price. And settlers seeking to purchase land from Indians were often taking large risks. Some were traveling to unknown or faraway places. Some were spending considerable time on what could prove to be fruitless negotiations. In some contexts would-be purchasers were risking their safety. One would expect that Englishmen who purchased land from Indians for resale to settlers would be compensated for assuming these risks: they would resell the land at prices substantially higher than they had paid for it. Even in a perfectly fair market, Indians would have sold land to the English at much lower prices than the English sold land to the English. Land prices, meanwhile, were generally rising over the colonial period, as new waves of immigration drove up the demand for land. Land sales by the Indians necessarily came before land sales by the English, which is another reason to expect that the Indians sold at lower prices than the English. We cannot take a discrepancy between the two prices as evidence that the Indians were not receiving a fair return.

Lloyd's Neck, for example, in present-day Huntington, Long Island, was purchased from Indians in 1654 for three coats, three shirts, two cutlasses, three hatchets, three hoes, two fathoms of wampum, six knives, and two pairs of shoes and stockings. Four years later the purchasers sold the same land to an English settler for £100. A precise comparison of the prices would require knowing the value of each of the items conveyed to the Indians. In an era when all such goods were made by hand,

and when transporting them from England to Long Island was no simple matter, the collection of goods was worth more than one might think. Even so, it is doubtful that the combined value of the goods approached £100. The Indians almost certainly received much less for the land than the English reseller did. But that tells us little about the adequacy of the price. By 1666, only eight years after Lloyd's Neck sold for £100, the English purchaser resold it to another English settler for £450.[50] Much of the gap between the Indian selling price and the English selling price must have been due to the simple passage of time. The rest may have been attributable to the risk assumed by the initial purchasers. There is no way to know.

Without any way to assess prices directly, the best we can do is ask what the English thought about them at the time. By the eighteenth century, there seems to have been a widely shared belief among the English that they were buying Indian land for a song. In Pennsylvania a critic of the colonial government claimed, most likely with some exaggeration, that the colony would realize proceeds of more than £1 million from selling land it had recently purchased from the Indians for a mere £750. "The land is bought in such *lumping Pennyworths* of the Natives," he complained, and then "*huckster'd* out again to the King's Subjects." The report adopted by the delegates to the 1754 Albany Congress deplored "purchases of Lands from the Indians by Private persons for small Trifling Considerations" and concluded that the Indians had made such bad bargains that they "appear not fit to be intrusted at Large with the Sale of their own Lands." In South Carolina, another writer observed, the Indians had sold their land to the English for nothing more than "trifling Presents." This is a very small sample, filtered through the arguments of colonists with varying motives, so generalizations are perilous. William Johnson, who knew as much about land purchasing as anyone, believed that by the 1760s the Indians had come to realize the value of their land, and indeed had "grown so cunning, & tenacious of their property, that in short it is verry difficult to get Land from them without paying too much for it." A group of New Jersey settlers insisted that their ancestors had purchased land from the Indians not "for some few Bottles of *Rum*," but rather "at a dear Rate, and with a great Sum for the then Times."[51] But this seems to have been a minority view, held by people with an interest in defending the legitimacy of their own land titles. By the later colonial period the English seem to have believed that the Indians sold their land to the English for far less than the land's market value among settlers.

The most thorough treatment of the subject was undertaken in 1722 by the Massachusetts minister Solomon Stoddard, who asked: "Did we any wrong to the Indians in buying their Land at a small price?" Stoddard's answer was no, for two reasons. "Tho' we gave them but a small Price for what we bought," he explained, "we gave them their demands, we came to their Market, and gave them their price." Here Stoddard was anticipating a way of thinking about prices that would grow more widespread as the century progressed. If a buyer and a seller agreed on a price, the price was fair; there was no need to inquire further. But Stoddard did go on to think about the substantive justice of the sales. He was satisfied on this score as well. At the time the English bought the land, Stoddard concluded, "it was worth but little: And had it continued in their hands, it would have been of little value. It is our dwelling on it, and our Improvements, that have made it to be of Worth."[52] The value of land depended on what one did with the land. The prices paid to the Indians by the English may have seemed low, Stoddard reasoned, but in truth they were not, because the land was still in its natural state. It was the settlers' own hard work that had caused land values to rise, *after* the land had passed into English hands.

Ezra Stiles, a Connecticut minister and the president of Yale, pressed Stoddard's point even further. "The protestant Europeans have generally bought the native right of soil, as far as they have settled, and paid the value ten fold," he declared. Those settlers "are daily increasing the value of the remaining Indian territory a thousand fold: and in this manner we are a constant increasing revenue to the Sachems and original Lords of the soil." Seen in this light, English land purchasing had been a net *gain* to the Indians. They were lucky the English had come. And if the Indians' real estate had appreciated due to English settlement of the eastern seaboard, just imagine how wealthy the Indians would be when settlers fanned out over the entire hemisphere. "How much," Stiles wondered, "must the value of land, reserved to the natives of North and South-America, be increased to remaining Indians, by the inhabitation of two or three hundred millions of Europeans?"[53] English settlement was, in Stiles's view, the best thing that could ever have happened to the Indians. They just had to sit back and wait for their land to grow more valuable.

The Indians themselves could not afford to be as optimistic. "We know our Lands are now become more Valuable," explained Canassatego, speaking on behalf of the Six Nations in 1742, to Pennsylvania lieutenant governor George Thomas and the colony's provincial council. But rising real estate prices were small consolation when most of the land had already been sold and the proceeds used up. "The white People don't think we know their Value," Canassatego continued, "but we are sensible that the Land is Everlasting, and the few Goods we receive for it are soon Worn out and Gone." The adjoining land still retained by the Six Nations was rising in value too, just as Ezra Stiles predicted, but that was more a curse than a blessing. The price of land was a function of aggregate demand for it, and increasing English demand for Indian land only led to more frequent and more intense trespassing on the part of settlers. The Six Nations "are not well Used with respect to the Lands still unsold by Us," Canassatego protested. "Your People daily settle on these Lands and spoil our Hunting. We must insist on your removing them." Rising land value, as measured in the settlers' real estate market, was only driving the land's Indian owners deeper into poverty. "It is Customary with us to make a Present of Skins whenever we renew our Treaties," Canassatego concluded, but that tradition was getting harder to follow. "We are ashamed to Offer our Brethren so few, but your Horses and Cows have eat the Grass our Deer used to feed on. This has made them Scarce, and will, We hope, plead in Excuse for our not bringing a larger Quantity." Proximity to the English had driven up the value of the Six Nations' land, and as a result, he apologized, "we are really poor."

Lieutenant Governor Thomas had an immediate response, one that Solomon Stoddard or Ezra Stiles would have endorsed, and one that would probably have commanded the assent of a large majority of Anglo-Americans. "It is very true that Lands are of late become more Valuable, but what raises their Value?" Thomas asked. "Is it not intirely owing to the Industry & Labour used by the white people in their Cultivation and Improvement?" Decades earlier John Locke had made the point even more emphatically, in arguing that two otherwise identical parcels of land, one farmed by an Englishman and the other owned (and, Locke presumed, not farmed) by an Indian, should fetch drastically different prices. If one could divide the value of material things into "what in them is purely owing to *Nature,* and what to *labour,*" Locke reasoned, "we shall find, that in most of them 99/100 are wholly to be put on the account of *labour.*"[54] If the fairness of Pennsylvania's land purchases was to be reckoned by the relative value of the Indians' land and the settlers' work, Thomas and his colleagues could be confident that the Indians had not been imposed upon.

There was another way to assess the adequacy of land prices, of course, and Thomas turned to it next. "What you say of the Goods that they are soon worn out is applicable to every thing," he pointed out to the Six Nations, "but you know very well that they cost a great deal of Money, and the Value of Land is no more than what it is worth in Money."[55] Within his own cultural frame of reference, Thomas was undoubtedly right. Money was a scale allowing otherwise incommensurable things to be compared. If land was worth a given amount of money, and a collection of goods cost the same amount of money, then a swap of the land for the goods was a fair trade by definition. Thomas and his colleagues could interpret Canassatego's speech as the complaint of someone who had taken a gamble and lost. Anglo-Americans also sometimes regretted their past transactions, but they weren't allowed to undo them. Why treat the Six Nations differently?

But the Six Nations would likely not have agreed that "the Value of Land is no more than what it is worth in Money." They had never exchanged land for money before the English arrived. Land inhabited by domesticated cows was worth more, measured in money, than land populated by wild deer, but if the Six Nations had the power to choose, they would doubtless have taken the deer. Deer allowed them to persist in their traditional ways of life, independent of English domination. Cows would require them to assimilate not only into the English economy, but into an English political structure in which they would lack any voice, and into an English society in which they would be the victims of pervasive discrimination. The Six Nations' land rose in price as it became more valuable to the English, but it was simultaneously becoming less valuable to the Six Nations themselves.

This difference between cultures in how value was constructed was itself part of the engine that drove land sales. If the value placed on a given piece of land could simultaneously rise for potential buyers and fall for potential sellers, any given purchase price would begin to look more attractive to the Indians, and any given sale price would become more attractive to the English. The range of possible prices at which to consummate a sale would widen. The result would be more sales, at prices kept near the bottom of that range by all the forces we have discussed. Parcel by parcel, the land would be sold, until little or none was left.

The Power to Enforce

In the colonial period the Indians sold an enormous amount of land to the English, but in the end they were poorer than when they began. They sold much of the land under the overt or latent threats of English expropriation and ecological destruction. They sold some under the misapprehension that the English intended to share it with them. The English defrauded them out of some. And much of the land was sold by individuals who lacked clear authority to sell. All of these factors conspired to keep land prices low, probably much lower than the prices at which the English bought and sold the same land among themselves.

The only reason these circumstances affected land prices, however, was that the English controlled the legal system within which these transactions were enforced. Indians dissatisfied with a sale to the English had to get the approval of English authorities before they could get any redress. Settlers seeking to enforce Indian sales, on the other hand, had no equivalent need to petition the Indians. The government was English, not Anglo-Indian; it was staffed entirely by Englishmen and was operated for the benefit of the settlers. Whether appointed from England or chosen locally, colonial government officials understood themselves as governors of the English colonists first and foremost, rather than as equally accountable to the English and the Indians. Even when colonial officials tried to be scrupulously fair in resolving disputes over land transactions, they were, at best, judges affiliated by social and cultural ties with English purchasers rather than Indian sellers. At worst they were English purchasers themselves.

That the English and not the Indians resolved disputes and enforced transactions was, of course, a product of the disparity in power between the two cultures. The English ran the legal system because of the same advantages in population and technology that allowed the English to colonize the Indians rather than vice versa. In the end, the acquisition of land in North America is a story of power, of the displacement of the weak by the strong; but it was a more subtle and complex kind of power than would have been necessary to seize land by force. It was the power to supplant Indian legal systems with the English legal system, the power to have land disputes decided by English officials using English

William Penn's land purchases from Indians in Pennsylvania were well known to whites in the eighteenth century as models of honorable relations between settlers and Indians, but Indians may well have viewed them differently. Engraving by John Hall, from a painting by Benjamin West.

law rather than Indian officials using Indian law. The threat of physical force was always present, but most of the time it could be kept out of view, because most of the time it was not needed.

The ability of the English to enforce contested transactions was a function of the degree to which the English were more powerful than the Indians. That power imbalance grew steadily over the colonial period. In the early 1600s, English settlers were dependent on the Indians for their very survival. As the English population grew and the Indian population shrank, the English gained the upper hand. It seems likely, therefore, that most of the factors depressing the prices at which the Indians sold their land grew stronger over time. We can suppose that, as the English grew more powerful relative to the Indians, more sales were made under the pressure of encroachment, there were more instances of fraud, and more land was sold by people who lacked clear authority to sell.

But if the English could use their increasing power over the Indians to purchase land cheaply, it was power exercised so subtly that English settlers and officials might not realize it was there. Most colonists would have found it distasteful to think of themselves as conquerors. The English could sincerely believe that Indian land was being purchased fair and square, just the way land was purchased back in England.[56] The fact that transactions were enforced according to English law was no cause for soul-searching. English property law was understood, by the English, as reason itself—it was sometimes complex, to be sure, but it was rooted in simple common sense. The Indians could hardly complain when it was applied to land transactions; indeed, the settlers would have been nearly unanimous in the belief that they were *helping* the Indians by bringing them English law—that they were leading the Indians along the path to civilization. The English could congratulate themselves on the honorable way they were populating North America. They could see the Indians growing poorer, but they did not conceive that they were the agents of the Indians' impoverishment. They were not taking the Indians' land by force of arms, after all. They were buying it on the open market.

3

FROM CONTRACT TO TREATY

FOR most of the colonial period, Indian land was purchased by a wide variety of individuals and groups—from ordinary farmers to large-scale real estate speculators, from towns to colonial governments. And Indian land was sold by an equally varied set of sellers—from individual Indians, to small groups, to entire tribes. In 1763, however, at the end of the French and Indian War, when the imperial government reorganized its relationships with the Indians, this era came to an end. From 1763 on, land purchasing became a task performed exclusively by colonial governments, in the name of the Crown, and land selling became a task reserved to tribes. Indian land sales were transformed from *contracts* into *treaties*—from transactions between private parties into transactions between sovereigns. After the American Revolution the government of the new United States would copy this feature of British Indian policy, and it has remained the foundation of land acquisition in the United States ever since.

The shift from contract to treaty was intended to smooth relations with the Indians in the short run, but in this respect it was an utter failure. Instead, the shift set in motion some unanticipated long-run changes in Anglo-American thought concerning the Indians and their land.

The Proclamation of 1763

When war against France broke out in the 1750s, and most of the Indian tribes sided with France, British colonial officials were forced to reflect

PRÆVALEBIT ÆQUIOR.

For most of the colonial period, as Britain and France competed for Indian allies, the British imperial government repeatedly and often ineffectually tried to restrain British settlers from trespassing on Indian land. In this 1757 woodcut, published in the *American Magazine* at the outset of the French and Indian War, Britain and France offer inducements to an Indian with a rifle: Britain (at left) offers a Bible and some cloth, while France offers gunpowder and a tomahawk. The need to stop antagonizing the Indians was the primary motivation for the Proclamation of 1763, which abolished private land purchasing.

on Britain's relationship with the Indians. Peter Wraxall, secretary to Indian superintendent William Johnson, knew what had "made numbers of them our Enemies, [and] sown a gloomy discontent and suspicion of our Intentions." The problem was land, or more precisely the devious ways settlers went about acquiring it. "An unaccountable thirst for large Tracts of Land," Wraxall explained, "hath prevailed over the Inhabitants of this and the neighbouring Provinces with a singular rage." Settlers increasingly seemed to be buying land from Indians with no right to sell it, making Indians drunk in order to get them to sign contracts, applying to colonial governments for patents stretching far beyond the limits of the land actually purchased, or even forging Indians' signatures on purchase documents. In 1757, when Johnson asked the Seneca Silver Heels "why the Indians in General seemed to Incline more of late to the French than usual," he got the same answer: the settlers' recent behavior had convinced the Seneca that the English "intended to dispossess them of all their Lands."[1]

The feeling seems to have been shared by tribes throughout the thirteen colonies. After meeting with members of several tribes in Pennsylvania, the missionary John Brainerd reported that "they understood that the White people were contriving a method to deprive them of their country." In Georgia, the Creeks began calling the English *Ecunnaunuxulgee*, or "People greedily grasping after the lands of the Red people." Under pressure from what Johnson called "the Pestilential Thirst of Land, so Epidemic thro' all the provinces," Anglo-Indian relations were worsening.[2]

With the perspective afforded by time, the English thirst for land was far from "unaccountable." Demand for Indian land was a function of the English population, and in the first half of the eighteenth century the English population of North America skyrocketed. There were only about 250,000 non-Indians in the colonies in 1700. That figure more than quadrupled in the next fifty years, until by 1750 there were nearly 1.2 million; by 1760 there were nearly 1.6 million. Areas that had been remote wilderness from the English point of view in 1700 were established towns by 1750. Settlers were pouring into areas even farther west. Anyone could see that there were immense profits to be made in acquiring blocks of land from the Indians and selling it out in parcels to colonists. The lower the initial purchase price, of course, the higher the profits, which created a powerful and ever-growing incentive to cheat the Indians.

Fraudulent land purchasing was nothing new, and colonial officials were long accustomed to meeting Indian complaints with professions of sympathy and little else, but the war with France gave the issue a new salience to colonial governments and to the imperial government. In the 1750s there was a distinct possibility that France, with the help of its Indian allies, would drive England out of North America. The English now had a heightened incentive not to antagonize the Indians. One way to achieve this end was to restructure the process of land purchasing. For more than a century the English authorities had allowed land to be purchased from the Indians by private individuals, who obtained patents from the colonial government. In the 1750s this tradition began to come under attack.

The problem was in part one of personnel. Many government officials were land speculators as well, so a certain amount of fraudulent purchasing would likely have taken place under any set of rules that had to be enforced by government officials. But much of the problem involved the rules themselves, and the institutional structure within which the rules operated. Indian land transactions often took place in the wilderness, sometimes far from tribe members who did not wish to sell, and often far from the colonial officials who in principle supervised the market by granting or withholding patents for the purchased land. When individual Indians sold land, the rest of the tribe might not learn about the sale until long afterward. When a purchaser applied for a patent, it could be impossible for the government to know anything about the circumstances of the sale. If the sellers whose names were on the contract had no right to sell the land, or if they were drunk at the time, or if the contract was forged, such matters might be discovered by the government only long after the patent had been granted, when the Indians' complaints finally reached the colonial capital. To ensure that land purchasing was conducted honestly, information had to travel quickly from the point of sale in two directions: to the tribe and to the colonial government. But communication over distance was slow and costly in the eighteenth century. Any reform would require eliminating the need for it.

Three solutions were proposed in the 1750s. The gap between Indian sellers and the rest of the tribe could be eliminated by prohibiting private sales—that is, by requiring sales to be made by tribes as a whole rather than individual Indians. The idea was first proposed by the Indians. Peter Wraxall reported in 1755 that "many years ago the Indians requested of our Governors, and indeed have earnestly repeated it to almost every Governor, that no Patents might be granted, but for Land sold at their general and public meetings." A ban on private sales quickly attracted the support of the colonial officials with responsibility for relations with the Indians. Charleston merchant Edmond Atkin, later appointed superintendent of the southern Indian tribes, proposed the same rule in his detailed report on Indian affairs to the Board of Trade. The colonial delegates to the 1754 Albany Congress agreed. They suggested that all future purchases ought to be made "from the Indians in a Body in their Public Councils." Thomas Pownall, a future governor of Massachusetts, was at the Albany Congress and included the same recommendation in his 1756 *Proposals for Securing the Friendship of the Five Nations*. "The Methods hitherto pursued in the Purchase of the Lands of the Indians," Pownall predicted, "will be attended with very bad Consequences" if continued too much longer.[3] If purchasing was brought out in the open, individual tribe members would no longer be able to sell the tribe's land secretly. Unscrupulous purchasers would no longer be able to ply prospective sellers with alcohol. Less land would be sold, and the land that was sold would fetch higher prices.

The gap between the point of sale and the colonial government could be eliminated by prohibiting private purchasing; that is, by requiring purchases to be made by colonial governments rather than individual settlers. This idea was suggested by the Board of Trade in a 1753 letter to the governor of New York, and it came up again the following year at the Albany Congress. It also appeared in Edmond Atkin's plan for re-organizing Indian relations.[4] Some of the colonial officials who would actually have to conduct the purchasing were not entirely above de-frauding the Indians, but they were less likely to do so than the least scrupulous of the private purchasers. The proposal doubtless held con-siderable appeal for colonial officials for a second reason, unrelated to protecting the welfare of the Indians: establishing colonial governments as the sole lawful purchasers of Indian land would allow the govern-ments to capture the profits from reselling the land to settlers, profits that under private purchasing flowed to individual speculators.

The third solution in circulation in the 1750s to the problem of dis-honest private land purchasing was to set aside an area in which land purchasing would be banned completely. If a boundary could be drawn between the settlers and the Indians, William Johnson reasoned in 1758, the major cause of friction between the English and the Indians would be removed. New York surveyor Alexander Colden suggested that pro-hibiting the purchase of at least part of the territory the Indians still owned would be the only way to prevent settlers from continuing to de-fraud the Indians.[5] The result would be, in effect, an Indian reservation.

In the midst of war against the French and many Indian tribes, how-ever, the colonies did nothing to modify the way settlers purchased In-dian land.[6] If anything, the situation only grew worse, as years of fighting against the Indians, combined with the constant westward migration pushed by a growing English population, made colonists more willing to disregard Indian property rights. Pennsylvania's governor James Hamil-ton discovered in the winter of 1760–61 that settlers from Connecticut had laid out townships the previous summer on the west side of the Delaware River, on land not yet purchased from the Indians. The news was bad for Pennsylvania, both because the colony would have to bear much of the cost of any renewed fighting with the Indians who owned the land and because Pennsylvania hoped eventually to purchase the very same land and sell it off to settlers, transactions that would become considerably more difficult if the land were already occupied by Anglo-Americans. Hamilton immediately sent a sheriff to warn the settlers off, but they refused to move. The worst thing about the standoff, Hamilton complained, was the way it must have looked to the Indians. "Indeed!" he exclaimed, "what can they think of us when they see the blood of our Inhabitants scarce covered, but we are quarrelling for Land that belongs to neither of us, but to them."[7]

In New York, the Indians of Conajoharie had the same grievance, that the years of war had made settlers even more aggressive in grabbing their land. They had sold many large tracts to the English in the past, a delegation of sachems reminded William Johnson and three local justices of the peace, and they had never disputed the validity of the sales. But this time, they complained, "we have been greatly Overreached." A few Indians, made drunk for the purpose, had sold a small tract to a group of settlers, who in turn had hired surveyors to mark out a much larger parcel—all the land the Indians had left. The Indians might never have learned about it, they explained, "had we not found out by mere Accident a Surveyors Staff stuck in the Ground, where he had been, during the night, surveying our Lands, without our Knowledge, and contrary to the usual Custom, when, as in all fair Purchases, Surveys are made in the Day, and in the Presence of some Indians." The surveyor had even chosen to do his work at a time of year when most of the tribe were away hunting. Had they not chanced upon the stick he left in the ground, New York would likely have granted away their land.[8]

As the war tapered off, imperial officials turned their attention to reform. In November 1761 the Board of Trade proposed to King George III that he do something to prohibit what the Board called "a Measure of the most dangerous Tendency"—the settlement of land not yet purchased from the Indians. The Board reminded the king that the primary reason most tribes had sided with France was "the Cruelty and Injustice with which they had been treated with respect to their Hunting Grounds, in open violation of those solemn Compacts by which they had yielded to us the Dominion but not the Property of their Lands."

(By "Dominion" the Board of Trade meant what we would today call "sovereignty." The Indians were within the area governed by Britain, the Board of Trade was saying, but they still owned their land.) The Board was particularly concerned that colonial governors were too freely granting licenses to purchase land from the Indians, and thereby authorizing too many people to migrate westward, beyond where they could be controlled by colonial governments, where settlers might omit to purchase land from the Indians and simply settle. The following month, the king instructed the governors of the seven royal colonies—the colonies governed directly by the Crown rather than by local proprietors or chartered entities—that they no longer had any power to grant licenses to purchase land from the Indians. All applications for licenses were to be forwarded to the Board of Trade, which would make the decision.[9] As of December 1761, part of the purchasing process was thus centralized. In seven colonies the power to approve purchases was placed in the hands of imperial officials far from the frontier, men much less likely than colonial officials to be speculating in land for their own account or to be susceptible to pressure from local speculators.

But relations with the Indians continued to deteriorate. Just when the war against France was winding down, war against Indian tribes broke out. In the south, the British began fighting the Cherokees in the early 1760s. In the north, a coalition of tribes led by Pontiac defeated British armies several times in the spring of 1763. The losses of early 1763 spurred the imperial government to further action.[10]

Already in circulation was the idea of drawing a western boundary for the colonies and prohibiting settlement beyond the line—not to prevent contact with the Indians, but rather to advance the mercantilist goal of keeping the colonists dependent on British manufactures. The farther from the Atlantic the settlers migrated, went the theory, the more difficulty they would have in importing British products, and the more likely they would be to begin manufacturing goods themselves. In June 1763 the Board of Trade first linked the proposed western boundary with the increasingly conspicuous need to placate the Indians, and suggested that drawing a line down the continent would create "an Indian Country, open to Trade, but not to Grants and Settlements." In August, alarmed by news of war with the northern Indians, the Board of Trade proposed that the king immediately issue a proclamation drawing a boundary and barring settlement to the west of it. The Privy Council went further, declaring that the proposed proclamation ought also to prohibit the private purchasing of Indian land, even east of the line.[11] Here were two of the three methods of restructuring the Indian land market that had been circulating in the colonies since the mid-1750s. The proclamation was drafted quickly and issued on October 7.

The Proclamation of 1763, as it has been known ever since, was one of the major events of British imperial history.[12] It included important changes in colonial policy in several areas related only tangentially to Indian land purchasing: It established governments for the various territories newly conquered from France; it authorized colonial governors to grant free land to all the soldiers who had fought in the war; and it set up a uniform system of licensing for the Indian trade. But the most fundamental of the changes instituted in 1763 was the complete overhaul of the process of acquiring Indian land. The Proclamation of 1763 included all three of the reforms that had been proposed in the 1750s.

The proclamation drew a line down the continent and prohibited new land grants and settlement west of the line. The proclamation explained, "It is just and reasonable," and, probably more to the point, "essential to Our Interest and the Security of Our Colonies," that the Indians "should not be molested or disturbed in the Possession of such Parts of Our Dominions and Territories as, not having been ceded to, or purchased by Us, are reserved to them." Colonial officials were accordingly instructed not to make any new land grants "beyond the Heads or Sources of any of the Rivers which fall into the Atlantick Ocean." The result was a line along the north–south ridge of mountains running through western New York, western Pennsylvania, western Virginia (including the eastern part of present-day West Virginia), western North and South Carolina, and the middle of Georgia.[13] The area west of the line was "reserved to the said Indians." Settlement in that area was forbidden without special permission from the Crown. Settlers already occupying land west of the line were ordered to leave immediately.

The placement of the boundary was a matter more of convenience than deliberation. Sitting in England, desiring to produce a proclamation quickly but lacking much firsthand information about the topography of the frontier or the actual locations of settlers and Indians, imperial officials chose a boundary that could be expressed in a single sentence and easily drawn on a map. There was no time to survey a boundary that genuinely divided the land the Indians had already sold from the land they had not. The drafters of the proclamation recognized that when the war was over they would have to send out surveyors to run a line more responsive to local conditions. They must also have foreseen that the colonies' rapid population growth was likely to require purchasing more land from the Indians in the future. They accordingly wrote this part of the proclamation, unlike the rest, in tentative, temporary language. The ban on land grants west of the line was to last only "for the present, and until Our further Pleasure be known." The reservation of that area to the Indians was also to endure "for the present as aforesaid." The temporary quality of the proclamation's language would prove to be important, because it would fuel the efforts of settlers and speculators to acquire land illegally, in the expectation that purchases unlawful in the present would become lawful in the future.

As to land east of the boundary, the proclamation banned private purchasing. "Great Frauds and Abuses have been committed in the purchasing Lands of the Indians," read the preamble of the relevant paragraph, and the proclamation accordingly instructed "that no private Person do presume to make any Purchase from the said Indians of any Lands." In the royal colonies, land was instead to be "purchased only for Us, in Our Name"—that is, only by colonial governors, on behalf of the Crown. In the proprietary colonies, where previous monarchs had already given away the right to purchase land, Indian land was to be "purchased only for the Use and in the Name of such Proprietaries." The point was to concentrate purchasing in the hands of a small number of people, who would tend to be more scrupulous than private purchasers were, and who could at least be more easily supervised from England. And it was hoped that even unscrupulous colonial officials would be less tempted to cheat the Indians if they were purchasing for the Crown rather than on their own account.

The proclamation also prohibited secret purchases of land from individual Indians. Purchases had to be made instead "at some publick Meeting or Assembly" of the selling tribe. If individual Indians could no longer sell the tribe's land and pocket the proceeds, a large class of abuses would be eliminated.

The combined effect of these measures was the complete reorganization of Indian land purchasing. Before 1763, land was often purchased in private, far to the west of any English town, by individual English buyers, from individual Indian sellers. After 1763, land could be lawfully purchased only out in the open, only by English units of government, only from Indian units of government, and only east of the mountains, closer to English towns. The Proclamation of 1763 was a genuine effort by the imperial government, in the wake of recurring wars against Indian tribes north and south, to remove the major cause of Indian dissatisfaction with English settlement.

The government's motives were no doubt more utilitarian than humanitarian. War was much more expensive than peace. The profitable fur trade depended on maintaining the Indians' cooperation. By disallowing settlement west of the mountains, and transforming land transactions from private deals into public meetings, the imperial government was giving up little or nothing. The military commander Thomas Gage said as much a few years later. "Let the Savages enjoy their Desarts in quiet," he declared. "I am of opinion, independent of the Motives of common Justice and Humanity, that the Principles of Interest and Policy should induce us rather to protect than molest them. Were they drove from their Forrests, the Peltry Trade would decrease." The interests of the imperial government and the Indians were aligned at least in this respect. Their common enemies were the settlers on the frontier.[14]

Whatever short-run gains the Indians anticipated from the proclamation, however, had to be balanced against a longer-term and less tangible loss. By banning the purchase of some of the Indians' land, and by banning the private purchase of the rest, the imperial government was for the first time imposing serious restrictions on the Indians' power to choose what they would do with their land. Individual colonies had long required purchasers of Indian land to obtain the colonial government's permission, but that requirement had never been onerous and had never prevented many sales from taking place. The Proclamation of 1763 was much more restrictive. The imperial government would never have dreamed of imposing similar restrictions on land owned by English settlers. After 1763, the Indians could do less with their land than the English could do with theirs. The proclamation marked the first time the imperial government treated Indian and English landowners in such a systematically disparate fashion.

When news of the proclamation reached North America, many of the colonial officials most knowledgeable about relations with the Indians were optimistic that it would achieve its goal of bringing peace with the Indians. They especially liked the boundary, which George Croghan, William Johnson's deputy superintendent, thought would "put an End, to dangerous Disputes" over land between settlers and Indians. William Franklin, the governor of New Jersey, foresaw peace for many years to come. "We shall avoid Many future Quarrells with the Savages by this

Salutary Measure," predicted Thomas Gage.[15] After more than a century of conflict with the Indians over land purchasing, they hoped, a more orderly and peaceful future was in sight.

Crossing the Line

First, however, the boundary had to be drawn. Running a line between the settlers and the Indians was necessary, Georgia governor James Wright knew, but he recognized that it "will be found a very delicate & difficult point," because wherever the line was placed, someone was likely to have a claim to land on the other side.[16] The concept of a boundary was simple, but actually locating the boundary was a task that would prove to be extraordinarily complex.

In July 1764 the Board of Trade circulated to colonial governors a proposed "Plan for the Future Management of Indian Affairs" intended in part to implement the broad changes announced by the Proclamation of 1763. The plan, although never formally adopted, summarized the expectations of the imperial government for the new land-purchasing regime. Land would be bought only by colonial governments or proprietors, not individuals. Land would be bought only at public meetings, from the "principal Chiefs of each Tribe," not in secret transactions from drunken tribe members. And most important, the Board of Trade specified that "proper measures be taken with the Consent and Concurrence of the Indians to ascertain and define the precise and exact boundary" beyond which no colonial settlement would be allowed.[17] The temporary mountaintop line established by the Proclamation of 1763 would be replaced with a more permanent boundary, based not on geography but on the actual pattern of landownership.

The difficulty in agreeing on a boundary was that so many inconsistent interests were at stake. Imperial officials seem to have envisioned a simple bilateral negotiation between Britain and the Indians, but neither Britain nor the Indians were a single unit when frontier land was at issue. In any given place, negotiations over the boundary's location involved at least three parties—a colony, an Indian tribe, and a group of settlers with claims based on an alleged purchase from the Indians. In many places there was more than one colony involved, because many of the colonies had overlapping and inconsistent claims to western territory, flowing from ambiguities in their original charters. Tribes also had overlapping and inconsistent claims to territory, so in many places there was more than one Indian tribe involved. There could be rival groups of settlers, with inconsistent private claims. Running the line often required complicated multilateral negotiations. The wonder is not that it took so long to survey the line, but that it was possible to draw a line at all.

John Stuart, the superintendent of Indian affairs in the south, began negotiating with tribes and colonial governments soon after news of the Proclamation of 1763 reached North America, despite lacking any formal instruction to do so. In late 1763 Stuart convened a meeting at Augusta, Georgia's westernmost town, between Georgia, the Chickasaws, the Choctaws, the Creeks, the Cherokees, and the Catawbas. All reached an agreement on a boundary, but the agreement began unraveling soon after, and there were repeated renegotiations for the next several years. A new line was surveyed in 1768, but that agreement also fell apart and a third line had to be mapped in 1773. By 1766 Stuart brokered a boundary agreement between South Carolina and the Cherokees, an agreement ratified at the Treaty of Hard Labour in 1768. The lines between the Cherokees and North Carolina, and the Cherokees and Virginia, were also ratified at Hard Labour, but the Virginia segment of the line was short-lived, because of pressure from western settlers. In 1771 Virginia purchased more land from the Cherokees to secure a boundary farther west. Boundaries also had to be drawn for the new colonies of East and West Florida, acquired in the French and Indian War. Stuart secured agreements in 1765 between East Florida and the Creeks, between West Florida and the Choctaws, and between West Florida and the Creeks, although much of the West Florida boundary was not actually surveyed until 1779, when England was on its way to losing the thirteen colonies to the north. After years of crisscrossing the wilderness all over the south, Stuart had produced a line separating the southern colonies from the Indians.[18]

William Johnson, superintendent of Indian affairs in the north, was meanwhile conducting similar diplomacy among the northern tribes and colonies, but with less success in the years immediately after 1763. Fighting in the north did not end until the fall of 1765, so the work could not even begin until then. There were many more tribes in the north than in the south, and the northern colonies had more inconsistent western claims than the southern colonies, so negotiations were more complex in the north. And Johnson felt more constrained than Stuart by the absence of any formal authorization to run the line. Johnson reached a provisional agreement with the Six Nations in 1765, but there would be no northern boundary line until 1768, when authorization from England finally came. In the meantime, the lack of a boundary despite years of promises caused English relations with the Indians to deteriorate further. By late 1767 George Croghan lamented that the northern tribes were "in so Sullen a Temper . . . [that he wished] that Boundary had never been Mention'd to them." In early 1768 the Pennsylvania Assembly sent a letter to England pleading with the government to establish the boundary. "The Natives have warmly complained," the Assembly reported, that without a boundary English subjects were continually settling on land that had not yet been purchased.[19] To promise a line, but then to delay drawing one, was worse than not promising a line at all.

Finally, at the 1768 Treaty of Fort Stanwix, Johnson brokered an agreement among the northern tribes and the northern colonies. Gathered at Fort Stanwix, in northern New York, were thousands of people, representing several Indian and English jurisdictions: the constituent tribes of the Six Nations, a few smaller tribes, Virginia, New York, New Jersey, and Pennsylvania. Also present were land speculators and missionaries, who each had interests of their own. With so many sides to satisfy, the result was "a very difficult Negociation," as Johnson described it shortly afterward, but one in which he believed he had "at length obtained a very advantagious Boundary." In the treaty signed at the conference, Johnson purchased from the Six Nations on the Crown's behalf thousands of square miles of land, and the parties agreed on the northern segment of the boundary line separating English from Indian territory. But not all interested groups had been present. The Shawnees and the Cherokees both had claims, probably superior claims, to much of the land the Six Nations sold. Aware that the Six Nations' ownership of these areas was contested, but eager to get an agreement, Johnson had declined to invite the Shawnees or the Cherokees to Fort Stanwix. These tribes were, as Thomas Gage put it, "exasperated to a great Degree" when they heard the news. Johnson insisted that it would have been impractical "to Satisfy all the Wants or demands of every Nation who might for the Sake of presents set up a Title which they dare not pretend to in the presence of the True proprietors," but that was a more one-sided view of the matter than most later and less partial observers have taken. In drawing the boundary there was no way to avoid making contestable choices as to which tribes owned which land.[20]

After 1768 in the north, and by the early 1770s in most of the south, there was a boundary between the British colonies and the Indians defining the westernmost limits of colonial settlement. The key provision of the Proclamation of 1763 had been implemented on paper, the outcome of nearly a decade of complex multilateral diplomacy. Had the various treaties been enforced by the British government against its own subjects, the boundary might have served its purpose of forestalling conflict between settlers and Indians. With time, inconsistent tribal claims to the land east of the line might have been worked out. Settlers might have been encouraged to fill in sparsely populated areas east of the line rather than head west. British (and later, American) population pressure would eventually have pushed the line farther west, but for a time there might have been peace on the frontier.

But the boundary proved extremely porous. It was already an old story by the middle of the eighteenth century: colonial governments simply could not prevent settlers from heading west. Motivated by a belief (at variance with the formal law) that land and other natural resources were free for the taking and belonged to the first taker, settlers swarmed into the west. So many Virginians crossed the boundary and occupied unpurchased Indian land, contrary to the repeated admonitions of Governor Francis Fauquier, that in 1766 Fauquier announced that transboundary settlers "must expect no protection or mercy from Government, and be exposed to the revenge of the exasperated *Indians.*" There could hardly have been any greater evidence of Virginia's inability to restrain its own citizens than this admission that the Proclamation of 1763 would have to be enforced by the aggrieved tribes rather than by Virginia. Illegal settlement led, unsurprisingly, to recurring skirmishes between settlers and the Indians whose land they were occupying. "Such frequent Accounts are transmitted of the Violences committed upon the Indians and usurpation of their Lands by the Frontier People," Thomas Gage reported to the imperial government in 1767, "that we can scarcely be secure of the Duration of Peace." After years of warfare, many settlers and their descendants felt nothing but disgust for the Indians. One man executed in 1766 for the brutal murder of two Indian women proudly declared on the gallows his belief that it was "a meritorious act to kill Heathen, wherever they were found." A resigned William Johnson lamented that "this seems to be the opinion of all the common people."[21] In such a climate, many of the settlers felt no compunction about stealing the Indians' land.

Their only real deterrent, as Fauquier's proclamation suggested, was the threat of reprisal from the Indians, but that threat could never grow strong enough to prevent much settlement. A colonist settling illegally on unpurchased Indian land knew that while there he would enjoy all the benefits of that land. He knew that his own government was unlikely to do anything to remove him. But he also knew that he would not bear all the costs of defending his possession of the land, because in the event of an Indian attack he could expect the government to help him defend it by sending a military force to fight the Indians. So proclamations like Fauquier's were not completely credible, and settlers could enjoy all the gains from occupying Indian land while externalizing a portion of the costs. By fighting sporadic Indian wars, the British government was in effect subsidizing the illegal occupation of the Indians' land.

But the boundary was battered by more than just racism and land hunger. The Proclamation of 1763, and the subsequent negotiations over the placement of the line, came after years of transactions between settlers and Indians, transactions that had lingering consequences. Settlers had sold goods to Indians on credit, in the expectation of foreclosing on land if the Indians could not pay when the bill came due. The proclamation's ban on private land purchasing left the Indians' creditors unable to collect debts, because foreclosure required the transfer of land from individual Indians to individual settlers. The inability to use their land as security for debts must have made life more difficult for the Indians as well, because it would have made it harder for them to buy goods on credit. Settlers and Indians alike seem to have often ignored the ban on private purchasing, by continuing to secure debts with land. "Such dangerous and unwarrantable practices" had to be stopped, thundered Lord Hillsborough, secretary of state for the colonies, in 1771, but stopping them was no easy matter.[22]

Creditors were not the only colonists who believed they had been left hanging by the Proclamation of 1763 and the subsequent boundaries. Some settlers had already obtained patents from colonial governments to western land, the validity of which they had no reason to doubt at the time. They had already invested all their resources in building houses and laying out farms. Their homes had been on the front lines of the French and Indian War. As one group of settlers reported, "many lost their Lives, almost all of us our Effects." Now, just as they were rebuilding after the war, they were told that their land lay to the west of the line, and that they would have to leave immediately. Many chose instead to stay, preferring the risk of another war with the Indians to the likelihood of destitution back east.[23] Drawing a boundary between settlers and Indians required sacrificing the interests of some settlers, who in turn had little reason to respect the boundary.

Creating a boundary also required sacrificing the interests of some Indians. The Proclamation of 1763 could not change the economic reality facing many Indians. Land was their major asset. If they wanted to buy European products—tools, animals, food, and so on—they had to sell land. The proclamation made land sales more cumbersome and accordingly was as unwelcome to many Indians as it was to many settlers. The result was the creation of a black market in Indian land, as buyers and sellers found one another despite the illegality of the transactions.

Some of the buyers on the black market were settlers, seeking only enough land for themselves. Others were speculators looking for opportunities to buy up enormous tracts that could later be broken up and sold to settlers in smaller parcels at a large profit if western settlement were later to be legalized. As one wealthy Virginia speculator explained to an associate in 1767, it was simply good business to buy Indian land "notwithstanding the Proclamation that restrains it at present," because "I can never look upon that Proclamation in any other light (but this I say between ourselves) than as a temporary expedient to quiet the Minds of the Indians." He had no doubt that the proclamation would be revoked within a few years. When that happened, the demand for western land would increase, and the price would rise. "Any person therefore who neglects the present opportunity of hunting out good Lands and in some measure marking and distinguishing them for their own (in order to keep others from settling them) will never regain it." He accordingly instructed his associate to buy up as much Indian land west of the line as he could, and "to keep this whole matter a profound Secret" because of its illegality. That speculator was George Washington.[24]

Washington was hardly the only prominent North American buying Indian land on the black market in the decade following the Proclamation of 1763. Henry Laurens owned plantations in South Carolina and Georgia. In 1777 he would succeed John Hancock as president of the Continental Congress. Six years earlier he was in England, where he had taken his sons for their education after the death of his wife. While there, Laurens acted as an unofficial representative of the interests of South Carolina, which were in many respects congruent with his own.

But he kept an eye on western land. "I believe you may depend upon this for Truth and it will not fail you," Laurens advised a colleague. "If you can get the proper Men to cede to you, any body or Quantity of Land, within the Indian Lines"—that is, west of the boundary beyond which land purchasing was illegal—"that Property will be to all Intents and Purposes, absolutely yours and your Heirs for ever."[25] When men like Laurens and Washington were willing to buy land illegally, there could be little hope of preventing others from following.

Buying land from the Indians west of the line was illegal only in the sense that purchase contracts would be unenforceable in court and land titles derived from such contracts could be superseded by titles created later. Purchasing land was not a crime. *Settling* on Indian land was made criminal by some of the colonies, and in Pennsylvania it was even a capital crime (although there is no evidence that anyone was ever executed for it), but purchasing land was not. In buying land, George Washington did not risk being punished by the government; his only danger was that he might lose the purchase price if the government later granted the same land to someone else. The potential profits from reselling the land were large enough for Washington and other speculators to be willing to bear that risk.

The market in Indian land, like any black market, was also supported by an informal legal culture that permitted activity proscribed by the formal law. Some, like Benjamin Franklin, thought the Proclamation of 1763 exceeded the power of the British government. The Indians owned their land and had the right to decide whom to sell it to, Franklin argued. The government, with no claim to any property rights in the land, had no power to forbid its sale. The argument had considerable appeal for the speculators, who were outraged at the Proclamation of 1763. Their dissatisfaction with the imperial government was one of the first of many similar grievances that would follow in the next thirteen years. It would echo in the words of the Declaration of Independence, written by a man who himself had large investments in western land, Thomas Jefferson. Toward the beginning of the Declaration's list of complaints about George III was the accusation that the king was placing onerous "conditions" on the "new Appropriations of Lands," a process that began with the proclamation. In retrospect, one can see the claim that the British government had exceeded its authority in prohibiting western settlement as an early instance of the broad category of argument that

Britain was governing its American colonies in new and unlawful ways, and thus as an early step in the development of the set of beliefs that would eventually lead to the Revolution.[26]

Franklin's argument would likely not have prevailed had it been litigated, but it was not frivolous. England's "constitution" was an unwritten amalgam of traditions rather than a document, so the outcome of litigation on the issue would not have been easy to foresee, but lawyers would have recognized the claim as plausible at the very least. If the Crown had tried to limit the power of *English* landowners in North America to sell their land, Anglo-American lawyers would have argued instinctively that the measure was an unconstitutional infringement of the rights of property. If the Crown lacked the power to prohibit English landowners from selling their land, and if the Indians owned their land just as the English did, then, speculators might have reasoned, how could the Crown have any power to prohibit the Indians from selling theirs? The question was not unanswerable. Crown lawyers might have pointed out that colonial governments had long placed restrictions on the sale of Indian land that were not placed on land owned by colonists. But the answer was not a simple one, and it would not have been universally convincing. In their rejection of the legality of the Proclamation of 1763, the land speculators were well within the mainstream of conventional legal thought.

The widespread belief (or fervent wish) among speculators that the Proclamation of 1763 was beyond the imperial government's authority is the only possible explanation for what would otherwise be an implausible sequence of events. Circulating among the American land speculators was a legal opinion ostensibly written by two of the most eminent English lawyers of the era, Charles Pratt and Charles Yorke. Pratt served as lord chancellor of England from 1766 to 1770, Yorke from 1770 to 1771. In 1757 they were, respectively, England's attorney general and solicitor general. That year, in response to a petition from the East India Company, Pratt and Yorke issued an official opinion explaining that in India a grant from the Crown was not a prerequisite to a valid land title. Land in India could instead be purchased directly "from the Mogul or any of the Indian Princes, or Governments." At some point between 1757 and 1773, probably much closer to 1773, someone in North America transcribed a misleading version of the opinion. References to the East India Company and to the Mogul were omitted, and the rest of the passage was edited to make it seem as if it referred to "Indian Princes or

Governments" in North America rather than in India. The result was a text, purporting to have been written by two of England's leading government lawyers, that authorized land purchases directly from the Indians, contrary to the Proclamation of 1763. American speculators were quick to pounce on the doctored opinion as support for their purchases. George Washington inscribed a version of the opinion on the flyleaf of his 1773 diary. The speculator William Murray carried a copy of the opinion to Illinois, where he presented it to a skeptical British military commander and, unsuccessfully, claimed it as authority to begin negotiating with the Indians.[27]

Without a preexisting climate of thought in which the Proclamation of 1763 was of dubious legality, no one could have believed the alleged Pratt-Yorke opinion was genuine. Anyone familiar with the Proclamation of 1763 and the subsequent negotiations over the boundary—and the big speculators were all familiar with these issues—would have immediately seen something fishy in a legal opinion so blatantly at variance with the proclamation and the tenor of imperial Indian policy for the preceding ten years. In the early 1770s, though, the atmosphere was just right for the opinion to appear authentic.

Speculators and settlers, in any event, hardly needed a fake legal opinion to obtain Indian land west of the boundary. No government, colonial or imperial, was strong enough to stop them. "Shall we, can we, permit these Banditti, these abandoned Men" to settle on Indian land?, Virginia governor John Blair asked the colony's House of Burgesses in 1768. After years of bloody fighting against the Indians, would the government allow illegal settlers "to open afresh those Sluices of Blood, whose flowing hath been so lately stopt" by the negotiation of a boundary? The answer, more often than not, was yes, because the settlers greatly outnumbered the military forces at the disposal of colonial governments. The imperial government repeatedly instructed colonial officials to put a stop to unlawful settlement. In 1766 the Earl of Shelburne, secretary of state, sent a circular to all the colonial governors, complaining that "Settlements have been made on the Back of the Provinces, without proper authority and beyond the Limits prescribed by His Majesty's Royal Proclamation of 1763," and urging each governor to "apply yourself in the most earnest manner, to remedy and prevent those Evils." But all the earnestness in the world would not have been enough. Officials could hope only to score small victories here and there. In 1767, for example, the commander at Fort Pitt destroyed the huts of a group of settlers illegally occupying Indian land in western Pennsylvania. But more settlers were on their way. By 1769 even William Johnson had to admit that "whatever Laws are made will fail in the Execution for reasons that are Obvious." The precise location of the boundary made little difference, Thomas Gage concluded, because even if the line could be moved to the west, the economics driving westward migration would be the same. "Lands still being dear, the People would have the same Temptation as they have now, to emigrate beyond the Boundary."[28] The most obvious effect of the Proclamation of 1763 was to replace legal land acquisition with illegal land acquisition.

The proclamation had been intended to secure peace with the Indians, but it was a dismal failure. A measure many had thought "was finally to put an end to all Our Disputes with the Indians," Hillsborough remarked in 1770, had only made things worse, by giving the Indians a "new Ground of Disgust"—the English failure to live up to the promises made in the boundary treaties. The proclamation most likely deterred some settlers from crossing the line. Speculators like George Washington were probably right in assuming that there would be more emigrants if western settlement could be done legally, with formal land titles. If so, then by somewhat stemming the tide of emigration, the proclamation most likely reduced the frequency of clashes between settlers and Indians. But the proclamation's possible benefits were overshadowed by one big cost—Britain had led the Indians to expect that there would be no new western settlement, but had not put that promise into practice. As a result, Hillsborough concluded, the proclamation had "so entirely failed in its Object, as to have produced the very Evils to which it was proposed as a Remedy."[29] Relations with the Indians had grown worse than ever.

From Contract to Treaty

The Proclamation of 1763 changed the legal method of acquiring land from the Indians, and that change would have important effects in the long run. From 1763 on, legal land purchasing was concentrated in the hands of the government. That practice would be continued by the independent state governments after 1776, and then in 1790 the first United States Congress would further centralize Indian land purchasing by establishing the new federal government as the only legal purchaser. The federal government has possessed the exclusive right to buy Indian land ever since. The ultimate effect of the Proclamation of 1763 was thus to transform the land market. Before 1763, land purchasing was largely a matter of *contract*, of private bargaining between individual groups of buyers and sellers. After 1763, land was lawfully conveyed only by *treaty*, in highly formalized transactions between units of government.[30] And that change, in turn, would begin to influence the way Anglo-Americans thought about Indian landownership.

With all the attention government officials paid to illegal land acquisition in the 1760s and 1770s, it is easy to forget that most of the big players in the market were following the law. They were trying to buy Indian land legally, according to the procedures set forth in the Proclamation of 1763. Formal land titles were much more important to speculators than to settlers, because speculators were hoping to sell parcels to prospective emigrants back east, and trying to sell shares to investors. Without formal titles they had little to offer a prospective emigrant, who had no reason to pay an intermediary for a pseudo-title when he could get one himself simply by occupying the Indians' land. Without the prospect of profits it would be impossible to attract investment. If they hoped to resell Indian land in the foreseeable future, speculators had to play by the rules.

Speculators accordingly redirected their efforts from buying land to lobbying the government to buy it. Once the land was purchased, the government could then grant it to the speculator. In 1771, for example, Jelles Fonda and his associates petitioned the government of New York to purchase from the Indians a forty-thousand-acre tract in Albany County. Fonda declared that he and his partners were "willing and desirous at their own Expence to vest the Indian Right and Title to the said Lands in the Crown." Of course, Fonda's proposal was not to buy land for the Crown. When the purchase had been completed, Fonda intended "to pray for and obtain his Majesty's Letters patent for the said Lands, and to cultivate and improve the same."[31] The government of New York would be a mere intermediary, a conduit passing land in one direction and money in the other, wedged between the Indians and Jelles Fonda to satisfy the formal requirements of the Proclamation of 1763.

Colonial officials were only too happy to play the role. The Crown was the sole lawful land purchaser under the proclamation, but the imperial government had not appropriated any new money for that purpose. Colonial governors and legislators faced strong popular pressure to acquire land. Without public funds, they had to fill the gap with private money. As New York governor William Tryon explained in 1773, he had been given no budget with which to buy land, and so "recourse has always been had to the subject, with whose money advanced on the faith of a licence from the governor with the advice of the Council the price was paid." The Indians would transfer their land to the Crown, "and the purchasers who advance the money derive no other advantage from it than a claim upon the honour and justice of government to a preference in letters patent." The purchasers would then file a second petition asking that the land bought with their money be granted to them, and the government would do so.[32] The form of the transaction changed after 1763, but the substance was the same.

In their efforts to lobby government officials to buy Indian land on their behalf, speculators had a tool more powerful than persuasion. The middle decades of the eighteenth century saw the formation of several well-capitalized land companies, as the possibility of buying up the territory won from France attracted wide investment. It became a standard practice after the Proclamation of 1763 for land speculators to offer shares in these enterprises to the government officials who had the power, or at least were close to those with the power, to decide whether land would be purchased. Many public officials accordingly became investors in land companies in the 1760s and 1770s.[33] Among them were Richard Henry Lee, a shareholder in the Mississippi Company and a member of the Virginia House of Burgesses; William Franklin, who had 10 percent of the Illinois Company while governor of New Jersey; Franklin's more famous father Benjamin, another Illinois Company shareholder while representing Pennsylvania's interests in England; Indian Superintendent William Johnson and his deputy George Croghan, who owned shares in the Illinois Company and the Indiana Company; Jonathan Trumbull, governor of Connecticut and shareholder in the Susquehannah Company; and Thomas Jefferson and Patrick Henry, both of whom invested in several western land ventures while they were members of the Virginia House of Burgesses.

A list of famous names does not even convey a sense of how closely government was intermingled with land speculation. More revealing is to consider a single colony and a single company. Of the twenty-five Virginians who were at one time or another shareholders in the Ohio Company, twenty were members of the House of Burgesses. Of those twenty, nine were members of the Council (as were the fathers of two of the others, the brothers of a few more, and other close relatives of most), two were presidents of the Council, one was lieutenant governor, and one was acting governor. At all times between 1748 and 1774 there was at least one Ohio Company shareholder on the Council. Public officials sometimes tried to keep their involvement secret, but with so many investing so much, secrecy could not last long.[34] It made little difference, in any event. In that era, it was not illegal to profit as a private citizen in the areas over which one governed as a public official. The absence of "conflict of interest" rules, from a modern perspective, was not unique to Indian affairs. It was a feature of government generally. Where Indian land was concerned, the lack of a sharp distinction between public and private interests greased the wheels of the land purchase system that evolved in response to the Proclamation of 1763.

Under the new system, individual landowners derived their title from the Crown, not from the Indians. Before 1763, many Anglo-Americans' claims to ownership of land were based on prior ownership by an Indian or a tribe, because the first recorded conveyance of the land had been from an Indian or a tribe to a settler. If the Indians had not owned the land, no one following them in the chain of title owned it either. A landowner's chain of title sometimes also required a patent from the government, but in most of the colonies, at most times, the patent alone did not create a property right; it only authorized the holder to purchase the property right from the Indians. Not all land titles required tracing a chain of individual purchases back to the Indians; some land had simply been occupied without the Indians' consent, some had been taken in war, and much had been purchased from the Indians by colonial governments rather than private individuals. But there was a large amount of private purchasing, and private purchasing usually presupposed a recognition that the Indian sellers owned the land they were selling. Until 1763, therefore, there was always a significant bloc of Anglo-Americans who had a strong financial incentive to believe that the Indians were truly the owners of their land. On that belief rested the validity of many landowners' titles.

Beginning with the Proclamation of 1763, no new titles depended on Indian ownership. All new landowners derived their titles from the Crown. Inserting the Crown between the Indians and the ultimate Anglo-American landowner made the validity of the Indians' title irrelevant to the landowner. In earlier times an "Indian deed"—the document evidencing the sale from the Indians to the first colonial purchaser—had often been the basis of title, but not any longer. Now "the Indian deed makes no part of the subject's title," Governor William Tryon explained; "it is of no other moment than to satisfy the claim of the native occupants."[35] Now a patent from the Crown was not just an authorization to acquire a property right from the Indians. The patent *was* the property right.

As a strict legal matter, the change in procedure had no bearing on whether the Indians owned their land before they sold it. The only thing different was the identity of the purchaser. But the fact that all new land titles derived from the Crown rather than from the Indians had some subtle long-run effects on the way Anglo-Americans thought about the Indian ownership of land.

The Proclamation of 1763 marked the beginning of a gradual erosion of the political base for recognizing Indian property rights. After 1763, the percentage of North America owned by people who traced their titles back to the Indians could only shrink. Every person who acquired land obtained from the Indians after the proclamation was one more person who had no reason to care whether the Indians had once owned the land. The rise in the number of such landowners was in part counterbalanced by the growth in population back east, which required the subdivision of some of the older eastern parcels acquired from the Indians in private purchases. But it seems unlikely that the number of new landowners basing their title on that of the Indians could ever have exceeded the number of new landowners whose title was derived entirely from the government. By the early 1800s some of the new western states had populations exceeding those of the much older eastern states. The 1820 census found that Ohio and Kentucky each had higher non-Indian populations than nine of the original thirteen states. Very few of these new westerners based their title on that of the Indians. Before 1763, landowners who needed to believe that the Indians had property rights in their land represented a latent but potentially powerful political force. By the first few decades of the nineteenth century, that force had dwindled away.

When the Indians were no longer allowed to sell their land to private purchasers, it became easier for settlers to think of the Indians' rights to the land as something less than full ownership. Ordinary landowners—people who, in legal jargon, owned their land in "fee simple absolute"—could sell the land to anyone they chose. English and American property law had long favored the free alienation of land. At any given time, much of the land in England and North America was owned in forms other than fee simple absolute; the alienation of such land might be subject to various restrictions, but these restrictions had been imposed at some point in the past by the landowner himself, as a means of deriving some future benefit he considered more valuable than the freedom of alienation. They were not restrictions imposed by the government. The Indians, by contrast, could sell their land only to the government, because of a restriction that had been placed on that land by the very same government. Before 1763, many colonists believed that Indian landownership was identical to Anglo-American landownership. After 1763, by contrast, Indian landownership was easier to perceive as a kind of second-class property right, something less complete than the full ownership enjoyed by Anglo-Americans. It became possible to think of "Indian title" as something different from ordinary title.

As the purchasing of Indian lands became exclusively a function of government, and as a grant from the government became the sole root of new land titles, it became easier to think of the original transaction between the government and the Indians as being less a transfer of ownership than a prudent military strategy, a way of mollifying the Indians while taking their land. It became possible to think of the money and goods transferred from the government to the Indians not as a purchase price required by law, but as gifts, not required at all but instead prompted by a shrewd calculation of how much it would take to forestall violence on the frontier.

One early marker of this shift in thought can be found in a document in Thomas Jefferson's possession, which the editors of Jefferson's papers date to 1773 or 1774. The document, captioned "Vindication of Virginia's Claim Against the Proposed Colony of Vandalia," is an anonymous rebuttal to a claim by one of the big land companies that it had purchased Indian land in western Virginia. Such purchases were clearly invalid under the Proclamation of 1763, but the author of this rebuttal seems to have been trying to come up with a reason for their invalidity that did not depend on the proclamation. Perhaps Jefferson or someone associated with him was anticipating independence and the need for a basis, other than the orders of the imperial government, upon which to reject speculators' claims to Indian land. The theory proposed by the author of the "Vindication" bears a striking similarity to the theory that would be adopted fifty years later by Chief Justice John Marshall in *Johnson v. M'Intosh*. "When America was first discovered by the Europeans," the "Vindication" posited, "a general notion prevail'd, that the first discoverers of any particular part, had a right to take possession, in the name of that Kingdom or State of which they were Subjects; and that such discovery and formality of taking possession conferred a Title." That notion did exist in the early seventeenth century, as we have seen, but it was far from "general," and in any event it had largely died out by the end of the seventeenth century. But the author of the "Vindication" assumed that discovery had consistently been deemed to confer title on the discovering nation, and used that assumption as the basis for denying the Indians the power to sell land to speculators. "Exceptionable as such a maxim may seem in its first establishment," he noted,

> all our Titles in America are derived from it; and it is impossible to argue against it now, without renouncing the Claim of Europe to America and dissolving those principles, upon which the rights of Individuals as well as the Claims of the different European Nations have been adjusted and ascertained. And altho' upon any disputes between the inhabitants of the British Colonies in America and the Native Indians, it is certainly more consistent with Justice and Humanity and even with our own Interest to compromise matters amicably with them by purchases, rather than extort from them by force; Yet such purchases have never been considering as operating in the least against the original Title of the British Crown. The Inhabitants of these Colonies derive their Titles not from Indian, but from British Monarchs.[36]

By the mid-1770s, someone in Virginia was already thinking of the Crown as the root of all land titles, and of the countless land purchases from Indians over the previous two centuries as legally meaningless charades.

This document was never published, perhaps because it would not have been persuasive to lawyers at the time. The theory it put forward would have invalidated the purchases of land speculators, but only by rendering pointless the ban on private purchasing instituted by the Proclamation of 1763. If the Crown was the true owner of all the Indians' land, there would have been no reason for the imperial government to prohibit private purchasing. It could simply have reminded colonists that the Indians did not own their land and that colonists accordingly ought not to try to buy it from them. The actual proclamation, of course, looked quite different. It reminded colonists that the Indians *did* own their land, and set down strict rules governing the transfer of ownership from tribes to the Crown. The "Vindication" was ahead of its time. It proposed a theory of landownership that became plausible sometime around the turn of the nineteenth century but was not plausible when it was written. In retrospect, it was a very early indication that the end of private land purchasing was beginning to influence the way Americans thought about transactions in Indian land.

At the time, the ultimate result of these changes in how Americans thought about Indian property ownership still lay well in the future. It would be a few decades before conventional American legal thought would unambiguously deny the Indians full property rights in their land. The changes were set in motion, however, by the Proclamation of 1763.

➤ 4

A REVOLUTION IN LAND POLICY

IN THE SPRING of 1783 the Continental Congress sent General Philip Schuyler to tell the Six Nations the Revolution was over. Schuyler knew the New York Indians well, after years of war against the tribes that had allied with Britain. In 1783 he was at the peak of his authority: he was simultaneously a member of the federal government's Board of Indian Commissioners, a New York state senator, and the state's surveyor general. If anyone was qualified to tell the Six Nations what the war's end meant for them, and how the victorious Americans intended to treat the Indians, it was Philip Schuyler.

Schuyler began with the good news. "The great spirit above has helped and given us success," he related, "and with the assistance of France [we] have conquered the King of England." But very quickly Schuyler's message grew darker. "We are now Masters," he told the assembled Indians, "and can dispose of the lands as we think proper or most convenient to ourselves." Most of the tribes in North America had fought on the losing side, the side of Britain. For more than a century, most Anglo-Americans had disclaimed any right of conquest and had purchased Indian land rather than taking it by force, but not any longer. Now, explained Schuyler, Indian tribes would be considered as defeated enemies, and their land would be appropriated. "As we are the Conquerors," Schuyler declared, "we claim the lands and property of all the white people as well as the Indians who have left and fought against us." The Indians had long looked to the imperial government back in England for protection against land-hungry settlers on the frontier, but Schuyler pointedly reminded his listeners that now they faced the settlers on their own. "We enquired of the King what he intended to do for the Indians," Schuyler needled, "as we expected that he would have been very particular about them. He being the person that should have considered their situation; but the King answered, *What can I do? Nothing! You have conquered me therefore do with them what you please.*"[1]

The American Revolution changed much of American life, and this newly aggressive land policy was one of the biggest changes. The immediate justification for it, as Schuyler told the Six Nations, was retribution for the decision of most tribes to fight for Britain against the colonists. But the Revolution contributed to the new land policy in other important ways as well—by giving birth to new units of American government that were desperately short of cash, by increasing the political power of land speculators and western settlers, and by removing the restraining hand of the imperial government, which in the colonial period had often been the Indians' ally against the colonists. As a result, in the first few years after the end of the Revolution, the Confederation government abandoned the English policy of purchasing Indian land and recognizing the Indians as property owners. In a series of "treaties" dictated to the Indians in the mid-1780s, the Confederation government confiscated Indian land without paying any compensation.

This new American land policy could not be maintained in full force for very long. In the late 1780s, to avoid unnecessarily antagonizing the Indians and to remove some of the threat of war, the government resumed paying the Indians for their land, in transactions that took the form of freely negotiated contracts, with the Indians exchanging land for money and goods. But in substance many of these transactions resembled the worst abuses of the pre-1763 private purchasing era. Mounting complaints from the Indians testified to a system of land acquisition in which land was "purchased" from small groups of sellers who lacked the authority to convey the tribe's land, in which purchasing agents employed by the federal government made promises that were never fulfilled, and in which the Indians' agreement to transactions was sometimes obtained by the threat of force. By the 1790s the United States government was purchasing Indian land, not seizing it by force. But the government was resorting to some of the same techniques employed by the least scrupulous private land purchasers of the mid-eighteenth century, the techniques that had prompted the imperial government to ban private purchasing in 1763. Now, however, the Indians could no longer look to the imperial government for protection. The ultimate authority over land purchasing rested with the very same federal government that was the sole lawful purchaser.

Continuities, 1776–1783

Independence from Britain, by itself, had not produced any substantial change in Indian land policy. Colonial governments had turned themselves into independent state governments, but generally they had continued to treat the Indians as owners of their land. Most of the circumstances that had produced this aspect of British policy remained as strong as ever, and independence had even added some new reasons to respect Indian property rights.

Anglo-Americans were still heirs to the same strands of thought that had predisposed them to recognize the Indians as property owners during the colonial period. The Indians had not ceased to farm, and for millennia educated Europeans had associated agriculture with the ownership of land. Some tribes laid out their fields just as common fields were organized in England, in parallel strips farmed by individual families. Common field farming was largely extinct on the East Coast of North America by the late eighteenth century, but many Anglo-Americans would have remembered the common fields of England, because the enclosure of the remaining English common fields was still a salient controversy at the time. In these respects, American thought did not change after independence.

Nor did independence immediately influence the material circumstances that had long impelled the English to respect Indian property rights in land. Land was still abundant and still cheap, much cheaper than land in England, and it was still true that the lower the price, the more likely Anglo-Americans would be willing to pay for land. There were still a great many Anglo-American landowners who traced their title back to an original purchase from the Indians and who thus could not question the legitimacy of the Indians' property rights without questioning the legitimacy of their own. These landowners still formed a latent but powerful political force capable of defeating any effort to stop recognizing the Indians as property owners.

Most important, it was still far less costly—in money, time, and lives—to purchase Indian land than to seize it by force. Indeed, the onset of the Revolution made it all the more important for Anglo-Americans on both sides of the conflict to maintain good relations with the

Indians, because both sides recognized that the Indians could be valuable allies. In the early years of the fighting the Continental Congress desperately tried to enlist the Indians on the American side, or at least to keep them neutral. "We desire you to remain at home, and not join on either side," a congressional delegation pleaded with the Six Nations in 1775, "but keep the hatchet buried deep." Such pleas from American officials rarely worked. The Indians could hardly be blamed for choosing the imperial government over the settlers, when the settlers were the source of all their problems and the imperial government a weak but often well intentioned friend. But during the Revolution the Indians occupied the same pivotal position between the colonists and the English as they had occupied between the English and the French before the French and Indian War.[2] Neither side could afford to antagonize a tribe before it had declared its allegiance to one side or the other.

Independence also created some *new* reasons to respect Indian property rights in land. In the debates that raged through colonial pamphlets and newspapers in the late 1760s and early 1770s, American polemicists questioned the power of Parliament to legislate for, and especially to tax, the colonies. That was a legal question, the answer to which depended on how one viewed the relationship between Britain and the colonies. One of the arguments offered by defenders of parliamentary authority was that the colonists had obtained their land from the Crown, and that the charters granting the land had incorporated the colonies within a unitary British empire with Parliament at its center. Critics of parliamentary power over the colonies disagreed with the notion that the charters had conveyed any land. The Crown had no power to grant land in the charters, they responded, because the land was not the Crown's to grant, but rather had belonged to the Indians. The land, and with it the power to govern, had been purchased from the Indians. The method by which property rights in North America had originally been acquired thus became a topical issue. It suddenly made a great deal of difference whether the earliest settlers had obtained their land from the Crown or from the Indians.[3]

Just before the Revolution, then, Americans had a new motive for believing that the Indians owned their land. "How, in common sense," asked John Adams in 1774, "came the dominions of King Philip, King Massachusetts, and twenty other sovereigns, independent princes here, to be within the allegiance of the Kings of England, James and Charles?" It could not have been by virtue of the colonial charters,

Adams argued, because discovery alone "could give no title to the English king, by common law, or by the law of nature, to the lands, tenements, and hereditaments of the native Indians here." The land belonged to the Indians, not to the Crown. "Our ancestors were sensible of this," Adams added, "and, therefore, honestly purchased their lands of the natives." Adams acknowledged the consensus among lawyers that the acts of Parliament carried force in newly discovered, uninhabited lands, but he hastened to add that the American colonies were hardly uninhabited. "America was not a vacant country," Adams reminded his readers; "it was full of inhabitants; our ancestors purchased the land."[4]

The press of political events prompted Benjamin Franklin to express the same sentiments. While reading Matthew Wheelock's defense of Parliament's supreme authority in North America, a defense premised on the assumption that the earliest colonists had acquired their land from the Crown, Franklin noted in the margin: "The British Nation had no original Property in the Country of America. It was purchas'd by the first Colonists of the Natives, the only Owners." In the margins of another pamphlet making a similar argument, Franklin scrawled: "False! The Lands did not belong to the Crown but to the Indians." Franklin eventually vented his frustration on this point in a 1773 letter published in the *Public Advertiser*, in which he insisted that "the Fact is well known, that Britain had not a Foot of Land in New-england; and that when the first Settlers went into that Country, they found it possessed by various Tribes of Indians."[5] The controversy over the authority of Parliament had given rise to a new reason to think of the Indians as property owners.

Independence meant the end of British authority in the colonies, and that created another new reason for arguing that the Indians owned their land. The newly independent states were no longer legally bound by the Proclamation of 1763 and its requirement that land be purchased by the government rather than private individuals. Land speculators hoping to make purchases from the Indians had always been among the most ardent defenders of Indian property rights, because without government recognition of Indian property rights the speculators would have nothing to buy. The prospect that independence might mean the resumption of private land purchasing brought the speculators' arguments for Indian ownership back into circulation. As early as August 1775, Edward Bancroft was already getting back in practice. "The aborigines of America being the Primitive Occupiers of that Continent,"

he argued, they "were by the Laws of Nature and Nations justly inti-
tuled to the full and Absolute Dominion and Property of that Continent." One can almost hear Bancroft calculating his future profits as he
declared that "the American Indians must still have an indisputable Title to the Jurisdiction and Property of all Parts of that Continent, which
have not been obtained from them by Purchase, Cession, or justifiable
Conquest."[6]

Once independence had been declared, such arguments became
common. Thomas Burke, representing the interests of speculators in
the Virginia House of Delegates in 1777 (and possibly a speculator himself), insisted that the "Indians have a right in the grounds they occupy,"
a "right which god and nature gave them," a right of which he hoped
they would shortly be relieved by the Transylvania Company. Burke reported his indignation at the Proclamation of 1763, a "tyrannical . . . prohibition." A representative of the Indiana Company likewise declared in
1781 that the Indians' title to their land "is the first and best in the
world. The Indians were the original proprietors of that tract of country.
It was conveyed to them by nature and providence." Not coincidentally,
the Indians had just reconveyed it to the Indiana Company.[7] Land acquisition was a motive for defending Indian property rights that had
been mostly dormant since 1763, but it reawakened with independence.

The speculators would be disappointed. Freed from the restrictions
of the Proclamation of 1763, the independent states nevertheless continued to prohibit private purchasing, for the same reason the imperial
government had. Independence did not alter the economics of land purchasing. It was still in the interest of speculators to purchase Indian land
as cheaply as possible, so speculators would be as tempted as ever to cut
corners by purchasing from tribe members with dubious authority to sell
and by deceiving sellers as to the extent of the land being bought.
There was still good reason to fear that such tactics would antagonize
the Indians and bring on war, and peace was still far less costly than war.
Independence did not change state governments' incentive to prohibit
private purchasing.

In Virginia, Thomas Jefferson's draft of the state constitution thus
included a prohibition on acquiring Indian land by any means other
than purchase, and by any purchaser other than the state, a requirement
that with some modification was incorporated in the document the Virginia Constitutional Convention adopted in June 1776: "no purchases of
Land shall be made of the *Indian* Natives but on behalf of the Publick,

by authority of the General Assembly." Similar provisions became part of the first constitutions of North Carolina and New York. In 1777, when George Walton and George Taylor claimed to have purchased a tract from a group of Indians purportedly acting on behalf of the Six Nations, the Continental Congress's Committee on Indian Affairs immediately declared the purchase void. Private purchases from the Indians were "wholly ineffectual to pass a title," the Virginia judge Edmund Pendleton declared on another occasion. The Proclamation of 1763 no longer possessed any *legal* effect after independence, but the concept of concentrating land purchasing in the hands of government persisted, because it was widely considered to be wise policy.[8]

Accordingly, the practice of land purchasing continued much as before independence, as a function performed by governments rather than individuals. In 1782, for example, Virginia's Council approved the expenditure of up to seven hundred pounds for a tract the Chickasaw Nation wished to sell, because of what the Council saw as "the advantages that may result from cultivating their friendship and judging that a fair purchase of the said Lands would be conducive to this end."[9] The pace of land purchasing slowed during the Revolution—in part because American governments were spending their money on the war instead, and in part because they were fighting against some of the very people who in peacetime would have been the sellers. But when land *was* purchased after independence, it was purchased the same way as before.

Before independence there had been settlers and even some colonial governments willing to appropriate Indian land without the Indians' consent, and independence brought no change to those facts either. The Mohegan chief Zachry Johnson complained in 1781, for example, of "the unaccountable spoils and devastations committed by Strange Indians and disorderly white people, on the Mohegan Lands." The imperial government had tried, with little success, to stem these incursions on the rights of the Indians. After independence the Continental Congress stepped into that role, as the only institution with any ability in principle to restrain state governments from taking the Indians' land or to urge state governments to restrain their own residents. The Continental Congress was no more successful than the imperial government had been. In 1779 the Continental Congress learned from Colonel Daniel Broadhead, who was commanding an army in western Pennsylvania and Virginia, that settlers had crossed the Ohio River and built huts on land owned by the Indians. Broadhead related that he had "ordered the trespassers to be apprehended and the huts to be destroyed." But such successes were few, in the face of repeated trespassing. Most of the time the Continental Congress was reduced to the same ineffectual gestures resorted to by the imperial government in earlier days, such as its 1777 resolution "earnestly" recommending to the government of Georgia that it "forthwith enact laws inflicting severe penalties" on Georgians settling on Indian land. Nothing happened. The pre-Constitution central government was simply too weak to impose much restraint on the states.[10]

Solving this problem required giving the central government exclusive control over Indian relations, a step that would eventually be taken in the Constitution of 1787. Before then, repeated efforts to strengthen the hand of the central government in matters concerning the Indians were all unsuccessful. In the proposal for a confederation of states he presented to Congress in 1775, Benjamin Franklin suggested that the central government should have the power to set Indian policy. John Dickinson's initial draft of the document that became the Articles of Confederation, submitted to Congress eight days after the Declaration of Independence, included the same idea. Dickinson's draft gave the government of the United States the sole power to purchase Indian land. But the final version of the Articles of Confederation adopted by Congress in 1777 was much weaker, because the states were unwilling to give up their authority. The Articles of Confederation gave the United States only "the sole and exclusive right and power of . . . regulating the trade and managing all affairs with the Indians not members of any of the states; provided that the legislative right of any State within its own limits be not infringed or violated." The states retained their authority over interactions with the tribes located within the state, including matters of land acquisition. For example, in New York, much of which was still owned by the Six Nations, the state government acquired large tracts of land in the 1780s.[11]

Within its limited sphere—Indian affairs in the area west of the thirteen states—the Continental Congress exercised what power it had been given. In 1783 Congress prohibited unauthorized settlement on or purchase of Indian land outside "the limits or jurisdiction of any particular State." In 1784, in an ordinance providing for the eventual division of western land into new states, Congress recognized that the only land that could be incorporated into new states was land that had been "already purchased, or shall be purchased, of the Indian inhabitants."[12]

These provisions were restatements of what had been English policy before the Revolution.

But just like the imperial government, the Confederation government was far from the frontier it ostensibly governed and was virtually powerless to prevent trespassing on Indian land. In 1783, for example, the Continental Congress learned that "sundry persons are preparing to settle on lands within the U.S. which have not been purchased from the Indian natives by which proceedings the present frontier inhabitants must be greatly endangered and the U.S. may be involved in war." A committee accordingly proposed a resolution that "all persons of whatever description be strictly enjoined against making purchases of or settlement on lands claimed by Indians." But of course a resolution on paper was no bar to westward migration. By 1785, Congress, like the imperial government two decades earlier, was reduced to relying on the Indians themselves to deter illegal settlement, by explicitly authorizing the Indians to treat settlers "as disorderly persons and compel them to retire." The distance between the central government and the settlers was so great, and the central government was so weak, that many settlers might not even have been aware that occupying Indian land was unlawful. Josiah Harmar, the American commander at Vincennes, reported in 1787 that when he posted copies of Congress's 1783 prohibition of unauthorized settlement, the news "amazed the inhabitants exceedingly." They had never heard of any such prohibition before.[13]

The central government was even weaker when the trespasses were condoned by a state, because the Continental Congress had no ability to prevent state governments from acting. In 1787 John Jay could look back on more than a decade of nearly uninterrupted war with the Indians and have little difficulty discerning the cause. "Not a single Indian war has yet been produced by aggressions of the present federal government, feeble as it is," Jay observed in *Federalist* No. 3; "but there are several instances of Indian hostilities having been provoked by the improper conduct of individual States . . . unable or unwilling to restrain or punish offences" by their citizens.[14] The imperial government had faced the same difficulty before the Revolution in trying to counteract colonial governments that had done little to thwart trespassing on Indian land or had even encouraged it.

There were thus many continuities, from before independence to after, in the ways Anglo-Americans thought about Indians and land. Had independence come peacefully—had independence not been followed by years of fighting—the Indian land policy of the 1780s might not have looked too different from that of the 1760s. But the war would produce some important changes.

From Consent to Compulsion

In much of North America, the Revolution was more a war against the Indians than a war against the British. Tribes found themselves drawn into the conflict, unable to stay neutral, because much of the fighting was taking place on their land. Forced to choose between the settlers who had long been trespassing on their land and the imperial government that had long been ineffectual in restraining them, most tribes sided with Britain as the lesser of evils. By 1777 the Continental Congress was receiving reports of losses on the western front, of massacres inflicted by "savage tribes of Indians . . . instigated by British agents and emissaries." But the Americans were winning some battles as well, and with these victories over the Indians came the beginning of a new way of thinking about the Indians' land.[15]

War with the Indians was nothing new. Colonists had fought sporadic wars with the Indians ever since colonization began, wars the colonists believed had been initiated by the Indians rather than by themselves. The colonial wars were not conceived of as wars of conquest designed to obtain the Indians' land; but after winning, colonial governments had often taken land as compensation. This pattern continued in the Revolution. At the 1777 Treaty of DeWitt's Corner, the Cherokees were forced to acknowledge that troops from South Carolina "did effect and maintain the conquest of all the Cherokee lands, eastward of the Unacay Mountain," lands that now belonged to the state. Later that year, at the Treaty of Long Island of the Holston, the Cherokees were forced to cede more land to North Carolina.[16] The newly independent state governments were doing what their colonial predecessors had always done.

As the war continued, however, the conquest of Indian land came to be a primary reason for fighting. Rawlins Lowndes reported in the summer of 1778 that for residents of Charleston, South Carolina, the prospect "of Sharing the Indian Lands renders a War with those People a desireable Object not considering or Caring what expence is incured or by what means it is defrayed." In Georgia, George Galphin urged an attack on the Creeks. "It will be an Exepensef warr," he counseled, "but there may be Lands got from them to pay a great part of it."[17] Particularly in the west, where issues of land acquisition loomed larger than the questions of taxation and representation that preoccupied easterners, the goal of freedom from British rule could be superseded by the goal of freedom to settle on Indian land.

And as the eventual outcome of the war became clearer, Americans began to think of *all* the Indians' land as conquered territory, not just the areas that had been scenes of fighting. After recent victories against the Six Nations, John Jay told George Clinton in late 1779, "some People have affected to speake of that Country as a conquered one, and I should not be surprized if they should next proceed to insist that it belongs to the united States, by whose Arms it was won from independent Nations in the Course and by the Fortune of War." Jay's prediction was right. By the end of the war, the desire to exact retribution against the Indians was very strong. The Indians were "aggressors in the war, without even a pretence of provocation," a committee of the Continental Congress insisted in 1783. "A bare recollection of the facts is sufficient to manifest the obligation they are under to make atonement for the enormities which they have perpetrated." The most obvious form in which to take revenge against the Indians was to confiscate their land. As Pennsylvania's delegation to the Continental Congress declared in 1783, the Indians' land now belonged "to the United States who claim it by Conquest."[18]

This climate of thought meant that the 1783 Treaty of Paris, the document bringing the Revolution to a formal close, was generally understood by American officials to strip the Indians of all property rights in their land, even though the treaty did not say a word about the Indians or their land. In the relevant clause Britain merely recognized the Mississippi River as the western boundary of the United States. Had it been written before the Revolution, this clause would have been interpreted as conferring upon the United States (and the individual states themselves) sovereignty, but not property rights, in western land—that is, the right to govern, but not ownership of the land. So understood, the treaty would have had no bearing on Indian property rights; it would merely have confirmed that the Indians, like other property owners, now owned land located within a sovereign entity that was no longer part of Britain. After the war, however, Americans saw the treaty as confirming the American conquest of all Indian land east of the Mississippi. As the United States commissioners told the Indians assembled at Fort Stanwix in 1784, "the Indian nations will perceive that the King of Great

Britain renounces, and yields to the United States all pretensions, and claims, whatsoever" in the land the Indians still believed was theirs. At Fort Stanwix the Indians protested that their rights were nowhere mentioned in the Treaty of Paris, and that even if they had been mentioned, Britain hardly possessed the power to divest the Indians of their property. The American commissioners had a ready answer. "You are mistaken in supposing that having been excluded [from the treaty] you are become a free and independent nation, and may make what terms you please," they responded. "It is not so. You are a subdued people; you have been overcome in a war."[19]

The Indians were outraged to learn that the British could treat them so treacherously as to give away their land, after they had helped the British so much during the war. The Indians "told me they never could believe our King could pretend to cede to America what was not his own to give," British brigadier general Allan Maclean reported. "If it was really true that the English had basely betrayed them by pretending to give up their country to the Americans without their consent or consulting them," they told Maclean, "it was an act of cruelty and injustice that Christians *only* were capable of doing."[20] It is not clear, though, that the British believed themselves to have given away the Indians' land. Government officials in London, if they even thought about the Indians at all, would most likely have perceived the treaty as a mere transfer of sovereignty having nothing to do with the Indians' ownership of their land. That is how it would have been understood two decades earlier. By the mid-1780s, however, opinion in North America had changed. The Indians were believed to have lost their land by conquest.

In this respect the Indians were in the same position as their Anglo-American allies. Land was also confiscated from Loyalists—colonists who had sided with Britain during the Revolution.[21] During and immediately after the war, the Indians lost their property rights because they had picked the losing side of the Revolution, not because they were Indians. (Land was not confiscated from the few tribes that had sided with the colonists in the war.) But the Indians and the Loyalists were obviously not the same. Confiscating the Loyalists' parcels and reselling them to the highest bidders was a program that could be completed in a relatively short time. The Loyalists themselves were mostly gone, having fled to Canada or Britain, and so were in no position to interfere. The Indians, by contrast, had not gone anywhere. They were still on their land, and indeed in some places they were still fighting against the

United States. Long after the Loyalists' land had all been confiscated, American officials still faced the question of how to acquire the Indians' land.

Although the desire to exact retribution against the Indians for siding with the British was the primary cause of the new belief that the Indians' land could simply be taken, it was not the only cause. In the 1780s there were several other factors that contributed to an aggressive federal Indian land policy that denied the Indians any power to refuse to give up their land. All were indirect results of the Revolution, but all would endure long after the Revolution had become a distant memory, and long after the desire for retribution against the tribes that had sided with Britain had faded.

Before the Revolution, the imperial government had been the major restraint, apart from the Indians themselves, on settlers' demand for the Indians' land. It was often an ineffective restraint, to be sure, but it was stronger than anything local colonial governments could provide, because officials in London were completely insulated from democratic accountability to North American residents. Even appointed colonial governors had to pay some attention to local preferences, but imperial officials in England were free to institute policies that ran counter to the interests of the majority of settlers. The Revolution removed the imperial government as a restraint on settler behavior. The federal government that took its place was to some degree also insulated from accountability to settlers, certainly more so than the local officials elected by the settlers themselves. But the federal government was far more representative of the settlers than the imperial government had been.

Many American officials themselves were investors in western land. In an era before there were many business corporations, western land was the main speculative investment available in North America. Anyone with money and a taste for risk, including government officials, found western land attractive. Their interest was in acquiring land quickly and cheaply from the Indians so it could be resold at a profit, which was exactly the interest of the settlers on the frontier, the people to whom speculators hoped to sell the land. That had also been true before the Revolution, but then the power of American officials had been checked by the imperial government, which was staffed by men far less likely to have invested their money in western land.

Elected American officials thus felt considerable pressure, from their constituents and from their own interests, to acquire Indian land to keep up with the pace of western settlement. "Such is the rage for speculating in, and forestalling of Lands on the No. West side of the Ohio," George Washington complained in 1784, "that scarce a valuable spot within any tolerable distance of it, is left without a claimant. Men in these times, talk with as much facility of fifty, a hundred, and even 500,000 Acres as a Gentleman formerly would do of 100 acres." And this was land still occupied by the Indians. The only way to avoid war, Washington advised, was for the federal government to keep up with the settlers, and to "purchase, if possible, as much Land of them immediately back [i.e., west] of us, as would make one or two States."[22] Wherever settlers went, they formed a concentrated political bloc in favor of obtaining Indian land as soon as possible.

The federal government would continue to feel this kind of pressure for more than a century, as settlers kept moving toward Indians. When residents of western Tennessee, for example, discovered that the Chickasaws and Cherokees lived between them and the Gulf of Mexico, they obtained from the Tennessee Assembly an instruction to the state's congressional delegation to press the federal government to acquire the Chickasaws' and Cherokees' land. "The people of this state consider themselves entitled to the right to pass and repass to and from the waters leading to the ocean, in the nearest practicable routes both by land and water, with their produce and merchandise," the resolution explained.[23] That sense of entitlement to this particular land could not have existed before settlers arrived nearby. Each acquisition of new territory only led to more settlement and pressure from the settlers to acquire even more land.

Some recognized early that if the government were to keep up with settler demand for Indian land, it would be locked into an endless cycle of land acquisition. In 1785, when James Wilson repeated the conventional wisdom—that the government ought to buy Indian land as fast as Americans could settle on it, to prevent them from bringing on war by settling on land still possessed by the Indians—Timothy Pickering was already skeptical. "But if Mr. Wilson's reason for extending the purchase, be a good one," Pickering wondered, "where shall we stop? If we purchase to the Mississippi, still there will be Indian lands to the Northward, as far as the Lake of the Woods—and farther still, beyond any limits that can be named." Part of the problem, Pickering recognized, was that the people who emigrated to the frontier were the very sort most likely to antagonize their Indian neighbors. They "are the least worthy subjects in the United States," he complained. "They are little less savage than the Indians." They may have been savage, but they were also smart. Settlers on the frontier knew very well that initiating conflict with the Indians was the surest way to prod the federal government to buy the Indians' land, in order to reduce the likelihood of war. On the Georgia frontier, complained Benjamin Hawkins, the federal government's emissary to the southern Indians, "the doctrine" among settlers "was, let us kill the Indians, bring on a war, and we shall get land." From its founding, the United States government could not avoid responding to this kind of pressure, a pressure it felt more acutely than had its imperial predecessor.[24]

Settlers were not the only political force advocating land acquisition. The federal government also felt pressure from merchants who had extended credit to the Indians in the past and knew that the Indians' only possible medium of repayment was land. In the early years after the Revolution such creditors were too widely scattered to be an effective political force, but by the 1790s a single firm—Panton, Leslie and Co.—had bought up and consolidated many of these small debts owed by members of the southern tribes. Panton, Leslie then began lobbying the federal government in favor of a triangular scheme whereby the Indians would cede land to the United States, the United States would pay the Indians' debt to Panton, Leslie, and Panton, Leslie would release its claims against the Indians. The firm's pressure finally bore fruit in a group of 1805 treaties between the United States and the Choctaws, Chickasaws, Cherokees, and Creeks, in which the United States acquired nearly eight million acres of land.[25]

In the aftermath of the Revolution the federal and state governments faced another kind of pressure as well. The war had been expensive. American governments were close to bankruptcy. During the war, when the money had run out, they had paid soldiers with promises of land. Now those promises were due, but the governments had no land to give and no money with which to buy it from the Indians. The Continental Congress started receiving many petitions from soldiers asking for their land. "The faith of the United States stands pledged to grant portions of the uncultivated lands as a bounty to their army," a nervous committee of the Continental Congress reported in 1783, "and the public finances do not admit of any considerable expenditure to extinguish the Indian claims upon such lands." State governments had made the same promises, and they were in the same position. Pennsylvania, for instance, had paid its troops in "depreciation certificates" redeemable in land, but Pennsylvania had no unowned land. Governments in desperate need of land to pay off demobilized soldiers began looking closely at the Indians.[26]

Federal and state governments also had large money debts. In the short run they needed assets that could be sold to pay creditors. In the longer run, if they hoped to be able to borrow in the future, they would need a conspicuous stream of income to entice creditors to lend. The most obvious source of money in both the present and the future was the sale of public land. "The public creditors have been led to believe and have a right to expect," the Continental Congress concluded, "that those territories will be speedily improved into a fund towards the security and payment of the national debt."[27] But the government had to acquire land before it could sell land, and the only people from whom land could be acquired were the Indians.

In the first few years after the Revolution, the widely felt desire to exact retribution against the Indians coincided with these strong political pressures to acquire land quickly and cheaply. The result was a dramatic change in the method of obtaining Indian land. The federal government began to dictate to tribes the extent of land they would be allowed to occupy.[28]

The first of the forced treaties was signed at Fort Stanwix, New York, in 1784. After reminding the Six Nations that they had been defeated in war, and that the United States accordingly claimed their land by right of conquest, the American commissioners announced: "We shall now, therefore declare to you the condition, on which alone you can be received into the peace and protection of the United States. The conditions are these." The commissioners then recited what became the text of the Treaty of Fort Stanwix. Section 2 of the treaty allowed the Oneidas and Tuscaroras, the two tribes that had sided with the colonists, to remain on their land. Section 3 asserted that the four tribes that had fought alongside the British—the Senecas, Mohawks, Onondagas, and Cayugas—had to give up much of western New York. The United States paid them no compensation. In the eyes of the American commissioners, the tribes who were compelled to cede land were lucky that the United States was so magnanimous in victory. "The King of Great Britain ceded to the United States *the whole*," they insisted, and "by the right of conquest they might *claim the whole*. Yet they have taken but a small part, compared with their numbers and their wants."[29]

The Treaty of Fort Stanwix marked a second important change as well. In previous transactions with the Indians, the document signed by the two sides had defined the boundaries of the area the Indians conveyed, just like deeds transferring land from one person to another. The Treaty of Fort Stanwix instead defined the boundaries of the land *not* conveyed. All else was ceded to the United States. This reversal was consistent with the American position that the Indians now retained no land other than what was given them by the grace of the government. The land reserved to the Indians was not termed a "reservation" in the treaty, but that is what it was. The Six Nations had long been bounded to the east by land owned by Anglo-American governments and citizens; now they were bounded by Anglo-American land to the west as well.

American commissioners repeated the performance the following year at Fort McIntosh, in western Pennsylvania, to representatives of the Delawares, Wyandots, Chippewas, and Ottawas. The chiefs of those tribes "held out an idea to the Continental Commissioners that they still looked upon the lands which the United States held by the treaty with Great Britain as their own," Josiah Harmar related, "but the Commissioners have answered them in a high tone, the purport of which was, that, as they had adhered during the war to the king of Great Britain, they were considered by us as a conquered people and had therefore nothing to expect from the United States, but must depend altogether upon their lenity and generosity." In the Treaty of Fort McIntosh the United States obtained much of present-day Ohio, again without compensation.[30] Again, the treaty defined not the land conveyed by the Indians to the United States but rather the land the United States allotted to the Indians. That the Indians were left any land at all was again understood by American officials to be a result of American mercy, not a result of any Indian property rights.

At Fort Finney in 1786, the United States commissioners dictated the same kind of treaty to the Shawnees. "You joined the British King against us, and followed his fortunes," the commissioners recalled. "We have overcome him, he has cast you off, and given us your country; and Congress, in bounty and mercy, offer you country and peace. We have told you the terms on which you shall have it; these terms we will not alter, they are liberal, they are just, and we will not depart from them." The commissioners warned the Shawnees that if they refused to agree, "we shall consider ourselves freed from all the ties of protection to you, and you may depend the U.S. will take the most effectual measures to

protect their citizens, and to distress your obstinate nation." The Shawnees were allotted a parcel of land.[31]

The treaties with the southern tribes followed the same pattern. The
committee of the Continental Congress responsible for supervising relations with the southern Indians instructed the American commissioners
to tell the Indians that they "are now in our power and at our mercy."
The commissioners were to declare "that we might return their cruelty
on their own heads, but that we prefer clemency to severity."[32] The
United States accordingly confiscated land from the Cherokees, Choctaws, and Chickasaws at the 1785 and 1786 Treaties of Hopewell.[33]

The first Indian treaties signed after the end of the Revolution, between 1784 and 1786, were thus very different from pre-Revolutionary
treaties. American officials no longer believed themselves bound to negotiate with the Indians for their land or to offer the Indians any compensation. They claimed, by conquest, the right to appropriate all the
Indians' land. The years of war had created a revolution in Indian land
policy.

From Conquest to Purchase

The new land policy was, unsurprisingly, felt as a serious blow by the Indians themselves. After the announcement of peace between Britain
and the United States, the Creek chief Alexander McGillivray recalled,
"the Georgians sent up an invitation to our chiefs to meet them in treaty
at Augusta, professing it was with an intention of burying the hatchet."
But when the Creeks arrived, "the leading people of the upper parts of
that State made a demand of a large cession of lands, comprehending
our best hunting grounds." This unexpected demand "was enforced by
bands of armed men, who at the same time surrounded them, threatening them with instant death if it was refused." The Creeks had never
been treated so badly before. The Creek chief Tallassee "had always
been a friend to the white people," he explained, and when, "after the
war, he was invited to Augusta," he "expected to be treated like a
friend; instead of which, the white people, their long knives in their
hands, insisted on his making a cession of land." The Creeks did not believe that they had been conquered. There were certainly no outward
signs of conquest. The Creeks were still living in the same places as before. Britain had signed a treaty ceding its claims in North America, but
the Creeks had not, and for that reason the swaggering attitude of Amer-

ican officials must have seemed to the Creeks to rest on the faulty premise that Britain somehow had the authority to surrender the Creeks' land. The other tribes compelled to cede land in the mid-1780s felt the same way. The "Indians have expressed the highest disgust," one American official reported, "at the principle of conquest, which has been specified to them, as the basis of their treaties with the United States."[34]

Indian tribes from north to south accordingly began preparing once again for war, to defend themselves against the newly bellicose demands of the United States. "The uniform tenor of the intelligence from the Western Country, plainly indicates the hostile disposition of a number of Indian nations, particularly the *Shawanese, Puteotamies, Chippewas, Tawas*, and *Twightees*," a committee of the Continental Congress reported in 1786. "These nations are now assembling in the Shawanese towns, and are joined by a banditti of desperadoes, under the name of *Mingoes* and *Cherokees*." All these tribes were "labouring to draw in other nations to unite with them in a war with the Americans." American officials were well aware that the new land policy was the primary cause of the Indians' unhappiness. "They appear dissatisfied with their late Cessions to us," John Jay observed, with some understatement, in July 1786. "There is Reason to apprehend Trouble with them." By December, Jay's outlook had grown even more pessimistic. "The public Papers will tell you how much Reason we have to apprehend an Indian War," he wrote to Thomas Jefferson (who was in Paris). It was becoming apparent that Americans, flush with victory over Britain, had underestimated the Indians' ability to fight back when their land was seized.[35]

If war against the Indians was to begin again, the person most responsible for conducting it on the American side would be Henry Knox, the secretary at war. Knox had been a general during the Revolution and was George Washington's successor as commander of the much-reduced army when the Revolution was over. Drawing on that experience, Knox recognized that a war against all the aggrieved tribes would be very costly. He estimated that fighting the Indians would take two years and would require twenty-five hundred to three thousand men each year. Raising and equipping two armies of that size, he calculated, would cost at least two million dollars, and that figure did not even take into account "the invaluable lives which would be sacrificed on the occasion, and the immense distress and loss to the nation by the abandonment of the frontiers" by settlers fleeing the fighting. Rather than fighting, he

suggested, it would be much less expensive for the United States simply to purchase from the tribes all the land it had recently confiscated.
The total cost of all that land, he reckoned, would be under twenty
thousand dollars, less than 1 percent of the cost of a war. "It may be wise
to extinguish with a small sum of money, a claim which otherwise may
cost much blood and infinitely more money," Knox advised the Continental Congress. He reminded Congress that such had been the practice before the Revolution. "A recurrence to the custom of Britain on
this point," he noted, "will evince, that they thought a treaty and purchase money for land, was the most prudent measure and in no degree
dishonorable to the nation."[36]

Knox was not the first to recommend abandoning the new Indian land
policy. George Washington, who also had experience fighting against the
Indians, had been against it from the start. Purchasing their land rather
than confiscating it "is the cheapest as well as the least distressing way
of dealing with them," Washington had pointed out back in 1783, as
"none who are acquainted with the Nature of Indian warfare, and has
ever been at the trouble of estimating the expence of one, and compar-
ing it with the cost of purchasing their Lands, will hesitate to acknowledge."[37] But while Washington had temporarily retired to his farm, Knox
was in a position to make a difference. And when Washington returned
to public life as president under the new Constitution, he kept Knox on
as secretary of war, which allowed Knox to stay in power long enough to
have an effect.

Through the late 1780s Knox repeatedly urged Congress to return to
the British practice of respecting Indian property rights and purchasing
the Indians' land, as a way of saving money and lives. "The practice of
the British government . . . previously to the late war, of purchasing the
right of the soil of the Indians, and receiving a deed of sale and conveyance of the same, is the only mode of alienating their lands" that would
be acceptable to the tribes, Knox argued in 1788. "The doctrine of conquest is so repugnant to their feelings, that rather than submit thereto,
they would prefer continual war." But a war so expensive, "and with an
exhausted treasury, would be an event pregnant with unlimited evil." If
such a war was to be fought without adequate resources, there was a
good chance the Indians would win, particularly because they could expect the assistance of the British troops who still occupied Canada and
the northwest.[38]

Recognizing the Indians as owners of their land, Knox insisted, could

be done "without the least injury to the national dignity." To the contrary, he suggested shortly after the Constitution went into force, "it
would reflect honor on the new Government, and be attended with
happy effects, were a declarative law to be passed, that the Indian tribes
possess the right of soil of all lands within their limits, respectively, and
that they are not to be divested thereof, but in consequence of fair and
bona fide purchases." Knox may have been primarily motivated by a calculation of the relative cost of purchasing and fighting, but he was also
driven by the late eighteenth-century American idealism that grew out
of the Revolution, the feeling that Americans had an opportunity to start
fresh, and to build a government on a virtuous foundation. "A nation solicitous of establishing its character on the broad basis of justice, would
not only hesitate at, but reject every proposition to benefit itself, by the
injury of any neighboring community, however contemptible and weak
it might be," Knox reported to Congress in 1789. That sentiment counseled a policy of noblesse oblige toward the Indians, who, "being the
prior occupants, possess the right of the soil." To dispossess the Indians
by any means other than purchase "would be a gross violation of the
fundamental laws of nature, and of the distributive justice which is the
glory of a nation." (Here Knox prudently added that if confiscating
the Indians' land "should be decided, on an abstract view of the question, to be just, . . . the finances of the United States would not at present admit of the operation.")[39]

Knox's efforts first bore fruit in the summer of 1787, when the Continental Congress adopted the Northwest Ordinance. In establishing the
framework for new state governments in the northwest, Congress included a promise that represented a break from the practice of the preceding years: "The utmost good faith shall always be observed toward
the Indians; their lands and property shall never be taken from them
without their consent." A few months later, when the governor of the
new Northwest Territory was told to inquire whether the northwestern
tribes would be willing to enter into a treaty, his instructions reflected
Knox's position. "Altho the purchase of the Indian right of Soil is not a
primary object of holding this treaty," the instructions read, "yet you
will not neglect any opportunity that may offer of extinguishing the Indian rights to the westward as far as the river Mississippi." Here was the
first official recognition by the government of the United States that the
Indians owned their land and that the government would pay the Indians for it. In July 1788 Congress appropriated six thousand dollars for

"extinguishing by purchase Indian titles" in the Northwest Territory.[40] Land policy, at least as expressed in official documents, had reverted back to its pre-1783 form.

The first treaties to incorporate the new (or rather, the old) view that Indian land had to be purchased were the two 1789 Treaties of Fort Harmar, one with the Six Nations and the other with the Wyandots, Delawares, and four other tribes. For the Six Nations' land the United States paid three thousand dollars in goods; for the land of the other tribes, six thousand dollars in goods. This was the very same land the government had claimed by right of conquest just a few years before, in the Treaties of Fort Stanwix and Fort McIntosh in 1784 and 1785. As a satisfied Henry Knox explained afterward, in looking back on the federal government's Indian treaties since 1783, the United States was finally acquiring land the right way.[41]

> By having recourse to the several indian treaties made by the authority of Congress since the conclusion of the War with Great Britain, excepting those made January 1789 at Fort Harmar, it would appear, that Congress were of opinion that the treaty of peace of 1783 absolutely invested them with the fee of all indian lands within the limits of the United States— That they had the right to assign, or retain such portions as they should judge proper.
>
> But it is manifest, from the representations of the confederated indians at the Huron Village in December 1786 that they entertained a different opinion, and that they were the only rightful proprietors of the soil—and it appears by the resolve of the 2d. of July 1788, that Congress so far conformed to the idea as to appropriate a sum of money solely to the purpose of extinguishing the indian claims to lands they had ceded to the United States, and for obtaining regular conveyances of the same—This object was accordingly accomplished at the treaty of Fort Harmar in January 1789.
>
> The principle of the indian right to the lands they possess being thus conceded, the dignity and interest of the nation will be advanced by making it the basis of the future administration of justice towards the indian tribes.[42]

By the time the first Congress of the new United States government convened in New York in 1789, equipped by the Constitution with the power to "regulate Commerce . . . with the Indian Tribes," one aspect of that commerce was thus understood to involve purchasing land. The doctrine of conquest in effect from 1783 to 1786 had been abandoned.

Knox's colleagues in Washington's administration shared Knox's view

that the Indians owned their land. Everyone hoped that the sale of public land would become a source of substantial income for the treasury,
but Treasury Secretary Alexander Hamilton included, in his 1790 *Report
on Vacant Lands,* an admission that the lands concerned were not really
vacant. "No Indian land shall be sold," he insisted, "except such, in respect to which the titles of the Indian tribes shall have been previously
extinguished." Thomas Jefferson had incorrectly declared back in 1786,
while the Confederation government was in the midst of confiscating
Indian land, that "not a foot of land will ever be taken from the Indians
without their own consent. The sacredness of their right is felt by all
thinking persons in America as much as in Europe." Jefferson was in
France at the time, so he might not have been up-to-date on what the
federal government was doing, or he might have been lying in order to
keep French opinion favorable to the United States. In any event, Jefferson was able to put his idealism into practice as Washington's secretary of state, agreeing with Knox and Hamilton that the Indians' land
could be obtained only by purchase.[43]

Even in Congress in the 1790s there seems to have been wide support
for Knox's change of policy, as a matter of both principle and expediency. The Indians "are the natural owners of the soil," Elias Boudinot of
New Jersey proclaimed on the floor of the first Congress. "It is theirs by
every principle of justice and propriety, and before you can convey it to
your creditors, you must purchase it of the lawful owners." Perhaps
more members of Congress would have agreed with Josiah Parker of Virginia. Regardless of who owned what, he advised, "it will cost much less
to conciliate the good opinion of the Indians than to pay men for de-
stroying them." Pennsylvania senator William Maclay made the point
more sarcastically. "Here is a fine scheme on paper," he scoffed, when
war with the Creeks seemed imminent: "to raise 5,040 Officers noncom-
missioned Officers & Privates at the charge of $1,152,000 for a Year to go
to War with the Creeks, because the Commissioners being ignorant of
indian affairs failed of making a Treaty." By the early 1790s federal officials were in agreement that the confiscations of 1784 through 1786
had been a mistake.[44]

Treaties after Fort Harmar were accordingly structured as purchases,
not forced cessions of land. While sending Brigadier General Rufus
Putnam to negotiate with the Wabash and the Illinois in 1792, Knox ordered Putnam, in the only italicized portion of his lengthy instructions,
to "*make it clearly understood, that we want not a foot of their land, and that it*

is theirs, and theirs only; that they have the right to sell, and the right to refuse to sell, and that the United States will guaranty to them their said just right." In the treaty Putnam signed with the Wabash and the Illinois, he duly included an article stating exactly that: "The United States solemnly guaranty to the Wabash, and the Illinois nations, or tribes of Indians, all the lands to which they have a just claim; and no part shall ever be taken from them, but by a fair purchase, and to their satisfaction. That the lands originally belonged to the Indians; it is theirs, and theirs only. That they have a right to sell, and a right to refuse to sell. And that the United States will protect them in their said just rights." In 1793, when Knox gave instructions to the commissioners appointed to negotiate with the northwestern tribes, he likewise directed that "the Government considers the Six Nations . . . and other Western Indians, who were the actual occupants of the lands, as the proper owners thereof; that they had a right to convey the said lands to the United States . . . with their free consent and full understanding."[45]

Some of the treaties of 1789 and after did, however, retain one element of the forced treaties of 1784–1786: they defined enclosed areas the Indians retained instead of areas the Indians conveyed. Such treaties included the Treaties of Fort Harmar, as well as the 1794 Treaty of Canandaigua, which referred to the land of the Oneidas, Onondagas, and Cayugas as "reservations." Even under the new plan of compensation, the Indians were gradually being hemmed in by the land acquired by the United States.

As the entity with the ultimate authority over Indian relations, the federal government occupied the same position once held by the imperial government, and the first Congress promptly replicated the most important component of pre-Revolution Indian land policy. The Intercourse Act of 1790 declared that "no sale of lands made by any Indians, or any nation or tribe of Indians" would be valid unless "made and duly executed at some public treaty, held under the authority of the United States." This was the same power the Crown had claimed for itself in the Proclamation of 1763. It was widely called the right of "preemption," but that was a misleading name; it was not a right to buy land from the Indians *before* other purchasers, but instead a denial of the ability of other purchasers to purchase at all, without the consent of the United States. Preemption became an enduring feature of federal Indian policy, reenacted in a series of subsequent statutes. It is still in force today.

The federal government's right of preemption was controversial, because by claiming the sole right to purchase Indian land the federal government was taking rights away from others. Among the others were *state* governments, which had grown accustomed in the previous decade to purchasing Indian land within their borders. New York, a state encompassing large tracts of yet unpurchased Indian land, was particularly defiant of the federal government in the 1790s. As secretary of state, Thomas Jefferson responded that preemption "is become a principle of the law of nations, fundamental with respect to America." (If so, it had become fundamental very quickly, having been proclaimed by Britain only in 1763.) Before the Constitution, Jefferson argued, state governments might have claimed a right of preemption, but by ratifying the Constitution they had ceded that sovereign right, along with a host of others, to the federal government. That was the constitutional basis for preemption, but New York's elected officials faced considerable pressure from New Yorkers who clamored for the state to buy Indian land faster than the federal government was willing to. In 1794, for example, the state legislature received a petition from the white inhabitants of Brothertown, who were farming land they had leased from the Indians. "From the insecurity of our title," they pleaded, "we are placed in a disagreeable and unfortunate situation." Without permanent ownership, they explained, they could not make investments in schools, churches, and the other institutions of civilized life. Couldn't the state please purchase the land from the Indians and give it to the settlers, or at least sell preemption rights in the land to the settlers?[46] Requests like these resulted in several purchases by New York that clearly violated the various Intercourse Acts because they lacked the approval of the federal government. Two centuries later, these purchases would come back to haunt the government of New York, which would find itself the defendant in several suits brought by Indian tribes.[47]

Preemption was also objectionable to the many settlers and speculators who wished to purchase—and who sometimes actually *did* purport to purchase—land from the Indians directly. The long tradition of private land purchasing had been driven underground by the Proclamation of 1763, but it survived the Revolution because the economics of the frontier had barely changed. As a spokesman for the Oneidas and Tuscaroras complained in 1785, "were We to listen to all the Overtures that are made to Us for the Purchase of our Lands (and altho' some who are fond of Liquor are inclined to it), We should have none for our Posterity." But despite such condemnation from political leaders on both sides of the frontier, the black market persisted, as white purchasers and Indian sellers found one another. The missionary Samuel Kirkland reported several unlawful sales and leases among the Oneidas and neighboring tribes. Farther west, illegal transactions were probably even more common. Arthur St. Clair, the first governor of the Northwest Territory, was dismayed to discover upon his arrival that many of the settlers claimed land by virtue of purchases from the Indians. St. Clair rejected them all. He suspected there had been many other private purchases that had not even been brought to his attention. "If one Indian sale is approved," he supposed, "it is probable that a great many will be brought forward." Someone in Washington's initial cabinet, perhaps Jefferson, must have wondered whether there was anything the government could do to prevent such unauthorized purchases, because in Jefferson's papers is a legal opinion of Attorney General Edmund Randolph in which Randolph reluctantly concluded that the government was powerless. Although unauthorized private purchases were void, Randolph pointed out, they did not constitute a crime, and the United States could not bring civil suits against private purchasers because the United States did not suffer any damage from transactions that lacked legal effect. Congress corrected the oversight in the Intercourse Act of 1793, by making the unauthorized purchase of Indian land a misdemeanor punishable by up to a year in prison.[48]

Underground private purchasing nevertheless continued, because the areas where Indians owned the most land were also the most difficult to police because they were so far away from the centers of government. In 1794 the Quaker James Emlen, traveling through western New York, met a man who proudly showed him the estate he had personally purchased from the Indians. Although he had planted acres of corn, this western magnate "was under some apprehensions least his Title should hereafter be disputed," apprehensions that were well justified. In 1804 Charles Jouett reported from Detroit that the local residents still relied on private purchasing to obtain titles. As late as 1810 a group of settlers and Indians in western New York petitioned Governor Daniel Tompkins to give official recognition to the many long-term leases into which they had entered over the previous several years. They "did not know nor suppose that making such contracts was criminal," they argued. The white lessees had "expended nearly the whole of their small fortunes in making permanent improvements on said land," and "they now have crops of grain & grass growing the fruits of several years hard labor." If the leases were to be invalidated, and the land revert to the Indian sellers, they argued, it "must reduce them almost to a state of beggary." It was impossible to keep willing buyers and sellers of Indian land apart.[49]

But of all the grievances arising from the federal government's right of preemption, the most justifiable was held by the Indians themselves. From the Indian perspective, preemption presented the same anomaly in the 1790s as it had in the 1760s. If the Indians truly owned their land, what right did the government have to tell them to whom they could sell it? Surely members of Congress would never have dreamed of imposing the same restriction on land owned by Americans of European descent. Representatives of the northern tribes aired this grievance while meeting with the commissioners Knox sent in 1793. The three commissioners had thought they would be giving the Indians good news, that the federal government no longer claimed to have been ceded the Indians' land by Britain under the Treaty of Paris. The commissioners of a few years before had "put an erroneous construction on that part of our treaty with the King," the 1793 commissioners admitted. "As he had not purchased the country of you, of course he could not give it away; he only relinquished to the United States his claim to it." That claim, the commissioners explained, was nothing more than the right of preemption. As a result, "the King, by the treaty of peace, having granted this right to the United States, they alone now have the right of purchasing . . . to the exclusion of all other white people whatever."[50]

If the American commissioners were proud to work for a government so honorable as to admit and rectify its mistakes, the Indians were far less impressed. "You want to make this act of common justice a great part of your concessions," they responded, "and seem to expect that, because you have at last acknowledged our independence, we should, for such a favor, surrender to you our country." The Indians then pointed out the inconsistency of purporting to recognize the Indians as property owners while simultaneously denying them the right to sell their land to anyone other than the federal government. "We never made any agreement with the King, nor with any other nation, that we would give to either the exclusive right of purchasing our lands," they protested; "and we declare to you, that we consider ourselves free to make any bargain or cession of lands, whenever and to whomsoever we please." The Treaty of Paris could hardly require the contrary, because the Indians had not been a party to it. "If the white people, as you say, made a treaty that none of them but the King should purchase of us, and that he has given that right to the United States," the Indians argued, "it is an affair which concerns you and him, and not us: we have never parted with such a power."[51] But landownership was ultimately determined in American courts, using American law, which denied legal effect to a land title obtained from the Indians by any purchaser other than the United States. Indians within the boundaries of the United States were powerless to sell land to anyone else.

By the 1790s the Indian land policy of the new United States looked, on paper, very much like the Indian land policy of the late colonial period. The central government declared itself committed to recognizing the Indians' property rights and purchasing the Indians' land, and refused to recognize the validity of purchases made by others. The desire for retribution against the Indians that had fueled the confiscatory treaties of the immediate postwar years had perhaps dimmed a bit, and that allowed the treaties of 1789 and after to be structured as purchases, like colonial treaties had been.

But the other circumstances that had contributed to the aggressive land policy of 1784–1786 were still in full force. American government officials were still democratically accountable to an electorate that included many settlers and investors in western land. Many officials were investors themselves. They accordingly continued to feel pressure to acquire land to keep up with the pace of western settlement. The federal government was still expected to derive a significant part of its income from the sale of public land, so there was pressure from that source as well. (Sales of public land in fact amounted to a negligible fraction of federal revenue through the 1790s, but they were expected to contribute more, and they eventually did.[52]) There were still merchants who were creditors of the Indians and were lobbying the federal government to give them the Indians' land in payment. Settlers on the frontier still despised the Indians. They were still prone to trespassing on Indian land and provoking sporadic wars between the United States and various tribes. These circumstances were long-term in nature. They could not vanish in a decade; indeed, they would still be strong in the twentieth century. In the 1790s and after, they put pressure on federal officials to acquire land whether or not the Indians wished to sell it. The way the Indians' land was actually acquired could thus look very different from the consensual purchases that were, in theory, required by law.

Another Name for Liar

Timothy Pickering was an American emissary to the Six Nations in the early 1790s, responsible for, among other things, attempting to purchase land. He knew all too well that the Indians did not trust him. "Indians have been so often deceived by White people," he informed George Washington, his employer, "that *White Man* is, among many of them, but another name for *Liar*. Really, Sir I am unwilling to be subjected to this infamy. I confess I am not indifferent to a good name, even among Indians." They did not trust Washington either, Pickering explained; "they viewed, and expressly considered *me*, as *'your Representative';* and my promises, as the promises of *'the Town Destroyer.'*" By 1795 Pickering had succeeded Henry Knox as secretary of war, but he had not changed his frank view of the way Knox's land policy was being received by the Indians. He recognized that the 1789 Treaties of Fort Harmar, the first of the post-Revolution treaties structured as voluntary purchases, were not being adhered to by the western Indians, who held that the Indian signatories had lacked the authority to speak for the selling tribes. The apparently enlightened policy of purchasing rather than confiscating Indian land was beginning to draw complaints from the Indians that the ostensible "purchases" had in fact been accomplished through trickery or coercion. There was sometimes considerable tension between what American officials believed they were doing and what the Indians perceived was being done.[53]

The volume of complaints seemed to grow over the years, particularly after the conclusion of the War of 1812 drove British troops out of the United States and removed a major reason to conciliate the Indians. Some of the complaints regarded unfulfilled promises. In the 1794 Treaty of Canandaigua, part of the price of the Six Nations' land was that "useful artificers" would be sent to reside among them. The Seneca chief Red Jacket despaired years later that "we were promised on the part of your government that different kinds of mechanics, blacksmiths and carpenters should be sent among us to improve us in these arts," but no such people ever came. The Cherokees sold land in Georgia to the United States in 1804, but, they complained in 1824, they had never received the annuities that were the purchase price. Indian tribes were far less powerful than the government of the United States. They had no way to force the government to live up to its obligations.[54]

Some of the complaints concerned purchases of land from one tribe where a different tribe believed itself entitled to that land, as when the Muskogees learned that the United States had purchased their land— from the Choctaws. The fluidity of tribal boundaries had yielded intertribal collective action problems during the colonial era, and those problems continued to plague tribes in the early republic. In 1816, for example, when the federal government sent Return J. Meigs to persuade the Cherokees to sell land lying on the north bank of the Tennessee River, Meigs expected to exploit precisely this weakness. "Nothing but a cession of the lands," he planned to tell the Cherokees, "will put an end to the Chickasaw claim to the same lands." He hardly needed to add that if the Cherokees turned him down he could approach the Chickasaws with the same offer.[55]

Some of the complaints concerned government negotiators who took advantage of their superior literacy and knowledge of English. In 1793 the missionary Jacob Lindley met a delegation of Cherokees who told him about their treaty with the United States from two years earlier, at which the government draftsman "inserted the free navigation of the Cherokee river, without their knowledge." But that wasn't the worst of it. The American negotiator also "bribed the interpreter to read, ten miles around Nashville village, where forty was inserted [in the written text]. There was a large extent of country, for which the natives required three thousand dollars per annum, but he assured them his power would not permit him to go so high; but for the present, he would insure two thousand dollars, and had no doubt of obtaining the whole sum, by an application to Congress. But in the article it was read, two thousand dollars, where one thousand only was entered. And after all, the survey far exceeded the limits of the land agreed on." A group of Cherokees had traveled to Congress to make their case in person and had been assured that matters would be put straight. But they returned home only to discover settlers building mills and forts on the disputed land. The Cherokees whom Lindley met had journeyed hundreds of miles north to see if they could enlist the help of the British in Canada.[56]

And some of the complaints were of outright force. According to John Badollet, an American official at Vincennes, recent treaties with the Miamis had "been concluded under circumstances not very short of compulsion." In one instance, at the bidding of Governor William Henry Harrison, the young Potawatomi chief Winamac had threatened the Miamis that if they did not sign the treaty Harrison had offered, Winamac "would drive them into the lake." The catalog of tricks employed by agents of the federal government quickly grew to resemble those used by private purchasers in the middle of the eighteenth century, the tricks that had contributed to causing the French and Indian War and had eventually prompted the imperial government to ban private purchasing.[57]

Federal land purchasers immediately adopted the primary technique used by devious private purchasers a half century earlier, that of exploiting the collective action problem within tribes by securing "consent" to sales from a small number of tribe members who had not been authorized to speak for the tribe as a whole. In 1790 the brand-new federal government began paying bribes to tribal leaders willing to sell their tribes' land, in order to separate the leaders' interests from those of the tribes as a whole. That year the Treaty of New York with the Creeks, in which the United States purchased much of Georgia, included "Secret Articles" guaranteeing the Creek chief Alexander McGillivray a perpetual salary of twelve hundred dollars per year, and giving assorted lesser chiefs perpetual salaries of one hundred dollars per year. To obtain an 1805 land cession from the Chickasaws, the federal government paid nearly five thousand dollars to tribal leaders. Agents of the Holland Land Company bribed individual Senecas with money and alcohol to obtain their assent to the sale of much of the tribe's land in western New York. The transaction was ostensibly supervised by U.S. Indian Commissioner Jeremiah Wadsworth, who had to approve the purchase on behalf of the federal government before it could be consummated. Wadsworth was not entirely disinterested, however—he and his family were among the most prominent land speculators in the region. Decision-making power within Indian tribes was less centralized than it was in the United States or its constituent parts. As in the colonial period, Indian tribes had great difficulty preventing small groups from purporting to sell the tribe's land.[58]

And as in the colonial period, tribes sometimes discovered, to their horror, that their land had been sold by tribe members who lacked the permission of the tribe as a whole. In 1825, for example, an outraged Creek delegation complained to Secretary of War James Barbour that the recent Treaty of Indian Springs, in which nearly all remaining Creek land had been sold, had been signed by an unauthorized minority of the tribe. Federal commissioners had purchased the land from a minor chief named William McIntosh, but, charged the Creek delegation, the commissioners knew very well that the tribe's head chiefs, the Little Prince and the Big Warrior, had already refused to sell the same land. "Were not the Commissioners at Broken Arrow met by a vast body of chiefs and then told the Nation had no land to sell?" the delegation asked, as part of a crescendo of angry rhetorical questions.

> Was it right after the sense of the nation was then given to appoint a meeting within the Jurisdiction of Georgia, and that at short notice?
> After a meeting was so convened & the authorized Chiefs dissented and invited the Commissioners within the Nation if they had any communication to make, to treat with the Nation, was it reasonable to hold intercourse with unauthorized individuals? . . .
> When all were gone except McIntosh and his party, what right had the Commissioners to pronounce the Council to be a legal one . . . ?
> If McIntosh and his party were the reigning authority of the Nation and he an Idol of the Nation, why did the Commissioners promise him protection in the Treaty?[59]

When government purchasers were willing to cut corners, and accept as representatives of the tribe any tribe members willing to sell the tribe's land, and even offer to protect the sellers against the rest of the tribe, there was little a tribe could do to undo the transaction.

Before 1763, private land purchasers had sold goods to the Indians on credit and deliberately encouraged the Indians to take on debt, in order to obtain the Indians' land as payment. It did not take long for the government of the United States to discover the same tactic. The best way to overcome the Indians' reluctance to sell land, President Thomas Jefferson observed privately in 1803, would be to establish government-run trading houses near them. "We shall push our trading houses," he explained, "and be glad to see the good and influential individuals among them run in debt, because we observe that when these debts get beyond what the individuals can pay, they become willing to lop them off by a cession of lands." If the United States could become the creditor of enough Indians, Jefferson predicted, "our settlements will gradually circumscribe and approach the Indians, and they will in time either incorporate with us as citizens of the United States or remove beyond the Mississippi."[60] The establishment of trading houses became a standard feature of federal Indian policy.

Private purchasers before 1763 had also been able to take advantage of settlers' frequent trespassing. The more settlers illegally occupied the Indians' land, the more willing the Indians would be to sell it. The United States enjoyed the same advantage, because trespassing never ceased. "We have held several treaties with the Americans, when Bounds was always fixt and fair promises always made that the white people should not come over," the Cherokee Hanging Maw complained, "but we always find that after a treaty they Settle much faster than before." Henry Knox recognized that the Indians' constant protests were justified. "The desires of too many frontier white people, to seize by force or fraud upon the neighboring Indian lands," he admitted, "has been, and still continues to be, an unceasing cause of jealousy and hatred on the part of the Indians." In the Mississippi Territory, Ephraim Kirby reported to Jefferson in 1804, the settlers, "for want of good land, have effected most of their cultivation upon ground where the native right remains unextinguished." The federal government sometimes tried to restrain trespassing settlers, but the settlers greatly outnumbered the troops that could be sent to drive them off the Indians' land, and once driven off there was no lingering military force to prevent them from trespassing once again. Boundaries between the settlers and the Indians simply could not be enforced.[61]

The difficulty in preventing settlers from trespassing was in part a problem of limited government resources, but it was even more a product of representative government. Elected officials were accountable to the settlers, not to the Indians, who could not vote. The local militias who might have been given the responsibility of enforcing the boundaries were composed of the very same settlers who coveted the Indians' land. The correspondence of Tennessee governor John Sevier, for example, shows how strongly his sympathies and his political future lay with the trespassing settlers rather than with the Indians. As federal officers prepared to evict settlers from Cherokee land, Sevier urged them to show "paternal, benevolent, and favorable indulgences towards those unfortunate people, by Granting them all the time and suitable opportunity adequate to a preparation for their removal." He asked Andrew Jackson "to use your utmost exertions in behalf of these distressed people." When the settlers were about to be evicted, Sevier sent them an apologetic warning, in which he made clear that the eviction was the work of the federal government, not the government of Tennessee. In such a political climate, trespassing was a constant and ineradicable problem.[62]

The settlers, for their part, were certain that the Indians were the ones responsible for all the troubles on the frontier. "I have been intimately acquainted with this district," Judge Harry Innes reported from Kentucky, in a typical settler account. "I can with truth say, that . . . the Indians have always been the aggressors; that any incursions made into their country have been from reiterated injuries committed by them." The settlers had to retaliate indiscriminately against the first Indians they found, Innes explained, because "the depredatory mode of war and plundering carried on by them, renders it difficult, and almost impossible, to discriminate what tribes are the offenders."[63] The settlers and the Indians were locked in a vicious circle, in which trespassing by the settlers provoked violence from the Indians, which caused the settlers to trespass even more. Most of the time the federal government was very far away.

Before 1763, private land purchasers had been able to exploit settlers' trespassing by snapping up land the Indians were having trouble retaining, because from the Indians' perspective it was better to sell land before the land was lost completely. In the early republic the federal government did the same. But now the Indians were even worse off than they had been before 1763, because they could no longer look to the imperial government for protection. The United States was the sole lawful purchaser and also had the sole authority to regulate the process of purchasing.

For all these reasons, the prices at which the United States purchased land from the Indians were normally much lower than the prices at which the same land sold on the settlers' real estate market. "What is the Federal Government itself but a hard-hearted speculator of the first magnitude, and most inexorable temper?" asked Thomas Hart Benton on the floor of the Senate. "It buys land from the Indians at *two cents*, or *less*, for the acre, and sells it to the People for *one hundred and twenty-five cents*, to the acre, or *more*."[64] Benton was not speaking up for the Indians. He was defending the land speculators, by pointing out that they could hardly be faulted for doing what their government did on a far grander scale.

Neither Birds nor Fish

By the 1790s the pieces of the federal land acquisition system were in place. Land was purchased by the federal government, from Indian tribes, just as the imperial government had purchased land after 1763. For the next century and more, the federal government gradually bought the United States parcel by parcel. In the first three decades of the nineteenth century, there were ninety-one such transactions with various tribes, or an average of approximately three per year.[65] Land acquisition became routine.

The Indians still had good reasons to sell land. It was still their primary asset, so they still needed to sell it if they hoped to buy anything else. As Jefferson told Congress in 1804, for example, a recent purchase from the Delawares had been desired by the Delawares themselves, in order "to convert superfluous lands into the means of improving what they retain," with "animals and implements for agriculture." The Delawares, like other tribes in the same position, were trying to adapt to a new economic environment they had no power to avoid. The Iowas were probably doing the same in 1815 when they spontaneously offered to sell part of their land to the United States in exchange for the annuities that neighboring tribes were already receiving. We know the strategy did not work well in the long run, but it is likely that any other strategy would have been worse. From the Indians' perspective, there was nothing irrational about selling land.[66]

But the federal government's actual purchases were often induced by bribery, debt, and trespassing, just as many private purchases had been induced before 1763. The Indians now experienced the worst of both schemes. They had to sell to the federal government. The lack of competition among purchasers most likely drove land prices down. But the Indians were also subjected to all the old techniques of unscrupulous private land purchasers. Relations between the Indians and the United States grew increasingly worse.

Looking back in 1792, George Mason recognized how things had gone wrong. Americans had once been satisfied to acquire land slowly and peacefully, by gradually spoiling the Indians' environment. "When our ancestors first settled on the American Shores," he recalled,

> they purchased, or obtained by Treaty (in some few Instances by force) from the Indian Nations, a small Tract of Country: the Settlement of this was the Means of destroying, or driving away the wild Game, and render-

ing the adjacent Country unfit for the savage Life. The Indians removed farther back for the Convenience of hunting; and sold, upon easy terms, the Lands, which were no longer of much Use to them. And thus, by making Purchase after Purchase, our Settlements gradually advanced; and the Indian Natives, following the wild Game, gradually retired; so imperceptibly, that we are now at a Loss to know, what became of the numerous Tribes of Indians, who once inhabited Virginia; very few of them, comparatively speaking, having been destroyed by Wars with us.

Had we continued to pursue this safe and easy Plan, we shou'd have saved a great deal of Money, and prevented many horid Scenes, with the Effusion of much Blood.

But Mason understood that the pace had quickened. Americans now wanted to obtain the Indians' land more quickly, too quickly for the old method of patient, parcel-by-parcel purchasing. There were now too many emigrants to the west, and too much need for the federal revenue the land promised to bring in, to wait for the game to be driven away.

Unfortunately, the Avidity of Individuals to engross large Tracts of Land, and the vain Expectation of raising a Fund, from the Sale of the Western Lands, for the Extinction of the public Debt, extended our Views to the Indian Country over the Ohio, before we had settled the adjacent Lands. Our people began to settle upon the Indian hunting Grounds, yet full of Game. . . . it is no Wonder, that it has created a general Confederacy of the Indian Tribes against us.

Mason was aware that the cycle of trespassing and purchasing was laying the foundation for a long period of hostility between the United States and the Indians.

We attempted, indeed, to form Treaties with the Indians, and to make Purchases. But in doing this, we conducted ourselves rather as Proprietors of the Soil, than as Purchasers; and prescribed certain Bounds, beyond which we wou'd still suffer them to live. These Bounds were extended much further westward, than was Yet necessary for our Settlements; and was therefore an unnecessary Intrusion upon their Room for hunting; which is their Means of Subsistence. The Indians, not thinking themselves in a Situation to make effectual Resistance, accepted our Presents, and seemed, tho' reluctantly, to acquiesce in what we thought fit to dictate; but the Sense of Injury lay ranklin in their Hearts; and they have almost ever since, at various times, been carrying on a clandestine Predatory War against our frontier Inhabitants.

The United States was not quite seizing the Indians' land, but it was not quite purchasing it either. Land policy had settled somewhere in the middle, in a position that satisfied neither the frontier settlers nor the Indians.[67]

The Cherokee chief Tickagiska, meanwhile, offered to President Washington the perspective of the Indians. The Cherokees had already ceded some land in treaties. Much of the rest was being occupied illegally by trespassing settlers. "At our last treaty," Tickagiska reported, "we gave up to our white brothers all the land we could any how spare, and have but little left to raise our women and children upon, and we hope you won't let any people take any more from us without our consent. We are neither birds nor fish; we can neither fly in the air, nor live under water; therefore we hope pity will be extended toward us."[68] Through a process midway between purchase and conquest, the United States was divesting the eastern tribes of their remaining land.

By the 1790s the United States had settled on the method of acquiring Indian land that would remain in effect for a very long time. The transactions were structured as contracts, but to the Indians they often felt more like conquest. This outcome may well have represented, from the point of view of the United States government, the optimal method of obtaining the Indians' land.[69] Outright conquest would have been costly, in terms of money and of life, as Henry Knox recognized. A policy of scrupulous respect for Indian property rights would have been costly too. The government probably would not have been able to obtain land quickly enough to satisfy all the people—settlers and public creditors, present and future—who had a stake in expanding the public domain. A course in the middle, the policy the government settled on in practice, incurred both kinds of costs. The government had to fight some wars against the Indians and had to acquire land more slowly than some citizens wished. But it was less expensive to fight *some* wars than to embark on a continent-wide campaign of outright conquest, and it was less costly to disappoint *some* settlers and public creditors than to disappoint them all. All these costs are unmeasurable, but it may be that the sum of these two reduced costs was smaller than either the full cost of conquest or the full cost of scrupulous purchasing would have been. If so, then we might interpret the outcome as an extraordinarily clever and successful method of acquiring land, accomplished at great cost to the Indians but at least cost to the United States.

It would be too much, however, to conceive of that result as having been intended by anyone. Federal Indian land policy came about not by plan but by compromise. On the frontier, many settlers hated the Indians and wished to grab their land by force (and indeed to kill as many of them as possible in the process). In the east, on the other hand, there were Americans who genuinely wanted to treat the Indians more honorably, and some of these, like Henry Knox, were in positions of power. Even if they considered the Indians inferior, even if they assumed that the Indians would have to assimilate with Anglo-Americans in order to survive, they wanted to respect the Indians' property rights in the meantime. Just as one could oppose slavery without liking the slaves, or oppose cruelty to animals without considering animals one's equals, or oppose capital punishment without befriending criminals, one could oppose seizing the Indians' land without having much regard for the Indians themselves.

Indian land policy, as it came to be carried out in practice, embodied a compromise between these two views—a compromise between the desires of well-placed easterners and of western settlers, between the force of idealism and the force of self-interest on the frontier. One group had the formal authority to make the rules; the other had the power to nullify some, but not all, of those rules on the ground. The outcome was a muddle, somewhere between consent and compulsion, that satisfied neither group, even as it may have advanced their collective interest in obtaining the Indians' land.

5

From Ownership to Occupancy

In the early 1790s, American lawyers and government officials considered the Indians the *owners* of their land. By 1823, however, when the United States Supreme Court declared in *Johnson v. M'Intosh* that the Indians were in fact *not* the owners of the land but had merely a "right of occupancy," that conclusion was utterly unsurprising, because it was already the conventional wisdom. A major change in American legal thought had taken place during the intervening three decades. In the early 1790s the land not yet purchased from the Indians was thought to be owned by the Indians; by the early 1820s that land was thought to be owned by the state and federal governments. Like many transformations in legal thought, this one was so complete that contemporaries often failed to notice that it had occurred. They came to believe instead that they were simply following the rule laid down by their English colonial predecessors, and that the Indians had *never* been accorded full ownership of their land. And that view, expressed most prominently by the Supreme Court in *Johnson v. M'Intosh*, has persisted right up until today.

The transition from ownership to occupancy would have been hard to predict in the early 1790s. The members of George Washington's cabinet responsible for relations with the Indians understood the Indians to own their unsold land. The Indians "possess the right of the soil," explained Henry Knox, the secretary of war, using a common phrase that connoted outright ownership, free from the claims of all others. Secretary of State Thomas Jefferson agreed. The United States government had the right of preemption—the sole right to purchase land from the

Indians—but Jefferson considered "our right of preemption of the Indian lands, not as amounting to any dominion, or jurisd[ictio]n, or paramountship whatever." The United States possessed the right of "preventing other nations from taking possession" of the Indians' land, but nothing more. Alexander Hamilton, the secretary of the treasury and one of the era's most sophisticated lawyers, cautioned that "the titles of the Indian tribes" had to be purchased before their land could be resold to settlers. Knox, Jefferson, and Hamilton did not speak of any "right of occupancy" midway between ownership and non-ownership. They considered the Indians to be landowners.[1]

So did their contemporaries on the bench, so far as one can tell from the limited evidence. In 1795 the Pennsylvania Supreme Court affirmed that both before and after the Revolution "the soil belonged to the aborigines" until they sold it.[2] The Indians held "title" to their land, they possessed the "right of soil"—in the earliest years of the United States, judges and government officials used the same words to describe landownership by Indians as they used to describe landownership by Anglo-Americans. The Indians owned their land.

In thinking of the Indians as landowners, early Americans were following their English colonial predecessors, who had long done the same. The Americans who were the most knowledgeable about Indian policy, men like Henry Knox, knew what English policy with respect to Indian land had been, and they agreed with it. In the early 1790s they could not have foreseen the dramatic change that would come.

No Traces of Agriculture

James Sullivan was a Massachusetts lawyer in the late eighteenth and early nineteenth centuries. For nearly two decades he was the state's attorney general, and he was briefly its governor in the last year of his life. Meanwhile he wrote books about government and the economy. His last book, *The History of Land Titles in Massachusetts*, published in 1801 while he was attorney general, included a detailed discussion of the nature of property, from someone who knew the nuts and bolts of the subject but was also interested in the broader issues it implicated.

Sullivan began his history of land in Massachusetts at the beginning, with the Indians. "There were no traces of agriculture, in this part of North America," before Europeans arrived, Sullivan affirmed, "excepting that on soft and yielding pieces of ground." But even there, he insisted, the Indians' fields were so "carelessly tilled" that they "did not seem to afford any evidence of an exclusive permanent claim in him, who expected to gather the promised harvest." On this point Sullivan was wrong. Seventeenth-century colonists observed quite a bit of Indian agriculture. They knew that the Indians were careful and skillful farmers and that they possessed exclusive rights to their own crops as well as exclusive rights to farm the land allotted to them for so long as the tribe remained in that location. But having claimed that the Indians were sporadic and sloppy farmers, Sullivan could derive the proposition that the Indians did not own their land. "As property is defined by Mr. Locke, and other great men," Sullivan went on, "there may be a question, how far the savages had acquired one [i.e., a property right] in the soil of this wilderness." To the extent that the Indians had any rights in the land, he argued, it "resembles that which is sometimes claimed in particular parts of the ocean." People sometimes claimed exclusive rights to fish in certain places, but "the water there cannot be considered his property, while it continues to be part of the sea." By the same reasoning, Sullivan concluded, the Indians' "precarious and transient occupancy" of land did not make them the land's owners.[3]

Sullivan's *History of Land Titles* is one of the earliest statements of a view that would be orthodoxy two decades later—that the Indians had only a right of occupancy, not full ownership of their land. By incorrectly claiming that Indians were halfhearted farmers, Sullivan arrived at a legal conclusion different from that which had prevailed for most of the preceding two centuries. But why would someone as intelligent and well informed as James Sullivan believe that the Indians were not really farmers?

Sullivan was hardly alone in making this mistake. In the early nineteenth century, Americans frequently expressed the view that the Indians had never been farmers. "The wandering savage who traverses the wilds of America," as the minister Levi Frisbie described him in 1804, became a common image of the Indian. The eastern Indians had been almost exclusively hunters, DeWitt Clinton informed members of the New-York Historical Society at their annual meeting in 1811. Magazine articles in the 1810s contrasted the stock types of the Indian hunter and the European farmer. By the 1820s the wandering Indian hunter was such a cliché that Lydia Sigourney could begin her 180-page poem *Traits of the Aborigines of America* with an evocation of a pre-Columbian world in which "the Indian rov'd, free and unconquered." A century or two earlier, English colonists knew very well that the Indians were farmers. By the early nineteenth century, in the popular American imagination, the Indians had become nomadic hunters.[4]

The shift must be partly attributable to its practical consequences. If the Indians did not practice agriculture, it would be easier to consider the land unowned and available for the taking. Anyone seeking to obtain land on which Indians still resided would have found congenial an image of the Indian as a nomadic hunter. When Richard Johnson of Kentucky declared on the floor of the House of Representatives that "we shall change a wilderness, through which barbarians roamed, to a cultivated and populous region," he had in mind a specific region, Florida, and specific "barbarians," the Seminoles, who were there still. It could be very convenient to forget the long history of Indian agriculture.[5]

The shift is probably also attributable to simple ignorance. By the early nineteenth century, American intellectuals in places like Boston or New York had little or no contact with any Indians. The Indians were almost all gone. Susannah Willard Johnson of New Hampshire had been a captive among the Indians in the 1750s, but by the 1790s she could reflect that "the savages are driven beyond the Lakes, and our country has no enemies. The gloomy wilderness, that forty years ago, secreted the Indian and the beast of prey, has vanished away; and the thrifty farm smiles in its stead." Missionaries charged with saving Indian souls in New England reported the need to expand their operations, either to Indians elsewhere or to other destitute New Englanders, because there just weren't enough local Indians left. Most easterners had no direct experience of what Indians were like, or of what they did, or of how they procured their food. As the British military captain Gavin Cochrane observed as early as 1764, "those who live in Towns, even some men of sense, who have had no experience in what concerns the Indians, tho they often talk of them, are as ignorant of them as of the Inhabitants of China or Tartary." Eastern intellectuals most likely derived much of their understanding of Indian life from reading books by European writers who had no more firsthand knowledge of the Indians than they did. From Adam Smith, or from Vattel, or from the Scottish historian William Robertson, or from the Comte de Volney, the French historian, Americans could learn that the Indians were not farmers, and that North America had been an uncultivated wilderness before Europeans arrived. In 1700 the residents of Massachusetts might have laughed to read such nonsense, because they would have known that these accounts were wrong. By 1800, men like James Sullivan believed what they read.[6]

But there was more to the erasure of Indian agriculture than settler self-interest and the ignorance of eastern intellectuals. The surest sign of this is that many of the missionaries to the Indians in the early nineteenth century, people who were trying to help the Indians *keep* their land, also emphasized the Indian "habit of depending on game for precarious subsistence" and their "itinerant and wandering mode of life" as the causes of their poverty. The missionaries and their benefactors considered their task "not only to carry the Gospel among the Indians," explained the Boston pastor John Lathrop in 1804, "but to inculcate, on the natives of the wilderness, the order which Jehovah gave to the first of our race, '*Replenish the earth*, and subdue it.'" Missionaries consistently urged the Indians to abandon the hunt and turn to agriculture. "It is the duty of all men to be industrious," Lemuel Covell told the Tuscaroras in 1803, "and to work at some calling or business that will help subdue the earth, and make it fruitful." They rejoiced when the Indians followed their advice. "They have for four years past made wonderful improvements in agriculture," exulted William Jenkins, missionary to the Oneidas, in 1811. "They have ploughed up much of their open ground, and likewise cut down and cleared off the timber from considerable large tracts of land." A Quaker missionary reported similar success among the Senecas, who had "followed the counsel of Friends, and . . . have cut down the woods, made good fences, raised wheat, Indian corn, oats, and flax, and have got oxen, and cows." (He did not reflect on the irony that the Quakers were teaching Indians to grow "Indian corn.") All these efforts by missionaries to teach the Indians agriculture suggests that the views of James Sullivan and his contemporaries were not entirely fanciful. In the early nineteenth century there must have been some reason to believe that the Indians were not farmers.[7]

To the extent that easterners could actually see Indians in the early nineteenth century, more often than not they were seeing the remnants of communities that had been nearly destroyed by a century or more of contact with Europeans. By 1800 a substantial fraction of eastern Indians had been killed by microorganisms from Europe. Many more had migrated far from their homes. Traditional social structures and labor patterns had changed dramatically. Americans familiar with early colonial accounts of the Indians recognized that Indian life had once looked very different, and that one of the major differences involved agriculture. "If our present Indians are the same race with those described by the historian of De Soto," Ezekiel Sanford pointed out in 1819, "they once derived their chief subsistence from vegetable food. Their planted fields were numerous and extensive." But not any longer. Now "the few tribes, which remain on this side of the Mississippi, are at length penned up in reservations," too poor and demoralized to begin farming again. The essayist Anne MacVicar Grant explained that the Indians had been "very active and industrious" when they were "in their original state," and that their reputed indolence was a recent development. Part of the widespread perception in the early nineteenth century of the Indians as nonfarmers is attributable to the decline, over the eighteenth century, of eastern Indian villages.[8]

There were still some eastern tribes, like the Cherokees, who were farming in traditional ways, but even they could be perceived as non-farmers because Indian agricultural techniques looked so different from the methods to which Americans were accustomed. The most glaring difference was that in most Indian communities farming was a task for women, not men. By the nineteenth century there was already a long Anglo-American tradition of criticizing Indian men as lazy and exploit-ative for this reason. When missionaries and others wishing to reform In-dian life spoke of teaching the Indians to farm, what they often meant was teaching Indian *men* to farm. Within Indian communities, however, the social pressures to retain the traditional gendered division of labor could be very strong. It was often difficult for reformers to persuade In-dian men to take up what they perceived as women's work. And that was not the only difference between the two cultures in agricultural techniques. Traditional farming among the Cherokees, for example, did not employ plows or horses, or all the paraphernalia that went along with them. Cherokees were unaccustomed to farming in fields located far from towns, as Euro-Americans were. Indian tribes were learning to raise the animals Europeans had brought with them, animals like pigs and cattle that Euro-Americans instinctively interpreted as markers of a properly run farm. When reformers spoke of teaching the Indians to farm, they often meant teaching the Indians to farm *differently*—in the Euro-American style. Many of the critics of traditional Indian agri-culture were well intentioned. They were trying to help the Indians by making their farms more productive. But it could be easy for less-than-careful observers of the Indians to conclude that they did not farm at all.[9]

Easterners' perceptions of Indians in the early nineteenth century were also strongly influenced by the many reports coming back from the early western explorers. Some of the tribes on the Great Plains practiced agriculture, but some did not. Some were nomadic. Early nineteenth-century travelers to the west knew that their readership was intensely interested in the land and how it might one day be acquired, so they made careful observations of land use and conceptions of property among the tribes they encountered. Lewis and Clark, along with other explorers, reported finding some tribes who "have no idea of an exclusive possession of any country," and others who lacked "any idea of exclusive rights to the soil." Of one western tribe, the early explorers observed that they "have no land, nor claim the exclusive right to any, nor have any particular place of abode, but are always moving." Of another, "they never remain in the same place more than a few days, but follow the buffaloe." These were the first descriptions of tribes west of the Mississippi to be widely disseminated in the eastern United States. They depicted Indians who neither farmed nor conceived that they owned the land beneath them.[10]

Other western travelers provided similar accounts. Stephen Long encountered the Kiowas and Cheyennes in 1820 and found that "they have no permanent town, but constantly rove, as necessity urges them, in pursuit of the herds of bisons." Thomas Nuttall journeyed to Arkansas in 1819 and met the Quapaws, who were industrious hunters "but pay little attention to agriculture." Henry Marie Brackenridge was disappointed, after navigating up the Missouri River, to find the plains inhabited by only "a few wretches . . . constantly roaming abroad." If there was one thing about the western Indians that became common knowledge in the early nineteenth century, it was that they were nomadic and did not practice agriculture. This view was not unanimous: John Bradbury visited the Arikaras and thought them "excellent cultivators," and William Wells found individual property ownership among the tribes of the old northwest. But the image of western Indians as nonfarming nomads was prevalent in the eastern United States. It is likely that easterners formed their opinions about Indians generally from such accounts, even about eastern Indians, whose agricultural practices had once been very different.[11]

For all these reasons, educated Americans of the early nineteenth century increasingly came to think of the Indians as nomadic hunters rather than the farmers they had once been. This change in perception had important consequences for Indian land policy.

The image of the nonfarming Indian opened the possibility of rethinking the legal relationship between the Indians and their land. The fact that the Indians were farmers was one of the reasons the British had treated the Indians as owners of their land. Since ancient times, educated Europeans had perceived a link between agriculture and land-ownership. A society of farmers necessarily stayed in place for years at a time, and its members necessarily mixed their labor with the land, providing the criteria for ownership cited by countless writers before and after Locke. But a society of hunters had a very different relationship with its land. Hunters followed the chase, never staying in any one location long enough to give rise to a claim of property. Hunters never mixed their labor with the land. The more the Indians were perceived as hunters instead of farmers, the less Anglo-Americans would recognize them as owners of the land beneath them.

Even when Americans acknowledged that the Indians did *some* farming, the perception of agriculture as only a minor part of Indian life allowed the resurrection of a legal argument that had scarcely been heard for half a century—that the Indians lacked any rights in their uncultivated land. The question of whether the Indians owned their hunting grounds and other unfarmed land had been controversial in the early colonial period. By the mid-eighteenth century, official British policy was settled: the Indians owned all their land, regardless of the purpose to which it was put. The policy was often violated in practice, as settlers continually trespassed on uncultivated Indian land, but as a statement of the formal law it remained true, even after the Revolution: if Americans wanted Indian hunting grounds, the land would have to be purchased. In the early nineteenth century, however, this understanding of the law began to come under attack.

In 1802, for example, John Quincy Adams, just beginning his political career, spoke of Indian property rights in a speech commemorating the anniversary of the Pilgrims' landing at Plymouth. No colony had been kinder to the Indians than Plymouth, Adams declared. The Pilgrims had purchased land rather than seizing it. "At their hands the children of the desert"—that is, the Indians—"had no cause of complaint." Purchasing the land had been an act of generosity, Adams reasoned, because the Indians owned only a tiny fraction of it. "Their cultivated fields; their constructed habitations; a space of ample sufficiency for their subsistence, and whatever they had annexed to themselves by personal labor, was undoubtedly, by the laws of nature, theirs," Adams conceded, in a Lockean style. But such land accounted for a very small percentage of the territory the Pilgrims purchased. Most land, insisted Adams, had been used for hunting. And "what is the right of a huntsman to the forest of a thousand miles over which he has accidentally ranged in quest of prey?" To recognize the Indians as owners of all that land would authorize them to refuse to sell it, which would endow the Indians with resources disproportionate to their numbers. "Shall the liberal bounties of Providence to the race of man be monopolized by one of ten thousand for whom they were created?" Adams asked. "Shall the exuberant bosom of the common mother, amply adequate to the nourishment of millions, be claimed exclusively by a few hundreds of her offspring?" Even worse, recognizing Indian ownership threatened to choke off progress in the new United States, because economic growth and the spread of civilization depended on access to all that land. Adams painted a dark picture of the consequences. "Shall the lordly savage not only disdain the virtues and enjoyments of civilization himself, but shall he control the civilization of a world?" Adams asked.

> Shall he forbid the wilderness to blossom like a rose? Shall he forbid the oaks of the forest to fall before the axe of industry, and to rise again, transformed into the habitations of ease and elegance? Shall he doom an immense region of the globe to perpetual desolation, and to hear the howlings of the tiger and the wolf silence forever the voice of human gladness? Shall the fields and the valleys, which a beneficent God has formed to teem with the life of innumerable multitudes, be condemned to everlasting barrenness? Shall the mighty rivers, poured out by the hand of nature, as channels of communication between numerous nations, roll their waters in sullen silence and eternal solitude of the deep? Have hundreds of commodious harbors, a thousand leagues of coast, and a boundless ocean, been spread in the front of this land, and shall every purpose of utility to which they could apply be prohibited by the tenant of the woods?

Of course not, Adams concluded. The Indians were accordingly not the owners of their hunting grounds, but only of the land they actually cultivated and built houses on.[12]

Adams's view never became the law. The United States would always recognize the Indians as holding *some* kind of right in their hunting grounds, even if it was not full ownership. But the opinion expressed by

Adams seems to have grown more common in the years around 1800. Tennessee governor John Sevier, referring to the Indians, declared in 1798 that "by the law of nations, it is agreed that no people shall be entitled to more land than they can cultivate." President James Monroe's annual message to Congress in 1817 included a similar assertion. "The hunter state can exist only in the vast uncultivated desert," Monroe explained. "It yields to the more dense and compact form and greater force of civilized population, and of right it ought to yield, for the earth was given to mankind to support the greatest number of which it is capable, and no tribe or people have a right to withhold from the wants of others more than is necessary for their own support and comfort."[13] The motives behind such statements varied. John Sevier was democratically accountable to frontier settlers who stood to gain directly if the United States were to declare Indian hunting grounds open for the taking. James Monroe was much less dependent on votes from the frontier, John Quincy Adams (then a state senator from Boston) scarcely at all. Settlers bordering on Indian hunting grounds, and the politicians for whom they voted, had always disparaged Indian property rights, but it had been a long time since eastern intellectuals and policymakers had agreed. When men like Monroe and Adams began to doubt that the Indians owned their uncultivated land, that was a sure sign that Indian property rights were weakening.

As the Indians came to be increasingly perceived as nomadic hunters, and as sentiment spread that the Indians lacked property rights in land they did not farm, it became possible to think of reducing Indian landholdings as a benefit to the Indians themselves. If the Indians would only switch from hunting to farming, Thomas Jefferson reasoned in 1803, "they will perceive how useless to them are their extensive forests, and will be willing to pare them off from time to time in exchange for necessaries for their farms and families." Indians would be wealthier on less land. Indeed, the process could work as well in reverse: *forcing* the Indians to get by on less land would be an effective way of inducing them to switch to farming. "A cession of a considerable part of their unoccupied lands," suggested Secretary of War William Crawford in 1816, "will diminish the temptation to waste in the chace, the time which could be more profitably employed in husbandry." Less land would accordingly "furnish the means of prosecuting their agricultural labours with the greatest success." Here was yet another argument pressing in favor of weakening Indian property rights.[14]

Conventional thought about Indians changed in the early nineteenth century, as the common perception of the Indian gradually transformed from farmer to hunter, and that had the effect of weakening support among educated Americans for recognizing Indian property rights. Meanwhile another kind of change was taking place that would also influence the way Americans thought about Indian land—a change in the mechanics of land purchasing.

Airey Sales and Purchases

William Strickland was a gentleman farmer from Yorkshire who traveled through the United States in 1794 and 1795, keeping a journal all the while. He was astonished by all the land speculation he encountered. "The value of lands both in the old settled country and in the new country has doubled within the past two years and is rapidly increasing," he reported: "these land speculations are carried on to a degree of madness." In Albany, New York, he met some speculators who explained to him the rules of the game. Much of the speculation was in land still possessed by the Indians, they told him. Private purchasers like themselves had no right actually to buy the land from the Indians, they conceded. That right—the right of preemption—was reserved to the government. When speculators traded in Indian land, what they were buying and selling was not *land*, or even the right to *buy* land from the Indians, but rather the prospect of being the owner of the land once the *government* bought the land from the Indians. "American jurisprudence holds valid many such airey sales and purchases as this," Strickland noted in his journal. These transactions existed because states, including New York, were in the habit of granting to individuals the right to own particular parcels of land before those parcels had been purchased from the Indians. Such rights were called "preemption rights," Strickland learned, and were "continually passing from one hand to another, and increasing in value as the prospect of possessing [the land] improves, or approaches, tho numerous tribes of Indians are still in possession." A preemption right would obviously grow more valuable the more likely the Indians were to sell the underlying land to the government, so the owner of a preemption right would be hopeful for "a fortunate war, or invasion of the small pox," or any equally happy event that would increase the odds that the government would acquire the land. The most unscrupulous speculators sometimes even took matters into their own hands by trying "to extirpate the much injured owners of the soil." Too often, Strickland despaired, "their destruction is persued with remorseless perseverance and their annihilation spoken of with atrocious pleasure." The market in preemption rights had the perverse effect of bringing speculators' financial incentives into alignment with their racism.[15]

The asset Strickland described was a new one. Before the American Revolution there was no such thing as a "preemption right" capable of being bought and sold, because colonial governments did not normally grant parcels of land before those parcels had been purchased from the Indians. The market in preemption rights sprang to life during and immediately after the Revolution, in the brief period when lawyers understood the American victory to have transferred the Indians' land east of the Mississippi to the federal or state governments by right of conquest. During and after the war, the states began granting out parcels of land not yet purchased from the Indians, because the prevailing belief was that the land did not have to be purchased from the Indians—the states already owned it. After the war, meanwhile, the federal government began entering into treaties with Indian tribes that reserved certain areas to the Indians, areas that sometimes included the parcels that state governments had already granted out. In South Carolina, for example, Governor William Moultrie received the text of the Treaty of Hopewell in early 1786 and realized that the area the treaty reserved to the Cherokees included many parcels he had already granted to settlers.[16] The federal treaty took precedence over the state land grants, but what did the grantees have now? Nothing? Or did the recipient of such a grant have the right to own the land in the future, in the event the Indians conveyed it to the government?

Things grew even more complicated in 1789, when federal Indian policy shifted back toward the recognition of the Indians as owners of all their unsold land. Now many of the recipients of the previous decade's land grants were left in an uncertain status. Were their grants void, on the ground that the states had no right to grant land before it had been purchased from the Indians? Were their grants valid, and superior to any Indian claims, on the theory that the grants had been lawful as of the time they were made? Or was the right answer in the middle? Did the grantees of parcels not yet purchased from the Indians have a right to own the land once the Indians were willing to sell it to the government?

It would be the latter. The first known American case to address the issue was *Marshall v. Clark*, decided in 1791 by the Virginia Supreme

Court. The lead plaintiff was Thomas Marshall, John Marshall's father, who challenged the validity of a grant Virginia had made to the war hero George Rogers Clark. (Marshall was acting on behalf of the state militia, which claimed the same land.) One of Marshall's arguments was that the grant to Clark was void because, when it took effect, the land the state purported to grant had not yet been purchased from the Indians. The Virginia Supreme Court rejected the argument. "The Indian title did not impede . . . the power of the legislature to grant the land," the court held. The grantee "must risque the event of the Indian claim, and yield to it, if finally established, or have the benefit of a former or future extinction thereof," the court reasoned, but these contingencies did not invalidate the grant. If the government ever acquired the land from the Indians, it would become Clark's. A few years later, the Pennsylvania and Tennessee Supreme Courts reached the same result. States had the power to grant land not yet purchased from the Indians.[17]

The effect of *Marshall v. Clark* and the subsequent cases was most likely to ratify a market in preemption rights that was already in existence, but it may also have expanded that market by giving it formal legal sanction. In the 1790s, transactions in preemption rights appear to have been commonplace. In 1795, for example, young Tennessee lawyer Andrew Jackson was trying to sell preemption rights in a parcel still owned by the Cherokees. His partner advised him to try to avoid giving any warranties to the purchaser, but in the event that a warranty was necessary, Jackson should make clear that it was "not understood to extend to any Tribe of Indians."[18] That is, Jackson was not to promise that the purchaser would acquire any rights superior to those of the Cherokees. All he could promise was the right to possess the land in the event that the Cherokees sold it to the federal government.

The growth of the market in preemption rights was facilitated by the federal structure of American government. State governments had the power to make land grants, but under the new Constitution only the federal government had the power to acquire land from the Indians. State governments had only a limited capacity to influence the speed at which the federal government purchased Indian land. In many states, elected officials faced considerable pressure to make land grants. Had the states been able to buy Indian land on their own, they might have done so before granting it to settlers. But under pressure from constituents to grant western land, and unable to purchase that land from the Indians, state officials continued granting it to settlers regardless of whether the Indians were still on it. The delay, they could tell would-be settlers, was the fault of the federal government, not the state.

When preemption rights came into existence, they were understood as contingent future interests in land still owned by the Indians. Lawyers of the period would have characterized the Indians' property right as a title in *fee simple*—the present right to possess the land for as long as they wished. Lawyers would have analogized a preemption right to an *executory interest*—the right to take possession of the land at some point in the future, should a particular event transpire. But as preemption rights came to be frequently bought and sold, the conventional legal understanding of them underwent a subtle transformation.

When Indian land could be bought and sold with the Indians still on it, the Indians' right to the land started to feel, to the buyers and sellers, less like fee simple ownership. Anglo-American real estate speculators were long accustomed to buying and selling land that was occupied by other people, but, like today, those other people were normally *tenants*, not fee simple owners. The fee simple owners were the people doing the buying and selling. When land occupied by A was also owned in fee simple by A, there was simply no occasion for B to sell that land to C, and indeed B would be committing fraud if he tried. But if A were merely a tenant, and B the fee simple owner, it would be perfectly natural for B to sell the land to C, who would take title subject to A's ongoing tenancy. In the market for preemption rights, A was the Indians; B and C were Anglo-Americans. In the period around 1800, when a speculator or a lawyer contemplated a transaction in preemption rights, the Indians must have intuitively felt like tenants.

In the years surrounding the turn of the nineteenth century, lawyers gradually began to think of the preemption right as the fee simple title, and the Indians' present right of possession as a kind of tenancy that would last as long as the Indians remained on the land. The purchaser of a preemption right, on this view, acquired, in the present, a fee simple title subject to the Indians' right of possession, rather than a contingent right to own the land in fee simple in the future. In practical terms, in the short run, the two ways of thinking about preemption rights had identical consequences. Either way, the Indians could stay on the land as long as they wished, and could sell only to the federal government, at which point the holder of the preemption right would become the land's owner. But to think of the preemption right as a fee simple title was to change the legal understanding of a land grant from the government.

The holder of a preemption right acquired it from a state government. For a preemption right to be a kind of fee simple title in land currently possessed by the Indians, therefore, the land occupied by the Indians had to be owned in fee simple by the state, not by the Indians—otherwise the state would lack the power to grant preemption rights. The shift to an understanding of preemption rights as fee simple titles was thus necessarily accompanied by a shift in the understanding of who owned the land *before* the preemption rights were granted. As preemption rights became more common, lawyers increasingly began to believe that the Indians had *never* held their land in fee simple. The land had *always* been owned by the government, subject to the Indians' right of possession.

A snapshot of one moment in this transformation in legal thought can be found in a revealing exchange on the floor of the House of Representatives in January 1795. The House was debating whether to award compensation to North Carolinians who in the 1780s had purchased, from North Carolina, parcels within an area that the federal government subsequently reserved to the Indians in the Treaty of Hopewell. Some had settled the land and begun farming, only to be evicted after the treaty was signed. "The Government of the United States has converted the property of the citizens of North Carolina to the uses of her Government," James Gillespie of North Carolina argued, and "compensation ought to be made out of the public purse." But Elias Boudinot of New Jersey objected to awarding compensation, on the ground that the claimants had not lost anything, because the state of North Carolina was never the owner of the land it had purported to grant them. "This claim of North Carolina to sell the lands was wrong," Boudinot insisted. "The Crown of Britain had never pretended to any right of this kind, nor ever thought it had a title to any lands till they were first purchased from the Indians. The question before the Committee was, have the United States taken away any claim which the purchasers of these lands had? And the answer is, that the United States have not. The State of North Carolina only had a right to sell the privilege of pre-emption. This was the only right which the purchasers obtained, and this right they still possess." Boudinot was defending the older view of Indian property rights. "The Indian right of soil," he concluded, "had always been acknowledged." The Indians had been the land's owner all along.

The debate began over whether to compensate specific claimants, but Boudinot's comments turned it into a broad-ranging discussion of whether the Indians owned their unsold land. William Vans Murray of Maryland agreed with Boudinot that settlers who purchased from North Carolina "never were possessed of any right but that which North Carolina could give them—the pre-emption right," which they had not lost by virtue of the treaty. But the members of Congress from North Carolina, and from the other southern states where similar disputes were arising, voiced the newer view of Indian property rights. "Much had been said about the Indian right" to their land, complained John Nicholas of Virginia, but they had no such right. "It could never have been the design of nature that these people should be termed the possessors of land which they were incapable to enjoy." Thomas Blount of North Carolina, himself one of the claimants to compensation, "denied that the Indians ever occupied the lands in question" in a manner sufficient to assert ownership. Indeed, he argued, the Indians had never been recognized as owners of their land. "He did not know of one purchase made in Carolina. It was all conquest, and so were nine-tenths of all the lands held by the white people in America." Nathaniel Macon of North Carolina and Thomas Carnes of Georgia declared that unsold Indian land in North Carolina belonged, not to the Indians, but to North Carolina. As Carnes put it, "the fee-simple of all the soil within the chartered limits belonged to the State." The House overwhelmingly voted not to compensate the claimants, which suggests that the older view of Indian property rights still prevailed, but both sides of the question had been vigorously aired. The Indians were beginning to lose ownership of their land.[19]

The issue returned to Congress a year later, while the House was debating the bill that would become the Intercourse Act of 1796. The bill included a clause that would have enforced the ban on surveying land not yet purchased from the Indians; the clause provided that any person holding a preemption right, who entered the land covered by his preemption right for the purpose of conducting a survey, would forfeit the preemption right. James Hillhouse of Connecticut, a lawyer, spoke in favor of this forfeiture provision. Forfeiture was appropriate, he argued, because the holder of a preemption right was in the same position as any other member of the public—he was a trespasser on land belonging to someone else. The Indians had "the fee simple of the lands," Hillhouse explained, taking the traditional legal view of Indian property rights. "Indeed, the right and title to the lands had been expressly recognised by the United States in the Treaties they had made with them. The God of Nature had given them the land." If the Indians were not the fee sim-ple owners of their land, Hillhouse asked, then "who were the propri-etors of this country previous to its being known to civilized nations (as they were called)? Were not those people?" And if the Indians had been the fee simple owners before European contact, "who gave us a right to call their title in question, or forcibly to thrust them out?" The Indians, he concluded, must still own their land in fee simple. A preemption right "is not a title, but a right only of becoming, in preference to all oth-ers, owners of the land, by some future grant or cession to be made by the Indians, who are the present proprietors."

But another lawyer, James Holland of North Carolina, sharply dis-agreed. Because North Carolina was one of the states that had been most aggressive in granting preemption rights in land not yet purchased from the Indians, Holland likely counted many holders of preemption rights among his constituents. North Carolina must have been a fertile soil for the new legal conception of Indian property rights. Holland ac-cordingly insisted that the Indians were not and never had been the fee simple owners of their land. "All titles to the soil were originally in the King," Holland declared. "The savages of these Provinces, when under the British Government, were considered a conquered people, and ten-ants at will." *Tenants at will* was (and still is) the legal term for tenants who could be evicted by the land's owner at any time, for any reason or no reason. The Indians held their land by "right of occupancy," Holland continued; theirs was "not the dignity of a fee simple." North Carolina had succeeded to the Crown's landholdings within the state's borders, and it was thus the state, not the Indians, that held the fee simple to the Indian land in North Carolina. The Indians were merely "tenants at will, and not tenants in possession of a fee simple estate." Citizens who had purchased preemption rights "had made a fair contract with the State of North Carolina, and a full payment for those lands." The hold-ers of preemption rights were now the land's fee simple owners, Holland concluded. The federal government had no right to take those land ti-tles away.

Here were clear statements of the legal understandings of Indian property rights that were in competition by the turn of the nineteenth century—the older view, expressed by Hillhouse, that the Indians owned their land in fee simple, and the newer view, articulated by Hol-land, that the Indians' land was owned by the government.

Other members of the House then jumped into the debate. If any representative was an expert in land speculation, it was William Cooper of New York, the founder of Cooperstown and father of the novelist James Fenimore Cooper. Cooper rightly observed that "the idea advanced by the gentleman from North Carolina, that Indian nations could not hold the fee of the countries they possess, was new." Not only was it new, Cooper continued, but it was "contrary to natural justice." The holders of preemption rights, he argued, "took them subject to the Indian claim, and they must wait until it is convenient for Congress to extinguish their title by Treaty." Until then, holders of preemption rights had no present interest in the Indians' land.

Next up was John Milledge of Georgia, another lawyer, and another representative from a state that had been aggressive in granting preemption rights to Indian land. Milledge supported Holland and the new view of Indian property rights. Jeremiah Crabb of Maryland sided with Hillhouse and the older view. Recipients of grants to Indian land "had nothing more than an unextinguished pre-emptive right," he urged, not a fee simple title. James Madison took the new view: if Indians owned their land in fee simple, he wondered, then what right did the federal government have to prevent them from ceding their land to foreigners? William Lyman of Massachusetts agreed. "The Indians ought certainly to be treated with humanity," he suggested, but he "did not believe they had any real title to land." The land "was the property of the United States, which they were suffered to enjoy, but to which they had no real title."

Theodore Sedgwick of Massachusetts had the last word. Sedgwick was a lawyer too, and after serving in Congress he would be a judge of the Massachusetts Supreme Court. Sedgwick was shocked at the legal doctrine espoused by Holland and the others—the notion that the government, not the Indians, owned the Indians' land. "Two hundred years ago," he remarked, "when cupidity gave a right to possession, and all the cruelties of Spain were exercised upon the innocent inhabitants, which [his] mind shuddered to think of, this doctrine might have been held." Sedgwick was right; the doctrine *was* held by many writers of the early seventeenth century. But Sedgwick could not believe that "at the close of the eighteenth century, and in this place, doctrines of this kind would have been held. Were they to say to the savages in their own country, you have no right to any land?" The new view of Indian property rights "would be a principle of plunder," he predicted, a principle "hostile to, and destructive of, all security in property."

The House was voting on whether to remove the forfeiture clause from the bill, not on the broader question of the nature of Indian land-ownership, so there is no way to know what other members thought. There were other reasons to remove the forfeiture clause from the bill besides the belief that the holders of preemption rights were the fee simple owners of the land. As a few members of Congress pointed out, for example, the most egregious trespassers on Indian land were people who did not even hold preemption rights, so the forfeiture clause would be no deterrent to the worst of the violators. So perhaps we ought not to infer too much from the fact that the House voted 33 to 28 to remove the clause from the bill—that is, that the advocates of the new legal understanding of Indian property rights were the winners.[20] But the exchange on the floor of the House captures a moment in a process of legal change, in which one way of thinking about Indians and land was in the midst of being replaced by another.

The shift in the conventional conception of Indian land title seems to have been prompted in the first instance by the new market in preemption rights. Once the shift was under way, it was facilitated by the growing perception that the Indians were hunters rather than farmers. There was an obvious counterintuition to the idea that the Indians were tenants. It was the one advanced by James Hillhouse—that the Indians were on the land first, and so had a superior claim to ownership. For the conception of Indians as tenants to take hold, there needed to be some hole in Hillhouse's logic, some reason the Indians' priority of occupancy did not give them fee simple title. The belief that the Indians were primarily hunters provided such a reason. It had been accepted for centuries that sedentary farmers owned their land but nomadic hunters did not. If a tribe of hunters occupied land first, and a group of farmers occupied the same land second, the farmers would be the owners. That was enough to dampen the force of arguments like Hillhouse's.

These two changes in thought took place simultaneously in the years around the turn of the nineteenth century. The result would be a new legal concept, the right of occupancy.

The Right of Occupancy

The earliest court opinions to adopt the new view of Indian property rights—that the government, not the tribes, was the fee simple owner of unsold Indian land—were given by state court judges in the first decade of the nineteenth century. The first reported case to confront the issue directly was *Strother v. Cathey,* decided by the North Carolina Supreme Court in 1807. Two parties claimed the same land, one by virtue of an 1803 grant from the state. The land was located within an area that the United States had purchased from the Cherokees back in 1791, in the Treaty of Holston. The opposing litigant argued that North Carolina had lacked any power to grant the land in 1803, because after the Treaty of Holston the land was owned by the federal government, the purchaser from the Cherokees. The North Carolina Supreme Court rejected the argument, on the ground that the United States could not have acquired title to the land in 1791—the title was not the Cherokees' to sell. The federal government had the power under the Constitution to extinguish the Indians' claim to land, Judge Francis Locke held, but "it does not follow that title rests in" the federal government, because the state had owned the land all along. Judge David Stone, a future North Carolina governor and United States senator, addressed the nature of Indian property rights more explicitly. The federal government could not have purchased fee simple title from the Cherokees, he explained, because "neither the European governments, nor the government of the United States, nor that of North Carolina, have considered the Indian title other than a mere possessory right." The land was owned by the state, subject to the Cherokees' "possessory right," and this possessory right was all the United States had acquired in the Treaty of Holston. "The treaty of 1791, with the Cherokees," Stone concluded, "cannot be considered, therefore, as conveying a title to the soil of this land to the United States." North Carolina thus had the power to grant fee simple title to the land whether or not the Cherokees were still on it, and whether or not the Cherokees had conveyed their interest in it to the United States. *Strother v. Cathey,* decided sixteen years before the United States Supreme Court decided *Johnson v. M'Intosh,* appears to be the first reported American court decision holding that unsold Indian land was owned by the government, subject only to a lesser right of "possession" or "occupancy" held by the Indians.[21]

The issue arose again the following year, in New York. In *Jackson v. Hudson,* one party claimed land by virtue of a 1731 patent from the colony of New York, at a time when the land was still occupied by the Mohawks. His opponent argued that the patent was invalid; if the land had not yet been purchased from the Mohawks, he reasoned, New York had nothing to grant. Chief Justice James Kent rejected the argument, but in a style so cautious as to suggest that Kent was aware of the question's difficulty. "The policy, or the abstract right of granting lands in the possession of the native Indians, without their previous consent, as original lords of the soil, is a political question with which we have at present nothing to do," Kent insisted. The court could avoid having to define the Indians' property rights, because neither claimant to the land traced his title back to the Indians. "What would be the effect of an Indian possession or title, in opposition to the grant under the patent, if they were to be brought into collision, is not a question before us," Kent concluded. The issue—whether the government or the Indians had the power to convey the Indians' land—was still an open one in New York.[22]

It would be closed the very next year. *Van Gorden v. Jackson* was another dispute over land in New York, this time involving a party who claimed the land based on, among other things, a few seventeenth-century deeds from Indian sellers to his predecessors in title. Chancellor John Lansing held that these deeds, by themselves, would not be enough to establish ownership. "Though Indian deeds were obtained for the purpose of proving that the rights of the natives, were extinguished," Lansing reasoned, such deeds "were never admitted, as of themselves, to be a source of legal title." Thus far Lansing had said nothing inconsistent with the older view of Indian property rights, that the Indians owned their unsold land. He was correct that in the colonial period a person wishing to own Indian land needed both a purchase from the Indians and a patent from the government to acquire title. But Lansing's next sentence revealed the subtle change in legal thought that was taking place. In the colonial period, patents from the government had been understood as confirmations of a transfer of ownership that took place, from Indians to settlers, when the land was purchased from the Indians. By 1809, however, Lansing could characterize the *patent* as the transfer of ownership, a transfer from *the government* to the settler. Deeds signed by the Indians "were presented to government as an inducement to extend its bounty by grant," Lansing declared, "but the firm and unbending principle has uniformly been, that all titles must be derived, either mediately or immediately, actually or presumptively, from the crown." This was a less explicit statement of Indian non-ownership than the one provided by David Stone two years earlier in North Carolina, but the point would have been clear enough to lawyers at the time. The Indians were not, and indeed never had been, the owners of their unsold land.[23]

The case that sealed the issue was *Fletcher v. Peck*, decided by the United States Supreme Court in 1810. *Fletcher* is a case well known to constitutional lawyers, for reasons having little to do with the Indians. It was the first of the great nineteenth-century Contract Clause cases, in which the Court found state laws unconstitutional for "impairing the Obligation of Contracts." The state law at issue in *Fletcher v. Peck* was a 1796 Georgia statute repealing a massive and corrupt land sale from the previous year. In 1795 the Georgia legislature had passed a law selling thirty-five million acres of the state's western land to four companies of speculators for less than a penny and a half per acre, a price far too low even then. Virtually all the legislators voting to approve the sale had been bribed by the speculators. At the next election, after the fraud was revealed, the corrupt legislators were voted out, and the new legislature promptly repealed the sale. In the intervening year, however, the specu-lators had hastily sold much of the land to others. These subsequent purchasers claimed a right to the land despite the repeal of the original sale. Eventually, after years of political maneuvering, the case landed in court.[24]

The land under dispute had not yet been purchased from the Indians, but when *Fletcher v. Peck* was tried in federal court in Massachusetts in 1807, neither side had any incentive to argue that the Indians were the land's owners. The litigation was collusive; both Fletcher and Peck were veteran speculators who stood to gain if the corrupt 1795 grant were up-held. They structured the case as a breach-of-contract suit by Fletcher, who claimed that when he had purchased a tract within the disputed area from Peck, Peck had falsely promised that he was the land's owner. In fact, Fletcher asserted, Peck did not own the land he purported to sell, because he took the land at the end of a chain of conveyances that had begun with the fraudulent 1795 sale, and that sale was invalid. The object of the suit for both sides was for Fletcher to lose—that is, for the 1795 sale to be upheld. Fletcher alleged four reasons the 1795 sale had not passed the land from Georgia to the purchasing speculators, only one of which is remembered today—that the sale had been nullified by the 1796 repeal. (This was the argument the Court would reject on the ground that the 1796 repeal violated the Contract Clause.) But another of Fletcher's arguments was that Georgia was not even the land's true owner in 1795. Fletcher argued instead that *the United States* owned the land, subject to the Indians' right of occupancy. Peck replied that Geor-gia had indeed owned the land in 1795, again subject to the Indians' right of occupancy.[25] The Indians, of course, had no voice in *Fletcher v. Peck*, so no one argued that the land was owned by the Indians. Both sides could accordingly adopt the newer view of Indian property rights, without the older view being heard.

When the case arrived at the United States Supreme Court, the Indians figured more prominently in the arguments, but still neither side had any incentive to suggest that the land was owned by the Indians. Once again Fletcher argued that the land was owned by the United States, and Peck that it was owned by Georgia. The litigation was well funded, and both sides wanted Peck to win, so Peck's lawyers were an all-star team: John Quincy Adams, then between jobs as U.S. senator and ambassador to Russia; Joseph Story, who would become a Supreme Court justice himself a couple of years later; and Robert Goodloe Harper, one of the era's leading lawyers and later a member of Congress. Toward the end of the argument, one of the lawyers (the case report does not say which one) brought up the question whether Georgia had any right to grant land that had not yet been purchased from the Indians. "A doubt has been suggested," Peck's lawyer began, "whether this power extends to lands to which the Indian title has not yet been extinguished." The suggestion most likely did not come from Fletcher's lawyer, the elderly and alcoholic Luther Martin, who was being paid to lose, and who offered only the most cursory of arguments. It probably came from Justice William Johnson, who was (as we will see shortly) the only person present who was willing to defend the older view of Indian property rights. Peck's lawyer later referred to "a question which has been suggested from the bench whether the right which Georgia had before the extinguishment of Indian title, is such a right as is susceptible of conveyance," a remark that confirms that the source of the doubt was one of the justices. But whether it was Johnson or someone else who raised the issue, Peck's lawyer launched into the first discussion of the nature of Indian landownership ever to take place before the U.S. Supreme Court.

"What is the Indian title?" Peck's lawyer asked, and then he answered his own question. "It is a mere occupancy for the purpose of hunting. It is not like our tenures; they have no idea of a title to the soil itself. It is overrun by them, rather than inhabited. It is not a true and legal possession." Here was a concise summary of how early nineteenth-century American intellectuals had come to perceive the Indians, as nomadic hunters who did not stay in any one place long enough to own the land beneath them. There were few, if any, people in the courtroom who had enough personal acquaintance with real Indians to be able to disagree. The authorities cited by Peck's lawyer in support of this view of Indian property rights and food-gathering practices were not eyewitnesses to Indian life, or even the many colonial statutes regulating the process of land purchasing, but rather Vattel, Montesquieu, and Adam Smith, theorists who had never been to North America. Two centuries of observations of Indian farming, and the long legal tradition of recognizing the Indians as the owners of their land, had been nearly forgotten.

Once he had posited that the Indians did not own their land, Peck's lawyer had little trouble arguing that the land belonged to Georgia. The British, he asserted, "always claimed and exercised the right of conquest over the soil. . . . Even Penn claimed under right of conquest." This was not true. "All the treaties with the Indians were the effect of conquest. All the extensive grants have been forced from them by successful war. The conquerors permitted the conquered tribes to occupy part of the land until it should be wanted for the use of the conquerors." This was not true either. But it led to the conclusion that "the rights of governments are allodial"—that is, that the British government had owned all the land in its colonies, even the land not yet purchased from the Indians. "The Indian title is a mere privilege," he argued, "which does not affect the allodial rights." These rights, the actual ownership of the land, belonged now to Georgia, as the successor to the Crown.

Chief Justice John Marshall's majority opinion included only two sentences about the Indians, but they would prove to be influential. Most of the opinion was about whether the 1796 legislature had the power to undo the grant made by the 1795 legislature. Only after Marshall had established that the repeal was unconstitutional did he turn to the question of whether Georgia even owned the land in 1795. The opinion covered the issue very quickly, in a discussion that assumed that the land's owner was either Georgia or the United States, and decided in favor of Georgia. And only then, at the very end of the opinion, did Marshall address Justice Johnson's suggestion that the Indians were the land's true owners. "It was doubted," Marshall remarked offhandedly, "whether a state can be seised in fee of lands [i.e., whether a state can possess lands in fee simple], subject to the Indian title, and whether a decision that they were seised in fee, might not be construed to amount to a decision that their grantee might maintain an ejectment for them, notwithstanding that title." Johnson must have been worried that if the Court held that Georgia was the fee simple owner of the land, Georgians receiving land grants would then have the power to evict the Indians, just like any landowner might evict tenants at will. Marshall tried simultaneously to assuage Johnson's fears and to establish Georgia's authority to grant fee simple titles to others. "The majority of the court is of opinion," he reported, "that the nature of the Indian title, which is certainly to be respected by all courts, until it be legitimately extinguished, is not such as to be absolutely repugnant to seisin [i.e., possession] in fee on the part of the state." In plainer language, Georgia and the Indians both had rights in the land: Georgia was the fee simple owner, while the Indians had something called "Indian title," a right to occupy the land, but not ownership of it. The newer view of Indian property rights, not yet even two decades old, had been officially adopted by the Supreme Court.

The fate of the Indians was a very minor part of *Fletcher v. Peck* in the minds of John Marshall and the other Justices who joined his opinion, so Marshall did not explain in any detail what he meant by "Indian title." From the phrase's context, however, we can make some plausible guesses as to what he meant. The Indians could evidently stay on the land, and if their right to do so had to be "respected by all courts," presumably that right would be judicially enforceable. Indian title would last until it was "legitimately extinguished." Marshall did not say which methods of extinguishing Indian title were legitimate and which were not, or even who had the power to extinguish it, but the purpose of this sentence was to make clear, in response to Justice Johnson's critique, that neither the state of Georgia nor Georgia landowners could forcibly evict the Indians. Because everyone knew that Georgia and its landowners had no power to *purchase* Indian land either—by statute the only lawful purchaser of Indian land was the federal government—Marshall was in effect saying that Indian title could not be "legitimately extinguished" by Georgia or by Georgia landowners at all. The United States was the only entity that could put an end to Indian title. There was no occasion in *Fletcher v. Peck* to say exactly *how* the federal government could legitimately extinguish Indian title. Purchase, obviously, was legitimate. But could the United States "legitimately" seize Indian land by force? Or was Indian title something that could be asserted in court against the federal government as well as a state? That question was not yet answered.

William Johnson dissented, alone, on two points. Public dissent was unusual on the early Marshall Court. The norm was to suppress dissent and speak with a unanimous voice—Johnson was the only early justice to publish more than a handful of dissenting opinions, but even he published very few by modern standards—so Johnson must have felt strongly about the case. His first point of disagreement with the majority was over whether Georgia could revoke its land grant. He agreed that it could not, but he found the source of that prohibition in natural law rather than in the Contract Clause. His more substantial point of disagreement concerned the nature of Indian landownership. Georgia did not own the Indians' unpurchased land in fee simple, Johnson insisted. Instead, "the interest of Georgia in that land amounted to nothing more than a mere possibility" of ownership, in the event the land was acquired from the Indians. Until then, when Georgia purported to grant the Indians' land to settlers, "her conveyance thereof could operate legally only as a covenant to convey"—that is, as a promise to grant the land in the future, should it come into the state's possession. Johnson was reasserting the older view of Indian property rights, the view that had once been dominant in American law. "The correctness of this opinion will depend upon a just view of the state of the Indian nations," Johnson explained. For centuries Anglo-Americans had obtained Indian land by purchasing it from the Indians. This "uniform practice of acknowledging their right of soil, by purchasing from them, and restraining all persons from encroaching upon their territory, makes it unnecessary to insist upon their right of soil." And if the Indians owned the land, how could Georgia own it too? "Can, then," asked Johnson, "one nation be said to be seised of a fee-simple in lands, the right of soil of which is in another nation? . . . In fact, if the Indian nations be the absolute proprietors of their soil, no other nation can be said to have the same interest in it." Britain had claimed only a right to purchase the Indians' land, to the exclusion of all competing purchasers, and upon American independence Georgia had succeeded to that right, but not to anything more. "The interest in Georgia was nothing more than a pre-emptive right . . . nothing more than a power to acquire a fee-simple by purchase." And even that right had been ceded by Georgia to the United States upon ratification of the Constitution. The Indians owned their land in fee simple, the United States had the sole power to buy it, and all Georgia possessed was the possibility of granting it to settlers in the future.[26]

But William Johnson's was a lone voice in *Fletcher v. Peck*. In two sentences tacked on to the end of an opinion addressing other issues, the rest of the Supreme Court had embraced the newer view of Indian property rights. Over the last decade of the eighteenth century and the first decade of the nineteenth, Indian ownership had turned into occupancy.

The lower courts quickly fell into line. In 1813 the question of Indian ownership came before the Pennsylvania Supreme Court, in a dispute over land that Pennsylvania had granted to two different people. James Johnston traced his title to a grant from Pennsylvania in 1773, before the land had been purchased from the Indians. John Thompson claimed the land by virtue of a grant in 1785, after the land had been purchased from the Indians. A decade or two earlier, the case might have been easily decided in Thompson's favor, on the ground that the 1773 grant was void, because in 1773 Pennsylvania was not yet the owner of the land. That ground was unavailable, however, after *Fletcher v. Peck*. Thompson ended up the winner, as it happened, but for a different reason. Pennsylvania was indeed the fee simple owner of the land in 1773, Chief Justice William Tilghman and Justice Hugh Henry Brackenridge declared. The Indians had never owned it. "From the first discovery of the continents or islands of America," Brackenridge explained, incorrectly, "these Aborigines were not considered as having any right, not being Christians, but mere heathens and unworthy of the earth." But as a matter of Pennsylvania colonial law, the court reasoned, the colony's proprietors had established the policy (except in this instance, evidently) of granting no land before purchasing the Indian title. The 1773 grant was invalid, but the court nevertheless affirmed that unpurchased Indian land in Pennsylvania was owned by Pennsylvania rather than the Indians.[27]

The point was made in several cases in the following decade. In an 1815 Supreme Court case involving a dispute over property in Tennessee, John Marshall asked one of the lawyers: "Does the question arise in this case whether a grant is good before extinguishment of the Indian title?" When the lawyer assured Marshall the question did not arise, Justice Joseph Story chimed in. "That question," he pointed out, "has been decided in the case of *Fletcher v. Peck*." Two years later, while riding circuit in Massachusetts, Story decided a case involving some of the same land that had been at issue in *Fletcher v. Peck*. He cited *Fletcher* for the proposition that states were fee simple owners of land not yet purchased from the Indians, and that states had the power to convey that land to others with the Indians still on it. Justice Bushrod Washington, riding circuit in Pennsylvania, instructed a jury along the same lines.

Paraphrases of the last two sentences of *Fletcher* began appearing in the arguments of counsel, in cases involving the legitimacy of a grant of Indian land.[28]

Not everyone agreed, and among the dissidents were some distinguished lawyers. Only a few months after *Fletcher* was decided, James Kent, then the chief justice of the New York Supreme Court, declared it "a fact too notorious to admit of discussion or to require proof, that the Oneida Indians still reside . . . upon lands which they have never alienated, but hold and enjoy as the original proprietors of the soil." Kent admitted that his affirmation of Indian property rights had no bearing on the case he was deciding, which had to do with the validity of a sale that was clearly forbidden by a state statute regardless of the nature of Indian landownership. His statement is comprehensible only as a way of registering his disagreement with *Fletcher v. Peck*. Philip Barbour would later be a justice of the U.S. Supreme Court, but he was still a congressman from Virginia in 1819 when he defended Indian landownership on the floor of the House of Representatives. "The Indians were the aborigines of this land: they were its proprietors," he argued, in the course of attacking the punitive Treaty of Fort Jackson, in which the Creeks were forced to cede a vast amount of land in Georgia and Alabama as retribution for siding with Britain in the War of 1812.[29]

Even Attorney General William Wirt, asked in 1821 to opine on the legality of a proposed survey of land occupied by the Senecas, insisted that a survey would be illegal because Senecas were the land's owners. "So long as a tribe exists and remains in possession of its lands, its title and possession are sovereign and exclusive," Wirt instructed. Indian tribes "do not hold under the States, nor under the United States; their title is original."[30] Wirt would later become an advocate for Indian tribes in some celebrated cases, when he was no longer in office. The opinion on the Seneca lands he produced as attorney general was carefully worded, to state the case for Indian ownership as strongly as possible without saying anything explicitly inconsistent with *Fletcher*. But expressions like those of Kent, Barbour, and Wirt were unusual in the years following *Fletcher*. An opinion of the United States Supreme Court simply could not be disregarded.

Indeed, the view that Indians had only a right of occupancy in their unpurchased land—that the land was owned instead by the government—seems to have become commonplace in the 1810s and early 1820s, even among nonlawyers. Hugh Montgomery was a marginally literate employee of the state of Georgia, who reported on frontier conditions to Governor William Rabun in 1817. He observed some settlers renting land from the Indians, and knew enough to question the lawfulness of the practice. "My own impressions," he explained, "are that Indians have not a principle tittle to any Lands, that theirs is a mere occupant claim, that they are tenants at the will of the Government." Jedidiah Morse was a New England minister commissioned by the federal government to visit several western tribes in 1820 and report on what they were like. He knew enough law to recognize that "the *complete* title to their lands, rests in the government," and that the Indians had only "the *occupancy* of their lands." The point was made in popular magazine articles of the early 1820s—as one article put it, "that barbarous tribes have but a partial and imperfect right in the soil."[31]

Again, the view was not unanimously held. In 1819 the missionary John Heckewelder published the Indians' side of the story, an account in which land originally belonging to the Indians had been seized through repeated acts of fraud and force. Some reviewers accepted as true the implied critique of *Fletcher v. Peck*.[32] But this appears to have been a minority view by the early 1820s. Inside and outside the legal system, the Indians seem generally to have been understood to possess a right of occupancy short of full ownership. Their land was owned instead by the government. In the past twenty years there had been a tremendous change in conventional thought.

Johnson v. M'Intosh

For nearly two centuries now, lawyers have understood *Johnson v. M'Intosh* as the source of the foundational principle of American property law—that some government, whether state or federal, is at the root of all land titles in the United States, because the original fee simple owner of all the country's land was the government, not the Indians. That principle was already the conventional wisdom among American lawyers by 1823, when the Supreme Court decided *Johnson*. *Johnson* was the Court's first detailed discussion of the subject, however, so it is *Johnson*, rather than *Fletcher v. Peck* or any of the earlier state cases, that is remembered as the origin of the right of occupancy.

John Marshall's opinion for the Court claimed that the Indian right of occupancy had been part of English law since the earliest days of colonization. That claim was generally accepted as true by lawyers at the time and has continued to be so accepted by lawyers and historians ever since. Marshall's claim, however, was not true. The idea that the Indians possessed only a right of occupancy in their unsold land was a concept that was only three decades old in 1823. English colonial law had included no such concept, nor had American law before the 1790s. Unsold Indian land had once been thought to be owned by the Indians. But in *Johnson v. M'Intosh*, the Supreme Court put the final nail in the coffin of the older view of Indian property rights.

Johnson v. M'Intosh was a suit brought by a consortium of land speculators in an attempt to establish the validity of two enormous late-colonial purchases of Indian land.[33] In 1773, William Murray, acting on behalf of the Illinois Company, bought two tracts in present-day central and southern Illinois from a delegation of the Kaskaskia, Peoria, and Cahokia bands. In 1775, Murray, this time for the Wabash Company, employed Louis Viviat to buy from the Piankashaws two more tracts straddling the present-day border of Illinois and Indiana. Each of the four tracts was huge and imprecisely defined; together they amounted to several thousand square miles of land. The litigation was collusive, just like *Fletcher v. Peck*. The speculators' nominal opponent was an Illinois resident who was alleged to own a parcel within one of the Wabash tracts, which he purchased from the federal government, which in turn had bought much of the same land from the same tribes in the first decade of the nineteenth century.

The companies' purchases were clearly unlawful when they were made, because the Proclamation of 1763 prohibited private land purchasing. Land speculators remained active even after the proclamation, however, because they were gambling that the proclamation would eventually be repealed or modified, and that their purchases would eventually be confirmed retroactively by the government. In the mid-1770s, as conflict intensified between Britain and the colonies, the prospect of freedom from the proclamation loomed even larger, which made unlawful land purchasing even more attractive. When independence came only a year after his second land purchase, and sovereignty over the four tracts shifted from Britain to Virginia, Murray and his colleagues must have thought their gamble was about to pay off.

If so, they were wrong. Virginia reinstated the ban on private land purchasing, and when Virginia ceded the Northwest Territory to the United States, the federal government likewise prohibited private purchasing. The land claim of the United Illinois and Wabash Company (the companies merged in 1779) was no stronger after independence than before. But if the company's likelihood of success was very small, its potential gain was immense, and that was enough to spur the company on to decades of unsuccessful petitioning and lobbying, first in Virginia and then before Congress, seeking to have its purchases recognized. After repeated failure in Congress, the company switched to the only possible alternative forum, the Supreme Court. *Johnson v. M'Intosh* was the company's last-ditch effort to find a more receptive audience for its claim.

Johnson could have been a very easy case, decided in a very short opinion. The company's purchases were obviously void under any relevant law—whether that of Britain, Virginia, or the United States—regardless of the nature of Indian property rights. Even if the Indians were deemed the fee simple owners of their unsold land, the purchases would still have been unlawful. Rather than decide the case quickly and easily, however, John Marshall embarked on an extended discussion of the history of the colonization of North America, and a detailed elaboration of Indian property rights. None of it was necessary to dispose of the claims of the United Illinois and Wabash Company.

Marshall's expansion of *Johnson v. M'Intosh* into a treatise on Indian property rights has been a long-standing puzzle for commentators,[34] but when *Johnson* is placed in the context of the legal disputes that preceded it, the reason becomes clear. Marshall must have had an eye on all the cases involving the validity of state grants of preemption rights. By the early 1820s, states had been granting preemption rights—the right to own particular parcels of unsold Indian land once they had been purchased from the Indians—to settlers and to speculators for forty years. Preemption rights circulated in a thriving market. Whether the states had the authority to grant land still occupied by Indians, however, had been doubted by some prominent lawyers and had been challenged in lower courts. Did the recipient of a grant of unsold Indian land acquire fee simple ownership of the land, subject to an Indian right of occupancy? Or did the recipient of such a grant acquire only a right to become the fee simple owner in the future, once the *Indians'* fee simple title had been purchased by the government? The law had been moving from the latter to the former, but the Supreme Court had addressed the question only in the most cursory manner, in the final sentence of Marshall's majority opinion in *Fletcher v. Peck*, a sentence that had been sharply criticized by William Johnson in dissent. There was still some room, even if not a lot, for the argument that the Indians, not the government, were the fee simple owners of their unsold land. And if that argument were to prevail, thousands of land titles in the west would suddenly be thrown into question, and many westerners would be plunged into bankruptcy. In countless ordinary real estate transactions over the past forty years, settlers and speculators had understood themselves to be acquiring fee simple title to land occupied by Indians. Most of them probably did not realize that their claims to landownership rested on a legal foundation that was not yet entirely secure. The Supreme Court would be doing them a service if it could unambiguously declare them the fee simple owners of their land.

John Marshall was well aware of the issue. Like other wealthy Virginians, he was a speculator in western land himself. The very first reported American case on the lawfulness of preemption rights, *Marshall v. Clark*, had been litigated by his father. In *Fletcher v. Peck*, he had recognized the significance of the question to western land titles. And the issue was most likely near the front of John Marshall's mind in the early 1820s, because it was relevant to an ongoing conflict between Virginia and Kentucky over which state had the power to grant certain land recently obtained from the Chickasaws. *Johnson v. M'Intosh* came to the Court as a case about the validity of private land purchases from the Indians, but Marshall turned it into a case about an issue that he knew was much more important—the validity of state grants of land that had *not* been purchased from the Indians.[35]

Marshall thus wrote the Court's opinion as if the issue to be decided was whether American law recognized the Indians as the owners of their unsold land. In the early nineteenth century the justices did not circulate drafts of opinions to one another before publication, as they do today, so the other members of the Court had no occasion to agree or disagree with Marshall's decision to expand *Johnson v. M'Intosh* beyond the validity of the purchases of the United Illinois and Wabash Company. Marshall thus had more freedom to shape the opinion than a Supreme Court justice would have today.

To arrive at the conclusion that the Indians had merely a right of occupancy, Marshall pulled together several strands of early nineteenth-century legal thought, some old and some of relatively recent invention. He began with some historical propositions. The first was that during the era of European colonization, the European countries had in practice tacitly agreed to a principle for dividing the western hemisphere among them. The principle, as Marshall characterized it, was that the "discovery" of a particular area gave the discovering nation certain rights to that area, exclusive of all other European nations. It would have been more accurate to state the prerequisite as discovery *and settlement*—most English commentators of the colonial era had agreed that discovery without settlement was not enough to prevent colonists of another nation from settling—but otherwise Marshall was right. The English, for example, had in the seventeenth century been conscious of earlier Spanish and French settlements, and although there was no easy way to determine boundaries of the territory claimed by right of discovery and settlement, the English had generally tried to plant colonies in areas not already claimed by Spain or France.

What were these rights that were acquired by discovery? One was "the sole right of acquiring the soil from the natives, and establishing settlements upon it." Here Marshall was on solid ground. If purchasers representing the government of France, say, had purported to acquire Indian land within the boundaries of a British colony in North America, the British government would not have recognized the transaction as valid, and such an attempt might even have been an occasion for war. There was some ambiguity in Marshall's formulation of this exclusive right to purchase. He described it as belonging to "the nation making the discovery," which was accurate if he meant *colonists acting under the sovereignty of* the nation making the discovery, but inaccurate if he meant *the government of* the nation making the discovery (because there were many private purchases of Indian land before 1763), or even *colonists from* the nation making the discovery (because some of the British colonies were quite multicultural, and some of the colonists buying land from the Indians had come from European countries other than Britain). But the general point was accurate: each European nation claimed the right, exclusive of other European nations, to acquire land from the Indians within the boundaries of its colonies.

And then Marshall took the step for which *Johnson v. M'Intosh* is famous, the step that was necessary to secure the titles of all the western settlers who had obtained land grants from states within areas not yet purchased from the Indians. Also among the rights acquired by discovery, Marshall asserted, was the "ultimate dominion" of the land, the "power to grant the soil, while yet in possession of the natives." The Indians "were admitted to be the rightful occupants of the soil, with a legal as well as just claim to retain possession of it," he explained, but they were not the land's owners. Ownership was instead vested in the European nation by right of discovery, and when European nations granted land to settlers, the settlers became the owners. "These grants have been understood by all," Marshall reasoned, "to convey a title to the grantees, subject only to the Indian right of occupancy."

With these sentences, Marshall firmed up thousands of western land titles and put the Supreme Court's stamp of approval on the transformation in legal thought that had taken place over the preceding three decades. In the American legal culture as of 1823, Marshall's conclusions were not surprising. Most American lawyers by 1823 probably thought the Indians had only a right of occupancy, and that the states had the power to grant fee simple titles in land the Indians had never sold. It could not have helped the Indians that in *Johnson v. M'Intosh* the case for Indian ownership was being made by a group of land speculators defending purchases that were obviously illegal. But even if the plaintiffs had been a more sympathetic group with a stronger claim, Marshall's reasoning would probably have been just the same.

The crux of Marshall's opinion rested on a historical assertion: that in British North America the Indians had been accorded only a right of occupancy. But this assertion was flat wrong. During the colonial period the government had not granted land before it had been purchased from the Indians. A purchase from the Indians was in practice a *prerequisite* for a land grant. The British government "have always made an Indian Purchase the Basis or Foundation of all Grants," declared the Indian Superintendent William Johnson toward the end of the colonial period.[36] The practice of granting land before it had been purchased from the Indians originated only after independence. Colonial writers used the same words to describe Indian ownership as they used to describe European ownership. The Indians were the "owners," or the "proprietors," or the "possessors" of their land, just like Europeans. The right of occupancy was born only after independence. Yet the conventional legal understanding of Indian property rights had changed so decisively between the 1770s and the 1820s that Marshall could apparently sincerely believe that nothing had changed, and his contemporaries could sincerely agree.

The longest part of *Johnson v. M'Intosh* was Marshall's effort to support his historical claims with a survey of British colonial land policy, which he took almost entirely from his own history of the American colonies, published in 1804 as the first volume of his five-volume biography of

George Washington, a book that was in turn copied from earlier colonial histories of uneven reliability. The subject was on Marshall's mind when he wrote his opinion in *Johnson,* because Marshall was in the midst of preparing a new edition of this volume, which he would publish the following year as a freestanding *History of the American Colonies,* separate from the Washington biography.[37] To support the assertion that the British had considered themselves the owners of the Indians' unsold land, Marshall discussed several of the colonial charters, which did indeed "purport to convey the soil as well as the right of dominion to the grantees," as Marshall argued. But actual colonial land policy looked very different from the charters, which were drafted in England before colonial settlement took place, before local conditions could have any effect on practice. The rules that in fact governed colonial land acquisition were not taken from the charters, and indeed contradicted the charters. Like most other lawyers of his generation, Marshall appears not to have known this. It is not that Marshall favored a legal fiction embodied in the charters over the reality of the law as it was implemented in the colonies, but rather that he mistook the fiction for the reality.

Having established to his satisfaction that Britain had claimed the right "to appropriate the lands occupied by the Indians," only one question remained: "Have the American states rejected or adopted this principle?" The states did, of course, begin granting unsold Indian land after independence. Marshall, who was intimately familiar with Virginia's western land grants, recounted how the state opened a land office to sell off the area that later became Kentucky, "a country, every acre of which was then claimed and possessed by Indians." But such grants of unsold Indian land were a *change* from colonial practice, not a continuation of it. Having set forth a wrong account of British land policy, Marshall wrongly concluded that recent American practice was nothing new.

Accordingly, Marshall reasoned, the states had the right to grant fee simple titles to parcels not yet purchased from the Indians. The government owned the Indians' land; the Indians had only the right to occupy it. Marshall had accomplished what seems to have been his goal, to provide firm support for all the existing western land titles acquired in this manner.

He then went on to justify this conclusion, in what are today the most frequently quoted passages from the opinion. The justification came about indirectly, after Marshall insisted that the justice of the rule was none of the Court's business. "We will not enter into the controversy, whether agriculturalists, merchants, and manufacturers, have a right, on abstract principles, to expel hunters from the territory they possess," Marshall began. "Conquest gives a title which the Courts of the conqueror cannot deny, whatever the private and speculative opinions of individuals may be, respecting the original justice of the claim." Two important and related ambiguities lurk in that last sentence.

First, Marshall here slipped from *discovery* to *conquest* as the root of land title. Up to this point the opinion had said nothing about any right of conquest, or any consequences that flow from conquest. It had all been about discovery, and about *purchasing* the Indians' right of occupancy, not seizing it by force. The opinion made no effort to assert that the British claimed a right of conquest during the colonial era, or that the United States claimed such a right. The latter assertion would have instantly been recognized as implausible by contemporary lawyers, who were familiar with the federal government's practice of purchasing the Indians' interest in their land, even if what the government was buying was only a right of occupancy. Conquest was even less accurate than discovery as a theory denying the Indians ownership of their land. It is not clear why Marshall made this switch. He does not appear to have favored a policy of conquest or to have desired to encourage the federal government to begin conquering Indian tribes. In some of his later opinions Marshall would betray considerable sympathy for the Indians, at least by the standards of his day. Substituting conquest for discovery had no discernible implications for the status of the western land titles Marshall sought to solidify. Those titles would have been equally secure under either formulation. The switch could not have been a mere slip of the pen, because the rest of the opinion (there were still seventeen pages more) speaks of conquest rather than discovery. It must have been a deliberate change on Marshall's part.

The only conceivable explanation lies in the other ambiguity contained in Marshall's observation that "conquest gives a title which the Courts of the conqueror cannot deny." Marshall never specifies *why* courts cannot inquire into the legitimacy of titles obtained by conquest, but he most likely meant that there were certain kinds of disputes resolvable only by war (or perhaps by conflict generally, whether military or political), and that courts lack any capacity or authority to decide such disputes. He seems to have been stating an early version of what modern lawyers would call the "political question" doctrine, an amorphous, self-imposed limitation on the jurisdiction of courts to interfere in political disputes. This sort of restraint was useful to Marshall in *Johnson v. M'Intosh*, because it allowed him to disclaim any personal responsibility for a decision that he seems to have found a little distasteful. It was not his fault, after all, that colonization gave Britain the title to all the Indians' land. "It is not for the Courts of this country to question the validity of this title," he repeated, "or to sustain one which is incompatible with it."

The shift from discovery to conquest helped Marshall characterize the issue as one in which courts were powerless to intervene. If *discovery* conferred title, it was through a peaceful process that happened automatically, by operation of law, when a given area was discovered. The colonists and Indians might not even know title was passing, because the passage required no human agency. It was the law, not any human beings, that did the work. And if the government's title rested on law, courts would have the authority—indeed, the responsibility—to decide what the law was. If *conquest* conferred title, by contrast, it was through violent conflict. A court would have no more authority to second-guess the passage of title than it would to second-guess the outcome of a war. The implications of conquest were brute facts that had to be taken as true, while the implications of discovery were legal conclusions that could be evaluated and found wanting. If Marshall wanted to avoid responsibility for the outcome of *Johnson*, it was convenient to slip from discovery to conquest as the basis for the opinion.

Even so, this explanation is not entirely satisfying. Marshall may have sympathized with the Indians, but he probably sympathized even more with the settlers and speculators who had been granted parcels of unsold Indian land, a group that included himself, his family, and his friends.[38] It is not obvious that Marshall would have wanted to disclaim responsibility for the decision, or that he would have perceived any personal advantage in using the doctrine of conquest as a shield. He would have found it much more attractive to deny responsibility for the opposite kind of decision, a decision with the effect of *un*settling western land titles. And in any event, after going through all this effort to deny the Court any role in justifying its conclusions, Marshall went ahead and did exactly what he said was beyond the Court's authority. He offered a theory to justify why discovery or conquest *should* divest the Indians of their land.

The principles set forth in the opinion, Marshall suggested, "find some excuse, if not justification, in the character and habits of the people whose rights have been wrested from them." Marshall drew on the early nineteenth-century's conventional juxtaposition of European farmers and nomadic Indian hunters. "The tribes of Indians inhabiting this country" when Europeans arrived, Marshall asserted, "were fierce savages, whose occupation was war, and whose subsistence was drawn chiefly from the forest. To leave them in possession of their country, was to leave the country a wilderness." Europeans needed land, and the only way to get it from such a warlike people was to fight. "The Europeans were under the necessity either of abandoning the country, and relinquishing their pompous claims to it," Marshall reasoned, "or of enforcing those claims by the sword." The result was "frequent and bloody wars," in which "European policy, numbers, and skill, prevailed. As the white population advanced, that of the Indians necessarily receded." At the end of all this fighting, the Indians withdrew deeper into the forests, and the Europeans gained the land.

This was a wildly inaccurate account of colonial land acquisition. There had been fighting between settlers and Indians, to be sure, but before the Revolution the British did not conceive of these conflicts as wars of conquest, and the total amount of land gained by fighting was almost certainly far less than the amount of land acquired by purchase. Again, however, Marshall seems to have been motivated primarily by the desire to convey the impression that the Court had been constrained by events. "However extravagant the pretension of converting the discovery of an inhabited country into conquest may appear," he explained, "if the principle has been asserted in the first instance, and afterwards sustained; if a country has been acquired and held under it; if the property of the great mass of the community originates in it, it becomes the law of the land, and cannot be questioned." As a factual matter, of course, the country had *not* been acquired and held under any such principle. If anyone was guilty of "converting the discovery of an inhabited country into conquest," it was John Marshall in *Johnson v. M'Intosh*, not the British colonists or their government.

Marshall finished by addressing the remaining arguments in the case, including the claim of the United Illinois and Wabash Company to its purchases, the issue the case was actually about but which Marshall had so far neglected to discuss. These, however, were only applications of the general principles that had already been set forth: The state governments and the federal government, as successors to Britain, were the original owners of all the land in the United States. This was either because the British had discovered North America, the theory of the first half of the opinion, or because the British had conquered North America, the theory of the second half. Either way, the Indians had only a right of occupancy in the land they had not sold.

William Johnson was still on the Court, but he did not dissent as he had in *Fletcher v. Peck*, perhaps because he realized that the battle had been lost. There was no longer any point in sticking up for the older view of Indian property rights. Marshall was careful to repeat the assurances he had provided to Johnson in *Fletcher*, that the right of occupancy was substantial enough to prevent the Indians from being kicked off their land. He analogized the right of occupancy to "a lease for years" and suggested that it "might as effectually bar an ejectment." The actual strength of the Indians' right of occupancy would vary in later years, both in the Court's pronouncements and in actual practice. Fee simple ownership was an established legal concept with a well-accepted meaning, but the right of occupancy was something new and not fully defined. Its precise meaning and the implications of the theory of conquest would be disputed for years to come, and indeed are still disputed today.

The practical consequences of *Johnson v. M'Intosh* would have been hard to predict in 1823, because they would depend on the outcomes of those disputes. But after *Johnson v. M'Intosh*, the transformation in legal thought that had begun in the 1790s was complete. Ownership had been turned into occupancy.

A Well Known Fact

The second quarter of the nineteenth century was the golden age of American legal treatises, and *Johnson v. M'Intosh* quickly assumed a prominent place in them, as the authoritative statement of the foundations of American property law. James Kent's *Commentaries on American Law*, first published in the late 1820s and then again in many more editions over the rest of the century, included a lengthy summary of *Johnson*. Joseph Story, a member of the Court that decided *Johnson*, opened his 1833 *Commentaries on the Constitution* with a summary of Marshall's opinion. The right of occupancy became a "well known fact," as a committee of the House of Representatives put it in 1827, a fact that would be restated in every discussion of Indian land.[39] Amplified by repetition, *Johnson v. M'Intosh* became part of the canon of celebrated cases that all learned lawyers knew. The shift from ownership to occupancy had been virtually complete before *Johnson,* but after 1823 it would be *Johnson* that everyone remembered.

What had happened to the belief, shared by Anglo-American lawyers and government officials from the late seventeenth to the late eighteenth century, that the Indians were the owners of their land? It was not entirely gone. William Wirt thought the doctrine of *Johnson v. M'Intosh* "the strangest absurdity. It is said they have no other title [to their lands] than that of having chased their game over them," he pointed out. "And yet, we contend that an English, Spanish or French ship, having sailed along the coast, or entered the mouth of a river, gains a complete title by discovery to the sovereign of the navigator—not only to the coast seen, but to the unseen interior." The English traveler Calvin Colton found *Johnson* "an unatoneable outrage." As for what the Indians themselves thought about *Johnson v. M'Intosh,* the reaction of the Creeks was no doubt representative. They knew that "we now hold our land by right of occupancy only," the Creek council informed federal officials in 1824. But they still considered themselves "the original proprietors of the soil as an inheritance left to us by our forefathers."[40]

But such dissent from *Johnson v. M'Intosh* was rare, at least among non-Indians. The idea that the Indians owned their land had taken a series of blows, which cumulatively were fatal.

First was the Proclamation of 1763, which ended the private purchasing of Indian land. When the Indians were no longer allowed to sell land to buyers of their own choosing, it became possible to think of the Indians' property rights as something short of full ownership. The percentage of Anglo-American landowners who traced their titles back to an initial private purchase from the Indians, and thus the power of the latent political force behind recognizing the Indians as owners, meanwhile began to decline irreversibly.

Second was the American Revolution, during which the imperial government, normally the Indians' ally against colonists and colonial governments, lost the ability to influence American land policy. Just as bad, most Indian tribes had the misfortune to have chosen the losing side. Many Americans came to perceive the Revolution as a war of conquest, entitling them to the Indians' land. That belief did not last long as government policy—it persisted for only a few years, and was abandoned in 1789—but it most likely lingered in popular consciousness as a certainty that the government owned all the unallocated western land.

Third was the growth of the image of the nomadic, nonfarming Indian, the sort of person who did not stay in any one place long enough to develop property rights in land. As eastern Indian communities disintegrated, and as Americans encountered nomadic western tribes, American lawyers came to conceive of Indians as John Marshall depicted them in *Johnson*, as "fierce savages, whose occupation was war, and whose subsistence was drawn chiefly from the forest."

Finally, the most important blow to Indian landownership may have been the growing practice on the part of state governments of granting identifiable parcels of land to settlers before the land had been purchased from the Indians. This was partly a product of the Revolution, as state officials in the late 1770s and early 1780s believed the state actually owned the land they were granting. It was also partly a product of federalism. The state governments had the power to grant land, but only the federal government had the power to buy it from the Indians, and the states had little ability to influence the speed at which the federal government acquired land. Under political pressure to grant western land to settlers, and unable to purchase that land from the Indians, the states continued granting it to settlers regardless of whether the Indians were still on it. As this practice grew commonplace, lawyers increasingly came to think of the Indians as tenants on the land rather than owners of it.

The result was not just the right of occupancy, but the erasure of virtually all memory that things had once been different—that under American law the Indians had once been deemed the owners of their land.

6

REMOVAL

THE word *removal* conventionally denotes a distinct era in the history of United States Indian policy, from the late 1820s through the early 1840s. As the story is usually told, during that period the federal government, at the urging of President Andrew Jackson, forced most of the remaining eastern Indians to migrate west of the Mississippi River. Between 1828 and 1838, more than eighty thousand Indians were removed from the east to the west. The enduring image of the period is the Trail of Tears —the U.S. Army's internment and forced relocation of approximately sixteen thousand Cherokees in the fall and winter of 1838–1839, under circumstances so dire that four thousand are said to have died along the route between Georgia and what is now Oklahoma.[1]

Removal has accordingly taken on sinister connotations, sinister because of the mismatch between the word's surface blandness and the cruelty of some of the events it was used to describe. After a century in which Orwellian terms like *ethnic cleansing* and *the final solution* became commonplace, the very word *removal* sounds chilling today. It evokes the idea of a newly aggressive federal government opening a new chapter in its Indian relations by forcibly pushing American Indians west of the Mississippi in order to seize their land and parcel it out to white settlers.

In light of the story thus far, however, removal looks much more like a *continuation* of earlier Indian land policy than a departure from it. Removal, just like the acquisition of Indian land for the previous two hundred years, was structured as a series of voluntary transactions. The federal government went to considerable trouble to obtain the signatures of

Indians on treaties in which the tribes ostensibly consented to be removed. Government officials of course used a variety of underhanded tactics to secure some of these treaties, but they were the very same tactics that had been used to obtain the land cessions of the preceding decades and the private land purchases of the colonial era. After ceding their land in the 1820s and 1830s, the Indians had to move to new land in the west, but Indians had been moving west after ceding their land ever since Europeans arrived in North America. If one focuses on the methods by which land was transferred and on the consequences to the Indians of ceding their land, there was little new about removal.

What *was* new was the speed of the process and the attention being paid to it. In the late 1820s, conflict between Georgia and the federal government over the pace at which the federal government was extinguishing Indian title turned Indian land policy into a major national political issue. For the first time, the details of Indian land acquisition became enmeshed in national party politics and in debates about constitutional law. In the history of American politics, it makes sense to speak of the years around 1830 as an era of removal simply because the issue of Indian land acquisition received more attention from Congress, the Supreme Court, and the public than at any time before or since. But most of the features of U.S. government policy that are conventionally thought to make up Indian removal were nothing new. If the 1830s were an era of removal, so too were the previous two centuries.

Removal, before "Removal"

Today, *remove* is virtually always a transitive verb. We usually think of removing *something* or *someone*, normally by the application of force. Before the twentieth century, however, the word had a second, intransitive sense, a meaning that has nearly disappeared today. *Remove* was almost synonymous with *move*, but it had the specific connotation of a relocation from one place to another. Macbeth, to pick a famous example, declares that he will not fear defeat "till Birnam Wood remove to Dunsinane." Benjamin Franklin entitled his 1784 essay on emigration to the United States *Information to Those Who Would Remove to America*. In Jane Austen's *Emma* (1816), Emma hears that Frank Churchill and his aunt "were going to remove immediately to Richmond," a place more suitable for them than London. In this sense of the word, the subject of the sentence was doing the removing of its own accord. It was not being compelled to remove by someone else.[2]

In the early nineteenth century, when American officials spoke of the Indians *removing* to the west, they normally had the verb's intransitive sense in mind. In 1809, near the end of his presidency, Thomas Jefferson sent a message to the Cherokees in which he expressed his pleasure to learn that some members of the tribe "are desirous to remove across the Mississippi, to some of the vacant lands of the United States." The same year, William Crawford, one of Georgia's U.S. senators, reported to Georgia governor Jared Irwin that "10 towns of the lower Cherokees, & most of 12 towns of the upper Cherokees are disposed to remove to Louisiana & settle on lands of the U.S." *Removal* simply meant *emigration*. The word lacked the overtones of force it would later acquire.[3]

By the early nineteenth century, Indian removal, in this sense of the word, had been taking place for two hundred years, ever since the arrival of European settlers. For example, in the seventeenth century the Delawares lived in the river valley that still bears their name, in what is now New Jersey and eastern Pennsylvania. Over the course of the eighteenth century, they moved across the Allegheny Mountains into western Pennsylvania. After the American Revolution, they moved into Ohio, and then Indiana.[4] The Delawares had been removing for some time before removal became a subject of national debate. So had many other tribes. With each land transaction, more Indians had removed to the west.

Before the nineteenth century, removal was more a by-product of Indian land purchases than an articulated government policy. That changed with the Louisiana Purchase. In 1803, the United States suddenly acquired sovereignty over an enormous and thinly populated territory west of the Mississippi.[5] It was immediately evident that all this new land could be doubly useful in Indian land transactions: it was an asset that could be exchanged for Indian land in the east, and it would simultaneously give selling tribes a place to go when they sold their land. In early 1804, when Congress established a territorial government over the area obtained from France, Congress accordingly authorized the president "to stipulate with any Indian tribes owning lands on the east side of the Mississippi, and residing thereon, for an exchange of lands, the property of the United States, on the west side of the Mississippi, in case the said tribes shall remove and settle thereon." The authorization was meaningless as a legal matter; even without it, the government would have had the authority to trade land with the Indians, and the authorization did not deprive the Senate of its role in ratifying whatever treaties executive officials might reach. For years, Anglo-Americans had purchased Indian land with money and goods; now they would be purchasing it with other land. But if the 1804 statute was legally unnecessary, it may have been important in a political sense, as a statement from Congress of support for Indian removal. The Senate would pass a similar resolution, again authorizing land exchanges, in 1817.[6]

For the first two decades after the Louisiana Purchase, the executive branch officials responsible for dealing with the Indians tried whenever possible to exchange western land for eastern, without much attention from Congress or the public. In 1809, a group of more than a thousand Cherokees agreed to trade their land for land in Arkansas. The War of 1812 made westward migration unattractive, but when the war was over, more Cherokees headed west. "I am daily enrolling new recruits," Tennessee governor Joseph McMinn reported in 1818. "I have enrolled upward of 300 Families since the 20th October, and it's now progressing with unabated ardor." By 1820 approximately three thousand Cherokees, or about one-sixth of the tribe, were west of the Mississippi. Members of other tribes migrated westward as well, often without formal arrangements with the government. As the House Committee on Public Lands complained in 1818, many of the Choctaws were living on land west of the Mississippi without ever having given up their land east of the Mississippi. Many of the Shawnees, Delawares, and Kickapoos moved to Missouri, and groups from the southern tribes moved to what later became Texas. Between 1817 and 1821, the federal government engaged in ten exchanges with Indian tribes of western land for eastern.[7]

By the early 1820s, despite the emigration of several thousand Indians to the west, there were still tens of thousands of Indians living east of the Mississippi. Most were in the south, because of white settlement patterns. The northern states grew in population more quickly than the southern states, so it made sense to purchase Indian land in the north first. In 1790, for example, Connecticut had a non-Indian population density more than eighty times greater than that of Georgia. The Indians of Connecticut had lost virtually all of their land, while large portions of Georgia were still possessed by Indian tribes.

It was non-Indian population growth in Georgia that pushed the issue of removal into the public spotlight. The combined white and black population of Georgia nearly doubled between 1790 and 1800, and then more than doubled again between 1800 and 1820. Georgia's congressional delegation began complaining that the federal government was moving too slowly in acquiring land from the Indians—particularly the Creeks and Cherokees, who had the most. "The Indian title to fully one-half, and probably the most valuable half, of the lands within the boundaries of the State is yet unextinguished," Thomas Cobb of Georgia complained on the floor of the House in 1820. In 1802, when Georgia had ceded its western land (which later became Alabama and Mississippi) to the federal government, the United States had promised to purchase the parts of the state still retained by the Indians, "as early as the same can be peaceably obtained on reasonable terms." Eighteen years later Cobb argued that the federal government had failed to fulfill this obligation.[8]

It had not been for want of trying. For years the federal government had been attempting to buy out the Creeks and Cherokees and relocate them to the other side of the Mississippi, but most tribe members had been just as persistent in refusing to sell. President James Monroe declared in 1824 that he favored removal as much as anyone in Georgia. "My impression is equally strong," he explained, "that it would promote essentially the security and happiness of the tribes within our limits, if they could be prevailed on to retire west and north of our States and Territories, on lands to be procured for them by the United States, in exchange for those on which they now reside." But he insisted that the government had no authority to force the Indians to move. The Indians "had a right to the territory, in the disposal of which they were to be regarded as free agents," Monroe reasoned. All the federal government could do was to offer the Indians western land in exchange for eastern, and wait for the Indians to accept.[9]

Conflict between Georgia and the federal government over the Indians would grow through the 1820s. In early 1825 the War Department estimated the Indian population of the United States; the figures testified to the depth of white Georgians' grievance. Of the approximately 129,000 Indians known to live within the then-existing boundaries of the United States, nearly 54,000 lived in Georgia, Tennessee, Alabama, and Mississippi. (The War Department could not break the figure down by state in this region, because tribal boundaries did not coincide with state lines.) Virtually all the rest lived in the western territories that had not yet been organized as states. The other states had Indian populations that were tiny by comparison. Only New York's, at more than 5,000, was significant; the others were all less than 1,000.[10] The white residents of Georgia and the other states with substantial Indian populations believed themselves to be at an unfair disadvantage compared with the white residents of other states that had already cleared out their Indians. As they perceived it, agricultural land was growing scarce and development was being bottled up, all because the federal government was unwilling to meet its obligation to extinguish the Indian title to their land.

As Georgians protested the slowness of Indian land acquisition through the early 1820s, removal in the original sense of the word—not a constitutional crisis, not a hot national political issue, but simply the Indians' cession of their land, sometimes in exchange for new land west of the Mississippi—was still proceeding at a gradual pace. The Oneidas began moving from New York to Wisconsin in the early 1820s. In 1820 the Kickapoos accepted land in Missouri in exchange for their ancestral home in Indiana and Illinois, and the Choctaws traded land in Mississippi for land in Arkansas. The Creeks ceded a slice of Georgia in 1821, and then another slice in 1826, the latter in exchange for the federal government's promise to buy land west of the Mississippi for the Creeks, land that would eventually be located in present-day Oklahoma. Other tribes were ceding land, bit by bit, all along.[11]

Apart from the federal government's use of the land west of the Mississippi as part of the purchase price, these transactions were scarcely different from Indian land sales going back a century and more. The Indians were not exactly forced to sell their land, but they did not exactly want to sell their land either. The truth, as always, was somewhere in the middle. Alexis de Tocqueville toured the United States when the removal controversy was at its height and, characteristically, he came to understand the process of land acquisition better than many Americans. In exchange for the Indians' land, Tocqueville observed, the government offered them new land in the west, as well as more traditional inducements like firearms and liquor. "If, after the sight of all these riches, they still hesitate, it is hinted that they cannot refuse to consent to what is asked of them and that soon the government itself will be powerless to guarantee them the enjoyment of their rights. What can they do? Half convinced, half constrained, the Indians go off to dwell in new wildernesses, where the white men will not let them remain in peace for ten years. In this way the Americans cheaply acquire whole provinces which the richest sovereigns in Europe could not afford to buy."[12] "Half convinced, half constrained"—such had been the standard mode of Indian land purchase for a long time before Tocqueville wrote. The Louisiana Purchase had given the federal government western land to use as a new tool for doing the convincing, but otherwise little had changed.

The 1821–1827 transactions with the Creeks were a perfect example. In 1821, the Creeks sold about half of their land in Georgia to the federal government, for $50,000, plus thirteen years of annuities adding up to another $150,000, plus up to $250,000 in Creek debts to citizens of Georgia that would be assumed by the federal government. The ink was barely dry before federal commissioners were trying to persuade the Creeks to sell the rest. Creek leaders pleaded with the federal government not to send land purchasers. The tribe was "already confined in too small bounds, taking into consideration the vast quantity of barren soil which is within the limits we occupy," Creek chiefs explained. "We deem it impolitic and contrary to the true interest of this nation to dispose of any more of our country." But the purchasers came anyway, bearing a message that was simultaneously an offer and an implicit threat. "If you wish to quit the chase," advised the federal commissioners, "to free yourself from barbarism, and settle down in the calm pursuits of civilization, and good morals, and to raise up a generation of Christians, you had better go. The aid and protection of the government will go with you." If the Creeks had any doubt as to whether they could count on the aid and protection of the government if they stayed, it was resolved a moment later. "You must be sensible that it will be impossible for you to remain for any length of time in your present situation as a distinct Society or Nations, within the limits of Georgia," the commissioners told the Creeks. "Such a community is incompatible with our System and must yield to it."[13]

The Creeks did not give in, at least not immediately. They reminded the commissioners that just a decade earlier the federal government had solemnly promised to protect them in their landholdings. They could not believe that the United States would permit any coercion to be applied to them, they explained, "nor can we believe that our father the President will act otherwise than in good faith in the strict and faithful performance of treaty stipulations."[14]

In the past, when the leadership of a tribe refused to sell the tribe's land, it had not been unusual for purchasers to bribe dissident tribe members willing to put their names on a contract as the tribe's supposed representatives. Private purchasers had done so in the colonial era, and officers of the federal government had done so as well. It was none too surprising, then, that in the 1825 Treaty of Indian Springs, a dissident group of Creeks led by William McIntosh, without informing the rest of the tribe, purported to exchange all the Creeks' remaining land in Georgia for new land in Arkansas and cash. In a clause separate from the main body of the treaty, McIntosh received a side payment of $25,000 for his trouble.[15]

The Creeks' struggle was not over, but it was nearly over. The Creeks executed McIntosh for treason and reopened negotiations with the federal government. They managed to persuade the government to annul the Treaty of Indian Springs. The new treaties signed by the tribe's true leaders in 1826 and 1827, however, only ended up reconveying to the United States the same land McIntosh had purported to sell in 1825. By 1827, the Creeks had left Georgia, most for Alabama.

Removal was thus well under way by the time it gave rise to the political crisis we remember today as removal. Before Andrew Jackson became president, before Georgia and other southern states began stepping up the pressure on the Indians to leave, the federal government was going about its normal business of purchasing the Indians' land, using the same techniques it had employed since the 1790s—bribery, implicit threats of force, and a willingness to deal with groups other than the official government of a tribe. Until the late 1820s, the process received no more attention from Congress and from the press than it ever had. Removing Indians from the eastern United States, like running the postal service or paying pensions to war veterans, was part of the low-level background hum of operating the federal government.

Removal became a prominent political issue in the late 1820s, when the Georgia legislature, frustrated with the Cherokees' refusal to sell their land to the federal government, began enacting a series of statutes designed to harass the Cherokees into leaving the state. The Cherokees were not the largest of the southern tribes, nor the tribe with the most land. The federal government counted nine thousand Cherokees east of the Mississippi in 1825, as against twenty-one thousand Choctaws and twenty thousand Creeks. The Cherokees' territory of 5.2 million acres in Georgia was dwarfed by the 15.7 million acres retained by the Choctaws and Chickasaws in Mississippi. But the Cherokees were located on fertile land, most of which was in northwestern Georgia, surrounded by areas already settled by whites. The Cherokees would nevertheless withstand the pressures to remove longer than most of the other southern tribes.[16]

The Cherokees' greater resistance to removal is most likely attributable to the fact that their land was worth more than the land of other tribes, because the Cherokees had adopted Anglo-American farming methods more thoroughly than other tribes had. If we divide the value of land into two components, one derived from agricultural productivity and the other from emotional attachments, religious beliefs, and so on, and if we assume that the latter category of value was approximately equal across tribes, we would expect that the most productive tribes would value their land the most highly and thus be the least willing to sell it at any given price. By the 1820s, many of the Cherokees had cleared their land and were farming in the Anglo-American style. They were producing cotton and other crops for the market. They owned nearly eighty thousand head of livestock. They had built permanent houses and outbuildings. Hunting was not as important as it had once been.[17] The Cherokees had, in large measure, Americanized. Their land had become more productive. As a result it was worth more, and the Cherokees were accordingly less willing than other tribes to exchange it for undeveloped land in the west.

Would-be federal land purchasers tried the same combination of enticements and threats they had used on the Creeks and other tribes, but these tactics did not work with the Cherokees. United States commissioners offered land in the west. They emphasized that the Cherokees were dependent upon the federal government for protection. In 1824, Secretary of War John Calhoun even explicitly threatened to leave the Cherokees "exposed to the discontent of Georgia and the pressure of her citizens" if the tribe continued to refuse to exchange its land in Georgia for land west of the Mississippi. The Cherokees responded to each communication with statements of refusal that rested on a full understanding of their legal rights. "Sir," a Cherokee delegation addressed Calhoun after the threat to abandon them to the government and white residents of Georgia, "to these remarks we beg leave to observe, and to remind you, that the Cherokees are not foreigners, but original inhabitants of America; and that they now inhabit and stand on the soil of their own territory; and that the limits of their territory are defined by the treaties which they have made with the Government of the United

States; and that the States by which they are now surrounded have been created out of lands which were once theirs; and that they cannot recognise the sovereignty of any State within the limits of their territory." Despite years of offers and threats from the federal government, the Cherokees consistently refused to leave.[18]

By the end of 1826 the Georgia legislature had had enough. "The extinguishment of the Indian title to all the lands within the limits of Georgia is a matter of not only constant, but urgent expediency," the state legislature resolved. The legislature declared that it rejected the power of the federal government to prevent Georgia from doing what it liked to the Indians within its borders. "Georgia owns exclusively the soil and jurisdiction of all the territory within her present chartered and conventional limits," the legislature resolved, "and, with the exception of the right to regulate commerce among the Indian tribes, claims the right to exercise, over any people white or red within those limits, the authority of her laws."[19] The exception for commerce was a necessary concession to the United States Constitution, which explicitly conferred power over commerce to Congress, but it was an unprecedentedly narrow reading of the Constitution, which had always been understood to give the federal government virtually total authority over Indian affairs, particularly where necessary to protect the Indians' unsold land from encroachment by settlers encouraged by state governments. In this context, the Georgia legislature's assertion of complete control over Indian affairs was a threat to strip the Indians of accustomed rights.

The legislature soon followed through on the threat. It barred Indians from testifying in court and from entering the non-Indian parts of Georgia without a permit. It assigned the Cherokees' land to various Georgia counties, a move that had the effect of subjecting the Cherokees to state law, much of which, like the denial to nonwhites of the right to vote, was discriminatory. In late 1827 the legislature resolved that all the land in Georgia "belong to her absolutely; that the title is in her; that the Indians are tenants at her will, and that she may at any time she pleases, determine [i.e., terminate] that tenancy, by taking possession of the premises." The statute did not actually authorize anyone to take the Cherokees' land. Its obvious purpose was rather to force the Cherokees to the bargaining table, by sending the message that if the Cherokees refused to sell their land the state would simply seize it. When the Cherokees refused to give in, the legislature upped the ante. In 1828 it declared all Cherokee laws void and explicitly subjected the Cherokees to the law of Georgia. In 1830, after gold had been discovered in the Cherokees' territory, the legislature passed a statute authorizing the governor to take possession of all gold, silver, and other mines on the Cherokees' land, on the ground that the mines "are of right the property of Georgia." Two and a half weeks later the legislature authorized the seizure of *all* the Cherokees' land, and the distribution of that land to white settlers. As a final insult, the legislature made it illegal for the Cherokees to assemble for any purpose, specifically including that of passing legislation, and then the legislature voided all contracts entered into by Cherokees.[20]

These statutes sparked a national debate that would not be resolved for several years. Did Georgia have the authority to take these actions? Did the federal government have the responsibility to protect the Cherokees from Georgia? Did it even have the authority to do so? Indian removal was no longer just a matter of Indians and land; now it was a constitutional crisis too. A process that had been proceeding slowly and quietly offstage for some time suddenly moved into the spotlight. By the late 1820s, there was a vigorous national debate—not just about the relative power of Georgia and the federal government, but also over whether, and how, the Indians should be relocated west of the Mississippi.

White Opinion

There were really two debates about Indian removal in the late 1820s and early 1830s. They were sometimes conflated by participants, but it will be useful to treat them separately because their outcomes were different. One was a *legal* debate, over whether the government had the right to *force* the Indians to exchange their land for land in the west. The Indians won this debate. As a legal matter, it was generally accepted within the federal government and among lawyers that removal could be accomplished only by treaty. The other debate was over the *wisdom* of removal. What would be best for the eastern Indians: remaining where they were or moving west? This was a question on which Indians as well as whites were divided. Some concluded that they would be better off removing, while others determined to stay in place. Given the relative power of the two groups, it was white opinion that mattered, and in the end, after years of argument, the pro-removal position would prevail.

The result was an uneasy combination of conclusions—that removal was in the best interests of the Indians, but that it could be lawfully accomplished only if the Indians consented. This tension gave rise to the actual circumstances of removal. Southern state governments (and eventually the federal government) would gradually ratchet up the pressure on the tribes to sell, until it reached a point best described as extortion. The *form* of Indian consent would always be present, but the substance would disappear.

Given the long history of Indian land acquisition in North America, the outcome of the legal debate was unsurprising. But new legal theories always spring from strongly desired political consequences, and the new theories justifying forced removal were no exception.

Proponents of forced removal made two legal arguments, both of which were ahead of their time. One was articulated by the lawyer-turned-soldier Andrew Jackson as early as 1817, while he was fighting the Seminoles in Florida. "The wisdom of the Government has wisely provided, that the property of a Citizen can be taken for public use, on just compensation being made," Jackson pointed out, correctly, in a letter to the new president, James Monroe. This power of eminent domain was enshrined in the Fifth Amendment to the Constitution, which Jackson was paraphrasing in his letter. Why, Jackson wondered, shouldn't the same principle apply to the Indians? If the government could take a white person's land against his wishes, so long as the taking was for public use and just compensation was provided, why couldn't the government take the Indians' land by the same method? Surely, Jackson reasoned, the requirement of a public use would be satisfied "whenever the safety, interest, or defence of the country should render it necessary for the Government of the United States to occupy and possess any part of the Territory." Why then, Jackson asked, did the federal government insist on obtaining the Indians' consent? Why did it treat the Indians with more solicitude than it treated its own citizens?[21]

The answer to Jackson's question rested partly on history and partly on then-current law. For two hundred years, Anglo-American governments had normally obtained Indian land by contract, never by exercising the power of eminent domain. That principle had originated at a time when English settlers lacked the power to acquire the Indians' land without the Indians' consent, and when the Indians' unsold land was understood to be beyond the effective control of any European government. As Jackson's letter underscored, however, both of those conditions had changed. The federal government was strong enough to take at least some Indian land by eminent domain, and the land in question no longer seemed so far away—now some of it comprised islands of Indian territory within a sea of white-owned land. The historical rationale for the government's reluctance to take Indian land by eminent domain was growing weaker with the passage of time.

American lawyers of the era would have had two more objections to Jackson's suggestion, objections grounded not in history but in early nineteenth-century American law. Indian tribes were sovereign entities of a sort. Exactly what that sovereignty entailed was in dispute, but all agreed that Indian tribes had always governed themselves internally by their own laws. The United States had always respected that sovereignty by negotiating treaties with Indian tribes rather than regulating them directly. Most lawyers would accordingly have been more hesitant than Jackson to suggest that the federal government's power of eminent domain extended to the Indians' land. They would most likely have deemed the United States no more capable of taking Indian land than of taking land in Canada—both areas would have been understood to lie within the sovereignty of an entity other than the United States. Jackson was sharp enough to realize this. He knew he had to supplement his argument with the claim that the federal government was wrong to treat Indian tribes like sovereign states. "The Indians are subjects of the United States, inhabiting its territory and acknowledging its sovereignty," he argued to Monroe. "Then is it not absurd for the sovereign to negotiate by treaty with the subject[?]" On this point Jackson was ahead of his time. Later in the century, the law would catch up with him: Congress would put an end to the practice of holding treaties with Indian tribes and would begin regulating the tribes directly. In 1817, however, the tradition of obtaining land by treaty was too strong to dislodge.

Most lawyers would also have objected to Jackson's expansive reading of the "public use" requirement of the Fifth Amendment. Taking land from the Indians in order to build a highway, or a fort, or some such public project, might amount to a public use, they would have argued. But taking land from the Indians in order to distribute it to white farmers would not be a public use, most early nineteenth-century lawyers would probably have concluded; it would be merely the expropriation from one group of people for the benefit of another, a redistribution of wealth understood in the early nineteenth century to lie beyond the government's power of eminent domain. Here too Jackson was ahead of his time. In the twentieth century, as government became more explicitly redistributive, the conventional understanding of the public use requirement broadened, to include the redistribution of property from one group to another, so long as it was backed by a plausible public-spirited motive. In 1817, however, most lawyers would have considered Jackson's plan too much a private transfer to be within the government's power of eminent domain.

James Monroe was a lawyer too, but his response to Jackson revealed none of these doubts. "The view which you have taken of the Indian title to lands is new but very deserving of attention," Monroe began. "It has been customary to purchase the title of the Indian tribes," he recognized, but he agreed that the custom deserved rethinking, in light of what he saw as the Indians' misguided determination to retain their land and their traditional ways of life, a stubbornness that was only driving them to extinction. "A compulsory process seems to be necessary, to break their habits, & to civilize them, & there is much cause to believe, that it must be resorted to, to preserve them." If this was Monroe's private view, his public pronouncements adhered to the tradition of acquiring Indian land only with the Indians' consent. In his first annual message to Congress as president, delivered two months after he responded to Jackson, Monroe emphasized the twin goals of civilizing the Indians and obtaining the land east of the Mississippi they still retained. But he also emphasized the need to *purchase* the land. Throughout his administration, Monroe continued to resist demands from Georgians and others that the Indians' land be taken without their consent.[22]

Whatever Monroe's true preferences were, the idea that the Indians' land could be taken by eminent domain was never put into practice, even when Andrew Jackson became president, and it seems never to have gained much support. Most white Americans probably agreed that the land could be put to better use by white farmers, but the notion of seizing it, even with compensation to the Indians, seemed too extravagant. As an anonymous contributor to the *North American Review* put it at the height of the removal controversy, "the United States would contend with a very ill grace for the doctrine, that unsettled lands may be seized by those, who need them for the purposes of cultivation." The doctrine had some troubling implications, because the federal government itself owned a vast amount of unproductive land. "How many millions of the people of France, Germany and Ireland might appropriate to themselves good farms in the States of Indiana, Illinois and Missouri?

Why should they not take immediate possession?"[23] The Indians and their supporters won this branch of the legal argument.

Advocates of forced removal had a second legal argument, one that was voiced more often. After the Supreme Court's decisions in *Fletcher v. Peck* and *Johnson v. M'Intosh*, there was no doubt that state governments were the fee simple owners of the unsold Indian land within their borders. The Indians, the Court had held, possessed only a "right of occupancy" in the land. Georgia's congressional delegation used these decisions to argue that the federal government had the right to remove the Indians from Georgia by force. "The Indians are simply occupants—tenants at will," they reasoned. *Tenants at will* was a term of property law, referring to tenants who could be removed at any time, at the landlord's pleasure. "If a peaceable purchase cannot be made in the ordinary mode," Georgia's congressmen argued, "nothing remains to be done but to order their removal." They supported the argument with the passages in *Johnson* in which Chief Justice John Marshall had emphasized the government's "right of conquest" and the temporary, extinguishable nature of the Indians' possession. As time passed and Georgians grew more impatient with the federal government, the Georgia legislature and its supporters relied heavily on these passages of *Johnson* to argue that even *Georgia*, not just the federal government, had the power to force the Indians off their land.[24]

But this argument did not prevail either, because it was so inconsistent with two centuries of practice. The New England lawyer and reformer Jeremiah Evarts, one of the leading white opponents of removal, made the point as plain as possible in one of his widely read essays, published under the pseudonym "William Penn" in the Washington *National Intelligencer*. The law had never declared "that Indians are tenants at will," he pointed out. On the contrary, "the whole history of our negotiations with them, from the peace of 1783 to the last treaty to which they are a party, and of all our legislation concerning them, shows, that they are regarded as . . . possessing a territory, which they are to hold in full possession, till they voluntarily surrender it." In an 1829 memorial to Congress, the Cherokees made the same argument. "Your memorialists solemnly protest against being considered tenants at will," they insisted. "As we have never ceded nor forfeited the occupancy of the soil and the sovereignty over it, we do solemnly protest against being forced to leave it."[25]

The law was thus on the side of the Indians. Despite the increasingly belligerent claims of Georgia and nearby states, there was never room to make a serious legal argument that the Indians could be removed by force. Even the Andrew Jackson administration would pursue removal in the form of treaties rather than simply using the army to force the Indians to move.

The other removal debate was about removal's wisdom. The Indians had the legal right to stay where they were, but was that a right they should exercise? Or would it be in their best interest to exchange their land for new land west of the Mississippi?

Some of the arguments advanced by the white proponents of removal were of course grounded in the interests of white settlers, not Indians. Government officials often noted that the pattern of Indian land purchasing had produced a jagged frontier, with scattered white settlements separated by intervening Indian territory. Defense against Indian attack, they repeatedly pointed out, would be far simpler and less expensive if whites and Indians each occupied a single contiguous territory, the two separated by a single line. Some of the other arguments in favor of removal were equally self-serving. Senator Thomas Buck Reed of Mississippi complained that "the Indian territory in Mississippi affords a complete sanctuary for debtors and vagabonds and criminals from every part of the Union." Richard Henry Wilde of Georgia thought removal appropriate simply because, in his view, whites would do better things with the land. "Are we to check the human course of happiness," he asked, "obstruct the march of science—stay the works of art, and stop the arm of industry, because they will efface in their progress the wigwam of the red hunter, and put out forever the council fire of his tribe?" Some supporters of removal made no pretense of looking out for the Indians. They were interested only in promoting white settlement.[26]

Other proponents of removal claimed to be friends of the Indian, but made arguments so patently disingenuous as to undermine the claim. When the General Assembly of Indiana, for example, sent a memorial to Congress praying that the federal government extinguish the Indian title of the two tribes remaining within the state, the Assembly suggested that the Indians would find the territory west of the Mississippi "so much better adapted to their wants and their habits" than Indiana, "where they now acquire but a precarious and scanty subsistence." One may wonder whether the Indiana Assembly would have been as solicitous of the Indians' well-being had the Indians not occupied land coveted by the state's white residents. On the floor of the Senate, John

Elliott of Georgia provided a range of ostensibly humanitarian reasons the Indians ought to move west, but then undercut his own posture when, evidently warming to his subject, he began rhapsodizing over how much money the government would take in from selling all that land to settlers.[27]

With all this thinly disguised self-interest floating around, it is perhaps easy to be cynical about the motives of *all* the white proponents of removal. No doubt many of those who argued for removal were not nearly as interested in the welfare of the Indians as they claimed to be. And given what we know, with the benefit of hindsight, about the long-term consequences of removal, it is easy to suspect that those consequences were intended by the whites who urged the Indians to move west. But in the 1820s and 1830s, as in all periods of American history, whites were not as monolithic in their motives or their opinions with respect to Indians as we sometimes implicitly accuse them of being. There were many white Americans who advocated removal because they genuinely believed it was in the best interests of the Indians.

Proponents of removal began with the obvious truth that contact with white settlers had always proven disastrous for the Indians. "If ever one tribe of Indians has flourished" in close proximity to settlers, observed the Baptist missionary Isaac McCoy, "we will hope that the like may happen again. But if such an event has never occurred, we may confidently assure ourselves that it never will." Wherever whites settled in large numbers, most of the Indians eventually died or moved away. After two hundred years of such encounters, some tribes had been driven to extinction, and others were nearly there. Everyone knew that the white population of the United States was constantly increasing and that white settlement was pushing steadily westward. Barring a dramatic change in the federal government's Indian policy, the Indians' future looked dismal. James Barbour, the secretary of war under President John Quincy Adams, was just one of many who recognized the looming catastrophe. "Shall we go on quietly in a course, which, judging from the past, threatens their extinction?" he asked in a thoughtful 1826 memorandum recommending removal. Or was there something the government could do to save the Indians?[28]

Many feared along with Barbour that there would soon be no Indians left unless the federal government protected them from extinction. The only way to do that, they argued, was to encourage the Indians to relocate far from white settlers. The annual report of the commissioner of

Indian affairs was normally a dry statistical document, but in his report for 1828 Commissioner Thomas McKenney included an emotional appeal to Congress to act before it was too late. *"What are humanity and justice in reference to this unfortunate race?"* McKenney asked.

> Are these found to lie in a policy that would leave them to linger out a wretched and degraded existence, within districts of country already surrounded and pressed upon by a population whose anxiety and efforts to get rid of them are not less restless and persevering, than is the law of nature immutable, which has decreed, that, under such circumstances, if continued in, *they must perish?* Or does it not rather consist in withdrawing them from this certain destruction, and placing them, though even at this late hour, in a situation where, by the adoption of a suitable system for their security, preservation, and improvement, and at no matter what cost, they may be saved and blest?[29]

McKenney and others who were concerned about the fate of the Indians had motivations similar to those of the many people today who are concerned for endangered species of animals. Today it is widely believed that the government has a responsibility to protect animals from extinction, and that the best way to do that is to provide them a sanctuary where they will be safe from the noxious influences of civilization. In the early nineteenth century, long before there was common concern for the welfare of animals, many were worried about endangered human beings.

The geography of the United States suggested a solution. Across the Mississippi River lay an enormous region about which little was known other than that it was very sparsely populated. It was generally agreed (incorrectly, as it turned out) that this territory was so big, and so remote, that it would not see substantial white settlement for a very long time, perhaps centuries. West of the Mississippi lay the only long-term answer to the inevitable humanitarian disaster—enough land, far enough from whites. The territory acquired in the Louisiana Purchase could be "a land of refuge, where this unhappy race may find rest and safety," declared Lewis Cass in the *North American Review* shortly before he became the administrator of removal as Andrew Jackson's secretary of war. For two hundred years, Indian policy had been a series of ad hoc, small-scale removals, and the Indian population had steadily diminished. For removal's proponents, the Indians' choice was either more of the same, which would lead to extinction, or the replacement of multiple small removals with one final, major, permanent removal that would be the Indians' only hope of survival. As Thomas McKenney explained to a pro-removal organization formed in 1829 by clergymen and laymen of the Reformed Dutch Church in Manhattan, "we believe if the Indians do not emigrate, and fly the causes, which are fixed in themselves, and which have proved so destructive in the past, they *must perish!*" His audience then included the same message in a memorial to Congress. The Indians "appear to us as if standing on the very verge of ruin," they declared. Removal west of the Mississippi would be "the only alternative left."[30]

Religious organizations had long taken an active interest in the Indians' welfare, both in this life and the next, so it is not surprising that they were among the most vocal proponents of removal. The Baptists were particularly strong supporters. The *American Baptist Magazine* published repeated endorsements of removal. Local Baptist associations petitioned Congress to the same effect. Baptist advocates of removal were careful to remind readers that the Indians had the legal right to remain in place, and that removal would be legitimate only if the Indians voluntarily agreed to it. "Whether it is expedient for the Indians to remove," one explained, "is distinct from the question whether they possess a right to retain their lands." What the Indians *should* do, and what they could be *forced* to do, were two separate issues. "A man may think it for the good of the Cherokees themselves that they should follow their countrymen beyond the Mississippi," declared a Baptist correspondent calling himself "Roger Williams," in honor of the early defender of Indian property rights, "and yet feel grief and indignation at a violation of solemn treaties, or an attempt to force the Indians from their homes." Other religious organizations favoring removal emphasized the same distinction: the Indians would either move west of the Mississippi or face imminent destruction, but that was a choice only the Indians could make.[31]

But what exactly was the humanitarian thing to do? Many thought removal was only likely to drive the Indians *toward* extinction. Heman Humphrey, the president of Amherst College, insisted that removal was nothing but a plan "to drive 70,000 unoffending people from the soil on which they were born, into distant wilds, where most of them will perish."[32] Among well-meaning whites with the shared goal of protecting the Indians, there were two opinions about removal.

Opponents emphasized that removal would hardly be the clean operation implicitly envisioned by its supporters. "It is no slight task," one observed, "for a whole people, from helpless infancy to the decrepitude of age, to abandon their native land, and seek in a distant, and perhaps barren region, new means of support." Even if the logistics of mass migration could be managed, the Indians would only face more hardships once they arrived at their destination. No one could say for sure whether they would encounter other Indian tribes, who would be hostile to the newcomers.[33]

Nor was there any certainty that the land west of the Mississippi would be a sanctuary from white settlers for as long as the proponents of removal hoped. If the land was any good for farming, it would be coveted by whites soon enough. "If the lands to which you remove them are what you describe them to be," predicted Representative Edward Everett of Massachusetts, "you may as well push back the tide in the Bay of Fundy, as keep out the white population." If the land was unsuitable for farming, on the other hand, the Indians were being snookered into an unfair trade. Either way, argued a group of Massachusetts residents in a memorial to Congress, the concept of removal was "too visionary to require serious attention."[34]

Perhaps the most commonly voiced objection to removal was that it was utterly inconsistent with the government's long-standing policy of helping the Indians along the path toward civilization. For decades, the federal government had urged tribes to live more like Anglo-Americans—to settle in permanent towns, to build churches and schools, to make long-term investments in farm animals and equipment. Some tribes, especially the Cherokees, had done just that, and were gradually adopting a lifestyle similar to that of their white neighbors. After the Indians had made so much progress toward civilization, opponents of removal wondered, how could the government turn around and advise the Indians to migrate westward into the wilderness? "How will these facts tell in history?", one asked. "How ridiculous will it appear, when acts to civilize them and acts to drive them into the forest, are placed side by side? What faith will be given to our professions, that we really intended to prevent the extinction of this race of men?" As citizens of Farmington, Connecticut, pointed out in their memorial to Congress, "these tribes are rapidly acquiring a practical acquaintance with the arts and usages of civilized life, and embracing the principles and imbibing the spirit of Christianity." Removal would only "throw them back into their original state of barbarism." The inconsistency between the goals of civilization and removal was not lost on the Cherokees. "Where have we an example in the whole history of man," wondered Elias Boudinot, editor of the *Cherokee Phoenix*, "of a Nation or tribe, removing in a body, from a land of civil and religious means, to a perfect wilderness, *in order to be civilized*."[35]

Because of arguments like these, for every religious group that favored removal, there was another urging the Indians not to accept the trade, and pleading with the federal government to protect the Indians in the east today rather than promising protection in the west tomorrow. The most urgent pleas came from missionaries resident among the Cherokees, who repeatedly predicted that removal would pose a far greater threat to the Indians' well-being than anything they might encounter at home.[36] The religious organizations, like white humanitarian opinion generally, were divided over removal.

This division was important, because whenever Indian land policy was at issue, whites essentially divided into two camps. Many, particularly in the south and the west, were interested in obtaining the land and had little or no concern with the welfare of the Indians. Many others, particularly in the northeast, might loosely be called "humanitarians." Whatever their interest in acquiring the Indians' land, they were able to keep at least one eye on the Indians' well-being, and they had at least some desire to protect the Indians from the aggressions of white settlers. Such people often occupied important positions in the federal government. Henry Knox, the United States' first secretary of war, was such a person, as was Thomas McKenney, who was in charge of the federal government's relations with the Indians between 1816 and 1830.[37] These eastern humanitarians were the only significant political counterweight to the expansionists on the frontier. The state of relations between the United States and the Indian tribes at any given time normally reflected the balance of power between the two groups, and the extent to which easterners possessing nominal power were actually able to use that power to keep westerners under control.

Because the humanitarians were split over removal, they could not provide the ordinary counterweight to the southerners and westerners who advocated removal on expansionist grounds. Had the debate among whites over the wisdom of removal simply pitted expansionists against humanitarians, the outcome might have landed somewhere in the middle, as Indian policy so often did. The "middle" in this context would have been a continuation of the traditional piecemeal method of land acquisition that had prevailed for two centuries. But the debate over the wisdom of removal pitted some of the humanitarians on one side against strange bedfellows on the other—the rest of the humanitarians, joined by the expansionists. By 1830, if not earlier, it became clear that white opinion supported removal.

The result was an uncomfortable juxtaposition of outcomes. Most whites agreed that the Indians could not be removed against their will. But most also agreed that the Indians ought to exchange their land for land west of the Mississippi. And many within the latter group sincerely believed that such an exchange would be in the Indians' best interests, even if the Indians themselves had not yet realized as much. Many whites were thus of the view that they were justified in pressuring the Indians into voluntarily agreeing to remove.

This was partly a matter of assumed racial superiority. If Indians were less intelligent than whites, they might not perceive their own self-interest as clearly as whites did. Just as children could not make important decisions without guidance from adults, the Indians' own preferences about removal might be helped by guidance from whites.

But there was more at work than racial paternalism in the apparently widespread belief, especially among government officials, that they had no need to take the Indians' stated preferences at face value. At least as important was the general impression within the federal government that the opposition to removal expressed by tribal leaders did not reflect the views of the majority of tribe members. Cherokee and Creek chiefs consistently declined offers to remove, but federal officials were convinced that the chiefs were misrepresenting the wishes of their constituents in a desperate attempt to preserve their own status. "It is by no means unnatural for the chiefs of those tribes to oppose the going away of their people," Thomas McKenney assured Congress in his 1829 annual report. "In proportion to the reduction of their numbers does their power decrease; and their love of power is not less strong than other people's." The House Committee on Indian Affairs concluded in 1830 that the Cherokees were governed by an aristocracy of mixed-blood families that controlled the entire wealth of the tribe and spoke for the tribe in its dealings with the government, despite constituting no more than 5 percent of the tribe's population. The remaining nineteen of twenty Cherokees, the Committee found, "are the tenants of the wretched huts and villages in the recesses of the mountains and else-where, remote from the highways and the neighborhood of the wealthy and prosperous." These "common Indians" stood to gain from removal, the Committee believed, and would have already accepted the government's offer to remove, had their voices not been silenced and their preferences not dictated by the Cherokee aristocracy, who stood to lose their wealth and power if the tribe headed west. The parallel committee in the Senate agreed that the Cherokees' opposition to removal was in truth the view "of comparatively a few, who are either white men connected with the nations by marriage, or of those of mixed blood, born in the nation, who are well educated and intelligent, who have acquired considerable property." Most Cherokees, "the mass of the population, are as poor and degraded as can well be imagined," and would prefer to move west of the Mississippi, the Committee concluded, if the tribal leadership did not keep them in the dark as to the benefits of removal. Such views were self-serving but not without foundation. As Indian tribes acculturated to Anglo-American ways, wealth distribution within tribes was indeed becoming more unequal, and the interests of rich and poor tribe members were diverging more and more. Exacerbating the problem, in the view of some government officials, were the missionaries living among the Indians, who, more interested in maintaining their own positions than in helping the Indians, urged the Indians to resist the government's offers to remove.[38]

This was the climate of white opinion in the late 1820s when removal first became a major national issue. Among those capable of influencing the federal government's Indian policy, it was generally understood that removal would be in the best interests of whites because it would open up new land to white settlement; that removal would also be in the best interests of the Indians because it was the only measure that would protect them from extinction; that the Indians could not be removed by force, but only by treaty; and that when Indians refused to agree to treaties of removal, the refusal did not have to be taken too seriously because it did not express the true preferences of most Indians.

This combination of beliefs was a recipe for extortion. It was only a matter of time before frontier state governments, answerable to white settlers bordering on Indian land, began ratcheting up the pressure on the nonselling tribes by threatening to make life considerably more difficult for Indians who refused to sell their land. That pressure, and the federal government's response to it, gave rise to the series of events that has come to be remembered as "removal."

Extortion

When Georgia invalidated the Cherokees' laws, declared the Cherokees subject to Georgia law, and threatened to seize the Cherokees' land and distribute it to white settlers, everyone knew that the state legislature's real goal was to force the Cherokees to the bargaining table. The legislature carefully avoided announcing any intention to use physical coercion to get the Cherokees out of the state, but there was little doubt as to what state officials had in mind. "Is there no compulsion except military compulsion?" asked George Evans of Maine on the floor of the House of Representatives. "Can men be coerced by nothing but guns and bayonets? I say that those Indians are not to be left in circumstances, where they can act in an unconstrained and voluntary manner." When Alabama, following Georgia's model, asserted sovereignty over the Creeks, the Creeks were well aware of the Alabama legislature's intentions. The state's "ostensible object is not so much the exercise of sovereignty," the Creek leadership declared in a memorial to Congress, "but, under that pretension, to expel our nation from their country."[39]

The motive underlying these state laws was so easy to discern because the laws themselves were so clearly beyond the power of the states to enact, for several reasons that were immediately apparent to the Indians and their white supporters. The seizure of Indian land was inconsistent with the Indians' right of occupancy. As the Supreme Court had held in *Fletcher v. Peck* and *Johnson v. M'Intosh*, the only entity capable of extinguishing the right of occupancy was the federal government. John Marshall's opinions had been less than clear as to whether the federal government could seize Indian land over the Indians' objection, but the opinions had made it plain that a *state* could not do so. The invalidation of Indian laws, and the subjection of Indian tribes to discriminatory state laws, were likewise contrary to the established understanding of the general division of power between the states and the federal government, and also contrary to the specific terms of statutes Congress had enacted and Indian treaties the federal government had concluded under that power. The text of the Constitution merely gave Congress the authority to regulate "Commerce . . . with the Indian Tribes," but that passage had consistently been interpreted to invest the federal government with virtually plenary authority over Indian affairs, even as to Indian tribes located within the boundaries of existing states. Using that authority, the federal government had concluded many treaties with the Indians in Georgia over the years, including several with the Cherokees themselves, some of which explicitly prohibited whites from settling on Indian land. Congress had passed statutes to the same effect. The tribes had always been allowed to govern themselves within their own unsold territories. No state government had ever thought it possessed the authority to strip an Indian tribe of this power of self-government and exert its own sovereignty over members of the tribe.

The state laws that precipitated the removal crisis could only be justified, in the constitutional sense, by rejecting forty years of precedent. And that is just what the Georgia legislature did. The entire history of the federal government's relations with the Indians in Georgia, the legislature asserted, had been unconstitutional all along, as an invasion of the prerogatives of the state of Georgia. All the treaties, all the statutes—the federal government had been acting outside its proper sphere of authority the whole time.[40]

In adopting aggressive tactics to push the Indians off their land, Georgia was playing a familiar role within the structure of intergovernmental relations that characterized the United States and the British Empire before it. Settlers on the frontier, and the units of local government most closely accountable to them, had a long history of pursuing more aggressive Indian policies than the central governments that in principle had the authority to keep those policies in check. In the colonial era, the imperial government in London had consistently, if ineffectually, exhorted colonial governments to restrain their citizens from trespassing on the Indians' land. After independence, the government of the United States had stepped into that role, as the only check on the tendency of frontier states like Georgia to pay insufficient attention to Indian property rights. In the late 1820s, when Georgia stepped up the pressure on the Cherokees, the Cherokees knew where to look for relief. As so many tribes had done in the past, the Cherokees appealed to the federal government to intervene in their behalf.

But it was the Cherokees' great misfortune that the new president, taking office in early 1829, was Andrew Jackson, one of the most enthusiastic proponents of removal. Historians disagree as to whether Jackson was motivated primarily by a racist hatred for the Indians or a humanitarian desire to save them from extinction—he provided ample evidence of both—but whatever his motive, Jackson decided not to protect the Cherokees from Georgia.[41] In an April 1829 letter to the Cherokees, Secretary of War John Eaton announced that the Jackson administration agreed with Georgia's novel interpretation of constitutional law. Georgia had every right to void the Cherokees' laws and seize their land, Eaton explained, and even if Georgia lacked that right, the federal government was powerless to intervene. "Allow me to call your attention for a moment to the grave character of the course, which under a mistaken view of your own rights, you desire the government to adopt," Eaton lectured the Cherokees. "It is no less, than an invitation, that she shall step forward to arrest the constitutional acts of an independent state, exercised within her own limits." Eaton informed the Cherokees that the federal government would not block Georgia from harassing them. "This can never be done. The president cannot, and will not, beguile you with such an expectation. The arms of this country can never be employed, to stay any state of the union from the exercise of those legitimate powers which attach, and belong to their sovereign character."[42] Jackson and his colleagues were happy to sit back and let Georgia do the work of persuading the Cherokees to sell their land to the United States.

The justification offered by Jackson and Eaton—that the federal government lacked the constitutional authority to intervene in the dispute between Georgia and the Cherokees—was understood by opponents of removal as an insincere excuse to speed up the Cherokees' exit. "These legal distinctions and constitutional subtleties, repugnant to the common sense, and unpropitious to the common necessities of mankind, will be regarded as mere inventions for the purpose of covering up our participation in the plunder of the aboriginals," accused an anonymous pamphleteer in 1829. "The world will not believe, indeed it will not, that our constitution imposes insuperable obstacles to the preservation of national faith." Representative Isaac Bates of Massachusetts accused Jackson and his supporters of bad faith even more pointedly. "You cooperate with Georgia—you give effect to her laws—you put the Indians aside and trample your treaties with them in the dust," Bates alleged. "And it will be in vain you tell the world you did not set fire to the city, when you saw it burning, and would not put it out, though you were its hired patrol and watch." These accusations of insincerity were almost certainly right. When government officials insist that they lack the legal authority to do something, it is virtually always something they would prefer not to do, and that is especially true when it is something that previous administrations have always done. But of course that was no help to the Cherokees. The federal government, which in the past had often been the Indians' ally against settlers and frontier states, was taking Georgia's side.[43]

Congress had already been debating whether, and how, to move the Indians westward, since before Jackson's election, without producing any legislation. The standoff between Georgia and the Cherokees provided an impetus to take up the issue again. In early 1830, at Jackson's suggestion, committees of both houses of Congress reported the bills that by May would become the Removal Act of 1830, a statute that is often misunderstood. The Removal Act is conventionally said to have authorized removal, by empowering the president to trade land west of the Mississippi to Indian tribes in exchange for the Indians' land in the east. The president, however, *already* had the authority to trade western land for eastern, and indeed presidents had been doing so for some time. The parts of the Removal Act ostensibly authorizing removal did not change the law in the slightest. The act did not divest the Senate of its constitutional role in ratifying Indian treaties; the Senate would continue to ratify treaties involving the exchange of land long after 1830. If Jackson had only been interested in his authority to pursue removal, he would have had no need to ask Congress for a statute. The real motivation for the Removal Act was financial. Removal would be expensive, and the Office of Indian Affairs could not pay for it from its ordinary budget. As Thomas McKenney had explained in early 1828, before Jackson was elected, the Office of Indian Affairs was already spending its entire annual appropriation on food, clothing, and medical care for Indians. "It is not possible to sustain the direct demands upon this fund, and pay out of it, also the cost of emigration," McKenney advised. He suggested that Congress appropriate funds "*specifically*, to defray the cost of the movement." The most significant part of the Removal Act was thus its last section, which appropriated $500,000 for the specific purpose of removal.[44]

But while the nonmonetary parts of the Removal Act were meaningless in a legal sense, they became the focus of the national debate over removal. In February and March of 1830, memorials poured into Congress, most from northern opponents of the bill. Residents of Brown County, Ohio, declared that removal "would be cruel, unjust, and disgraceful to our Government." A group from Pittsburgh asked Congress to protect the Cherokees "against the enslaving and unjust decree" of

Georgia. The "Ladies of Burlington, New Jersey," deplored attempts to dispossess the Indians, after explaining that "they deem it no departure from the reserve and decorum benefiting their sex, briefly and unpresumingly to make known their opinion of measures, fraught, as they believe, with injustice and oppression, to an already wasted and suffering portion of the human race."[45] The New York merchant John Pintard told his daughter that "removal from the graves of their forefathers is an indelible disgrace to our country," and the sentiment was shared by a great many northerners.[46]

White residents of Georgia and the nearby states with large Indian populations viewed these earnest expressions of support for the Indians with considerable skepticism. Virtually all of the anti-removal petitions came from parts of the country whose residents had removed their Indians long ago. Opposition to removal, complained Wilson Lumpkin of Georgia, was the work of "Northern fanatics, male and female," who had "gotten up thousands of petitions . . . protesting against the removal of the poor dear Indians."[47] It was a little too easy for northerners to claim a superior humanity. Their ancestors had already done the dirty work.

The Removal Act squeaked through the House by only 5 votes out of 199 cast. The vote was largely along regional lines, after northern Democrats broke with Jackson and the party to vote against the bill. The Senate approved the bill by a wider margin, along straight party lines. The federal government now had the money for large-scale removal, as well as a statement of support from Congress.

The Cherokees, meanwhile, had only one hope left—to persuade the Supreme Court to take their side. For that purpose they retained former U.S. attorney general William Wirt, one of the most distinguished lawyers of the era. Getting the issue before the Supreme Court, however, was no simple matter. It would take Wirt three tries over three years to overcome the opposition of Georgia officials and frame a case in which the Court could intervene. And even when the Court sided with the Cherokees, Wirt's victory would have little practical effect. There would be an unbridgeable gap between the legal principles upheld by the Supreme Court and the power relations on the ground in Georgia.

Soon after the Cherokees hired Wirt, Georgia indicted a Cherokee named George Tassels for murdering another tribe member within the Cherokees' territory. The prosecution was based on the new Georgia statute extending state law to the Cherokees' land. Wirt realized that the case provided a route to the Supreme Court. Under Wirt's supervision, Tassels's lawyer challenged the jurisdiction of the state trial court by arguing that the new statute was unconstitutional. That challenge, as Wirt expected, provoked the trial court to uphold the statute's constitutionality. Wirt then sought review of that ruling in the Supreme Court. In December 1830, Chief Justice John Marshall granted a writ of error—that is, he agreed that the Court should hear the case—and ordered both sides to appear before the Court for argument in January. A Supreme Court decision on the constitutionality of Georgia's actions seemed imminent. Tassels, in the meantime, had already been tried and sentenced to death. In a normal case, his execution would have been stayed until the Supreme Court had ruled. But this was not a normal case. The Georgia legislature voted to defy the Court and proceed with Tassels's execution. Tassels was hanged in late December. The case was moot.[48]

Wirt was not surprised. Back in June he had predicted that Georgia officials would use whatever tricks they could to prevent him from getting a case to the Supreme Court. If the case originated in the Georgia courts, Wirt realized, state officials might have the ability, by pleading strategically, to keep the case from falling within the Supreme Court's jurisdiction. They could even refuse to supply the Court with the trial record. Wirt was aware that the only way to bypass the Georgia courts was to structure the case to originate in the federal courts. That, however, was not an easy matter. The Eleventh Amendment barred individual tribe members from suing Georgia in federal court. There were only two routes to a federal court that did not go through the state courts. An individual Cherokee could sue an individual citizen of Georgia in a federal trial court. Or, if the Cherokees were a "foreign state" under Article III of the Constitution, the tribe itself could sue the state of Georgia directly in the Supreme Court.[49] The second option would get the Cherokees to the Supreme Court faster, and it would not require finding (or manufacturing) a dispute between an individual tribe member and an individual Georgian. Wirt accordingly filed suit in the Supreme Court, on behalf of the tribe, against the state, seeking to have the aggressive Georgia statutes of the late 1820s declared invalid, as contrary to the Constitution, contrary to the treaties between the United States and the Cherokees, and contrary to the federal Intercourse Act of 1802.

The resulting Supreme Court opinion—*Cherokee Nation v. Georgia* (1831)—would become one of the most famous in the Court's history, because John Marshall provided the Court's first extended discussion of the nature of Indian tribal sovereignty and set out some basic principles that remain the law today. The Cherokees lost the case. Indian tribes, the Court held, are *not* foreign states and thus lack the power to bring suit directly in the Supreme Court. Of course, as the Court recognized, Indian tribes are not American states either. Instead, Marshall held, they are *sui generis*. "They may, more correctly, perhaps, be denominated domestic dependent nations," Marshall concluded. "Their relation to the United States resembles that of a ward to his guardian."[50] Because the Court lacked jurisdiction, Marshall did not reach the merits of Wirt's argument on the constitutionality of the Georgia statutes. Only Justices Smith Thompson and Joseph Story, who argued in dissent that the Cherokees *were* a foreign state and thus that the Court *did* have jurisdiction, reached the merits. They sided with the Cherokees.

It did not take Wirt long to find a new case. Samuel Worcester, a Congregationalist missionary living among the Cherokees, was one of the most vocal white opponents of removal. In late 1830 the Georgia legislature tried to drive people like Worcester away by making it illegal for whites to reside within the Cherokee Nation without a license from the state. In 1831, soon after the Supreme Court's decision in *Cherokee Nation v. Georgia*, Worcester was convicted of violating this law. He was sentenced to four years of hard labor in the state penitentiary. Wirt promptly asked the Supreme Court to hear the case, and the Court agreed. This time there was nothing Georgia could do to stop it. The Court clearly had jurisdiction, and because Worcester had been sentenced to prison rather than death, the state could not moot the case by executing him.

Worcester v. Georgia (1832), the opinion that resulted, was an astonishingly pro-Indian document for the era. The winner in a technical sense was Worcester, whose conviction was reversed, but Chief Justice Marshall's opinion vindicated the Cherokees' position on virtually every point in their long dispute with Georgia. Marshall must have been bothered by the way Georgia officials had relied on passages from his opinions in *Johnson v. M'Intosh* and *Fletcher v. Peck*, because his opinion in *Worcester* included none of the ambiguity and vacillation of his earlier pronouncements. Marshall began by mocking "the extravagant and absurd idea, that the feeble settlements made on the sea coast" by early English colonists had given England any right to govern the Indians or occupy their land. All that colonial settlement entitled the English to do, Marshall insisted, was to purchase "such lands as the natives were willing to sell." And until the Indians decided to sell their land, he concluded, the English (and thus the United States as well) had only the most limited kind of power with respect to the land. They had the right to keep agents of other European sovereigns away, but that was all. England, and later the United States, had no authority to interfere with the Indians' ownership of the land or their sovereignty over it. "Our history furnishes no example," Marshall declared, "from the first settlement of our country, of any attempt on the part of the crown to interfere with the internal affairs of the Indians." He cited the federal government's treaties with the Indians, and the various statutes respecting the rights of Indian tribes, as proof that this recognition of Indian sovereignty had continued throughout the history of the United States. As a result, Marshall concluded, "the Cherokee nation, then, is a distinct community occupying its own territory, with boundaries accurately described, in which the laws of Georgia can have no force, and which the citizens of Georgia have no right to enter." The law under which Samuel Worcester was convicted was accordingly void.[51]

In *Worcester v. Georgia*, John Marshall led the Supreme Court in a ringing declaration of Indian sovereignty. The crux of *Worcester* contradicted some of what Marshall had said in his earlier opinions. The idea that colonial settlement gave England sovereignty over North America, for example, may have been "extravagant and absurd," but it was an idea that Marshall himself had played an important role in propagating nine years earlier in *Johnson v. M'Intosh*. In *Johnson*, Marshall had been primarily concerned not with Indians but with white settlers who had received grants of unsold Indian land from state governments. In *Worcester*, by contrast, when the removal controversy was at its height and the fate of the Cherokees seemed to hang in the balance, Marshall revealed much more sympathy for the Indians.

There is a legend that Andrew Jackson responded to news of *Worcester v. Georgia* by saying "John Marshall has made his decision, now let him enforce it." The myth reflects a pervasive misunderstanding of the case. Jackson is often faulted by historians for "failing to enforce" or "failing to execute" the Court's judgment in *Worcester*, as if the opinion imposed some kind of legal duty on the federal government that Jackson contrived to shirk.[52] It is certainly true that the federal government continued to refuse to intervene to protect the Cherokees from the aggression of Georgia, aggression that took the form of statutes the Court found unconstitutional in *Worcester*. It is nevertheless a mistake to accuse Jackson of failing to enforce the Supreme Court's judgment in *Worcester*. The

Court's opinion declared Samuel Worcester's conviction void, but, given the procedural context of the case, the opinion could not have ordered the federal government to do anything. The Court lacked the power to invalidate acts of the government of Georgia that did not contribute to Worcester's conviction, and it certainly could not order the federal government, which was not a party to the case, to intervene. The Court's decision imposed on Georgia a legal obligation to release Samuel Worcester from prison, an obligation that Georgia (not the federal government) shirked for several months, but by the end of 1832 the governor of Georgia pardoned Worcester and ordered that he be released. That put an end to any lingering effect of *Worcester v. Georgia.* The state had done all the Supreme Court would ever tell it to do.

The episode thus provides a parable of the limits on the ability of courts to effect social change, given all the structural constraints the legal system places on them.[53] Even if the Jackson administration had been willing to obey a Supreme Court order to intervene to help the Cherokees, there was simply no mechanism within the American legal system for the Cherokees to secure such an order. The constraints of litigation required the Cherokees to proceed bit by bit, to challenge individual acts on the part of Georgia depriving particular plaintiffs of some cognizable interest in liberty or property. In each case, the only remedy available was a court order like the one in *Worcester v. Georgia*, requiring Georgia to free a particular plaintiff or to restore a particular plaintiff's property. Few nineteenth-century American lawyers, if any, would have conceived that courts had the power to issue an order to a state government as broad as "stop harassing the Cherokees." And even if the courts had been thought capable of issuing so broad an order, the order's proper target would almost certainly have been Georgia, not the United States.

John Marshall himself had recognized the first half of this problem the year before in *Cherokee Nation v. Georgia.* A court could decide who of two competing parties is the true owner of land, Marshall explained. But a court could not "control the legislature of Georgia" or "restrain the exercise of its physical force," because such a sweeping claim of authority "savours too much of the exercise of political power to be within the proper province of the judicial department." In asking the Supreme Court to intervene, the Cherokees were grasping for the only hope left to them, but it was an effort that was doomed from the start—not just by the political atmosphere and the attitude of the Jackson administration, but by the structural limits American lawyers placed on their courts.[54]

John Ross, here in an 1843 lithograph, led the Cherokees' resistance to removal in the 1820s and 1830s. After more than a decade of controversy, the Cherokees were forced to move from Georgia to present-day Oklahoma. Removal was structured on paper as a series of voluntary transactions but was compulsory in practice. This divergence between legal form and actual substance was already a common feature of Indian land transactions by the early nineteenth century.

But if the apocryphal quote attributed to Jackson makes no sense as a legal matter, it does capture the spirit of Jackson's continuing refusal to intervene on the Cherokees' behalf. Samuel Worcester was out of prison, but otherwise the Supreme Court's opinion in *Worcester* changed nothing. Georgia continued to make life difficult for the Cherokees, and the federal government continued to offer to purchase the Cherokees' land. John Ross, the Cherokees' principal chief, continued in vain to enlist the federal government's help. He proposed a deal to Andrew Jackson: if the Cherokees could become U.S. citizens and receive the same protections from the federal government as were enjoyed by whites, the Cherokees would give up part of their land and allow Georgia to govern them on the rest. He considered moving the tribe to Mexico, in the hope of finding a more friendly government.[55] But none of these plans worked out. In the end, after all the hubbub surrounding removal, the federal government resorted to the oldest trick in the book: it signed a treaty with a group of dissident Cherokees in which the United States purported to purchase all of the tribe's land in exchange for land in present-day Oklahoma.

The Treaty of New Echota, signed in 1835, was an exercise in despair on both sides. The Cherokees who took part knew full well that they spoke for a minority of the tribe, but they were convinced that the tribe's only hope was to sell before it was too late. As Elias Boudinot, one of the Cherokee signers, pointedly asked John Ross, "what is the prospect in reference to *your* plan of relief, if you are understood at all to have any plan? It is dark and gloomy beyond description." Removal, Boudinot had come to believe, was the lesser of evils. If the Cherokees remained in Georgia, Boudinot argued, "the time will come when there will be only here and there those who can be called upon to sign a protest, or vote against a treaty for their removal—when the few remnants of our once happy and improving nation will be viewed by posterity with curious and gazing interest, as relics of a brave and noble race."[56] The United States commissioners also knew they were treating with a group that spoke only for a small minority of the tribe, but they agreed with Boudinot that removal was the Cherokees' only hope, and they had grown frustrated with years of trying to persuade the majority of the tribe to agree.

And even then, the Cherokees hung on as long as they could. Ross spent most of the next three years repeatedly proving what the government already knew—that the signers of the Treaty of New Echota did not speak for the tribe. Finally, in 1838, while a delegation led by Ross was away in Washington still trying to negotiate with representatives of the Martin Van Buren administration, the Army rounded up the Cherokees and interned them in forts, to await transportation west of the Mississippi. Ross had to give up. The Cherokees would join the Choctaws, the Creeks, and Chickasaws, who had already left the southeast for present-day Oklahoma. The Seminoles would follow soon after. Meanwhile the smaller and more numerous northern tribes were moving west as well—some to Michigan and Wisconsin, and others across the Mississippi. In some of the treaties the United States secured from the northern tribes, like the 1838 Treaty of Buffalo Creek, in which the Seneca ceded nearly all their remaining land in New York, the government resorted to the same dubious tactics it used with the Cherokees at New Echota.[57]

Moving tens of thousands of very poor people several hundred miles would be a massive logistical operation even today, and it was considerably more difficult in the first half of the nineteenth century. The Cherokees' journey to Oklahoma—the Trail of Tears—is the one most remembered today, but many tribes suffered through the actual process of removal. The Army was in charge, and official reports tended to emphasize how smoothly things were proceeding, but, as always, the devil lay in the details. In principle, Indians were supposed to be compensated for their houses, their livestock, and the other property they had to leave behind. In the chaos of removal, little compensation was awarded, and most Indians seem to have headed west with little apart from the clothing on their back. The military officers responsible for herding the Indians westward obtained food and other supplies from contractors along the way, by the normal government method of purchasing from the lowest bidder. Even when the government got what it paid for, it didn't pay for much, and often it got even less because of the fraud that permeated the process. A physician who accompanied the Creeks reported that food was in such short supply that the Creeks were reduced to "eating every green thing they can find on the road," a practice "which occasioned much dysentery and cholera amongst them." The Creeks had so little clothing, another white witness to their removal observed, that many were naked, and thousands shoeless, while walking across the frozen ground of Mississippi in the winter of 1836. Government contractors supplying the emigrating Potawatomis engaged in so much fraud, one Boston magazine reported, that "goods were boxed up and marked with large sums on the outside, but when opened were found to contain not one tenth part of the value." Removal, as a concept, was in part a humanitarian ideal, intended to protect the Indians from being victimized by whites. But removal as an actual process was a humanitarian disaster.[58]

This was yet another old story. Fraud had been a basic element of Indian land purchasing since the seventeenth century. As long as whites had purchased their land, Indians had often received less than they had bargained for, because there had always been white purchasers and contractors willing to exploit the Indians' lack of equal access to the legal system within which promises were enforced. For two centuries, Indians had trudged westward after ceding their land, and many had died along the way. Because removal was managed by the Army and covered by the press, we have more evidence of the death and disease suffered by the Indians during removal than during earlier post-cession migrations, so it is difficult to compare the amount of death and disease in different periods. There can be little doubt, however, that moving long distances to new land entailed suffering in any era. On the long journey across the Mississippi, the Indians were replaying countless similar journeys over the preceding two hundred years.

Constant Removal

By the middle of the nineteenth century the eastern Indians had ceded virtually all their land. The pace of land purchasing accelerated in the 1830s, to 5.5 transactions per year, up from 1.7 per year in the 1820s. The federal government completed purchasing Alabama and Mississippi in 1832; Florida and Illinois in 1833; Georgia, North Carolina, and Tennessee in 1835 (in the Treaty of New Echota); and the final parts of Indiana in 1840 and Ohio in 1842.[59] When these transactions were added to the federal government's many earlier purchases, and those of the states and colonies and private purchasers in earlier eras, the land east of the Mississippi was almost entirely possessed by non-Indians.

After ceding all this land, Indians had headed west. In 1855 the Office of Indian Affairs counted approximately 315,000 Indians in the United States. All but 8,500 lived west of the Mississippi or in Michigan or Wisconsin. These numbers should be taken with a grain of salt: by the Office's own admission, it knew little about the Indian population in the west, and the Office was not even counting an estimated 350,000 Indians who had "lost their tribal character or amalgamated with whites or blacks." Most of these "amalgamated" Indians lived in the east, and many had retained their "tribal character" to a degree unappreciated by the Office of Indian Affairs. Still, most members of the largest eastern tribes had moved west of the Mississippi. There were 17,500 Cherokees in the territory "west of Arkansas" and only 2,200 back east. There were 25,000 Creeks west of Arkansas and only 100 in Alabama. There were many more Oneidas in Wisconsin than in New York, many more Seminoles in Oklahoma than in Florida.[60]

What if there had been no removal crisis? Suppose Georgia had never enacted all those unconstitutional statutes in the late 1820s, Congress had never enacted the Removal Act of 1830, and the Supreme Court had never decided *Cherokee Nation v. Georgia* and *Worcester v. Georgia*. By 1855, would the Indians have retained more land east of the Mississippi? Would the Indian population east of the Mississippi have been any higher? The answer to both questions has to be no. Had there been no removal crisis, the land cessions of the 1830s might have taken a bit longer to consummate, because the government's acquisition of Indian land might have continued to be as gradual and piecemeal as it had been in earlier decades. We might remember Martin Van Buren or John Tyler, rather than Andrew Jackson, as the president who presided over the removal of the Indians from the eastern United States, or the process might have been too steady even to encompass within a single administration. But removal was going on long before the so-called era of removal, and it would go on long afterward.

The actual land transactions that constituted removal were indistinguishable from earlier Indian land purchases, with the sole exception that the purchase price was western land rather than money or goods. From the Indians' perspective, removal, like earlier land sales, took place within circumstances constructed by whites to yield a state of affairs in which selling was the lesser of evils. In 1835 the *North American Review* described the removal of the northern tribes in words that could have been written at any time in the preceding century.

> We state the following as the means by which cessions of land are usually obtained of the Indians. The whites encroach and settle upon their territory. They increase greatly in number in a short time, and representations are soon made to the government, concerning the value of the land and the necessity of buying it. Commissioners are sent, large presents are made to the chiefs, (formerly whisky was copiously distributed,) and their ears are filled with the glory and power of the whites. Such representations are not, however, needed to convince them either of the ability or the will of the United States to oppress them, and they usually sell, what they think would otherwise be taken by force.[61]

The Indians who removed to the west, like earlier Indian land sellers, were caught midway between force and consent. As in so many earlier transactions, the government had the power to make an offer the Indians could not refuse.

$\Rightarrow$ 7

RESERVATIONS

REMOVAL had been based on the assumption that the West was big enough to provide the Indians a sanctuary from settlers for hundreds of years, but that assumption turned out to be spectacularly wrong. Settlers were crossing the Mississippi in large numbers, some headed as far as California, within a decade or two. By the late 1840s it became clear that the systematic removal of the 1830s would provide no more permanent a solution to the conflicts between settlers and Indians than the piecemeal removals of the preceding two centuries. The "Indian problem" had not disappeared; it had only moved west. But now there was no place left to push the Indians.

The result was the Indian reservation, an island of Indian territory within a sea of white settlement. The creation of reservations took place during a time of very rapid federal land acquisition. By the 1880s the pattern of land tenure in the West had been completely transformed—the Indians retained virtually no land that was not part of a reservation. By then, however, the optimism surrounding the creation of the earliest reservations had faded away. In the 1840s, reservations had offered promise to both sides of an uneasy coalition of white supporters—those seeking to protect the Indians from whites, and those seeking to protect whites from Indians. By the 1880s both sides were disillusioned.

During this same period there was recurring warfare between Indian tribes and the United States. Indeed, except during the Civil War and its immediate aftermath, fighting Indians was the main thing the U.S. Army did. This was the era of George Custer and Philip Sheridan (remembered most for declaring that "the only good Indians I ever saw were dead"), of Crazy Horse and Geronimo, of the Sand Creek Massacre and the Battle of the Little Big Horn—the era described in Dee Brown's *Bury My Heart at Wounded Knee* and portrayed in countless movie westerns.[1] It was no coincidence that all this fighting took place when the federal government was actively purchasing Indian land and creating reservations, because the fighting was about land. The federal government never stopped structuring land transactions, including those involving reservations, as voluntary sales by the Indians, but everyone on both sides of the frontier knew that the contractual form was a sham. There had always been inconsistency between the form and the substance of Indian land transactions, but the contrast was never greater than in the second half of the nineteenth century.

Overrun

Long before the word *reservation* acquired the specific meaning of an area set aside for Indians, it was a term of property law referring to the act of retaining for oneself rights in land one was conveying to another. When a person granting a parcel of land wished to retain a portion of the parcel, for example, or perhaps the right to possess the parcel for a certain time, or the right to continue using the parcel for certain purposes, his lawyer would include a reservation in the deed, a clause *reserving* the relevant rights to the grantor. Over time, the land or the rights retained by the grantor also came to be called a *reservation*. If A conveyed land to B but retained some for himself, for instance, the land still owned by A was a *reservation;* A had reserved it from the grant to B. Reservations in this sense were routine elements of land transactions, whether grants from the government to individuals or sales from one individual to another.

The idea of setting land aside for Indians was also very old by the nineteenth century. In seventeenth-century Massachusetts, many of the Indians were already living in "Indian villages" or "praying towns" established specifically for Indian habitation, and there were similar areas set aside for the Indians in other colonies. After the Revolution, Britain continued to set aside parcels of land for the indigenous inhabitants of its other colonies.[2] Some of the earliest treaties between Indian tribes and the United States, from the 1780s and 1790s, defined zones of land reserved for the Indians that were surrounded by areas open to white settlement. Such zones were referred to as "reservations" as early as the

1794 Treaty of Canandaigua, because they were reservations in the old sense of the word—parcels the tribes retained while ceding the rest of their land to the government. As the white population increased and the Indians sold more of their land, it became increasingly common for tribes to be living on reservations in this sense, surrounded by whites, inhabiting their last remaining tracts of unceded land.

After removal, many relocated tribes now lived on reservations in a new sense of the term—land the *government* had selected from *its own* land and reserved for the Indians' use. The areas to which eastern tribes were removed consisted of land the government had only recently purchased from western tribes. These were parcels that would have been part of the public domain, waiting to be sold to white settlers, had they not been set aside for the incoming eastern Indians.

In the 1840s, land possessed by Indian tribes formed a solid wall from Minnesota down to Texas.[3] There was no overland route west that did not enter the Indians' land, much of which had been granted to the relocated tribes only a decade or so earlier, during the course of removal, back when the West seemed so enormous and so far away that there would be room for all.

By the mid-1840s, however, the West was beginning to look much smaller. Settlers were already heading west in numbers that "could not, perhaps, have been anticipated twenty years ago, when the plan [of removal] was formed," the *United States Magazine* recognized in 1844. The more whites traveled west, the more they would perceive that the Indians were in their way. "The snowy heights of the Rocky Mountains are already scaled; and we but apply the results of the past to the future, in saying that the path which has been trod by a few, will be trod by many. Now the removed tribes are precisely in the centre of this path." The problem became even more acute a few years later, when the United States acquired California, and California turned out to contain gold. Removal, "when adopted, seemed wise and humane," reflected a report of the House Committee on Indian Affairs, but the policy had been overtaken by events. "Its authors never anticipated the rapid progress of the extension of our settlements and population westward. It was supposed that the Mississippi would, for many long years, mark the western confines of this Union." The 1850 census found 93,000 non-Indians in California alone, and many more were on the way. What would happen when so many whites crossed land belonging to Indians?[4]

The need to clear Indians off the white emigration routes to the West quickly became a recurring theme of the annual reports of the Commissioner of Indian Affairs. "Material changes will soon have to be made in the position of some of the smaller tribes on the frontier," William Medill declared in his 1848 report, "so as to leave an ample outlet for our white population to spread and to pass towards and beyond the Rocky mountains." Medill proposed creating two large "colonies" of Indians, one in the North and the other in the South, in order to free up the space between for whites to emigrate. Medill's successor was Orlando Brown, who reported the following year that the Indians living between Missouri and the Rocky Mountains "consider the whole country their own, [and] have regarded with much jealousy the passing of so many of our people through it, without any recognition of their rights, or any compensation for the privilege." White emigrants were not merely trespassing; they were also killing the buffalo, a matter which "has also caused much dissatisfaction among them." Brown repeated Medill's suggestion to move the Indians out of the way. So did Brown's successor as commissioner, Luke Lea. Lea's successor, George Manypenny, pointed out a related problem: all those emigrants had to settle somewhere, but there was nowhere for them to stop that was not possessed by Indians. Relocating the Indians would open up land for white settlement as well as emigration.[5]

Moving the Indians was only one of three possible solutions. The second would have been to police the frontier to prevent conflicts from arising between Indians and settlers. The Office of Indian Affairs, however, was far too weak and distant to prevent either side from disturbing the other, or indeed to exert much influence on anything that was happening in the West. The third alternative, of course, would have been to stop whites from emigrating. But few whites seriously entertained the idea that the Indians might have the power to choke off westward migration. The *New York Times* was hardly alone in finding it "quite evident, that with civilization spreading across the continent, we never can submit to the roaming and reckless habits hitherto permitted to the Indians. A broad zone of travel, including the railroads and the emigrant routes, must be made absolutely free from the incursions of the marauders." Luke Lea made the point even more firmly in one of his annual reports as Commissioner of Indian Affairs. "When civilization and barbarism are brought in such relation that they cannot coexist together," Lea explained, "it is right that the superiority of the former should be asserted and the latter compelled to give way."[6]

It was this perceived need to keep Indians from interfering with white emigration that gave rise to the idea of confining the Indians to specified locations, but once the idea was in circulation, many suggested that it would benefit Indians as much as whites. As with some of the ostensibly humanitarian reasons offered for removal, some of the arguments in favor of confining the Indians to reservations were no doubt disingenuous. But whites were no more monolithic in their attitudes toward Indians in the 1840s and 1850s than they had been in earlier periods.[7] As always, many were genuinely concerned with the Indians' welfare. By the late 1850s, many such people were just as convinced as the most ardent Indian-haters of the desirability of moving Indians to reservations.

Some argued that reservations would be the lesser of evils—that the Indians would be killed unless they got out of the settlers' way. "The border tribes are in danger of ultimate extinction," Lea warned in 1850. "If they remain as they are, many years will not elapse before they will be overrun and exterminated." The same weighing of alternatives had motivated the humanitarian support for removal back in the 1830s. In the 1850s, it suggested a form of internal removal, into areas where the Indians could be protected from the dangers of contact with whites. In 1856, when Commissioner of Indian Affairs George Manypenny looked back over a decade of growing western cities and expanding western railroads, he was apprehensive about the Indians' future. They would be "blotted out of existence," Manypenny predicted, "unless our great nation shall generously determine that the necessary provision shall at once be made, and appropriate steps be taken to designate suitable tracts or reservations of land, in proper localities, for permanent homes for, and provide the means to colonize, them thereon." Proponents of moving the Indians to reservations could sincerely think of themselves as humanitarians, as people altruistically interested in the Indians' well-being rather than their own.[8]

A second humanitarian argument in favor of reservations was the potential they offered for a more permanent land tenure. The Ojibwa writer and lecturer Kahgegagahbouh—also known by his English name, George Copway—lamented "the perpetual agitation of mind" among many tribes caused by the ever-present "fear of being removed westward by the American government. None but an Indian can, perhaps, rightly judge of the deleterious influence which the repeated removals of the Indians has wrought." Indians were reluctant to invest the labor and money in their land necessary to engage in agriculture, Copway reported, because they remembered what had happened to the eastern tribes who had done so. "Having seen the removal of many tribes," Copway related, Indians were "conscious of the fact, that the government may, and doubtless will, want more land, and they be obliged to sell at whatever price the government may see fit to give, and thus all improvements they have made become valueless to them." Copway accordingly recommended establishing a large permanent Indian territory in present-day South Dakota, where the Indians would be secure enough to farm. The point was repeated several times in the 1850s by various commissioners of Indian affairs. The argument suffered from an obvious weakness: while it was no doubt true that security of title would provide a greater incentive toward investment, why should the Indians believe that *this* relocation would be any more permanent than the earlier ones? Still, the idea that reservations would provide the Indians with more secure land tenure—that things really would be different this time—was powerful enough to endure through the middle decades of the century.[9]

The reservation promised a third benefit as well. White humanitarians were primarily interested not in preserving traditional Indian life but in changing it to more closely resemble their own. They wanted to teach the Indians Christianity, agriculture, literacy, thrift, work discipline—all the practices they summed up as civilization. This sort of education was difficult to provide, however, when Indians were roaming here and there. The reservation, they believed, would aid in civilizing the Indians, by keeping them within a compact space where they could be more easily instructed. "There are many objections to allowing them to live dispersed, in this, their first stage of improvement," argued the Indian agent Benjamin Wilson, sent to California in 1852 to report on the condition of the local tribes. "It interferes too much with education, and deprives them measurably of instruction in religion." Wilson advised forcing the Indians to live together in towns, where they could be compelled to labor a fixed number of hours per day and thus taught to act more like white Americans. "The time has arrived when our Indians are to be gathered into reservations," agreed the Philadelphia philanthropist William Welsh, "and trained in the habits of civilized people, that the Christian Church may exert its holy influences over them." The reservation, in the view of reformers, would be a classroom for the Indian.[10]

On the back of this undated and otherwise unlabeled photograph are the words "Indian payment, Odanah, Wisconsin." If this caption is accurate, the photograph may depict members of the La Pointe Band of the Chippewa of Lake Superior receiving one of the annual payments due under an 1854 treaty. In that treaty, the Chippewa ceded the northeastern corner of Minnesota, along the north shore of Lake Superior. In exchange they received several reservations, including this one in northern Wisconsin (the present Bad River Reservation), as well as the promise of twenty annual payments of money and goods. The creation of Indian reservations became a common feature of land transactions in the early 1850s.

By the early 1850s, for all these reasons, federal Indian policy turned to the reservation.[11] Virtually all Indian land cessions from then on resulted in the designation of a circumscribed area in which the selling tribe was to live. The federal government no longer simply purchased land from the Indians, as settlers had done since the early 1600s. Now land transactions typically had two components, a cession from the Indians to the United States and the delineation of a reservation for the Indians. Many of the reservations were created by treaty, when tribes, while selling part of the land in which they held an original right of occupancy, retained the rest. Many others were created by executive order, when the president designated an area of public land that would be withdrawn from the pool available for sale to settlers and reserved for a particular tribe.

Between the 1850s and 1880s, the federal government acquired Indian land at unprecedented speed. By 1870 all the land in Iowa, Minnesota, Texas, and Kansas had either been ceded to the government or designated as a reservation. By 1880 the same was true of Idaho, Washington, Utah, Oregon, Nevada, Wyoming, Nebraska, and Colorado; by 1886 it was also true of Montana, Arizona, and New Mexico. It had taken whites 250 years to purchase the eastern half of the United States, but they needed less than 40 years for the western half. The rush of settlers that had created the reservation policy was also driving the pace of land acquisition. At the same time, whites' growing interest in experiencing uninhabited "natural" landscapes caused the federal government to acquire even more Indian land, to be set aside as national parks once the Indians had been expelled. The East had been acquired in small bits, but some of the transactions in the West involved immense areas of land. More than 75 percent of Nevada, for example, was acquired in two bites; the large majority of Colorado in three. It was not long before the West was dotted with Indian reservations.[12]

By 1881, when a Senate committee considered a bill that would have regulated Indian affairs in certain areas, including "lands to which the original Indian title has never been extinguished, but which have not been specifically reserved by treaty, act of Congress, or otherwise, for the use of the Indians," this quoted phrase raised some eyebrows. A few decades earlier, most of the West would have fallen within that classification, as land the government had neither purchased from the Indians nor set aside as an Indian reservation. In 1881, however, legislators realized that the quoted passage had become unnecessary. They struck it from the final version of the bill, they explained, because "they believe that there are no such lands in the United States." As the political scientist Robert Weil concluded a few years later in his treatise *The Legal Status of the Indian*, few, if any, tribes "now live upon territory that has not been ceded to the United States." Instead, Weil reported, "most of them live upon reservations."[13]

There were two broad reasons for creating reservations, however, and in some respects they were at cross-purposes. Some proponents of the reservation were primarily interested in keeping the Indians from interfering with whites; others were primarily interested in keeping whites from interfering with the Indians. That tension would prove to be important in determining what life on the reservation was actually like. If a reservation was to keep Indians away from whites, the boundaries of the reservation would face inward. The purpose of the reservation would be to confine the Indians, in order to increase the settlers' freedom of movement. On the other hand, if a reservation was to keep whites away from Indians, the boundaries of the reservation would face outward. The purpose of the reservation would be to confine the *settlers*, in order to increase the *Indians'* freedom of movement. A reservation could be a prison, if the lock was on the outside, or it could be a haven, if the lock was on the inside. Everything depended on what the reservation was supposed to accomplish.

Nations Die like Men

In principle, no reservations could be created without the Indians' consent. All through the nineteenth century, the U.S. Supreme Court continued to declare that Indians held their lands by right of occupancy, which the Court defined in 1835 as "a perpetual right of possession in the tribe or nation inhabiting them, as their common property, from generation to generation." The government of the United States, as the land's fee simple owner, had the exclusive right to purchase the Indians' right of occupancy whenever a tribe was willing to sell, but the government could not force a sale. In *Johnson v. M'Intosh*, the 1823 case in which the Court first discussed Indian property rights in their unsold land, John Marshall's opinion had left open the possibility that the government could extinguish the Indians' right of occupancy by fiat as well as by purchase, but the later cases emphatically rejected that notion. Rather, the Court insisted, "their right of occupancy is considered as sacred as the fee simple of the whites." When Congress in the 1860s granted to the state of Kansas for railroad purposes a tract that included some land the Osages still held by right of occupancy, the Court found the Osages' land implicitly exempted from the grant. "The perpetual right of occupancy, with the correlative obligation of the government to enforce it, negatives the idea that Congress, even in the absence of any positive stipulation to protect the Osages, intended to grant their land," a majority of the justices held. "For all practical purposes, they owned it." Three dissenters would have found that Congress merely intended to grant fee simple title in the land subject to the Indians' ongoing right of occupancy, but even that, the majority argued, would "involve a gross breach of the public faith" owed by the government to the Osages. There was no room to doubt, as a legal matter, that the only way the government could acquire the Indians' land was to purchase it.[14]

Indeed, in a series of cases in the 1850s the Court made it clear that the Indians' right of occupancy entitled them to bring suit to eject, as trespassers, settlers who had purchased the government's fee simple title to land the Indians had not yet sold, but that settlers had no similar right to evict the Indians, even from land the Indians had already sold, a right the Court held was reserved to the federal government.[15] A person conversant with the Supreme Court's cases, but not with actual practice in the West, would have believed it impossible for an Indian reservation to exist unless a tribe wished to live there.

Land acquisition looked very different close up. In the Colorado Territory, for example, Colonel John Chivington was less impressed with the sanctity of the right of occupancy than the lawyers were. Some of the Cheyenne chiefs had agreed in 1861 to give up much of the tribe's land in return for a reservation on the Arkansas River in the southeastern part of the Territory, but others had not. By 1864, as white immigration into Colorado continued and tension between settlers and the remaining Cheyennes was running high, Chivington led a military expedition into a Cheyenne settlement near Sand Creek. What followed was best described, not by any advocate for the Indians, but by the Joint Committee of Congress formed to investigate.

> And then the scene of murder and barbarity began—men, women, and children were indiscriminately slaughtered. In a few minutes all the Indians were flying over the plain in terror and confusion. A few who endeavored to hide themselves under the bank of the creek were surrounded and shot down in cold blood, offering but feeble resistance. From the sucking

THE NEW INDIAN WAR.
NOW, NO SARCASTIC INNUENDOES, BUT LET US HAVE A SQUARE FIGHT.

Indian land policy has always been a subject of controversy among whites. In this 1878 *Harper's Weekly* cartoon, "The New Indian War" is fought between Carl Schurz, the secretary of the interior, and General Philip Sheridan, the leader of several campaigns against Indian tribes in the 1860s and 1870s, representing the War Department. "The Noble Red Man" in the middle holds, in his pockets, a peace pipe pointing at Schurz and a tomahawk pointing at Sheridan.

babe to the old warrior, all who were overtaken were deliberately murdered. Not content with killing women and children, who were incapable of offering any resistance, the soldiers engaged in acts of barbarity of the most revolting character; such, it is to be hoped, as never before disgraced the acts of men claiming to be civilized. No attempt was made by the officers to restrain the savage cruelty of the men under their command, but they stood by and witnessed those acts without one word of reproof, if they did not incite their commission. For more than two hours the work of murder and barbarity was continued, until more than one hundred dead bodies, three-fourths of them women and children, lay on the plain as evidences of the fiendish malignity and cruelty of the officers who had so sedulously and carefully plotted the massacre, and of the soldiers who had so faithfully acted out the spirit of their orders.[16]

The survivors moved to the reservation. This was not the process envisioned by the Supreme Court.

Over the next two decades there were several other episodes in which the Army forced Indians onto reservations at the point of a gun. The same year as the Sand Creek Massacre, the Army marched the Navajos into a new reservation against their will. The Crows underwent a similar compelled resettlement in the early 1880s, after the local Indian agent Henry Armstrong decided that "the time has come when the Indians ought to be *governed* and there is no way to govern them but by force."[17]

Perhaps the best remembered of the forced relocations was that of the Sioux, after gold was discovered in the Black Hills in 1874. The Black Hills were within the Sioux Reservation, the boundaries of which had been defined only six years earlier. By the winter of 1875–76, however, gold had lured fifteen thousand white trespassers into the reservation. When the Sioux refused to sell the Black Hills, the Army attacked. The United States and the Sioux fought a series of skirmishes through the spring and summer of 1876, during the most famous of which, at Little Big Horn, George Custer and all the men under his command were killed. Congress responded by cutting off food to the Sioux until they agreed to cede the Black Hills. Facing the prospect of starvation, the Sioux finally gave in.[18]

Even in the absence of overt force, the treaties creating reservations often suffered from the same problems that had infected Indian treaties for centuries. Sometimes promised compensation was never paid. Sometimes the signatures of chiefs were obtained by bribery. There had always been some distance between the formal law and actual practice; in the mid-nineteenth century, that gap grew very wide.

Actual practice diverged from the formal law most sharply in California, where the white population increased so quickly in the 1850s and 1860s that the pace of formal land acquisition could not keep up. The government could not even adhere to the pretense of obtaining land and creating reservations by treaty. Robert Stevens, sent by the federal government to California to report on Indian affairs, found several Indian reservations, all of which had been created when whites had seized Indians' land by sheer force. "As is well known," he explained, "there have been no formal ratified treaties with the Indians, or extinguishment of title in this State, any more than by the inherent extinguishment conferred by the natural rights of man, evolved in the necessities of the continually incoming emigrants, who wish to occupy and develop the soil." Stevens himself thought the absence of any treaties a good thing. "The men of the past must give way to the men of the present," he concluded. "After all, nations die like men."[19] But this was not the way reservations were supposed to be created as a legal matter. In principle, the Indians of California had the same right of occupancy as Indians anywhere else. The government was supposed to be purchasing it.

The reservations had been set up to serve inconsistent purposes, and by the 1870s it was obvious that the goal of confining the Indians was winning out over the goal of protecting them. In some cases the government compelled tribes to cede land and accept reservations; in others, the government forced dissident members of tribes onto reservations they did not wish to inhabit. These actions were sometimes justified on paternalistic grounds, as being for the Indians' own benefit. William Welsh considered himself a pro-Indian activist, for instance, and he was quite concerned that individual Sioux were leaving their reservation without first obtaining the permission of the government's Indian agent.[20] But it would take an extreme form of paternalism to excuse all the slaughter that accompanied the forced relocations of the 1860s and 1870s. In many of the new reservations, the lock was all too clearly on the outside.

The nature of the reservations was displayed most starkly whenever the Army tracked down Indians who had escaped from reservations, a task soldiers were repeatedly asked to perform. The Comanches, for example, regularly slipped away from their reservation, and were just as regularly chased by troops and brought back.[21] The notion of *escaping* from a reservation—even the idea that Indians would need permission to leave—would have been inconceivable to the early humanitarian proponents of reservations, who could not have imagined that the reservation would be used to incarcerate the Indians.

Three celebrated escapes in the late 1870s focused public attention on the issue. In 1877 a Nez Percé band led by Chief Joseph was herded back onto the Nez Percé Reservation in Idaho after attempting to flee to Canada. The Northern Cheyennes had been forced onto a reservation in present-day Oklahoma, but in 1878 a group of three hundred Northern Cheyennes escaped and fled to the north, back toward their home. The Army caught up with some of the Cheyennes in Nebraska. Others made it as far as Montana before they were captured, six months after the escape. Those who were not killed were forced to return to the reservation. Even more spectacular was the escape of the Poncas, a small tribe who had likewise been moved to a reservation in Oklahoma. In 1879 the chief Standing Bear led many of the Poncas north. Again, the Army pursued them, and captured them in Nebraska. With the help of white sympathizers (including General George Crook, their captor, who was carrying out an order he personally found unjust), the Poncas brought suit in federal court. They persuaded the court to grant a writ of habeas corpus ordering their release. "I have searched in vain," Judge Elmer Dundy concluded, "for the semblance of any authority justifying" the government "in attempting to remove by force any Indians, whether belonging to a tribe or not, to any place." The government had the power, and indeed the obligation, to keep trespassers *out* of a reservation, Judge Dundy held, but no power to keep Indians in. By then the Poncas' story was headline news. Their cause was taken up by white reformers, all the while confirming the growing impression that Indian reservations were doing more to wall Indians in than to keep settlers out.[22]

These repeated escapes testified to the hardships of life on many of the reservations. Some reservations housed multiple tribes with little in common—even tribes with a long history of animosity toward each other—because the government was not particularly careful about which tribes would be placed with which. Peter Pitchlynn, a Choctaw emissary to Congress, pointed out the difficulties involved in consolidating several tribes in a single place. Each tribe was accustomed to its own sovereignty, Pitchlynn explained. "They have been separate and independent of each other from time immemorial, and are exceedingly sensitive in relation to any matters that may affect this independence." But that was only the start of it. Some tribes were agriculturalists, while others were hunters. "Their languages are wholly different; most of the tribes do not understand each other. . . . Their laws and customs are wholly different."[23]

Tribes accustomed to hunting found it difficult to continue when confined to a reservation. Agricultural tribes had trouble growing traditional crops in a new location. "The bringing of us here has caused a great decrease of our numbers, many of us have died, also a great number of our animals," reported the Navajo Barboncito, after the tribe was relocated to the Bosque Redondo Reservation. "Our grandfathers had no idea of living in any other country except our own and I do not think it right for us to do so." The problem was "this ground we were brought on, it is not productive. We plant but it does not yield. All the stock we brought here have nearly all died." The Navajos had given up planting crops. When they ran out of food they ate their animals. After a few years at Bosque Redondo, the Navajos were destitute. The land was more fertile on the Wichita Reservation, so the Caddos and Wichitas were more successful at growing crops and raising livestock, but they too found it impossible to produce enough to feed themselves, so, like many tribes, they were dependent on meager government rations for survival, and their population steadily declined. Life on the reservation, many found, was considerably worse than life had been before.[24]

Making matters worse, the reservation had promised to shelter the Indians from encroaching whites, but the federal government proved no better at keeping white trespassers off the Indians' land than it had ever been. A formal declaration that a given tract of land was an Indian reservation could not change the reality on the ground: the trespassers were scattered over an enormous area, they greatly outnumbered the relatively small number of soldiers who had the responsibility of removing them, and in any event those soldiers were, most of the time, more interested in protecting the settlers than the Indians. Some of the federal government's Indian agents genuinely wanted to evict trespassers, but they knew they lacked the power. "The Indian Country is being filled up with squatters," agent B. F. Robinson complained in 1854; "I am at a loss to know how to proceed." As the white population of the West grew, varieties of encroachment multiplied. In the Southwest, for example, white farmers diverted scarce water from Indian farms. White miners took minerals from beneath Indian lands. A reservation was a line on paper. It was no barrier to the appropriation of the Indians' resources.[25]

And sometimes settlers took more than land or water. "Neither our territorial nor military authorities ever punish white men, according to law, for robbing, and especially murdering Indians," charged a broadside published by the New York–based American Indian Aid Association. "The Indian race is not being diminished in consequence of any decree of manifest destiny, as has been most fallaciously asserted by border settlers and other interested persons; but by very different instrumentalities, such as the rum, the rifle, the revolver, and contaminations of their white aggressors."[26] As always, however, the matter looked different from the point of view of the settlers, who tended to think of themselves as peaceful pioneers surrounded by savages. A satirical poem in the New York humor magazine *Punchinello*, titled "The Indian Question (As Viewed in the West)," summarized the settler perspective:

> This is *our* business, understand!
> You Eastern folks, with tempers bland
> All get your views at second-hand.
> *We* are the ones that take the brunt
> Of every lively Indian-hunt,
> So don't be angry if we're blunt.
> If any body's scalped it's *us!*
> So we've a well-earned right to cuss,
> And you've *no* right to make a fuss.
> Talk as you please about their "rights;"
> That don't include their coming nights,
> And cutting out our lungs and lights.[27]

There was nothing new about this sentiment, but that is the point—the existence of reservations could hardly alter the incompatible incentives and perspectives that had always characterized the frontier.

There were many whites who sympathized with the Indians, as in all prior periods, and by the 1870s and 1880s they were firing a steady barrage of criticism at the government for forcing the Indians to cede their land and live on reservations. "It is scarcely necessary to say, what is universally conceded," argued the poet and journalist John Greenleaf Whittier, "that the wars waged by the Indians against the whites, have, in nearly every instance, been provoked by violations of solemn treaties, and systematic disregard of their rights of person, property and life." "We ought to have learned something from past experience in regard to the removal of Indians from their homes to satisfy the convenience or greed of the white man," declared Charles C. Painter on behalf of the Indian Rights Association, the most important of the reform organizations. "The Nez Perce war of 1877 was caused by an attempt to force Joseph's band of Lower Nez Perces to abandon their own home," Painter recalled. "All our troubles with the Chiracahua Apaches since 1876 have come from our attempts to remove them from their native mountains. . . . The war with the northern Cheyennes came from an attempt to make them stay in the Indian Territory." And of course "the shame and disgrace of the Ponca removal is yet fresh in mind." The *New York Times* likewise recalled "the miseries and the wars that are due to coaxing or coercing Indians from their ancestral homes." "Our Indian policy," the *Times* concluded, "is usually spoliation behind a mask of benevolence." The most famous of the reformers was Helen Hunt Jackson, who filled her 1881 classic, *A Century of Dishonor,* with story after story of tribes forced to give up their land. A few decades earlier, reformers like these had been among the most enthusiastic proponents of the reservation. They had not expected reservations to be created and maintained by violence.[28]

The law governing the acquisition of land from the Indians had always been at odds with the actual practice of obtaining land, going back to the early colonial period, but the divergence between the two reached its widest point in the second half of the nineteenth century. The size of the gap between theory and practice had always been a function of the relative power of settlers and Indians. By the late nineteenth century, the settlers were more powerful relative to the Indians, in terms of numbers and technology, than they had ever been. The white population of the United States was increasing very fast. Many were heading to the West. The government was democratically accountable to the settlers but not to the Indians, who could not vote and who would have been greatly outnumbered even if they could.

The interesting question, then, is not why there developed such a large gap between the law on paper and the law in practice, but rather why the law on paper did not change. As a matter of Supreme Court doctrine, the Indians continued to enjoy the right to live on their own land as long as they wanted to. They had the power, in theory, to refuse to convey their land to the government, to refuse to move to a reservation, and to leave a reservation so long as they were not trespassing on someone else's land. As accounts of forced relocations and foiled escapes filled the newspapers, and as Congress held hearings into atrocities committed by United States soldiers in the course of herding the Indians into reservations, Supreme Court justices could hardly have avoided learning the reality of life in the West. Yet the Court continued to adhere to the fiction that Indian land transactions were void unless voluntarily entered into by the Indians.

The Supreme Court did little, to be sure, to stop the government from exploiting its superior power over the Indians. Instead, in a series of cases beginning in 1870, the Court consistently held that Congress has the power to enact statutes that abrogate Indian treaties. In the first of these cases the Court upheld the validity of a federal tax on tobacco produced on the Cherokee reservation, despite the existence of a treaty granting the Cherokees immunity from such taxes. Later cases applied the same principle to permit Congress to take land away from reservations and grant it to non-Indians. In the most notorious of these cases, *Lone Wolf v. Hitchcock*, the Court refused to consider the complaint of the Kiowas that Congress had deprived the tribe of land in a manner clearly inconsistent with the 1867 Treaty of Medicine Lodge. "It was never doubted that the *power* to abrogate existed in Congress," Justice Edward White's opinion reaffirmed, and "as Congress possessed full power in the matter, the judiciary cannot question or inquire into the motives which prompted the enactment of this legislation." The Court's passivity ensured that the Indians' property rights were far stronger in principle than in practice.[29]

It is conventional today to criticize the Court for cases like *Lone Wolf*, and to suggest that the justices of the era were accomplices to the forced dispossession of the Indians. One historian, for example, calls *Lone Wolf* "the culmination of the late-nineteenth-century attack by the federal legislature and judiciary on Native American political and legal rights." While the justices were no doubt men of their era, with attitudes toward Indians that would be out of step with prevailing beliefs a century later, such criticism is overdrawn. The idea that Congress could abrogate Indian treaties was not devised as a method of harming the Indians. It followed from the well-established doctrine that Congress had the power to abrogate treaties with foreign countries. Such a power was necessary, American lawyers realized, because otherwise Congress would be unable to declare war (which is often inconsistent with existing treaties) or to respond in other ways to changing aspects of the international climate. By the late nineteenth century, lawyers were accustomed to thinking of international treaties as capable of being repealed, like any other laws, by a subsequent act of Congress. The justices instinctively placed Indian treaties in the same category.[30]

The analogy was not perfect: Indian tribes were far more dependent on the federal government's promises than was any foreign country, and so they were far more vulnerable when Congress abrogated a treaty. One might have argued, in cases like *Lone Wolf*, that the consequences of a broken treaty were more dire to Indian tribes than to foreign countries, and that Congress should accordingly be held to its promises.[31] But if Indian treaties differed in some respects from treaties with foreign countries, they were also similar in many ways. Federal officials perceived the same need for flexibility with respect to Indian tribes (to fight wars, for example, when relations soured) as with respect to foreign countries. Perhaps most important to a legally trained mind, Indian treaties, like foreign treaties, were, in a formal sense, agreements between sovereigns. Although Indian tribes had largely lost the power associated with real sovereignty, in the law they were still sovereign entities. To a late nineteenth-century lawyer, it would have seemed anomalous to grant Congress any less power to break an Indian treaty than it already had to break a foreign treaty. The line of cases exemplified by *Lone Wolf* was driven as much by a lawyerly desire for consistency as by any racism or land hunger on the part of the Supreme Court.

Meanwhile, the *Lone Wolf* line of cases existed alongside another line that was more favorable to the Indians. Even as events in the West were at their blackest, the Court continued all the while to insist that Indians possessed an inviolable right of occupancy in their unceded land.[32] One could, perhaps, understand such statements in a Machiavellian way, as deliberately ineffectual blather intended to cover up the actual conquest going on in the West. But it is hard to see why justices bent on conquest would have perceived a need to cover it up. The Court's consistent reiterations of the right of occupancy are more convincingly interpreted at face value, as genuine reports of what the justices perceived the law to be. In part this was a product of the inherent conservatism of the law, the standard reluctance to depart from precedent unless the circumstances absolutely require it. The Court's reaffirmation of the right of occupancy must also have been in part attributable to the ambivalent nature of the eastern intellectual climate. The justices would have read newspaper accounts of actual events in the West, but they would also have been familiar with eastern humanitarian opinion. They knew of the Sand Creek Massacre, but they also knew the shock that it provoked among eastern intellectuals. As in any period, it would be a mistake to treat white policymakers as monolithic in their attitudes toward the Indians.

In the second half of the nineteenth century, then, the Supreme Court was playing a standard role in an old drama. It was the conscience at the center of government, too far from the frontier to have much real influence, issuing rules for the humane treatment of the Indians that would largely be ignored in the field. This was the role played by the imperial government in London before 1776, and by certain executive branch officials of the federal government in the early republic. In the middle and late nineteenth century, while the Army was slaughtering Indians and herding them into reservations, the Supreme Court was keeping alive an old legal tradition of recognizing the Indians' property rights. That would prove crucial in the twentieth century, when better times came for the Indians and some tribes were able to use that legal tradition to their advantage.

From Treaties to . . . What?

It was increasingly apparent by the middle of the nineteenth century that many of the treaties in which tribes ostensibly consented to live on reservations were not treaties in the full sense of the word, but documents papering over the exercise of force. This growing realization led, in 1871, to a change in the legal form by which Indian land was acquired.[33]

Indian treaties had been the subject of steady criticism since the early 1800s, on the ground that it was anomalous to enter into treaties with inhabitants of one's own country. The point had long been made by people like Andrew Jackson and John Calhoun, who argued that Indians should instead be regulated directly by the government, just like white Americans were. That sort of criticism had never died out. Commissioner of Indian Affairs William Dole, for example, took up the argument in his annual report for 1862. "It may well be questioned whether the government has not adopted a mistaken policy in regarding the Indian tribes as quasi-independent nations, and making treaties with them for the purchase of the lands they claim to own," Dole suggested. "They have none of the elements of nationality; they are within the limits of the recognized authority of the United States and must be subject to its control." The Seneca Ely Parker, the first Indian to be appointed Commissioner of Indian Affairs, made the same point in his annual report for 1869. "A treaty involves the idea of a compact between two or more sovereign powers, each possessing sufficient authority and force to compel a compliance with the obligations incurred," reasoned Parker, but Indian tribes lacked the strength to compel their own members to comply with treaties. "It is time that this idea should be dispelled, and the government cease the cruel farce of thus dealing with its helpless and ignorant wards." On this view, Indian treaties were a vestige of a time when tribes were much like foreign states—when they controlled a territory separate from the area inhabited by settlers, and when regulating their members directly would have been militarily impossible. Those days, the critics suggested, were long gone. "There is not a civilized nation on the face of the globe that undertakes to make treaties with roving bands of savages," declared William Lawrence of Ohio on the floor of the House of Representatives. The Indians, he concluded, "are dependent tribes, within our jurisdiction and subject to our laws."[34]

As Lawrence's remark suggested, many also found Indian treaties anomalous for a second reason: the Indians were simply too primitive to treat with. After eighteen months among the Sioux, the Indian agent D. C. Poole concluded that the Indian "has a childlike interest in the present and small care for the future." George Custer, who pointedly gave his autobiography the subtitle *Personal Experiences with Indians*, mocked the romantic image of the Indian as portrayed by armchair writers like James Fenimore Cooper. Out on the plains, Custer insisted, "we see him as he is, and, so far as all knowledge goes, as he ever has been, a *savage* in every sense of the word; . . . one whose cruel and ferocious nature far exceeds that of any wild beast of the desert." On this view, negotiating treaties with Indians made no more sense than negotiating treaties with animals. If the Indians were savages, *Harper's Weekly* noted, "let us act accordingly. There is no prohibition upon hunting the buffalo. Every hunter rides and shoots at his own risk. We propose no buffalo treaties; we have no buffalo reservations." Why treat the Indians differently? *Harper's* was joking, but Custer was not, and he was hardly alone in his view.[35]

Observations like these were attributable in part to a hardening belief that Indians were biologically inferior to whites. Although it is impossible to measure changing attitudes with any certainty, it seems likely that the prevailing view a century earlier was that whites were merely farther along the path to civilization than Indians, and that with time and appropriate instruction the Indians might close the gap. By the second half of the nineteenth century, however, a growing interest in evolution and heredity, and a growing acceptance of biological explanations for racial differences, caused many whites to believe that differences between themselves and the Indians were permanent parts of the natural order. Indian treaties were once understood as devices for civilizing the Indians, but now many saw no point in even trying.

This sort of criticism of treaties can also be traced to the changing characteristics of the Indian tribes that settlers encountered. It was one thing to enter into a treaty with a large group like the Cherokees. It was quite another to sign a treaty with some of the tiny tribes of the West. "One of these treaties which has been made in Oregon was with the Umpquas," remarked an amused Aaron Augustus Sargent of California. "There are thirty-eight individuals, men, women, and children, all told, as shown by the census of the 'great nation' of Umpquas! Another of the treaties has been made with the Calapooias, binding us to pay, year after year, several thousand dollars to them. They number two hundred and eighty-two souls, men, women, and children. Another of these great nations, with which the treaty-making power has made treaties, are the Rogue River Indians, and we are bound to pay them thousands of dollars. They number altogether two hundred and thirty-six individuals. A great nation with whom treaties should be made!" Tribes like these were "simply the wards of the Government, to whom we furnish means of existence, and not independent nations with whom we are to treat as our equals," Sargent declared. "Ought not that fact to be admitted? Has not the comedy of 'treaties,' 'potentates,' 'nations,' been played long enough?"[36]

Indian treaties also affected the balance of power within the federal government in ways that created recurring conflict. The Constitution confers upon the Senate alone the power to ratify treaties, but requires the concurrence of the Senate and the House of Representatives for ordinary legislation. When Indian treaties committed the federal government to pay tribes in exchange for land cessions, as they often did, the House found itself forced to agree to appropriate money for purposes it had no voice in choosing. Worse, Indian treaties often reserved for Indians the very same land that congressional representatives wanted to grant to settlers, at a time when representatives were the only directly elected members of Congress and many represented districts in which reserving public land for the Indians could be a serious political liability. There were always members of the House who resented the institution of the Indian treaty.

Despite decades of criticism along these lines, the federal government had continued to enter into treaties with Indian tribes. There were always white humanitarian voices to speak up for treaties, because any other method of acquiring the Indians' land promised to leave the Indians even worse off. But the growing realization in the mid-nineteenth

By the late nineteenth century, land was acquired from the Indians by force, despite the retention of a contractual legal form, and even the more consensual land purchases of the early colonial period had come to be viewed with considerable cynicism. In this 1899 *Life* cartoon, "The Circumvention of the Native by William Penn," Penn trades trinkets for land, while at the lower left an Indian digs what is presumably his own grave.

century that many of the new treaties were shams had the effect of muting this kind of support. The Board of Indian Commissioners, a group of wealthy religious philanthropists appointed in 1869 by President Grant to oversee much of the government's relations with the tribes, concluded in its first annual report that the treaty system should be abandoned and "uncivilized Indians" treated as wards of the government. The Episcopal bishop Henry Whipple, perhaps the best-known white advocate for the Indians in the 1860s, thought the way treaties were negotiated was "one of those blunders which is worse than a crime. We recognize a wandering tribe as an independent and sovereign nation," Whipple argued:

We send ambassadors to make a treaty as with our equals, knowing that every provision of that treaty will be our own, that those with whom we make it cannot compel us to observe it, that they are to live within our territory, yet not subject to our laws, that they have no government of their own, and are to receive none from us; in a word, we treat as an independent nation a people whom we will not permit to exercise one single element of that sovereign power which is necessary to a nation's existence.

The treaty is usually conceived and executed in fraud. The ostensible parties to the treaty are the government of the United States and the Indians; the real parties are the Indian agents, traders, and politicians. The avowed purpose of the treaty is for a Christian nation to acquire certain lands at a fair price, and make provision that the purchase-money shall be wisely expended, so as to secure the civilization of the Indians. The real design is to pay certain worthless debts of the Indian traders, to satisfy such claims, good or bad, against the Indians, as have been or may be made, and to create places where political favorites may receive their reward for political service.

The Reverend T. S. Williamson agreed that "after treaties are solemnly made, we fulfil, modify or abrogate them as suits our own convenience." Men like Whipple and Williamson were the traditional white constituency for the Indian treaty. When even they started doubting the utility of treaties, the institution could not last very long.[37]

All that was wanting was a reason for members of Congress to focus their attention on the issue. That reason came in 1869, after a flurry of treaties caused the Senate to add several million dollars to the annual Indian appropriations bill, to pay for annuities and other goods promised to various tribes. These additional appropriations aroused so much opposition in the House that in the next session of Congress the House passed a bill prohibiting further Indian treaties. There was enough sentiment along those lines in the Senate for the Senate to agree. The statute eventually enacted in 1871 provided "that hereafter no Indian nation or tribe within the territory of the United States shall be acknowledged or recognized as an independent nation, tribe, or power with whom the United States may contract by treaty." Some members of Congress even wanted to abrogate all the old treaties, but Congress did not go that far. The statute made clear that "nothing herein contained shall be construed to invalidate or impair the obligation of any treaty heretofore lawfully made and ratified with any such Indian nation or tribe."[38] The old treaties would remain in force. After 1871, however, there would be no new Indian treaties.

But what would take their place? For two and half centuries, Indian land had been acquired in transactions structured as voluntary agreements between the buyers and the sellers—as treaties between sovereigns ever since the Proclamation of 1763, and as a mixture of treaties and private contracts before that. Now that treaties were illegal, how would land be acquired? Francis Walker, the commissioner of Indian affairs, recognized the problem in his annual report for 1872. For as long as the United States had existed, he explained, the nation "pursued a uniform course of extinguishing the Indian title only with the consent of those Indian tribes which were recognized as having a claim by reason of occupancy." Walker acknowledged that "wrong was often done in fact to tribes in the negotiation of treaties of cession. The Indians were not infrequently overborne or deceived by agents of the Government in these transactions." But "formally at least," Indian land had always been acquired in treaties.[39] What now?

The answer emerged very soon. For all the hyperbole in Congress and elsewhere about the incongruity of negotiating agreements with Indian tribes, there was really no other way to go about acquiring the Indians' land. The normative appeal of formally voluntary transactions was too great for them to be abandoned in an instant. Few in the federal government had the stomach to switch to an explicit policy of conquest. Instead, the government quickly adopted a set of techniques that have aptly been called "treaty substitutes."[40] These were methods of acquiring land and establishing reservations that were functionally identical to treaties but were not treaties in the technical legal sense. They were available because the 1871 statute had not prohibited all agreements with Indian tribes. It had only prohibited agreements called "treaties."

One obvious treaty substitute was to have *both* houses of Congress, rather than just the Senate, approve agreements with Indian tribes. Another substitute was for Congress to pass statutes acquiring a tribe's land provided the tribe consented. The land cessions of the 1870s and 1880s were accomplished by these techniques. From the Indians' perspective, they looked exactly like treaties. The only difference between treaties and treaty substitutes concerned the allocation of authority within the federal government. A third treaty substitute was the executive order, which had been used before 1871, alongside the treaty, to set aside public land for Indian reservations. After 1871, presidents simply used the executive order more frequently.

In the end, then, the abolition of the Indian treaty in 1871 was a change in the legal form, but not the substance, of land transactions. It did not affect the pace of land acquisition in the West or the frequency with which the government created reservations. Far more important than the demise of the treaty would be another phenomenon that was taking place at the same time—the growing dissatisfaction with the institution of the Indian reservation.

From Reservations to . . . What?

The concept of the reservation was coming under attack by the 1870s, as it became more and more evident that reservations were not advancing either of the goals that had motivated their creation. Whether one was interested primarily in helping whites settle without the hindrance of nearby Indians, or in helping Indians flourish without the hindrance of nearby whites, the reservation increasingly looked like a failure.

Reservations tended to be created in any given area soon after the area experienced its first significant white settlement, when it was hard to imagine that the land left for the settlers would ever be perceived as inadequate. But the West consistently filled up with settlers faster than expected. The population density of Colorado multiplied fivefold between 1870 and 1880. That of Montana tripled between 1870 and 1880 and tripled again the following decade. As more whites headed west, reservations created years before came to seem unfairly large to settlers who wanted land the Indians appeared to be wasting. In the Indian Territory, for example, tribes removed from the Southeast in the first half of the century held reservations encompassing nearly twenty million acres, one advocate for the settlers complained, while homesteads for settlers were growing scarce. Was it fair, settlers wondered, that a small number of Indians could monopolize so much land, when so many white farmers could put it to better use? "As well keep London in limits, to save orchards adjoining," suggested the Indian-fighting General Henry B. Carrington, "as to hold millions of acres intact for the *red man's hunt*. The tidal wave must sweep on."[41]

To be sure, there were always earnest expressions to the contrary. "These Indian reservations are not, as has been represented by those who covet them, to an unreasonable extent lying unused by the Indians," insisted the Board of Indian Commissioners. "Their owners are not a horde of savage nomads standing in the way of civilization, as they would have us believe."[42] But this sort of dissatisfaction with the reservations would be a constant refrain, one that could only grow louder as the white population of the West grew.

Also growing in volume over the second half of the century was the observation that Indians seemed to be using the land on reservations less productively than whites used their land. Critics suggested two different reasons why this was so, but both pointed to the institution of the reservation as the root cause.

One perceived problem was that even though the government was often careful in drawing the *external* boundaries of reservations, it normally said nothing about property rights *within* the reservation.[43] The land within a reservation was simply granted to the tribe as a whole. The absence of government-defined individual property rights, reformers argued, prevented hardworking Indians from enjoying the fruits of their labor, and so discouraged labor in the first place. "I have seen instances of it," explained J. B. Harrison in his treatise on Indian reservations, "when educated young Indians had married, built themselves a house, and laid in a stock of provisions for the winter, flour, meat, vegetables, fruit, sugar, coffee, tea, salt, soap, etc. While the young man is away at work, the old chiefs of the tribe, and their retainers, will come to the house and eat up, and carry away, every vestige of food, and every article of clothing and furniture, leaving the house bare and the young people destitute." The solution was to break up the reservation and vest ownership of land in individuals rather than in tribes as a whole.[44]

The inefficiencies of collective ownership are as familiar today as they were in the nineteenth century, but nevertheless it seems quite unlikely that the lack of government-defined individual property rights inhibited the productivity of reservations. Tribes accustomed to farming already had property systems of their own that allocated exclusive rights to individuals, and those systems still existed on the reservations. Among such tribes, hardworking farmers *did* enjoy the fruits of their labor. Tribes who were traditionally hunter-gatherers, on the other hand, lacked similarly well-established methods of dividing property among individuals. Like hunter-gatherers around the world, they tended to be governed by long-standing norms of sharing, according to which a person who killed an animal was obliged to share the catch with others.[45] These norms would not have transferred well to agriculture, of course, but there is no evidence that any tribe tried to transfer them. The troubles that the nonfarming tribes had in converting to agriculture seem to have been caused by the inherent difficulty of learning a new way of life, rather than by the retention of a vestigially communal system of property rights. The complaint that the absence of individual property rights slowed development on Indian reservations was common among reformers in the late nineteenth century, but it does not seem to have been accurate.

Perhaps the reason most commonly voiced for why the reservations were unproductive, however, was that the federal government was constantly redrawing their boundaries under the pressure of white settlement. "The practice of removing tribes has of course retarded their improvement," one critic noted as early as 1860. "Could it be expected that Indians would take much interest in cultivating land which they were destined to abandon to others?" Agriculture required investment for the future, but without assurance of being able to reap what one had sown, little sowing would get done. The Board of Indian Commissioners reported in 1871 that "the frequent removal of Indians has led to a general distrust of the designs of the Government with regard to them, and the fear of such removal has deprived them of all incentive to improve their lands." By the 1880s the point had been made again and again: land tenure on reservations was too insecure to encourage investment.[46]

The problem, strictly speaking, was not the reservation itself but the government's habit of moving reservations around. But the two issues were inextricably linked, because it was generally understood that the government would be far less likely to move Indians if the Indians owned their land by the same tenure as whites—as individuals rather than as tribes.[47] Under the Constitution, the government could not uproot a white landowner without paying for the market value of the land. If the same law applied to the Indians, they might be as secure as whites.

By the late nineteenth century, moreover, there was considerable sentiment that the reservations had become pockets of poverty and backwardness—the very opposite of what many reformers had hoped they would be a few decades earlier. "The reservation system runs a fence about a great territory and says to civilization, 'Keep off!'" insisted the Congregationalist minister Lyman Abbott, one of the best-known Indian reformers of the 1880s. "It holds back civilization and isolates the Indian, and denies him any right which justice demands for him." Reservations, another critic charged, had turned the Indians into a "race of involuntary prisoners and paupers." That the Indians were still savages was no fault of their own; rather, they were victims of a misguided policy. As one correspondent suggested in 1885, the same would have happened to anyone: "Place a few hundred white families of a low grade of intelligence upon an area as large as the State of New Jersey, keep everybody else off the territory, let these people know that the Government will provide them with blankets and with flour, beef, and sugar, if they are in want, and they or their descendants would become about as lazy and barbarous as the Indians in a short time."[48]

The reservation still had its defenders, who argued that the problem was not with the institution but with the way in which it was implemented in practice. The idea of separating Indians and whites was sound, they argued. If only the government could do something to stop settlers from trespassing, or if only the government could guarantee, in practice, that reservations would not be moved in the future, the institution might still serve its intended purposes. Among whites seeking to promote the welfare of Indians, however, and among the Indians themselves, there was little confidence that the government would ever be able or even willing to act so benevolently. Maybe, they began to think, the answer lay in assimilation rather than segregation. "Cease to treat the Indian as a red man and treat him as a man," Abbott insisted. "Treat him as we have treated the Poles, Hungarians, Italians, Scandinavians. Many of them are no better able to take care of themselves than the Indians; but we have thrown on them the responsibility of their own custody, and they have learned to live by living." Maybe the best way to protect the Indians was not to wall them off but to insist that they be treated like whites.[49]

By the 1880s, however, the West was dotted with all the reservations that had been created in the previous few decades. Property rights in these reservations had been guaranteed to Indian tribes by the federal government in treaty after treaty (before 1871) and then in treaty substitutes (after 1871). It was easy enough to say that the reservation was a failure. But what would take its place? This would be the central question of federal Indian policy for the next fifty years.

Allotment

EACH of the major programs that characterized nineteenth-century Indian land policy was supported by a coalition of the Indians' friends and foes, and each proved disastrous for the Indians. Removal, in the early part of the century, and reservations, in the middle, each had the support of two kinds of people—whites trying to protect the Indians by placing them apart, and whites trying to obtain their land. In each case, it was clear within a decade or two that only the latter group achieved its goal. This process took place yet again at the end of the century, when white humanitarians turned to what they hoped would be a different method of helping the Indians. In a variety of areas, from education to political participation, Indian policy turned from segregation to assimilation.[1] As applied to land, the ideal of assimilation took the form of the General Allotment Act, or Dawes Act, of 1887, which envisioned carving up the Indian reservations into fee simple plots owned by individuals and families, in the same way whites owned their land. The Dawes Act, as amended every few years, remained in effect until 1934.

From the Indians' perspective the result was, once again, disaster. Many supporters of allotment were trying to protect the Indians from losing more of their land, but allotment also had the support of many who wanted to accelerate land loss, and once again it was the latter goal that was achieved. Between 1887 and 1934 the Indians lost most of their remaining land—86 million acres out of the 138 million in their possession in 1887. One of the goals of allotment was to encourage Indian farming, but during the period of allotment the extent of Indian farming *declined,* both absolutely and relative to whites.[2] Making matters worse, by 1934 much of the Indians' remaining land was owned in patterns so complex as to impose debilitating consequences on the nominal owners, consequences that have persisted up through today. For the Indians and anyone concerned with their welfare, allotment was a failure so spectacular that it raises questions about the motivation and execution of the policy. How could so many people have genuinely believed in allotment? And how could it have gone so wrong?

Allotment, before "Allotment"

Like the previous installments of federal Indian land policy, allotment was far from a new concept when it became the focus of public attention. By the late nineteenth century, Anglo-Americans had been allotting land for hundreds of years, all over the world, including land belonging to Indians.

Land tenure in Britain itself and in much of the rest of Europe once resembled land tenure among American Indian tribes. Individuals and families tended to own rights to use particular resources in particular ways, not rights over all the resources in a given geographic space. A person might, for example, have the right to farm a given strip of land during the growing season, the right to pasture a certain number of animals in a certain field during certain times of year, the right to gather wood from a given forest, and so on. Between the fifteenth century and the nineteenth century, this functionally organized system of property rights was gradually transformed into the spatially organized system we know today, in which individuals and families own zones of land and are understood to command all the resources within the zone. In Britain this process was generally called *enclosure,* but it was similar to what in the United States would be called *allotment*—the replacement of one property system, in which any given geographic area was likely to contain property rights held by many people, with another, in which all the property rights in each geographic area were held by a single person.[3]

The arguments for enclosure were many, but the dominant theme was efficiency. Land divided spatially, it was argued, would be used more productively than land divided functionally. This usually turned out to be true. Land rents tended to rise after enclosure, which suggests that the land was producing more. But enclosure had distributive consequences as well. It harmed some of the poorest Britons, who lost their rights to use the old common fields, rights that had been the basis of their livelihood. This pair of results—greater agricultural efficiency and the detriment it caused to the poorest beneficiaries of the old system— would recur in many other places that underwent the same transition, including the United States.[4]

In Britain in the late eighteenth and early nineteenth centuries, as the number of landless people grew, there was considerable sentiment to give out small garden parcels to the poor, who would thereby be empowered to grow some of their own food, while also learning the values of hard work and thrift. These parcels were generally called *allotments*. Some were doled out by local governments, others by private philanthropists. Some exist to this day. The British allotment movement was highly visible all through the nineteenth century, particularly during the 1880s, when Congress was debating whether and how to divide up the Indian reservations. Indeed, in 1887, the year Congress passed the General Allotment Act, the British Parliament enacted an Allotments Act of its own, requiring local authorities to provide allotments when there was sufficient demand for them.[5]

The British were meanwhile settling throughout the world. They brought their ideas about property with them, and in many places they set out to convert indigenous property systems into the system they knew, through comprehensive programs that closely resembled enclosure. Beginning in the 1840s the nominally independent kingdom of Hawaii, under heavy influence from British and American settlers, reorganized its traditional system of land tenure by dividing much of the land into fee simple plots. In the 1860s the British colonial government of New Zealand established a Native Land Court for the purpose of replacing traditional Maori land tenure with fee simple titles to zones of space. Soon after, the British set up a similar institution in Fiji. These schemes were intended to serve two purposes. They would contribute toward the civilization of the indigenous inhabitants, by turning them into self-sufficient English-style farmers who appreciated the value of hard work. And simultaneously they would facilitate British settlement, by putting land into a form in which it could be purchased from its owners by incoming colonists. These twin goals would reappear in the United States in the late nineteenth century.[6]

While there was no comprehensive program of allotment in the United States until 1887, the allotment of parcels to Indians had been proceeding here and there, on an ad hoc basis, almost since the beginning of English colonization. A Massachusetts statute of 1633 provided that "for the civilizing and helping them forward to Christianity, if any of the Indians shall be brought to civility, and shall come among the English to inhabit, . . . such Indians shall have allotments amongst the English." Fee simple grants were a feature of the "praying towns" established for Indians converted to Christianity in colonial New England. This policy continued after the Revolution. The ministers Jeremy Belknap and Jedidiah Morse reported in 1796 that the Indians "of New Stockbridge and Brotherton have made a division of their lands, so that each one holds his landed property as an estate in fee simple." Belknap and Morse concluded that "this is the *grand reason* of their superiority in point of agricultural improvements to their brethren, the Oneidas, Tuscaroras, etc."[7]

As these comments suggest, it was conventional wisdom among whites that the Indians would be improved by owning plots of land in the Anglo-American style. The Indians would work harder, many believed, if they owned their land by the same tenure whites did. But the benefits of fee simple landownership were widely understood to be much broader than that. Private property was more than just an incentive to produce food. It was an essential component of civilization, something that any society had to adopt before it could progress beyond barbarism. "Were it possible to introduce among the indian tribes a love for exclusive property," George Washington learned from Henry Knox, his secretary of war, "it would be a happy commencement of the business." As civilization was inseparable from Christianity, there was an obvious link between landownership and religion. "It is impossible ever to convert them" to true faith, averred the Revolutionary general Benjamin Lincoln, "until they can be impressed with just notions of their own situation, as it regards an exclusive right to the soil." Of all the aspects of Indian life that might be reformed, James Madison insisted in his final year as president, it was "divided and individual ownership" of land that was most important in establishing "the true foundation for a transit from the habits of the savage, to the arts and comforts of social life." T. Hartley Crawford, the commissioner of Indian affairs, was even more emphatic in his annual report for 1838. "Unless some system is marked out by which there shall be a separate allotment of land to each individual," he declared, "you will look in vain for any general casting off of savagism. Common property and civilization cannot co-exist."[8]

The connection between individual landownership and civilization was so obvious to nineteenth-century Americans that they tended not to explore it very closely. Sometimes "civilization" was simply assumed to be a consequence of increased agricultural productivity, which in turn was assumed to be a consequence of allotment. "The foundation of all civilization commences with the plow," thundered the Minnesota Congressman William Phelps in 1859, while advocating the allotment of land belonging to the Winnebago. "In the same proportion that agriculture is promoted, wealth and the more refined sciences, together with a larger intelligence, are also promoted. It is the history of all nations."[9] Allotment produced agriculture, and agriculture produced money and culture.

In retrospect, the first link in this chain does not seem very strong. Contrary to the assumptions of some of the cruder proponents of allotment, the Indians were not communists. Individual tribe members had exclusive rights to farm particular areas and exclusive rights to gather their crops. Indian tribes already had a system of property rights. When tribes were unsuccessful farmers, their problems tended to be due to factors like poor land, a lack of capital for adequate machinery, or poor skills. The one thing they were *not* missing was the right to reap what they had sown.

Sometimes, though, nineteenth-century Americans understood the connection between individual property and civilization as something less utilitarian, something more diffuse, than the simple relationship between hard work and wealth. To be a humanitarian in the nineteenth-century United States was to believe that there was such a thing as progress, and that it proceeded more or less the same way for all societies. Whites, Indians—all peoples were progressing along the path, but some were farther along than others. The kindest thing whites could possibly do for Indians, on this view, was to help them catch up. "Civilization" was a broad set of attributes characteristic of the societies that had made the most progress, qualities such as Christianity, morality, and scientific knowledge. Such things might have made people wealthier, but they were also good in their own right, regardless of their consequences. Individual ownership of land was in the same category. Even apart from its capacity to promote thrift and hard work, private property was an attribute of civilization. It was something worth bringing to the primitive peoples of the world for its own sake.

If allotment promoted civilization, then it made sense to convert Indian land-tenure systems into the Anglo-American system whenever possible, and so allotment—in the sense of grants in fee simple to individual Indians—became a frequent feature of the United States' Indian treaties. The first appears to have been an 1805 treaty with the Choctaws that reserved two parcels to individual tribe members. In some of the treaties by which southeastern tribes were removed to the West, tribe members were granted plots in fee simple. The allotment of land in fee simple became especially frequent in the treaties of the 1850s, and continued right up to the Dawes Act. As Indian Commissioner William Dole proudly reported in 1862, "one by one, the tribes are abandoning the custom of holding their lands in common, and are becoming individual owners of the soil—a step which I regard as the most important in their progress towards civilization." By 1887, when allotment became the general policy of the United States, several thousand Indians had already received patents evidencing their ownership of land in fee simple, land that amounted to more than seventeen million acres.[10]

Some of these treaties placed restrictions on the Indians' ability to sell their land. An 1825 treaty with the Kansas Indians, for example, required the permission of the federal government before tribe members were allowed to sell their parcels, and in 1860 Congress stiffened this requirement, by specifying that the secretary of the interior, not the land's owners, was the one who would conduct the sale and decide how the proceeds should be spent to best serve the sellers' interests. The point was to protect the Indians from their own improvidence. Without such restrictions, the Supreme Court explained, "there would be no way of preventing the Indians from being wronged in contracts for the sale of their lands, and the history of our country offers abundant proof that it is at all times difficult, by the most careful legislation, to protect their interests against the superior capacity and adroitness of their more civilized neighbors."[11] Individual landownership could be a blessing or a curse: it was a step along the road to civilization, but it also offered a path to destitution, if the land was sold and the proceeds frittered away. This tension ran through the piecemeal allotment programs of the nineteenth century and would become even more important when allotment became the centerpiece of American Indian policy.

By the late nineteenth century, then, allotment had a long history, both in the United States and abroad. As the reservations came under increasing criticism—in part from whites concerned with the welfare of Indians, and in part from whites who simply coveted the land—allotment began to look more attractive by comparison.

Adding to the urgency of the issue was the growing realization that, contrary to widespread expectations, the Indians were not dying out. In the 1870s the Bureau of Indian Affairs began to report fragmentary statistics suggesting that in many tribes births were exceeding deaths. By the decade's end it was conventional wisdom among experts that the Indian population had hit bottom and was beginning to rise.[12] Evidently the "Indian problem" was not going to go away on its own. In the 1870s and 1880s, many began to consider whether Congress ought to pass a general allotment act, a law applicable to *all* Indians, that would break up the reservations into individually owned parcels of land.

A Bill to Despoil the Indians of Their Lands

As with earlier changes in policy, it would be too simple to see allotment simply as a program imposed by whites on Indians. There were whites and Indians on both sides of the issue, just as there had been whites and Indians on both sides of removal and on both sides of whether to create reservations. As before, however, it was white opinion that mattered, and by the late 1880s white opinion was running in favor of allotment.

Perhaps the most common argument for allotment was an old one—that private property would encourage the Indians to be more industrious farmers. "Their weak point is agriculture," the *New York Times* editorialized in 1873. "And why? Because the land is held in common, and, though there are several who would show an example if they were to receive the fruits of their labors, yet they will not work for the lazy ones of the tribe." That the Indians would work harder once their land was allotted was a recurring theme in the annual reports of the Indian commissioners of the 1870s and 1880s. "When everything is held in common, thrift and enterprise have no stimulus of reward, and thus individual progress is rendered very improbable, if not impossible," asserted Edward P. Smith in his report for 1873. "The starting-point of individualism for an Indian is the personal possession of his portion of the reservation." Hard work was a virtue in its own right, and it also promised to relieve the government of its burden of supporting those Indians who, under the reservation system, could not support themselves.[13]

As in earlier periods, arguments based on the higher productivity associated with private property often slid into arguments that private property would bring the Indians to civilization in a broader sense. The Indian commissioners of the era doubted, as John Q. Smith put it in his report for 1876, "whether any high degree of civilization is possible without individual ownership of land." The North Carolina Democrat Thomas Skinner, one of allotment's supporters in the House of Representatives, agreed that the reservations were only "postponing their civilization" by denying the Indians the benefits of title to their land.[14] The connection between landownership and civilization was as complex as ever, encompassing "progress" in all of its dimensions.

Not everyone, least of all the Indians themselves, agreed that Indians were lazy farmers or that the civilizing process was being hindered by a lack of property rights. The Cherokees, for example, lobbied against allotment for years, and one of their major themes was that the popular white conception of Indian life was utterly inaccurate. "We are not a roving band of Indians, without a local habitation," insisted a delegation of Cherokees in 1878, when the question of allotment came before the Senate. "On the contrary, we are a 'corporate body'—a 'political community or state'—a 'nation'—in the broadest sense, feeble in number it is true, nevertheless a nation." The Cherokee chief Dennis Bushyhead observed that "there are those who wish us well who are carried away by the doctrine of 'land in severalty.' I would say to them that to provide that our land shall be a chattel that can be sold, immediately or remotely, is not the best way of civilizing Indians." This was so, Bushyhead patiently noted, because the Cherokees already had private property—not in land itself, but in the *use* of land—and the Cherokee system was in some important respects superior to the proposed alternative. "In the Cherokee nation individual property rights are fully respected," Bushyhead explained.

> A Cherokee is entitled to all the land he can cultivate and the exclusive use of land a quarter of a mile outside his fence. These rights descend to children and heirs, or can be sold and are sold continually, but the right is in the use; the property is in the improvements, and the land is not itself a chattel that can be speculated on whether cultivated or not. If it is abandoned for two years it reverts to the public domain, and any Cherokee can take unoccupied portions. This, like the air and waters, is the heritage of the people; if it were otherwise, our domain would soon drift into the hands of a few, and our poor people, in a few years, would become like your poor people, most of whom, if they died to-morrow, do not own a foot of the earth's surface in which they could be buried. If this is the phase of your civilization, to which you are at present so nervously inviting us, can you wonder if we pause to study the present tendencies and probable future of this fearfully anti-republican system? Our people have been taught from remote ages to believe that the surface of the earth, apart from its

use, is not a chattel. We are neither socialists nor communists, but we have a land system which we believe to be better than any you can devise for us. Individual rights are fully respected, but the rights of the whole people are not destroyed. Cannot you leave us alone to try our plan while you are trying yours?

In the 1890s, when a federal commission arrived in Oklahoma to negotiate the allotment of the Cherokees' land, Bushyhead once again pointed out that if allotment meant individual property rights to use land, "the Cherokees have had a complete though simple system of allotment in satisfactory operation since they framed their first constitution in 1828. This system consists in securing to each and every citizen of the nation as much domain as he or she can make valuable by means of improvements and cultivation." The Cherokee version of allotment, however, did not permit the enormous inequalities in ownership that existed under the property law of the United States. "Intelligent Cherokees know," Bushyhead remarked, "that dividing the national domain so that each citizen may be enabled to permanently convey his interest to another will be as sure to result in a monopoly of real estate among the red race as it has been among the whites."[15]

Leaders of other tribes likewise emphasized that they already had well-functioning property systems. "Our system of land tenure has proven successful and satisfactory to us through all the years of our tribal existence," affirmed the Creek chief Isparhecher. "Never have we had a homeless wanderer during all that time. . . . We have had no suits about land titles, for our land title is not disputable." From New York, the Senecas reported that "agriculture flourishes, the houses and farms of the Indians are constantly improving, the people are contented and prosperous, and there are no paupers to be a burden on the community," all under a property system in which "the lands are owned in common, controlled by the national councils, and are permanently inalienable." The Choctaw chief Wilson Jones reminded supporters of allotment that if "civilization" included a respect for one's heritage and for stability over the long run, allotment would hardly be an improvement over the property law the Choctaws already enjoyed. "We own the homes and lands of our grandfathers," Jones declared. "This can be said of the people of no state. Why is this? It is because our forefathers were wise enough when our first treaties were made, to adopt our present land system." Allotment was conceived by many of its proponents as a way of conferring upon the Indians the benefits of private property, but, as the Indians kept pointing out, Indian tribes already had private property. Individuals owned rights to use land, not the land itself, but it was property all the same.[16]

These voices did not go entirely unheard. The Colorado Republican Henry Moore Teller, the leading opponent of allotment in the Senate, understood that an Indian reservation was not a commons, and that allotment would accordingly fail to provide any incentive for the Indians to farm more industriously than they already were. "There is a wide difference between holding land in common tenure and working the land in common," he explained to his colleagues.

> Each Indian goes upon the reservation and takes for himself such land as is unoccupied and works it, and he works it just as long as he sees fit. That is the rule among all the Indian tribes. That possession of an Indian, that appropriation by him is as sacredly protected and guarded among the Indians as though he owned a fee-simple title; but when he abandons it and goes away from it then any other Indian may step in and take his place. Knowing that fact, and knowing that the Indians protect these possessions with as much scrupulous honesty as we protect the fee-simple title, I say that when it is asserted that they will not work because the title is not secure, it is nonsense.[17]

But this was an unusually lucid view among whites seeking to help the Indians. Most seem to have taken it for granted that the Indians were suffering from a lack of property rights.

There would have been more to the argument that allotment would improve the productivity of the Indians' land, had the argument been formulated a bit differently. Allotment promised, not to bring property to the Indians, but rather to replace Indian property systems with the Anglo-American system. Neither was obviously better suited for the small-scale farming that allotment's proponents sought to encourage. Indian property systems, however, might well have made other kinds of land use more difficult. Any major project that required assembling a large area of unused land, such as the construction of a factory or a hotel, for example, would have been difficult to undertake without modifying Indian property law, which did not recognize any right to buy or even hold vacant land for future use. In the late nineteenth century, however, proponents of allotment were not thinking of large construction projects. They were hoping to turn the Indians into yeoman farmers.

The prospect of encouraging the Indians to be more industrious was, in any event, only one of several arguments in favor of allotment. One of the major criticisms of the reservation was that it left the Indians too vulnerable to having their land expropriated, and this provided a second reason to divide the reservations into individually owned parcels. Allotment, some argued, would put Indian land tenure on the same footing as white tenure, and so provide greater protection against both individual trespassers and a federal government that had proven its willingness to move reservations around to suit white settlement patterns. The Round Valley Reservation in California, the government's Indian agent reported, was "still occupied by settlers and trespassers to such an extent that it is almost impossible to increase our stock, or to protect our growing crops from destruction by their stock." With the prospect of allotment, he explained "the Indians were quite jubilant," and when an allotment bill failed in Congress, they were "much distressed, fearing that the friends of the trespassers are the cause of its defeat." When the Interior Department recommended allotment in 1879, the impossibility of preventing trespassing was its lead argument. "The government is impotent to protect the Indians on their reservations," admitted Commissioner of Indian Affairs Ezra Hayt, "whenever a discovery has been made rendering the possession of their lands desirable by whites." Indeed, Hayt conceded, one of the worst offenders had been "the government itself, whenever an active demand is made that the treaty stipulations under which the Indians hold their lands should be abrogated to open the way for white settlements." White landowners could not be pushed around so easily, by either trespassers or the government. If Indians owned their land the same way whites did, perhaps they would be as secure.[18]

But the relationship between trespassing and the forms of land tenure was hardly self-evident. As the minister William Harsha suggested in the *North American Review*, so long as the government stood by and permitted whites to take the Indians' property, allotment would make little difference. "What possible benefit would there be in endowing the Indians with lands in severalty, if their standing before the law remains unchanged?" Harsha asked. "Big Snake or Two Crow could as easily be put off a quarter section as the tribe off a reservation. The individual Indian could be robbed of his ponies as well as a tribe. The clamor of neighboring white men would not be any more likely to cease. . . . In fact, the condition of affairs would be worse. Opportunity for individual stealing would be increased, [and] the armies of the United States might not even pretend to be available for the help of single Indians."[19] The

Indians' security of possession depended more on the attitudes of the government officials charged with protecting them than on the formal law.

A third argument in favor of allotment was the expectation that, as fee simple owners of their land, the Indians would become more assimilated into American life. Assimilation was a pervasive ideal in the late nineteenth century, particularly with respect to recent immigrants. Many suggested that the melting pot ought to accommodate the Indians as well. "Do we not assimilate millions of ignorant and semi-barbarous foreigners, speaking different languages and bred under other institutions than our own?" asked one writer. "Shall we hesitate before a paltry quarter of a million of red Indians? Put the little savages into the mill and grind out American citizens!"[20]

The mechanisms by which allotment was thought to produce assimilation were varied. Some expected that tribal authority would weaken with allotment, as tribal leaders lost their power to allocate land and regulate its use. The power to regulate would be assumed by state governments and the federal government, who would govern individual Indians directly, as they did whites. "When the Indians are individual owners of real property," predicted former interior secretary Carl Schurz, "their tribal cohesion will necessarily relax, and gradually disappear. They will have advanced an immense step in the direction of the white man's way." Others hoped that the Indians would perceive themselves to have more of a stake in peace and stability once they owned their own land. "All persons with fixed property are conservative. It is generally the poor, starving, and naked men of any community who stir up strife, and bring about hostilities," observed a contributor to *Scribner's Monthly* magazine in 1875. "But few Indians now have more property than they can put upon their horses and carry away. Let them acquire property not portable, and they will be as adverse to war as we could desire." Landownership had long been associated with the capacity for full citizenship, so many of the calls for allotment were joined with calls to reclassify the Indians as United States citizens. Most, perhaps, simply assumed that assimilation was a matter of treating the Indians more like whites, and that allotment would, in itself, be a significant advance toward that goal. But whatever the process, there was considerable support among reform-minded whites for allotting the Indians' land as a means of assimilation.[21]

Assimilation looked quite different, of course, from the Indians' point of view. For European immigrants, assimilating meant adopting a new language, new modes of dress, new cultural interests, and so on. For Indians it meant all of that and more, because Indian tribes were not just sites of nonmajority culture. They were also sovereign entities, with powers of self-government that other minority groups did not have. Assimilation meant giving many of those powers away, to states and to a nation that were certain to govern the Indians less successfully, from the Indians' perspective, than the Indians could govern themselves. Allotment "would ultimately break up our tribal government and end in the absorption of our people by the great body of citizens in the United States," the Creek Council recognized. The Council opposed allotment for this reason. The Choctaws likewise rejected "any proposition looking to a change of the present system of holding their lands in common or any change in their present tribal government whatever."[22]

Again, these voices were not entirely unheard. Julius H. Seelye, president of Amherst College, criticized reformers who wished to break up the tribes for overlooking "that communal relationship, on which not only the very existence of human society depends, but in which is the germ of whatever is distinctively human." In the House of Representatives, Mississippi Democrat Charles Hooker predicted that "if this policy prevails and the allotments are made in severalty, and the tribal relation, which is the great bond of union holding these Indians together, is destroyed," the Indians could not long survive. But these were unusual statements for whites of the late nineteenth century. Assimilation was in the air. The Indian tribe was conventionally understood as a vestigial institution that would have to give way if the Indians were to make any further progress. Even many of allotment's white opponents favored assimilation; their only quarrel with allotment was that it was being proposed too soon, before the Indians were ready.[23]

Supporters of allotment often discounted the opposition of Indian leaders as an effort to maintain their own positions atop their tribes. Rank-and-file tribe members, many whites suspected, would come out ahead from allotment, but were being silenced by tribal leaders who stood to lose their political power and their effective control over a disproportionate percentage of the tribe's ostensibly communal property. The same phenomenon had taken place during the controversy over removal earlier in the century, when many white humanitarians believed that the chiefs were opposing removal for the same self-interested reasons. At the end of the century, the sense that the reservations were home to a chiefly aristocracy provided yet another reason to favor allotment, as a method of equalizing power and wealth among the Indians. "The rich Indians who cultivate tribal land pay no rent to the poorer and more unfortunate of their race," charged Indian Commissioner John Atkins. "In theory the lands are held in common under the tribal relation, and are equally owned by each member of the tribe, but in point of fact they are simply held in the grasping hand of moneyed monopolists and powerful and influential leaders and politicians." Atkins thought this accusation so important that he leveled it twice, in identical language, in successive annual reports. The most enterprising Indians, Indian Commissioner Thomas Morgan suggested, regarded allotment much as the wealthiest New Yorkers would have regarded a plan "to take all the real estate of New York City and divide it equally among its several inhabitants. It is not surprising," he concluded, "that there should be, on the part of the more aggressive, able, and prosperous Indians, very serious objections." When Chief Wilson Jones opposed the allotment of the Choctaws' land, the local newspaper explained that "Jones has a pasture that is about thirty-two miles around it, besides other pastures and farms. He is opposed to a change in this tribal government, as some poor homeless Indians will get good homes within his enclosures." Accusations like these, Creek chief Pleasant Porter admitted, had a ring of truth. "As we became a more agricultural and stock growing people," Porter recalled, "individuals with more ability and energy gradually possessed themselves of the use of larger portions of the public domain than the less industrious and more ignorant." Over time, inequality among the Creeks had increased, until "we awake to find that the few of our people, under our present laws are quietly possessing themselves of the lion's share of our common property." Proponents of allotment could thus think of themselves as advocates for the common man, seeking to break up land monopolies that favored a powerful few.[24]

This reason for allotment stood in considerable tension with the argument that allotment would turn the Indians into industrious farmers.[25] Some Indians were already *too* industrious, evidently, even without privately owned parcels of land. If advocates of allotment noticed this tension, however, they did not let on. The arguments were not entirely inconsistent. If pressed, supporters of allotment might have spoken of their desire to see all Indians, not just a privileged few, farming their land. That the debate never even progressed this far suggests the extent to which allotment had captured the imagination of whites.

Underlying all these reasons for allotment was another with much wider appeal. Whether or not allotment would make the Indians work harder or be more civilized, whether or not it would protect them from trespassing and removal, whether or not allotment would assimilate the Indians or make them more egalitarian, the one thing allotment was certain to do was free up much of the Indians' land for white settlement. The land set aside for the Indians was so vast, complained Senator John Mitchell of Oregon, that it amounted to a thousand acres for every Indian man, woman, and child in the United States, at a time when white settlers in the West were allocated only 160 acres per family, and millions of white and black Americans owned no property at all. Those more charitably inclined toward the Indians imagined the possibility of converting some of this land into money that could be spent to improve Indian life. If each individual Indian were allocated 160 acres, Thomas Morgan calculated, and if the land left over were sold at one dollar per acre, the result would be a sum so large that the annual interest alone would be sufficient to pay the full cost of educating all the Indian children in the United States. From any point of view, the Indians were sitting on a vast untapped resource.[26]

Allotment promised to free up this land in two different ways. First, assuming that land would be allotted in amounts somewhere near 160 acres per person, there would be enormous portions of the reservations left over. These could be sold to white settlers, and the proceeds used to benefit the Indians. Second, once allotment was complete, individual Indians would have the opportunity to sell their land, if they chose to. This was an opportunity most Indians had lacked for more than a century, since King George III prohibited private sales in the Proclamation of 1763.

Selling land posed considerable risks for the Indians in the long run, however, and the fear that allotment would cause too much land to be sold was perhaps the most pervasive theme among allotment's opponents. "This is a bill," declared Senator Henry Moore Teller, "that, in my judgment, ought to be entitled 'A bill to despoil the Indians of their lands and to make them vagabonds on the face of the earth.'" "If I stand alone in the Senate," Teller concluded, "I want to put upon the record my prophecy in this matter, that when thirty or forty years have passed and these Indians shall have parted with their title, they will curse the hand that was raised professedly in their defense to secure this kind of legislation." Teller indeed stood nearly alone in the Senate, but among the Indians his view was widely shared. Allotment was "the greatest blackmailing scheme of the century," one opponent charged, with "its object the parcelling out of the soil among eager, grasping land-harpies." The Seminole chief John F. Brown found allotment a "gigantic and monstrous fraud" intended to pry land away from the Indians. It did not take much foresight to recognize that land, as so often before, was the Indians' single most valuable asset, and that facilitating sales could prove extremely dangerous.[27]

Even the most enthusiastic proponents of allotment recognized as much. "Experience has shown that even the most advanced and civilized of our Indians are not capable of defending their lands when title in fee is once vested in them," Indian Commissioner Ezra Hayt explained.

> The reservations in such cases are infested by a class of land-sharks who do not hesitate to resort to any measure, however iniquitous, to defraud the Indians of their lands. Whiskey is given to them, and while they are under its influence they are made to sign deeds of conveyance, without consideration. They are often induced to sign what they are informed is a contract of sale for a few trees growing on their land, with a receipt for the consideration paid; or some party goes to them claiming to be an agent of the State or county, distributing funds to the poor. This party will pay the Indian five or ten dollars, and procure his signature to a pretended receipt for the same, when in reality the paper signed is a warranty deed, which is recorded, and generally the land is sold to a third and innocent party before the Indian discovers the fraud which has been practiced upon him.[28]

One could make the same point without disparaging the Indians' intelligence. The Indians were very poor. Land, once allotted, would be the only significant asset for most. Selling the land would be a convenient way to acquire money for food, clothing, shelter, and other necessities, not to mention the varied consumer goods that were increasingly becoming a part of American life. Anyone in such a situation, Indian or otherwise, would be sorely tempted to sell some land, even if he could predict regretting the transaction many years later, once the goods purchased with the proceeds had been consumed.

The solution, allotment's supporters argued, was simply to restrict the ability of individual Indians to sell land—for instance, by prohibiting sales for a certain number of years after the land was allotted, or by requiring the permission of the federal government for a sale, as had been done in some of the earlier treaties. The debate before 1887 tended not to descend to this level of detail, but the outcome of allotment would turn out to depend heavily on the precise restrictions imposed on allotted land, and on how federal government officials interpreted those restrictions.

The allotment debate in the 1870s and 1880s was about whether to turn a piecemeal treaty-by-treaty program into a general plan for all tribes, so there was a fund of experience available on which both sides could draw. The Bureau of Indian Affairs saw allotment as an unqualified success. "In no case where allotments have been made," proclaimed Commissioner Hiram Price in 1883, "have any other than the best results followed." Three years later, as the bill that would become the Dawes Act was making its way through Congress, Price's successor John Atkins provided a glowing account of allotment among the Omahas. Atkins concluded that "the success of the Omahas is such as to impress favorably friends of the Indians and believers in their civilization, and to afford to Indians everywhere the highest encouragement to adopt the same policy." Allotment, in the view of its supporters, was not a utopian plan. It had a proven track record.[29]

If one examined that record more closely, however, one could find a disturbing pattern. The Oklahoma tribes had firsthand experience with allotment, in treaties from early in the century. "Hundreds of Indians entitled to patents for land under those treaties have never secured a single acre," a delegation representing four tribes recalled in a petition to Congress. "Many more whose rights were recognized by the Government were shamefully wronged by the whites and have to this day been unable to obtain relief or redress."[30] The Creeks undertook a study of the outcome of allotment among tribes all over the country, which resulted in a detailed sixty-page memorial they sent to Congress in 1883. Their review yielded two conclusions: first, "that former experiments in allotment have had the effect in most instances of reducing the great body of the community subjected to the trial to a state of pauperism and beggary," and second, that in several instances "during the period of allotment, the death-rate in the bodies referred to increased and that it was diminished among the same Indians after their return to the tenure in common." The Creeks accordingly pleaded with Congress to leave their property system alone.[31]

The Creeks had no illusions about their influence. "In opposing the change of Indian land titles from the tenure in common to the tenure in severalty," their petition acknowledged, "your memorialists are aware that they differ from nearly every one of note holding office under the government in connection with Indian affairs, and with the great body of philanthropists whose desire to promote the welfare of the Indian cannot be questioned."[32] They were right about this. Scarcely any of the proponents of allotment took the trouble to inspect the details of how allotment had been carried out in the past, and even if they had, they would likely have concluded that the problems to which the Creeks referred were defects of implementation rather than design, flaws that could be corrected this time around. Allotment was too attractive in broad outline to be rejected for some distasteful details.

The Creeks might have added that many Indians disagreed with them as well. Field reports from the Interior Department's Indian agents were consistently filled with expressions of support for allotment from the Indians under their supervision. From the Crow Creek Agency in the Dakota Territory, Agent W. E. Dougherty reported in 1881 that "last spring the demand of the Indians for the subdivision of the land and the allotment of it in severalty became general." From the Santee Reservation in Nebraska, Agent Isaiah Lightner explained that the Santees felt the same way. A group of tribes gathered on the Round Valley Reservation in California petitioned the Interior Department in 1885 to allot their land. They "have been promised land in severalty for a great many years," they despaired, "but have been put off from time to time, until we have about come to the conclusion that the good time will never come." With accounts like these coming in year after year, Indian commissioners were confident that, as one put it, "the demand for title to lands in severalty by the reservation Indians is almost universal." Reformers outside the government were equally confident. The Indians were pleading for land in severalty, affirmed Merrill Gates, the president of Rutgers College. The humane thing to do would be to let them have it.[33]

There was doubtless some wishful thinking going on here, an eagerness to find more support among the Indians for allotment than actually existed, but there were too many such reports to dismiss them all as fanciful. Even if allotment did not command as much support among Indians as among whites, there were some Indians who favored it. Life on an Indian reservation in the late nineteenth century was not easy, so one might have expected at least some Indians to be optimistic about an alternative, even one with as dubious a history as allotment. We know how it would work out in the end, but of course they did not.

The Oglala Lakota leader Wašíču Tašunka, known to non-Indians as Chief American Horse, photographed in 1907 with a government allotting surveyor and an interpreter. American Horse was one of many Indians who favored allotment, in the hope that converting traditional land tenure to Anglo-American tenure would help prevent whites from trespassing.

Indeed, it bears emphasizing that white reformers' enthusiasm for allotment was more reasonable at the time than it may appear in retrospect, given our knowledge of allotment's consequences. In 1880 a person sincerely concerned with the Indians' welfare knew that a century of segregating the Indians had succeeded only in killing off many of them and demoralizing most of the rest. Assimilating the Indians, it must have seemed, could hardly do them any more harm than was already being done. Other ethnic minorities were being successfully assimilated. It was not crazy to suppose that the Indians' turn was next.

General allotment bills had been before Congress for several years when Congress finally passed the one sponsored by Henry Dawes, chairman of the Senate Committee on Indian Affairs. Each of the bills, including Dawes's, provided for allotment of a tribe's land only with the consent of the affected tribe, but at the last moment, after both houses had passed versions of an allotment bill, the consent provision was dropped without explanation by the conference committee charged with reconciling the two. As a result, the Dawes Act provided for allotment whether or not the Indians agreed. The mandatory nature of allotment was challenged by the Cherokees as an unconstitutional taking of property owned in fee simple by the tribe, but the Supreme Court rejected the claim on the ground that allotment changed only the form, not the substance, of the Indians' property rights. The Court did not elaborate, but to a lawyer of the era, compulsory allotment would have seemed much like the compelled distribution of a corporation's assets to its shareholders, an event that would destroy the artificial entity of the corporation but would leave the shareholders with exactly as much wealth as before, just owned in a different form.[34]

The Dawes Act authorized the Bureau of Indian Affairs to survey and allot any reservation land the Bureau deemed "advantageous for agricultural and grazing purposes." Each head of a family would receive 160 acres, each single adult or orphan child 80 acres, and every other child 40 acres. (In 1891 these amounts would be changed to 80 acres of agricultural land or 160 acres of grazing land per person, after many complained that the original scheme was unfair to married women and minors.)[35] Indians who had already improved land had the first shot at the land containing the improvements. The act left to the Bureau the task of figuring out how to allocate the rest. If, after four years, a person entitled to an allotment failed to select one, the Bureau was to assign one for him. The relatively small number of Indians not living on a reservation had similar rights, which they could exercise on any unappropriated land of the United States.

Explicitly exempted from allotment under the Dawes Act were the tribes who had objected most vociferously to it—the tribes in the Indian Territory, and the Senecas in New York. Land in the Indian Territory was too enticing for white settlement, however, for this exemption to last long. In 1893 Congress would authorize federal commissioners to begin negotiating with the tribes in the Indian Territory for the allotment of their reservations. When, after several years of negotiations, these tribes still refused allotment, Congress empowered the commissioners to undertake the allotment as soon as they had completed the tribal rolls—this time without mentioning the tribes' consent as a prerequisite. The tribes, recognizing that allotment was now inevitable and that they could influence the process only by cooperating, formally registered their agreement soon after.[36]

The longest, and in the end the most important, part of the Dawes Act was section 5, which governed the sale of the Indians' land. For at least twenty-five years, and longer in individual cases if the president saw fit, the federal government would own the land in trust for the individual Indian to whom it had been allotted. During this trust period, sales or leases of the land were not allowed. The purpose of this restriction was to prevent the Indians from dissipating the proceeds of allotment. Reformers hoped that after twenty-five years of owning land, the Indians would have learned to make prudent decisions in this regard. During and after the trust period, allotted land would become subject to state laws of descent in the event the allottee died. This provision seemed innocuous in 1887, but in time it would be of tremendous significance, because Indians were unaccustomed to writing wills. For individuals who died intestate, state laws of descent typically divided property equally among the children. A few generations later, much of the Indians' land would be owned in tiny fractions by large numbers of the original allottees' descendants.

Section 5 also specified what would become of those portions of the reservations that were left over after allotment had been completed. This land was to be purchased by the federal government, "on such terms and conditions as shall be considered just and equitable." Land adapted to agriculture was then to be resold, in tracts no larger than 160 acres per person, to white settlers. The proceeds of these sales were to be held in the Treasury, earning interest, and used "for the education and civilization" of the Indians from whom the land had been purchased. This too must have seemed an innocuous provision in 1887, but it would also prove very important in time, because the federal government would be an extraordinarily incompetent manager of the Indians' money. The Harvard law professor James Bradley Thayer was more prophetic than he could have realized when he remarked in 1888 that "one would feel a good deal surer of the proper application of that money if it were to be put into some trust company, upon specific and defined trusts."[37]

To complete the assimilation of the Indians, at the end of the twenty-five-year trust period, those who received patents to (i.e., full ownership of) their land would become United States citizens, and all members of tribes whose land had been allotted, even members who themselves were not landowners, would be subject to the laws of the state in which they resided. By this point African Americans had been citizens for nearly twenty years, since the Fourteenth Amendment was ratified in 1868. Indians would not become citizens generally, without regard to landownership, until 1924.

The Dawes Act was hailed by reformers as "the beginning of the new era in the status of the Indians." After a century of dishonor, they believed, the United States was finally set to treat the Indians with humanity and respect. "By the passage of this bill we have, as a nation, definitely pledged ourselves to the policy of ultimately making the Indian as one of us," exulted the Indian Rights Association in its annual report. "It is, accordingly, manifest to all who are at work for the Indian, that we stand at the beginning of a transitional period in his history." Charles Painter, the association's agent in Washington, predicted that February 8, the day the bill became law, would be a national holiday. "So long as the cosmopolitan population of this country shall remember and celebrate Runnymede and Magna Charta, Independence and Emancipation," Painter proclaimed, "will the 8th of February, 1887, also come in for proportionate claim for honorable mention and thrilling memories."[38]

Rarely have so many well-intentioned people been so wrong.

Rich in Land but Poor in the Necessities of Life

The work began quickly. By 1890 there had been more than 15,000 allotments. By 1899 there had been 17,000 more, amounting in all to nearly four million acres of freshly allotted land. The pace then quickened considerably. By 1934, when allotment came to an end, the government had made more than 240,000 allotments, adding up to more than forty million acres of land.[39]

The aggregate numbers conceal the complexity of allotment on the ground. The first step was to draw up a list of exactly which individuals were tribe members entitled to an allotment, a task that was often not easy, given the number of non-Indians, part-Indians, and Indians with ancestors from more than one tribe living on and near reservations, the attraction of a free grant of land, and the lack of any governing principle for deciding cases of mixed ancestry. Alice Fletcher, the anthropologist appointed as special agent in charge of allotting the Nez Percé reservation in Idaho, arrived only to find that the Nez Percés were unaware of the Dawes Act and doubtful of Fletcher's authority. Once that hurdle was overcome, she had trouble even ascertaining the personal names of tribe members, because the Nez Percés considered their true names to be sacred and not lightly revealed. Fletcher next had to learn the ancestry and family relationships of every applicant, in order to figure out who should receive an allotment and to discern who qualified as the "head of a family" entitled to the larger parcel conferred by the original Dawes Act. Meanwhile a surveying crew was out in the rocky canyons of the reservation, running straight lines for the boundaries of the parcels that would be allotted to tribe members. In some Nez Percé communities, residents were pleased to choose allotments, but in others they refused to participate, until Fletcher finally coerced their participation by persuading the commissioner of Indian affairs to forbid tribe members who had not received allotments from leaving the reservation to hunt.[40]

Allottees understandably tended to choose parcels of land in patterns that would permit them to change their lives as little as possible. Members of extended families picked allotments in groups, to create larger contiguous blocks. Many bands and villages remained together. Allotments clustered around sources of water and traditional meeting places. Tribes did what they could to reproduce traditional ways within the new framework of property rights.[41]

As one might expect from a government program of this scope, the process did not always work well. Because some reservations were too small to provide allotments for all their residents, some tribes were forced to disperse. Some of the federal agents and surveyors sent out by the Indian Bureau were careless or incompetent, and their work created parcels that were too small or were useless for agriculture. In many cases Indians inadvertently selected parcels miles from home, and in many others they discovered, when trying to pick the parcel on which they lived, that someone else had already been allowed to select it. Many Indians refused on principle to participate at all: as one of the Creeks despaired, "he would rather knock the brains of his children out against a tree than make application for them." Federal agents assigned allotments in such cases, but the land assigned was often very poor and very far away. Problems like these must have caused tremendous anguish in many communities. Allotment was far messier on the reservations than reformers had envisioned.[42]

In locating allotments, moreover, federal agents were not immune from the pressures exerted by nearby whites, who had much to gain if the most desirable land could remain unallotted. In Arizona, for example, the Bureau of Indian Affairs tried for years to convince the Yavapai, who lived on the Camp McDowell reservation near Phoenix, to accept allotments on the Salt River reservation instead. Yavapai resistance to the move was led by the physician and activist Carlos Montezuma, who recognized that the government's real goal was to acquire the water rights to the Verde River, which ran through the Camp McDowell reservation. In the end the Yavapai prevailed, but only after an impasse that lasted more than two decades, during which time the uncertainty must have deterred them from making any significant investment in the land.[43]

It soon became apparent, in any event, that allotment was not by itself the spur to farming that its proponents had expected. Land was only one input to agriculture. Without training, equipment, or animals, landowners were unlikely to make their land more productive. In some years Congress appropriated funds to provide these things, but in other years it did not, and the sums were far too small even when it did. Reformers began to second-guess the provision of the Dawes Act that prohibited allottees from selling or leasing their allotments during the twenty-five-year trust period. They began to suggest that it might be wiser to permit the Indians to lease some of their land, so they would have the money they needed to farm the rest. Some allottees, moreover, were too old or too young to cultivate land themselves. Some of the allotted land was suited only for mining, a business in which few Indians, if any, were equipped to engage. All this land was lying unused. Reformers began to suggest that such land should be opened for lease as well, on the theory that if the Indians could not farm it they should at least get some benefit from it.

This sort of thinking, combined with the constant support among would-be acquirers of Indian land for any loosening of restrictions, prompted Congress to amend the Dawes Act in 1891 to permit allottees to lease their land for up to three years for farming or grazing purposes, and up to ten years for mining, "whenever it shall be made to appear to the Secretary of the Interior that, by reason of age or other disability, any allottee . . . can not personally . . . occupy or improve his allotment." This seemed a minor technical amendment at the time and so occasioned virtually no debate, but it would prove to be extremely important. The local Indian agents who had the power to approve leases tended to interpret the "age or other disability" requirement very liberally, particularly after 1894, when Congress added an allottee's "inability" to use the allotment as a further ground for permitting leases. The

Indian agents were under considerable pressure to give their consent to leases from the prospective lessees of these allotments, who were often locally powerful people and businesses. The annual number of approved leases of allotments began to rise, from 295 in 1894, to 1,287 in 1897, to 2,500 in 1900.[44]

In his annual report for the last of these years, Commissioner William Jones conceded that "on some of the reservations leasing is the rule and not the exception, while on others the practice is growing. To the thoughtful mind it is apparent that the effect of the general leasing of allotments is bad." By 1892, most of the land on the Omaha reservation had been leased to whites, and the allottees were spending much of the proceeds on liquor. Leasing was so popular among the Sisseton Sioux and their white neighbors that when the alarmed Indian agent began denying approval, the only effect was to create a black market in which the rent was less than half of the market rate for legal leases, a result that did more to reduce the Sissetons' revenues than to promote Sisseton farming.[45] A law intended by humanitarians to provide only the narrowest of outlets for leasing had become the tool for a substantial transfer of the right to use land from Indians to non-Indians, because although the humanitarians had significant input into the legislative process, they had much less influence over how the law would be applied in the field. This was only the latest installment of a very old story. Indian policy was set in the capital, whether Washington or London, by a group of people that included some who were interested in the welfare of the Indians, but policy had to be implemented in the field by people who had, on average, far less sympathy for the Indians.

As the leasing of allotments intensified, so too did the pressure to reduce the twenty-five-year trust period during which allotments could not be sold. Permission for early sales, like early leases, began slowly, with the subset of allottees who had the least need for land and the most for the revenue the land could bring. These were the heirs of allottees who died during the trust period. Many were minors. Many were receiving fractional shares of an allotment, because of the way state intestacy law divided allotments among the allottee's children. Many already had allotments of their own. They needed money much more than they needed more land. In 1902, Congress amended the Dawes Act to permit such heirs (or their guardians, if they were children) to sell the allotments whether or not the trust period had expired.[46] As with leases, sales were subject to the approval of federal officials, but the same circumstances that encouraged Indian agents to be liberal in permitting leases encouraged them to be liberal about sales.

Once some sales were permitted, the steady demand for Indian land prompted questions about the possibility of others. What about allottees who had shown themselves competent to manage their own affairs? Was it fair to prohibit them from selling their land? "An Indian may desire to engage in business" rather than farming, one 1904 editorial put it; "some of the best business men in this nation are Creek Indians. To advise these men one way or the other is presumption." Other Indians were "rich in land but poor in the necessities of life." Why not let them sell 120 acres to get the funds to build a house, to live comfortably on the remaining 40? And what about allottees too old or incompetent to farm? What was gained by forcing them to hold on to their land for 25 years, when "it may be advisable for them to sell their land and enjoy the proceeds"? All Indians were obviously not alike, so why subject all to a uniform twenty-five-year trust period? Such questions were raised not just by the land-hungry but by sincere reformers as well, because they implicated the goal of assimilation that lay behind the Dawes Act. If the trust period was hindering some Indians from engaging in business or building houses, it was hindering assimilation as well.[47]

Congress accordingly opened up one valve, in the Burke Act of 1906, when it authorized the secretary of the interior to grant allottees a fee simple title, ending the trust period and empowering the allottees to sell their land if they wished, "whenever he shall be satisfied that any Indian allottee is competent and capable of managing his or her affairs." Congress opened a second valve the following year, by authorizing the Interior Department to sell the allotment of "any noncompetent Indian" and to apply the proceeds to the allottee's benefit.[48] These statutes terminated the trust period for the most competent and the least competent of allottees. The competence of any particular Indian was a question that could be decided only in the field, so the statutes of 1906 and 1907 inevitably granted considerable discretion to the local Indian agents to decide who would be allowed to sell.

The local agents proved as liberal in granting permission to sell as they were in granting permission to lease. The annual number of sales of allotments steadily grew, until in 1910 it reached 1,425 tracts, amounting to more than two hundred thousand acres of land. By 1934, heirs and incompetents receiving permission to sell under the 1902 and 1907 statutes had sold nearly four million acres. Allottees receiving fee simple patents had sold twenty-three million more.[49]

In allowing sales, local officials were generally encouraged by their superiors in Washington. In 1917, for example, Commissioner Cato Sells, an enthusiastic assimilationist, announced that "every Indian as soon as he had been determined to be competent to transact his own business affairs would be given full control over his property and have all his lands and money turned over to him, after which he would no longer be a ward of the Government." Two years later, impatient at the rate at which Indians were coming forward to be declared competent, Sells instructed the superintendents of all the reservations to compile lists of "all Indians of one-half or less Indian blood, who are able-bodied and mentally competent, 21 years of age or over, together with a description of the land allotted to said Indians," so that the Bureau could grant patents in fee simple to all of them. Not all commissioners felt this way. Sells's predecessor, Robert Grosvenor Valentine, was nervous that the Bureau was granting fee simple titles too quickly. "The greater number of successful applicants have made such haste to sell the land," Valentine reported, "that they have got considerably less money than they would have received from sales through the superintendents. In a period of idleness they have squandered the entire proceeds, and in a short time have had neither land nor a substitute for any part of it, but in fact have been morally and industrially the worse for ever possessing land." Valentine's assistant commissioner, Frederick Abbott, feared that "reservations have been allotted with too much thought merely of 'opening the reservation to white settlement' and with too little thought of making the allotment in each case a real factor in the civilization and advancement of its owner." The overall tone of the Bureau's leadership, however, was to encourage agents to give allottees full control over their land.[50]

Local pressures to do so were even stronger. Accounts of land purchasing from the period virtually always describe the Indians as easy prey for sharp whites, so even if we discount some of these stories for stereotyping there must have been a great many instances where the stereotype was based in fact. Some of the predators were land speculators who offered quick money to allottees, often before the restrictions on sale were even removed and before the allottees could develop a sense of the land's market value. Some of the predators were firms interested in the land's resources. Many of the allotments on the White Earth reservation in Minnesota, for example, were quickly bought up by lumber companies.[51]

There was considerable room for fraud in these transactions, partly because of the ignorance of many of the sellers, but largely because government officials and land purchasers could find it easy and profitable to work together. This was another very old story, going back to the colonial era. Government salaries were always low enough to make additional income welcome, and on the frontier, government officials and land purchasers were always part of the same small social circle, having much more in common with each other than with the Indians. Tams Bixby, for example, was chairman of the Dawes Commission, the government body responsible for allotting the land of the Oklahoma tribes. At the same time he was also president of the Canadian Valley Trust Company, a major purchaser of Indian land, whose offices happened to be in the same building as those of the Dawes Commission. Other members and employees of the Dawes Commission were also associated with the Canadian Valley Trust Company. "Thus it will seem," noted one sarcastic editorialist,

> that when Tams Bixby is upstairs he is a government functionary vigilantly zealous that no body shall get the better of the simple aborigine in a land deal. When he is downstairs he is a private citizen, whose interest will be subserved by acquiring the real estate of the simple aborigine at the lowest possible price.
>
> As in the case of the Honorable Pooh-bah of the village of Titipu it is important to differentiate between the private and the public functions of Tams Bixby in order to avoid misapprehension and possible trouble.
>
> There is [sic] intimations that the untutored child of the forest has not in all cases been able to do this. It is asserted that he ambles into the offices of the Canadian Valley Company and explains his business under the impression that he is dealing with functionaries of the Dawes Commission. The representatives of the company, momentarily forgetful, are said occasionally to omit to explain that they are, at the moment, acting as private citizens and not in an official capacity.

This may have been an especially blatant conflict of interest, but subtler instances seem to have been common.[52]

Some of the predators were lawyers, who discovered they could exploit the Indians' unfamiliarity with the American legal system. To obtain permission to sell land, Indians had to fill in the blanks on a short application, but many lacked sufficient literacy to do so. Lawyers rushed in to help, charging exorbitant fees for the simplest of tasks. "I fought hard to have our lands allotted," recalled the Cherokee rancher Richard Martin, but he realized his mistake too late. The main result of allotment, he concluded, had been "to turn this illiterate people into the Shark like Jaws of the greedy grafter who are here in large numbers with but the one Thought and that is gain."[53]

While individual Indians were selling their allotments, the government was purchasing from the tribes, for resale to white settlers, the parts of the reservations left over when all tribe members had received their allotments. In this manner, by 1934 the government had acquired approximately 60 million acres, of which 38 million were separated from the reservations and another 22 million were opened to white homesteaders within reservations. Between 1887 and 1934, Indian landholdings had been reduced from 138 million acres to 52 million acres.[54]

To make matters worse, allotment left many reservations with the inefficient checkerboard pattern of landownership that persists in many areas to this day. By 1934 a reservation might include land owned in fee simple by individual tribe members, land owned in fee simple by whites, land owned by the federal government in trust for individual living Indians, land owned by the federal government in trust for the heirs of deceased Indians, land owned by the tribe, land owned by the state, and land owned by the federal government. Much of what the Indians retained was divided into parcels too small to be used effectively for grazing or logging. As time went on, this problem of fractionated ownership grew steadily worse, as state intestacy laws further subdivided rights to land with each generation. By the second half of the twentieth century, one tract in South Dakota, worth eight thousand dollars, had 439 owners, a third of whom had shares so small that they received less than a nickel in annual rent. The owner of the smallest share was due a penny every 177 years.[55]

White reformers had hoped that allotment would encourage Indian farming, but its net effect was the opposite: by 1930, there were fewer Indian farmers, farming less land, than there had been in 1910. By the end of allotment, Indian agriculture lagged even farther behind white agriculture than it had at the beginning.[56] The Indians seemed no more assimilated in 1930 than in 1880.

These outcomes would eventually turn white humanitarian opinion against allotment, but not quickly. Reformers continued to favor allot-

INDIAN LAND FOR SALE

GET A HOME
OF
YOUR OWN
✻
EASY PAYMENTS

PERFECT TITLE
✻
POSSESSION
WITHIN
THIRTY DAYS

FINE LANDS IN THE WEST
IRRIGATED
IRRIGABLE
GRAZING
AGRICULTURAL
DRY FARMING

IN 1910 THE DEPARTMENT OF THE INTERIOR SOLD UNDER SEALED BIDS ALLOTTED INDIAN LAND AS FOLLOWS:

Location.	Acres.	Average Price per Acre.	Location.	Acres.	Average Price per Acre.
Colorado	5,211.21	$7.27	Oklahoma	34,664.00	$19.14
Idaho	17,013.00	24.85	Oregon	1,020.00	15.43
Kansas	1,684.50	33.45	South Dakota	120,445.00	16.53
Montana	11,034.00	9.86	Washington	4,879.00	41.37
Nebraska	5,641.00	36.65	Wisconsin	1,069.00	17.00
North Dakota	22,610.70	9.93	Wyoming	865.00	20.64

FOR THE YEAR 1911 IT IS ESTIMATED THAT 350,000 ACRES WILL BE OFFERED FOR SALE

For information as to the character of the land write for booklet, "INDIAN LANDS FOR SALE," to the Superintendent U. S. Indian School at any one of the following places:

CALIFORNIA: Hoopa. COLORADO: Ignacio. IDAHO: Lapwai. KANSAS: Horton. Nadeau.	MINNESOTA: Onigum. MONTANA: Crow Agency. NEBRASKA: Macy. Santee. Winnebago.	NORTH DAKOTA: Fort Totten. Fort Yates. OKLAHOMA: Anadarko. Cantonment. Colony. Darlington. Muskogee, Pawnee.	OKLAHOMA—Con. Sac and Fox Agency. Shawnee. Wyandotte. OREGON: Klamath Agency. Pendleton. Roseburg. Siletz.	SOUTH DAKOTA: Cheyenne Agency. Crow Creek. Greenwood. Lower Brule. Pine Ridge. Rosebud. Sisseton.	WASHINGTON: Fort Simcoe. Fort Spokane. Tekoa. Tulalip. WISCONSIN: Oneida.

WALTER L. FISHER,
Secretary of the Interior.

ROBERT G. VALENTINE,
Commissioner of Indian Affairs.

Allotment freed up sixty million acres of so-called surplus reservation land for sale to whites, including the land advertised by the Interior Department in this 1911 poster. Between the 1887 passage of the General Allotment Act and its 1934 repeal, Indians lost nearly two-thirds of their remaining land.

ment long after a close inspection of allotment's effects ought to have given them second thoughts. At the annual Lake Mohonk Conference of Friends of the Indian, the leading forum for the expression of sympathetic views, speakers continued to insist—as one 1914 speaker asserted, to several rounds of applause—that "since the Dawes bill was passed there has been more progress; since that time we have done more for the uplift of the American Indian than ever was done in the history of any race." *The Red Man in the United States,* a comprehensive survey of Indian life published in 1923 by a consortium of missionary organizations, still called allotment "a far-sighted and benevolent policy" that would insure the Indians' economic independence.[57]

The reformers may have lowered their sights between 1880 and 1920: rather than assimilating the Indians, some may have been content merely for whites to make good use of the Indians' resources, with the hope that assimilation would follow.[58] But much of the enduring support for allotment among reformers seems less a matter of changing goals than of limited attention. Allotment was one of those ideas that sounded better the less one knew about the details. If one stuck to the generalities—private property, independence, clear boundaries, hard work— there was little to dislike. Everywhere allotment was tried in the nineteenth century, however, from New Zealand to the western United States, the initial optimism about allotment turned sour among the people closest to it, white or native. In each of these places, allotment made most of its ostensible indigenous beneficiaries poorer. The winners were primarily white settlers and land speculators. By the end of the process, the only humanitarians still optimistic were the ones farthest away, the urban intellectuals who continued to tout the virtues of the generalities long after the ugly details were widely known. In this sense, the allotment of indigenous people's land was to the nineteenth and early twentieth centuries something like what Soviet-style communism would be to the middle of the twentieth—a system that sounded much better in theory than it worked in practice, and so a system that retained the confidence of far-off progressive intellectuals much longer than it retained the support of those who had to endure it themselves.

The End of Allotment

The Indian Reorganization Act of 1934 finally put an end to allotment. The statute provided, in its very first sentence, that "hereafter no land of any Indian reservation . . . shall be allotted in severalty to any Indian." Existing trust periods and restraints on alienation were to continue indefinitely. The Bureau of Indian Affairs was authorized to restore to the reservations the land that had been removed but not yet sold to white settlers.[59] The federal government committed itself to a set of policies precisely the opposite of those that had motivated allotment: now the goal was to preserve the tribes as living institutions, and to encourage tribal ownership, rather than individual ownership, of land.

It was an old story: allotment was yet another program embarked upon with high hopes, only to be recognized decades later as a dismal failure. In 1926 the Interior Department asked the Institute for Government Research (an independent research organization that would soon change its name to the Brookings Institution) to evaluate federal Indian policy. The Institute came back two years later with an 847-page indictment of nearly every aspect of the subject, including allotment. "It almost seems as if the government assumed that some magic in individual ownership of property would in itself prove an educational civilizing factor," the Institute's report charged, "but unfortunately this policy has for the most part operated in the opposite direction." The problem, the report concluded, was that "too much reliance was placed on the sheer effect of individual land ownership and not enough was done to educate the Indians in the use of land." The Institute recommended incremental reforms rather than the abolition of allotment.[60] The tide of white humanitarian opinion, however, was beginning to turn.

The spirit of change in Indian policy was very much in the air from the mid-1920s, but actual change would not come until Franklin Roosevelt took office and placed experienced pro-Indian advocates in key positions in the Interior Department. Harold Ickes, Roosevelt's secretary of the interior, had been one of the founders of the Indian Rights Association of Chicago. Nathan Margold, the solicitor of the interior (the department's chief lawyer), had represented the Pueblo Indians and had been a member of the ACLU's Indian Rights Committee. Most important of all, John Collier, the new commissioner of Indian affairs, had devoted most of his professional life to Indian causes. Collier was the driving force behind the bill that would become the Indian Reorganization Act.[61]

As in prior moments of major change in Indian land policy, arguments for ending allotment emphasized how poorly the Indians had fared under existing law. "Reduced to its simplest terms, the present bill would prevent any further loss of Indian lands," explained the Reorganization Act's sponsor in the House, Edgar Howard of Nebraska. "It stops the big hole through which 90,000,000 acres of land have passed from Indian ownership." The optimism that had surrounded allotment a generation earlier had completely vanished. "As everyone knows the plan failed to work out," the *Christian Science Monitor* editorialized. "In brief, the allotment act destroyed the native society, economy and organization." By 1934, allotment no longer had significant support from the eastern white humanitarians who had been its biggest advocates fifty years earlier.[62]

Opposition to the abolition of allotment came instead primarily from allotment's material beneficiaries. Some were whites who were enjoying long-term leases of allotments at favorable rents. (The end of allotment did not interfere with existing leases, but it raised the possibility that leases would not be renewed in the future.) Others were Indians. Allotment had not been good for Indians in the aggregate, but many individual Indians had come out of the process successfully, as fee simple owners of large parcels of land. When the Bureau of Indian Affairs explained the pending legislation on reservations throughout the West, the Bureau's agents discovered that opposition to allotment was far from unanimous. A typical account came from Charles Berry, the superintendent of the Cheyenne and Arapaho Agency in Oklahoma. "The Indians at this Agency seem to have divided themselves into three different groups as regards this proposed legislation," Berry explained in a letter to Collier. "One group favors the proposed legislation, and those in this class are principally Indians who do not have any land or any home. The second group is composed of the Indians who have land and homes and who, at this time, appear to be opposed to the plan. The third group, composed of land owners, and those who do not own land, state that they are neutral."[63] As with earlier changes in Indian land policy, it would be too simple to think of Indians or whites as a single bloc with uniform interests.

With the abandonment of allotment, the law governing the acquisition of the Indians' remaining unallotted land returned to its pre-1887 state, where it has stayed ever since. Land already allotted, patented, and sold was irretrievably gone. Land allotted and patented but not sold was still owned by individual Indians in fee simple, just like land owned by whites. As with land owned by any comparably sized group of people, some of it remains to this day in the families of its 1934 owners while much of it has been sold to others. Land allotted but not yet patented—that is, land still held by the United States government in trust for individual Indians—was frozen in that condition in 1934, and much of it is still in trust today, owned by the government as trustee for the descendants of the original allottees. And land that had never been allotted was once more to be possessed by tribes, not by individuals. This complex pattern of landownership, created by allotment and then allotment's repeal, remains in place today.

Epilogue

IN THE MIDDLE of the twentieth century, the rate at which land was transferred from Indians to non-Indians slowed considerably, and Indians were even able to regain some land.[1] The non-Indian population of the West was increasing quickly during this period. Before the mid-twentieth century, every other comparable change in the non-Indian population of any area caused the Indians to lose large amounts of land. But not any longer.

Indeed, the story of Indians and land over the past sixty years has primarily been that of tribes' efforts to get land back, or to be compensated for land wrongfully taken. Indians have directed land claims at every branch of the federal government—at Congress, at the courts, at the Interior Department, and, from the 1940s through the 1970s, at a purpose-built administrative agency called the Indian Claims Commission. Some of these claims have been remarkably successful, culminating either directly in court judgments or indirectly in legislative settlements. In 2001, to pick one recent example of a judgment, the Cayuga Nation was awarded $248 million (including $211 million in interest) in its suit against New York State, for illegal land transactions in 1795 and 1807.[2] Perhaps the most striking example of a legislative settlement was the Alaska Native Claims Settlement Act of 1971, in which Alaska Natives agreed to relinquish their land claims in exchange for more than forty million acres of land and nearly $1 billion. Outcomes like these would have been almost unimaginable in 1900, and utterly inconceivable in 1800. Much had changed in relations between the Indians and the government in the middle decades of the twentieth century. By the end of

the century, Indians wielded far more political power than they had possessed in the 1930s.[3]

The law governing the acquisition of the Indians' land, however, had
scarcely changed. As Indians filed successful lawsuits to recover land or
gain compensation, or as they used the threat of lawsuits as leverage to
extract legislative settlements, they usually relied on law that would
have been familiar to a lawyer in 1900 or even 1800. *Johnson v. M'Intosh*,
the 1823 case in which the Supreme Court firmly established the "right
of occupancy," is still the foundational case in this area of law. Some of
the suits filed by eastern tribes were for violations of statutes enacted by
Congress in the 1790s. If John Marshall or William Wirt were to come
back to life today, he could get straight to work.

The transformation that took place over the middle decades of the
twentieth century was thus not a change in the law. It was a change in
the relative political power of Indians and whites. From the early seventeenth century to the early twentieth, the divergence between formal
law and actual practice had been growing, as whites grew stronger relative to Indians. In the twentieth century, when the balance began to tip
back a bit toward the Indians, they gained the power to force practice to
move closer to the formal law. Lawyers and judges began taking their
claims more seriously. Legislators and executive branch officials began
fearing the consequences. The law did not change, nor did the nature of
the Indians' claims. Rather, those claims were now heard, and the law
was now implemented, within a new political framework in which Indians could no longer be ignored.

In this respect, Indian land claims are different from lawsuits filed by
other groups who have been mistreated in the past. African Americans,
for example, have not won reparations from the descendants of slave
owners, despite the acknowledged evil of slavery, because slavery was
not illegal when it was practiced. Seizing the Indians' land, by contrast,
was illegal when it was practiced. Where Indians have succeeded in land
claims, it has not been by showing that they were treated in ways that violate abstract notions of justice, or that they were treated in ways that
would violate the law today. Indians have succeeded by showing that
they were treated in ways that violated the law *at the time*—that a given
transaction, for example, was illegal when it occurred. If the Indians had
simply been conquered, and if Anglo-American law had held conquest
lawful at the time, Indians today would have no redress in the courts.

They would be in the same legal position as the descendants of African American slaves.

Indians, like other groups, were able to use their new political voice to achieve some changes in the law in the mid-twentieth century, but so far as land claims were concerned, they did not have to. The law, as words on paper, was already on their side. All they had to do was persuade government officials, for the first time in centuries, to enforce it as written.

NOTES

ACKNOWLEDGMENTS

INDEX

Notes

Abbreviations

AIUS   *The American Indian and the United States: A Documentary History,* ed. Wilcomb E. Washburn (New York: Random House, 1973)

ASP   *American State Papers: Indian Affairs* (Washington: Gales and Seaton, 1832)

ASU   Arizona Collection, Department of Archives and Manuscripts, Arizona State University, Tempe

DHFFC   *Documentary History of the First Federal Congress of the United States of America,* ed. Linda Grant De Pauw et al. (Baltimore: Johns Hopkins University Press, 1972–)

HL   Huntington Library, San Marino, California

JCC   *Journals of the Continental Congress, 1774–1789* (Washington: Government Printing Office, 1904–1937)

NA   National Archives, Washington

NL   Newberry Library, Chicago

NYA   New York State Archives, Albany

OU   Western History Collections, University of Oklahoma, Norman

PRO   Public Record Office, Kew, UK

PWJ   *The Papers of Sir William Johnson* (Albany: University of the State of New York, 1921–1965)

RC   *Revolution and Confederation* (1994), ed. Colin G. Calloway; vol. 18 of *Early American Indian Documents: Treaties and Laws, 1607–1789,* ed. Alden T. Vaughan (Washington: University Publications of America, 1979–)

Royce   *Indian Land Cessions in the United States,* comp. Charles C. Royce, in J. W. Powell, *Eighteenth Annual Report of the Bureau of American Ethnology to the Secretary of the Smithsonian Institution* (Washington: Government Printing Office, 1899)

SNA   *Southeastern Native American Documents, 1730–1842,* http://www.galileo.usg.edu (formerly www.galileo.peachnet.edu, visited 27 Feb. 2002)

Introduction

1. Kent McNeil, *Common Law Aboriginal Title* (Oxford: Clarendon Press, 1989), 108–110.
2. Previous mappers have tended not to acknowledge these difficulties, and have thus in effect favored the government in all cases of doubt. Francis Paul Prucha, *Atlas of American Indian Affairs* (Lincoln: University of Nebraska Press, 1990), 22–35; Royce, plates following p. 997.

1. Native Proprietors

1. William Cronon, *Changes in the Land: Indians, Colonists, and the Ecology of New England* (New York: Hill and Wang, 1983), 57; David Armitage, *The Ideological Origins of the British Empire* (Cambridge: Cambridge University Press, 2000), 97; Wilcomb E. Washburn, "The Moral and Legal Justifications for Dispossessing the Indians," in James Morton Smith, ed., *Seventeenth-Century America: Essays in Colonial History* (Chapel Hill: University of North Carolina Press, 1959), 15–32; Chester F. Eisinger, "The Puritans' Justification for Taking the Land," *Essex Institute Historical Collections* 84 (1948): 131–143.
2. Robert A. Williams Jr., *The American Indian in Western Legal Thought: The Discourses of Conquest* (New York: Oxford University Press, 1990), 221. For similar arguments, see Patricia Seed, *American Pentimento: The Invention of Indians and the Pursuit of Riches* (Minneapolis: University of Minnesota Press, 2001), 12–44; L. C. Green, "Claims to Territory in North America," in L. C. Green and Olive P. Dickason, *The Law of Nations and the New World* (Edmonton: University of Alberta Press, 1989), 1–139; Wilbur R. Jacobs, "British Indian Policies to 1783," in William C. Sturtevant et al., eds., *Handbook of North American Indians* (Washington: Smithsonian Institution, 1978–), 4:6–7.
3. *Johnson v. M'Intosh*, 21 U.S. 543 (1823).
4. *Tee-Hit-Ton Indians v. United States*, 348 U.S. 272, 279 (1955); Jesse Dukeminier and James E. Krier, *Property*, 4th ed. (New York: Aspen, 1998), 3, 11, 12, 18.
5. Joyce Chaplin, *Subject Matter: Technology, the Body, and Science on the Anglo-American Frontier, 1500–1676* (Cambridge, Mass.: Harvard University Press, 2001).
6. On the Spanish debate, see Lewis Hanke, *Aristotle and the American Indians* (Chicago: Henry Regnery, 1959); James Muldoon, *The Americas in the Spanish World Order: The Justification for Conquest in the Seventeenth Century* (Philadelphia: University of Pennsylvania Press, 1994); Anthony Pagden, "Dispossessing the Barbarian: The Language of Spanish Thomism and the Debate over the Property Rights of the American Indians," in David Armitage, ed., *Theories of Empire, 1450–1800* (Aldershot, UK: Ashgate, 1998), 159–178.
7. Susan Myra Kingsbury, ed., *The Records of the Virginia Company of London* (Washington: Government Printing Office, 1906–1935), 3:1–3.
8. William Crashaw, *A Sermon Preached in London* (London: William Welby, 1610), n.p.
9. William Symonds, *Virginia: A Sermon Preached at White-Chappel* (London: Eleazer Edgar and William Welby, 1609), 10.

10. The distinction between property and sovereignty can be blurred in the sources, which sometimes use the same words—*possession, title,* or *dominion*—to denote both concepts, but from the context one can usually discern which is intended. When Oliver Cromwell, for instance, mocked Spain's "imaginary title" to North America, and contrasted it with the English "right of possession" and "the justness of our title," he seems to have been talking about sovereignty, despite his use of terms that would connote property to a modern lawyer. William Cortez Abbott, ed., *The Writings and Speeches of Oliver Cromwell* (Cambridge, Mass.: Harvard University Press, 1937–1947), 3:888–889.

11. Anthony Pagden, *Lords of All the World: Ideologies of Empire in Spain, Britain and France c. 1500–c. 1800* (New Haven: Yale University Press, 1995); John Thomas Juricek, "English Claims in North America to 1660: A Study in Legal and Constitutional History" (Ph.D. diss., University of Chicago, 1970); CO 5/283, p. 10, PRO; Patricia Seed, *Ceremonies of Possession in Europe's Conquest of the New World, 1492–1640* (Cambridge: Cambridge University Press, 1995); Arthur Keller, Oliver J. Lissitzyn, and Frederick J. Mann, *Creation of Rights of Sovereignty through Symbolic Acts 1400–1800* (New York: Columbia University Press, 1938).

12. Opposition to colonization developed only later, and even then it was not widespread. Sankar Muthu, *Enlightenment against Empire* (Princeton: Princeton University Press, 2003).

13. Christopher Tomlins, "The Legal Cartography of Colonization, the Legal Polyphony of Settlement: English Intrusions on the American Mainland in the Seventeenth Century," *Law and Social Inquiry* 26 (2001): 315–372; Nicholas Canny, *Making Ireland British, 1580–1650* (Oxford: Oxford University Press, 2001); William Macdonald, ed., *Select Charters and Other Documents Illustrative of American History, 1606–1775* (New York: Macmillan, 1899), 10, 92–93.

14. William Strachey, *The History of Travaile into Virginia Britannia* (London: Hakluyt Society, 1849), 20 (probably written between 1612 and 1616); Kingsbury, ed., *Records of the Virginia Company,* 2:95; Robert Gray, *A Good Speed to Virginia* (London: William Welbie, 1609), 19; CO 1/4, p. 92, PRO.

15. Samuel Purchas, "Virginias Verger" (1625), in Samuel Purchas, *Hakluytus Posthumus or Purchas His Pilgrimes* (Glasgow: James MacLehose and Sons, 1906), 19:220; Hugo Grotius, *The Law of War and Peace* (1625), trans. Francis W. Kelsey (Indianapolis: Bobbs-Merrill, 1925), 550; Anthony Pagden, "The Struggle for Legitimacy and the Image of Empire in the Atlantic to c.1700," in Nicholas Canny, ed., *The Origins of Empire: British Overseas Enterprise to the Close of the Seventeenth Century* (Oxford: Oxford University Press, 1998), 1:40; Cotton Mather, *The Life and Death of the Renown'd Mr. John Eliot,* 2nd ed. (London: John Dunton, 1691), 72, 118, 117; Higginson quoted in John Palmer, *The Revolution in New England Justified* (Boston, 1691), in W. H. Whitmore, ed., *The Andros Tracts* (Boston: Prince Society, 1868–1874), 1:90; Jeremiah Dummer, *A Defence of the New-England Charters* (London: W. Wilkins, 1721), 14.

16. *Nova Britannia: Offering Most Excellent Fruites by Planting in Virginia* (London: Samuel Macham, 1609), 12, 14; Robert Wintour, "A Short Treatise Sett Downe in a Letter" (1635), in John D. Krugler, ed., *To Live like Princes* (Baltimore: Enoch Pratt Free Library, 1976), 28; *Journals of the House of Commons,* 1:488 (17 May 1614).

17. John Smith, *A Description of New England* (London: Robert Clerke, 1616), 33–34; William Loddington, *Plantation Work the Work of this Generation* (London: Benjamin Clark, 1682), 3–4.

18. Grotius, *Law of War and Peace*, 550; Clayton Colman Hall, ed., *Narratives of Early Maryland, 1633–1684* (1910; New York: Barnes and Noble, 1959), 440–41; Nathaniel B. Shurtleff, ed., *Records of the Governor and Company of the Massachusetts Bay in New England* (Boston: William White, 1853–1854), 4(2):176; Pagden, *Lords of All the World*, 63–102; *Thoughts on the Right of the North American Indians, to the Lands They Possess* (London, 1774), viii.

19. Keith Thomas, *Man and the Natural World: Changing Attitudes in England, 1500–1800* (New York: Oxford University Press, 1996), 42; Ferdinando Gorges, *America Painted to the Life* (London: Nath. Brook, 1658–1659), 2:49; William Bullock, *Virginia Impartially Examined* (London: John Hammond, 1649), 55; *A Relation of Maryland* (London, 1635), in Hall, *Narratives of Early Maryland*, 84; William P. Cumming, ed., *The Discoveries of John Lederer* (London, 1672; Charlottesville: University of Virginia Press, 1958), 25; Karen Ordahl Kupperman, *Indians and English: Facing Off in Early America* (Ithaca: Cornell University Press, 2000), 11; Loren E. Pennington, "The Amerindian in English Promotional Literature 1575–1625," in K. R. Andrews, N. P. Canny, and P. E. H. Hair, eds., *The Westward Enterprise: English Activities in Ireland, the Atlantic, and America, 1480–1650* (Detroit: Wayne State University Press, 1979), 175–194; David Murray, *Indian Giving: Economies of Power in Indian–White Exchanges* (Amherst: University of Massachusetts Press, 2000).

20. John Winthrop, "Generall Considerations for the Plantation in New England" (1629), in *Winthrop Papers* (Boston: Massachusetts Historical Society, 1929–1947), 2:120. See also R. F., *The Present State of Carolina* (London: John Bringhurst, 1682), 14; W. H. Whitmore, ed., *Letters from New-England, a.d. 1686 by John Dunton* (Boston: Prince Society, 1867), 166.

21. E. B. O'Callaghan, ed., *Documents Relative to the Colonial History of the State of New-York* (Albany: Weed, Parsons and Co., 1856–1887), 1:58.

22. Karen Ordahl Kupperman, *Settling with the Indians: The Meeting of English and Indian Cultures in America, 1580–1640* (Totowa, N.J.: Rowman and Littlefield, 1980), 81–84; George Parker Winship, ed., *Sailors Narratives of Voyages along the New England Coast 1524–1624* (Boston: Houghton, Mifflin, 1905), 19; Thomas Hariot, *A Briefe and True Report of the New Found Land of Virginia* (London, 1588), 19–20; David B. Quinn and Alison M. Quinn, eds., *The English New England Voyages, 1602–1608* (London: Hakluyt Society, 1983), 223; John Smith, *A True Relation of Such Occurrences and Accidents of Noate as Hath Hapned in Virginia* (London, 1608), in Philip L. Barbour, ed., *The Jamestown Voyages under the First Charter, 1606–1609* (Cambridge: Cambridge University Press, 1969), 173; William Bradford, *Of Plymouth Plantation, 1620–1647* (written 1630–1650), ed. Samuel Eliot Morison (New York: Alfred A. Knopf, 1952), 85; Linda S. Cordell and Bruce D. Smith, "Indigenous Farmers," in Bruce G. Trigger and Wilcomb E. Washburn, eds., *The Cambridge History of the Native Peoples of the Americas* (Cambridge: Cambridge University Press, 1996), 1(1):201–266.

23. John Smith, *A Map of Virginia* (Oxford, 1612), in Barbour, *Jamestown Voyages*, 355,

371; Alexander Whitaker, *Good Newes from Virginia* (London: William Welby, 1613), 26–27; Edward Winslow, *Good Newes from New England* (London, 1624), in Alexander Young, ed., *Chronicles of the Pilgrim Fathers* (Boston: Charles C. Little and James Brown, 1844), 361; William Penn, *A Letter from William Penn ... to the Committee of the Free Society of Traders* (London: Andrew Sowle, 1683), 6; John Lawson, *A New Voyage to Carolina* (London, 1709), 179.

24. *A True Declaration of the Estate of the Colonie in Virginia* (London: William Barret, 1610), 6.

25. Robert Cushman, "Reasons and Considerations Touching the Lawfulness of Removing Out of England into the Parts of America," in *A Relation or Journall of the Beginning and Proceedings of the English Plantation Setled at Plimoth* (London, 1622), ed. Dwight B. Heath (New York: Corinth Books, 1963), 91–93.

26. Daniel Gookin, *Historical Collections of the Indians in New England* (1674; Boston, 1792; New York: Arno Press, 1972), 39; CO 5/864, p. 520, PRO.

27. Thomas Budd, *Good Order Established in Pennsilvania & New-Jersey* (1685), 34; Robert Morden, *Geography Rectified: or, a Description of the World* (London: Robert Morden and Thomas Cockerill, 1693), 608; Nathaniel Crouch, *The English Empire in America* (London: Nath. Crouch, 1685), 105; Daniel Dulany, *The Right of the Inhabitants of Maryland to the Benefit of the English Laws* (Annapolis: W. Parks, 1728), 23.

28. Yasuhide Kawashima, *Puritan Justice and the Indian* (Middletown, Conn.: Wesleyan University Press, 1986), 46–50; O'Callaghan, *Documents*, 1:128; Increase Mather, *A Brief Relation of the State of New England* (London, 1689), in Whitmore, *The Andros Tracts*, 2:153; Penn, *Letter from William Penn*, 6; *Maine in the Age of Discovery: Christopher Levett's Voyage, 1623–1624* (London, 1628; Maine Historical Society, 1988), 45; New Haven governor quoted in James Warren Springer, "American Indians and the Law of Real Property in Colonial New England," *American Journal of Legal History* 30 (1986): 56; Robert Ferguson, *A Just and Modest Vindication of the Scots Design, for the Having Established a Colony at Darien* (Edinburgh, 1699), 96–97; Glen quoted in John Oliphant, *Peace and War on the Anglo-Cherokee Frontier, 1756–63* (Basingstoke,UK: Palgrave, 2001), 11.

29. The same thing happened in Connecticut, which in 1717 declared the king, rather than the Indians, to be the owner of all the land in the colony, but which nevertheless allowed land purchases from the Indians with the Assembly's consent. *Laws of the Colonial and State Governments, Relating to Indians and Indian Affairs* (Washington: Thompson and Homans, 1832), 178 (South Carolina), 41 (Connecticut).

30. Kingsbury, *Records*, 3:304; Shurtleff, *Records*, 1:394; J. Franklin Jameson, ed., *Johnson's Wonder-Working Providence, 1628–1651* (New York: Charles Scribner's Sons, 1910), 112; *New Englands First Fruits* (London, 1643; New York: Joseph Sabin, 1865), 14–15; CO 5/286, pp. 5–8, CO 1/17, p. 241, PRO.

31. O'Callaghan, *Documents*, 3:105, 3:188, 3:219, 3:823; CO 5/1041, pp. 277, 395, PRO.

32. CO 5/1040, p. 253, PRO; Peter R. Christoph and Florence A. Christoph, eds., *The Andros Papers: Files of the Provincial Secretary of New York during the Administration of Governor Sir Edmund Andros, 1674–1676* (Syracuse: Syracuse Univer-

sity Press, 1989), 129; CO 323/20, p. 23, PRO. For the same requirement in Virginia, see Leonard Woods Labaree, ed., *Royal Instructions to British Colonial Governors, 1670–1776* (New York: Appleton-Century, 1935), 467.

33. CO 1/62, p. 331, PRO; William Penn, *A Further Account of the Province of Pennsylvania* (London, 1685), 17–18; James Glen, *A Description of South Carolina* (London: R. and J. Dodsley, 1761), 60; McGillivray quoted in Dorothy V. Jones, *License for Empire: Colonialism by Treaty in Early America* (Chicago: University of Chicago Press, 1982), 145; *PWJ*, 3:319.

34. Some are published in compilations, such as Jeremy Dupertuis Bangs, *Indian Deeds: Land Transactions in Plymouth Colony, 1620–1691* (Boston: New England Historic Genealogical Society, 2002); George H. Budke, comp., *Indian Deeds, 1630 to 1748* (New York: Library Association of Rockland County, 1975); Sidney Perley, *The Indian Land Titles of Essex County Massachusetts* (Salem: Essex Book and Print Club, 1912); Harry Andrew Wright, ed., *Indian Deeds of Hampden County* (Springfield, Mass., 1905); and *Documents Relating to the Conveyance of Land, &c. on Long Island* (New York: Bell and Gould, 1850). Most probably lie unpublished in all the county offices and state archives where real estate records are stored. See, for example, the discussion of unpublished Delaware deeds in Leon deValinger Jr., *Indian Land Sales in Delaware* (Wilmington: Archaeological Society of Delaware, 1941).

35. *An Answer to the Council of Proprietor's Two Publications* (New-York: Catherine Zenger, 1747), 7.

36. Marshall Harris, *Origin of the Land Tenure System in the United States* (Ames: Iowa State College Press, 1953), 157–163; *Laws of the Colonial and State Governments*, 10 (Massachusetts), 41 (Connecticut), 53 (Rhode Island), 59 (New Hampshire), 133 (New Jersey), 138 (Pennsylvania), 149 (Virginia), 162 (North Carolina), 178 (South Carolina). Land purchasing in early Pennsylvania was initially reserved to the Penn family, but in 1700 it was opened to anyone with the Penns' permission. Virginia required the government's permission in 1658 but then banned all private purchasing in 1705.

37. Springer, "Law of Real Property," 25–58; CO 5/1049, p. 517, CO 5/1050, p. 13, CO 5/1056, p. 65, PRO.

38. J. Payne, *The French Encroachments Exposed* (London: George Keith, 1756), 6; Springer, "Law of Real Property," 44; *Essex Institute Historical Collections* 35 (1899): 142.

39. Francis Higginson, *New-Englands Plantation*, 3rd ed. (London: Michael Sparke, 1630), in *Massachusetts Historical Society Proceedings* 62 (1928–1929): 316; David E. Stannard, *American Holocaust: The Conquest of the New World* (New York: Oxford University Press, 1992); *The Planters Plea* (London: William Jones, 1630), 14; Jon Butler, *Becoming America: The Revolution before 1776* (Cambridge, Mass.: Harvard University Press, 2000), 12; Peter H. Wood, "The Changing Population of the Colonial South: An Overview by Race and Region, 1685–1790," in Peter H. Wood et al., eds., *Powhatan's Mantle: Indians in the Colonial Southeast* (Lincoln: University of Nebraska Press, 1989), 38–39; Daniel Denton, *A Brief Description of New-York* (London: John Hancock, 1670), 7.

40. Klaus E. Knorr, *British Colonial Theories, 1570–1850* (Toronto: University of To-

ronto Press, 1944), 41–48; Edward Williams, *Virginia: More Especially the South Part Thereof, Richly and Truly Valued* (London: John Stephenson, 1650), introduction; Richard Hakluyt, *Divers Voyages Touching the Discovery of America* (1582), in Louis B. Wright, ed., *The Elizabethans' America: A Collection of Reports by Englishmen on the New World* (Cambridge, Mass.: Harvard University Press, 1965), 21–22; *Good News from New-England* (London: Matthew Simmons, 1648), 15, 9, 6.

41. Thomas More, *Utopia* (1516; Basel, 1518), ed. George M. Logan and Robert M. Adams (Cambridge: Cambridge University Press, 1989), 56.

42. English cases discussing the proposition include *Geary v. Barecroft*, 82 Eng. Rep. 1148 (K.B. 1667), and *Holden v. Smallbrooke*, 124 Eng. Rep. 1030 (C.P. 1668). See also Thomas Wood, *An Institute of the Laws of England*, 3rd ed. (London: Richard Sare, 1724), 216. European theoretical treatments include Grotius, *Law of War and Peace*, 202, and Samuel Pufendorf, *De Jure Naturae et Gentium* (1688), trans. C. H. Oldfather and W. A. Oldfather (Oxford: Clarendon Press, 1934), 2:569–573.

43. Walter Raleigh, "A Discourse of the Original and Fundamental Cause of Natural, Arbitrary, Necessary, and Unnatural War," in *The Works of Sir Walter Ralegh, Kt.* (Oxford: University Press, 1829), 8:255; John Donne, "A Sermon Preached to the Honourable Company of the Virginian Plantation" (London, 1622), in George R. Potter and Evelyn M. Simpson, eds., *The Sermons of John Donne* (Berkeley: University of California Press, 1959), 4:274.

44. Purchas, "Virginias Verger," 19:222; John Cotton, *God's Promise to His Plantations* (London, 1634; Boston: Samuel Green, 1686), 4; William Penn, *A Brief Account of the Province of Pennsylvania* (London: Benjamin Clark, 1681), 1.

45. Raphe Hamor, *A True Discourse of the Present Estate of Virginia* (London: William Welby, 1615), 29; John Rolf, "Virginia in 1616," *Virginia Historical Register and Literary Adviser* 1 (1848): 105; George Percy, "Observations Gathered out of a Discourse of the Plantation of the Southerne Colonie in Virginia by the English, 1606" (approx. 1608), in Barbour, *Jamestown Voyages*, 141; Helen C. Rountree, *Pocohontas's People: The Powhatan Indians of Virginia through Four Centuries* (Norman: University of Oklahoma Press, 1990), 82; E. Merton Coulter, ed., *The Journal of Peter Gordon 1732–1735* (Athens: University of Georgia Press, 1963), 37. The same method is planned in Robert Mountgomry, *A Discourse Concerning the Design'd Establishment of a New Colony to the South of Carolina* (London, 1717), 7–9.

46. Robert Cushman, "Of the State of the Colony, and the Need of Public Spirit in the Colonists" (1621), in Alexander Young, ed., *Chronicles of the Pilgrim Fathers* (Boston: Charles C. Little and James Brown, 1844), 259; Denys Delâge, *Bitter Feast: Amerindians and Europeans in Northeastern North America, 1600–64*, trans. Jane Brierley (Vancouver: UBC Press, 1993), 251–252; James Kendall Hosmer, ed., *Winthrop's Journal* (New York: Charles Scribner's Sons, 1908), 1:294.

47. Daniel K. Richter, *The Ordeal of the Longhouse: The Peoples of the Iroquois League in the Era of European Colonization* (Chapel Hill: University of North Carolina Press, 1992), 23–24; James Axtell, *The European and the Indian: Essays in the Ethnohistory of Colonial North America* (Oxford: Oxford University Press, 1981), 47–48.

48. See, e.g., David Hume, *A Treatise of Human Nature* (London, 1739–1740), ed.

L. A. Selby-Bigge, 2nd ed. (Oxford: Clarendon Press, 1978), 507; Emer de Vattel, *The Law of Nations* (1758), ed. Joseph Chitty (Philadelphia: T. & J. W. Johnson, 1866), 97–100; Jack Scott, ed., *An Annotated Edition of Lectures on Moral Philosophy by John Witherspoon* (Newark: University of Delaware Press, 1982), 127 (written in the late 1760s).

49. J. M., *The Original Rights of Mankind Freely to Subdue and Improve the Earth* (Boston: Printed for the author, 1722), 6.

50. Thomas Hobbes, *Leviathan* (1651), ed. Richard Tuck (Cambridge: Cambridge University Press, 1996), 90, 101; Thomas Hobbes, *A Dialogue between a Philosopher and a Student of the Common Laws of England* (1681), ed. Joseph Cropsey (Chicago: University of Chicago Press, 1971), 72–73; John Bulkley, "Preface," in Roger Wolcott, *Poetical Meditations* (New-London: L. Green, 1725), xviii, xxv, xxx.

51. Paul J. Lindholdt, ed., *John Josselyn, Colonial Traveler: A Critical Edition of Two Voyages to New-England* (Hanover: University Press of New England, 1988), 103; George Alsop, *A Character of the Province of Mary-Land* (London: Peter Dring, 1666), 60; John Cowell, *The Institutes of the Lawes of England* (London: Jo. Ridley, 1651), 57; John Selden, *Of the Dominion, Or, Ownership of the Sea* (London, 1652; New York: Arno Press, 1972), 24–27.

52. Wright, *Indian Deeds*, 15; Shurtleff, *Records*, 4(2):213; William Cosby to Jacob Glen et al., 3 Nov. 1733, HM 1478, American Indian File, HL; O'Callaghan, *Documents*, 4:888; CO 5/65, p. 43, PRO.

53. Arthur O. Lovejoy and George Boas, *Primitivism and Related Ideas in Antiquity* (1935) (New York: Octagon Books, 1965); Thomas Cole, *Democritus and the Sources of Greek Anthropology* (Cleveland: American Philological Association, 1967), 36–38; Cicero, *De Officiis*, trans. Walter Miller (Cambridge, Mass.: Harvard University Press, 1947), 23; Seneca, *Ad Lucilium Epistulae Morales*, trans. Richard M. Gummere (New York: G. P. Putnam's Sons, 1920), 2:423; *The Geography of Strabo*, trans. Horace Leonard Jones (Cambridge, Mass.: Harvard University Press, 1917–32), 3:207; Horace, *The Complete Odes and Epodes with the Centennial Hymn*, trans. W. G. Shepherd (Middlesex: Penguin Books, 1983), 155; Julius Caesar, *The Gallic War*, trans. H. J. Edwards (Cambridge, Mass.: Harvard University Press, 1917), 347; Justin, *Epitome of the Philippic History of Pompeius Trogus*, trans. J. C. Yardley (Atlanta: Scholars Press, 1994), 27; Virgil, *Georgics*, trans. Smith Palmer Bovie (Chicago: University of Chicago Press, 1956), 10; Ovid, *The Erotic Poems*, trans. Peter Green (London: Penguin Books, 1982), 153.

54. Thomas Aquinas, *Summa Theologica* (Cambridge: Blackfriars, 1964–), 37:13; John F. Moffitt and Santiago Sebastian, *O Brave New People: The European Invention of the American Indian* (Albuquerque: University of New Mexico Press, 1996), 69–75; Peter Stein, "The Four Stage Theory of the Development of Societies," in *The Character and Influence of the Roman Civil Law: Historical Essays* (London: Hambledon Press, 1988), 395–409; Adam Smith, *Lectures on Jurisprudence*, ed. R. L. Meek, D. D. Raphael, and P. G. Stein (Oxford: Clarendon Press, 1978), 459 (Smith delivered these lectures in the 1760s); Ronald L. Meek, *Social Science and the Ignoble Savage* (Cambridge: Cambridge University Press, 1976); William Blackstone, *Commentaries on the Laws of England* (1765–1769), 9th ed. (London: W. Strahan et al., 1783), 2:7.

55. Anthony Pagden, *The Fall of Natural Man: The American Indian and the Origins of Comparative Ethnology* (Cambridge: Cambridge University Press, 1982), 4–6; Anthony Grafton with April Shelford and Nancy Sirasi, *New Worlds, Ancient Texts: The Power of Tradition and the Shock of Discovery* (Cambridge, Mass.: Harvard University Press, 1992); J. H. Elliott, *The Old World and the New, 1492–1650* (Cambridge: Cambridge University Press, 1970), 50; David Armitage, "The New World and British Historical Thought: From Richard Hakluyt to William Robertson," in Karen Ordahl Kupperman, ed., *America in European Consciousness, 1493–1750* (Chapel Hill: University of North Carolina Press, 1995), 63–64; Hugh Jones, *The Present State of Virginia* (London, 1724), ed. Richard L. Morton (Chapel Hill: University of North Carolina Press, 1956), 51.

56. David Grayson Allen, *In English Ways* (Chapel Hill: University of North Carolina Press, 1981).

57. Nancy Shoemaker, *A Strange Likeness: Becoming Red and White in Eighteenth-Century North America* (Oxford: Oxford University Press, 2004), 13–34; R. Douglas Hurt, *Indian Agriculture in America: Prehistory to the Present* (Lawrence: University Press of Kansas, 1987), 65–67; Anthony F. C. Wallace, "Political Organization and Land Tenure among the Northeastern Indians, 1600–1830," *Southwestern Journal of Anthropology* 13 (1957): 301–321; William Bartram, *Travels Through North & South Carolina, Georgia, East & West Florida* (Philadelphia, 1791), ed. Francis Harper (New Haven: Yale University Press, 1958), 325; John Bellers, *An Essay Toward the Improvement of Physick* (London, 1714), in A. Ruth Fry, ed., *John Bellers 1654–1725: Quaker, Economist and Social Reformer* (London: Cassell, 1935), 128; John Locke, *Two Treatises of Government* (3rd ed. 1698), ed. Peter Laslett, 2nd ed. (Cambridge: Cambridge University Press, 1970), 305.

58. Thomas Pownall, *The Administration of the Colonies*, 4th ed. (London: J. Walter, 1768), 265; *Pennsylvania Gazette*, 14 October 1736. On the British sense of vulnerability with respect to the Indians, see Linda Colley, *Captives* (New York: Pantheon, 2002), 137–202.

59. Archibald Kennedy, *The Importance of Gaining and Preserving the Friendship of the Indians to the British Interest, Considered* (New-York: James Parker, 1751), 6; CO 1/55, p. 108, PRO; *PWJ*, 1:928.

60. CO 324/17, pp. 67–68, PRO.

61. Terry L. Anderson and Fred S. McChesney, "Raid or Trade? An Economic Model of Indian–White Relations," *Journal of Law and Economics* 37 (1994): 39–74; CO 5/1040, p. 96, PRO; Alden T. Vaughan, *New England Frontier: Puritans and Indians, 1620–1675*, 3rd ed. (Norman: University of Oklahoma Press, 1995), 107–108; *A Further Account of New Jersey* (1676), 12, 6; George Scot, *The Model of the Government of the Province of East New Jersey in America* (Edinburgh: John Reid, 1685), 183.

62. CO 217/6, p. 39, PRO; Brendan McConville, *Those Daring Disturbers of the Public Peace: The Struggle for Property and Power in Early New Jersey* (Ithaca: Cornell University Press, 1999); Alan Taylor, *Liberty Men and Great Proprietors: The Revolutionary Settlement on the Maine Frontier, 1760–1820* (Chapel Hill: University of North Carolina Press, 1990).

63. Mary Lou Lustig, *The Imperial Executive in America: Sir Edmund Andros, 1637–*

1714 (Madison, N.J.: Fairleigh Dickinson University Press, 2002), 152–154; CO 1/63, pp. 119, 116, PRO; *The Declaration of the Gentlemen, Merchants, and Inhabitants of Boston* (Boston, 1689), in Whitmore, *The Andros Tracts,* 1:15–16 (emphasis in original); Palmer, *The Revolution in New England Justified,* in Whitmore, *The Andros Tracts,* 1:89. Existing property owners might have been satisfied had the nonrecognition of Indian title been applied only prospectively, but neither side appears to have proposed that compromise, perhaps because of the incoherence in declaring the Indians to be property owners before a certain date but not afterward.

64. "Councill's Opinions Concerning Coll. Nicholl's Patent and Indian Purchases," 1 July 1674, in Francis Jennings et al., eds., *Iroquois Indians: A Documentary History of the Diplomacy of the Six Nations and Their League* (Woodbridge, Conn.: Research Publications, 1984), reel 2.

65. Washburn, "The Moral and Legal Justifications for Dispossessing the Indians," 25; Herman Lebovics, "The Uses of America in Locke's *Second Treatise of Government,"* *Journal of the History of Ideas* 47 (1986): 579.

66. Roger Williams, *A Key Into the Language of America* (London, 1643), in *The Complete Writings of Roger Williams* (New York: Russell and Russell, 1963), 1:120. Williams here seems to imply that the Indians bought and sold land before the English arrived, a conclusion inconsistent with the great weight of opinion both then and now.

67. Roger Williams, *The Bloody Tenent Yet More Bloody* (London, 1652), in *Complete Writings of Roger Williams,* 4:461.

68. *Laws of the Colonial and State Governments,* 9–10.

69. John Cotton, *A Reply to Mr. Williams* (London, 1647), in *Complete Writings of Roger Williams,* 2:46–47.

70. Locke, *Two Treatises of Government,* 304–19.

71. Barbara Arneil, *John Locke and America: The Defence of English Colonialism* (Oxford: Clarendon Press, 1996), 24; PRO 30/24/48, no. 84, PRO 30/24/48, no. 55, p. 91, PRO 30/24/48, no. 35, PRO.

72. William L. Saunders and Walter Clark, eds., *The Colonial Records of North Carolina* (1886–1914) (New York: AMS Press, 1968–1978), 1:204.

73. E.g., James Tully, *An Approach to Political Philosophy: Locke in Contexts* (Cambridge: Cambridge University Press, 1993), 137–176.

2. Manhattan for Twenty-four Dollars

1. CO 5/1330, p. 272, CO 323/20, p. 17, PRO.

2. Thomas Jefferson, *Notes on the State of Virginia* (London, 1787), ed. William Peden (Chapel Hill: University of North Carolina Press, 1955), 96 n.*; Francis Jennings, *The Invasion of America: Indians, Colonialism, and the Cant of Conquest* (New York: W. W. Norton, 1976), 128–145; Jean M. O'Brien, *Dispossession by Degrees: Indian Land and Identity in Natick, Massachusetts, 1650–1790* (Cambridge: Cambridge University Press, 1997); Wilbur R. Jacobs, *Dispossessing the American Indian: Indians and Whites on the Colonial Frontier* (1972) (Norman: University of Oklahoma Press, 1985).

3. Robert L. Hale, "Coercion and Distribution in a Supposedly Non-Coercive State," *Political Science Quarterly* 38 (1923): 470–479; Robert L. Hale, "Bargaining, Duress, and Economic Liberty," *Columbia Law Review* 43 (1943): 603–628.

4. CO 1/62, p. 331, PRO; E. B. O'Callaghan, ed., *Documents Relative to the Colonial History of the State of New-York* (Albany: Weed, Parsons and Co., 1856–1887), 3:219, 3:823.

5. Bruce G. Trigger, "Early Native American Responses to European Contact: Romantic versus Rationalistic Interpretations," *Journal of American History* 77 (1991): 1195–1215; Christopher L. Miller and George R. Hamell, "A New Perspective on Indian–White Contact: Cultural Symbols and Colonial Trade," *Journal of American History* 73 (1986): 311–328.

6. Richard White, *The Roots of Dependency: Subsistence, Environment, and Social Change among the Choctaws, Pawnees, and Navajos* (Lincoln: University of Nebraska Press, 1983); CO 5/67, p. 184, PRO.

7. Robert A. Williams Jr., *Linking Arms Together: American Indian Treaty Visions of Law and Peace, 1600–1800* (New York: Oxford University Press, 1997); Neal Salisbury, "Native People and European Settlers in Eastern North America, 1600–1783," in Bruce G. Trigger and Wilcomb E. Washburn, eds., *The Cambridge History of the Native Peoples of the Americas* (Cambridge: Cambridge University Press, 1996), 1(1):399–460; Samuel Wilson, *An Account of the Province of Carolina in America* (London: Francis Smith, 1682), 15; Richard Aquila, *The Iroquois Restoration: Iroquois Diplomacy on the Colonial Frontier, 1701–1754* (Detroit: Wayne State University Press, 1983); Neal Salisbury, *Manitou and Providence: Indians, Europeans, and the Making of New England, 1500–1643* (New York: Oxford University Press, 1982), 184–185; James Kendall Hosmer, ed., *Winthrop's Journal* (New York: Charles Scribner's Sons, 1908), 1:139–140. See also *New-Englands Plantation* (London: Michael Sparke, 1630), 13 ("They doe generally professe to like well of our comming and planting here . . . partly because our being here will be a meanes both of reliefe to them when they want, and also a defence from their Enemies").

8. Michael Leroy Oberg, *Dominion and Civility: English Imperialism and Native America, 1585–1685* (Ithaca: Cornell University Press, 1999), 101–102; PRO 30/24/48, no. 35, PRO.

9. Nathaniel Crouch, *The English Empire in America* (London: Nath. Crouch, 1685), 105.

10. Robert Steven Grumet, "An Analysis of Upper Delawaran Land Sales in Northern New Jersey, 1630–1758," in William Cowan, ed., *Papers of the Ninth Algonquian Conference* (Ottawa: Carleton University, 1978), 25–35; Robert S. Grumet, "The Selling of Lenapehoking," in Charles F. Hayes, ed., *Proceedings of the 1992 People to People Conference* (Rochester: Rochester Museum and Science Center, 1994), 19–24; Robert S. Grumet, "Suscaneman and the Matinecock Lands, 1653–1703," in Robert S. Grumet, ed., *Northeastern Indian Lives, 1632–1816* (Amherst: University of Massachusetts Press, 1996), 116–139.

11. CO 5/66, p. 75, CO 5/1330, p. 253, PRO.

12. *PWJ*, 1:529–30.

13. James Logan to John, Richard, and Thomas Penn, 16 November 1729, Ayer MS 522, NL.

14. Virginia DeJohn Anderson, "King Philip's Herds: Indians, Colonists, and the Problem of Livestock in Early New England," *William and Mary Quarterly* 51 (1994): 601–624; Claudio Saunt, *A New Order of Things: Property, Power, and the Transformation of the Creek Indians, 1733–1816* (Cambridge: Cambridge University Press, 1999), 46–50; William Cronon, *Changes in the Land: Indians, Colonists, and the Ecology of New England* (New York: Hill and Wang, 1983), 98–107; Daniel R. Mandell, *Behind the Frontier: Indians in Eighteenth-Century Eastern Massachusetts* (Lincoln: University of Nebraska Press, 1996), 94; Catawba chief quoted in James H. Merrell, *The Indians' New World: Catawbas and Their Neighbors from European Contact through the Era of Removal* (Chapel Hill: University of North Carolina Press, 1989), 182.

15. Peter A. Thomas, "Cultural Change on the Southern New England Frontier, 1630–1665," in William W. Fitzhugh, ed., *Cultures in Contact: The Impact of European Contacts on Native American Cultural Institutions a.d. 1000–1800* (Washington: Smithsonian Institution Press, 1985), 131–161; O'Brien, *Dispossession by Degrees*, 173; J. Russell Snapp, *John Stuart and the Struggle for Empire on the Southern Frontier* (Baton Rouge: Louisiana State University Press, 1996), 39–44; William Stith, *The History of the First Discovery and Settlement of Virginia* (Williamsburg: William Parks, 1747), 140.

16. Alvin H. Morrison, "Indian Land-Deeds in the North-East: Some Ethnohistorical Basics," in William Cowan, ed., *Papers of the Twenty-Third Algonquian Conference* (Ottawa: Carleton University, 1992), 305; George S. Snyderman, "Concepts of Land Ownership among the Iroquois and Their Neighbors," in William N. Fenton, ed., *Symposium on Local Diversity in Iroquois Culture* (Washington: Smithsonian Institution, 1951), 15–34; George Bird Grinnell, "Tenure of Land among the Indians," *American Anthropologist* 9 (1907): 1–11; George Bancroft, *History of the United States of America* (Boston: Little, Brown, 1876), 1:456 ("the unlettered savage, who repented the alienation of vast tracts by affixing a shapeless mark to a bond, might deem the English tenure defeasible").

17. Kathleen J. Bragdon, *Native People of Southern New England, 1500–1650* (Norman: University of Oklahoma Press, 1996), 137–139; R. Douglas Hurt, *Indian Agriculture in America: Prehistory to the Present* (Lawrence: University Press of Kansas, 1987), 66; Daniel K. Richter, *The Ordeal of the Longhouse: The Peoples of the Iroquois League in the Era of European Colonization* (Chapel Hill: University of North Carolina Press, 1992), 23–24; James Axtell, *The European and the Indian: Essays in the Ethnohistory of Colonial North America* (Oxford: Oxford University Press, 1981), 47.

18. Marshall Sahlins, *Stone Age Economics* (Chicago: Aldine-Atherton, 1972), 1–39; John Locke, *Two Treatises of Government* (3rd ed. 1698), ed. Peter Laslett, 2nd ed. (Cambridge: Cambridge University Press, 1970), 314–315; Thomas Morton, *The New English Canaan* (Amsterdam, 1637), ed. Charles Francis Adams Jr. (Boston: Prince Society, 1883), 178.

19. Peter A. Thomas, "The Fur Trade, Indian Land, and the Need to Define Adequate 'Environmental' Parameters," *Ethnohistory* 28 (1981): 363; Alan Taylor, *Liberty Men and Great Proprietors: The Revolutionary Settlement on the Maine Fron-*

tier, 1760–1820 (Chapel Hill: University of North Carolina Press, 1990), 13; *A Brief and True Narration of the Late Wars Risen in New-England* (London: J. S., 1675), 3; Roger B. Ray, "Maine Indians' Concept of Land Tenure," *Maine Historical Society Quarterly* 13 (1973): 39; Shirley W. Dunn, *The Mohican World 1680–1750* (Fleischmanns, N.Y.: Purple Mountain Press, 2000), 69.

20. David H. Corkran, *The Cherokee Frontier: Conflict and Survival, 1740–62* (Norman: University of Oklahoma Press, 1962), 61; Tom Hatley, *The Dividing Paths: Cherokees and South Carolinians through the Era of Revolution* (New York: Oxford University Press, 1993), 76–77.

21. Sandra M. Gustafson, *Eloquence Is Power: Oratory and Performance in Early America* (Chapel Hill: University of North Carolina Press, 2000), 119–139.

22. Such is the conclusion of the scholars who have closely studied Indian land sales in individual places. Peter S. Leavenworth, "'The Best Title That Indians Can Claime': Native Agency and Consent in the Transferal of Penacook-Pawtucket Land in the Seventeenth Century," *New England Quarterly* 72 (1999): 275–300; Emerson W. Baker, "'A Scratch with a Bear's Paw': Anglo-Indian Land Deeds in Early Maine," *Ethnohistory* 36 (1989): 235–256; Shirley W. Dunn, *The Mohicans and Their Land 1609–1730* (Fleischmanns, N.Y.: Purple Mountain Press, 1994), 115–116.

23. Harry Andrew Wright, ed., *Indian Deeds of Hampden County* (Springfield, Mass., 1905), 12, 17; *The Proprietors' Records of the Town of Mendon, Massachusetts* (Boston: Rockwell and Churchill Press, 1899), 8. For other examples of early deeds in which Indian sellers reserved rights to specific resources, see James Warren Springer, "American Indians and the Law of Real Property in Colonial New England," *American Journal of Legal History* 30 (1986): 38–39; *Historical Indian–Colonial Relations of New Hampshire* (Manchester, N.H.: Pennacook/Sokoki Inter-Tribal Nation, 1977), 11, 12, 23; Joel N. Eno, *The Puritans and the Indian Lands* (New York, 1906).

24. James H. Merrell, *Into the American Woods: Negotiators on the Pennsylvania Frontier* (New York: W. W. Norton, 1999); Jane T. Merritt, *At the Crossroads: Indians and Empires on a Mid-Atlantic Frontier, 1700–1763* (Chapel Hill: University of North Carolina Press, 2003).

25. CO 5/646, pp. 113–119, 250, 266; CO 5/647, p. 12; CO 5/673, pp. 8, 94, 98, 212; CO 5/674, pp. 3, 41; CO 5/712, p. 10, PRO.

26. Hilary E. Wyss, *Writing Indians: Literacy, Christianity, and Native Community in Early America* (Amherst: University of Massachusetts Press, 2000); Ives Goddard and Kathleen J. Bragdon, *Native Writings in Massachusett* (Philadelphia: American Philosophical Society, 1988), 14; Elizabeth A. Little, "Three Kinds of Indian Land Deeds at Nantucket, Massachusetts," in William Cowan, ed., *Papers of the Eleventh Algonquian Conference* (Ottawa: Carleton University, 1980), 61–70.

27. CO 5/866, pp. 341, 377, CO 217/2, p. 113, CO 5/867, p. 177, PRO.

28. *PWJ*, 6:984; Mandell, *Behind the Frontier*, 134; Cotton Mather, *A Monitory, and Hortatory Letter, to Those English, Who Debauch the Indians, by Selling Strong Drink Unto Them* (Boston, 1700), 4; Peter Wraxall, *An Abridgment of the Indian Affairs* (1754), ed. Charles Howard McIlwain (Cambridge, Mass.: Harvard University Press, 1915), 179n1; *PWJ*, 3:339, 673–674, 4:112–114, 176.

29. Douglas Edward Leach, *The Northern Colonial Frontier 1607–1763* (New York:

Holt, Rinehart and Winston, 1966), 177; *Collections of the New-York Historical Society for the Year 1918* (New York: New-York Historical Society, 1919), 158; CO 323/20, p. 23, PRO; Leonard Woods Labaree, ed., *Royal Instructions to British Colonial Governors 1670–1776* (New York: Appleton-Century, 1935), 467.

30. O'Callaghan, *Documents*, 7:761–762; Ruth L. Higgins, *Expansion in New York* (Columbus: Ohio State University, 1931), 83–86. For a similar episode, in which another tribe discovered that a large tract had been granted to settlers who had in fact purchased only a small part of it, see CO 5/66, pp. 154–155, PRO.

31. Edith M. Fox, *Land Speculation in the Mohawk Country* (Ithaca: Cornell University Press, 1949); Georgianna C. Nammack, *Fraud, Politics, and the Dispossession of the Indians: The Iroquois Land Frontier in the Colonial Period* (Norman: University of Oklahoma Press, 1969), 86–106; Stanley Nider Katz, *Newcastle's New York: Anglo-American Politics, 1732–1753* (Cambridge, Mass.: Harvard University Press, 1968), 144–145.

32. Catherine Snell Crary, "The American Dream: John Tabor Kempe's Rise from Poverty to Riches," *William and Mary Quarterly* 14 (1957): 176–195; *PWJ*, 4:818, 4:864, 11:925.

33. E. B. O'Callaghan, ed., *The Documentary History of the State of New-York* (Albany: Weed, Parsons, and Co., 1849–1851), 3:236–238.

34. Anthony F. C. Wallace, *King of the Delawares: Teedyuscung 1700–1763* (Philadelphia: University of Pennsylvania Press, 1949), 18–30; Francis Jennings, "The Scandalous Indian Policy of William Penn's Sons: Deeds and Documents of the Walking Purchase," *Pennsylvania History* 37 (1970): 19–39; James Axtell, *After Columbus: Essays in the Ethnohistory of Colonial North America* (New York: Oxford University Press, 1988), 139.

35. O'Callaghan, *Documents*, 7:302; *PWJ*, 4:748.

36. Mandell, *Behind the Frontier*, 45–46.

37. Harry Andrew Wright, "The Technique of Seventeenth Century Indian-Land Purchasers," *Essex Institute Historical Collections* 77 (1941): 185–197; John Strong, "Tribal Systems and Land Alienation: A Case Study," in William Cowan, ed., *Papers of the Sixteenth Algonquian Conference* (Ottawa: Carleton University, 1985), 183–200.

38. Hurt, *Indian Agriculture in America*, 65; Eric Hinderaker, *Elusive Empires: Constructing Colonialism in the Ohio Valley, 1673–1800* (Cambridge: Cambridge University Press, 1997), 120–122. For an example from New York, a case in which colonial officials enforced a sale by a group whose authority to sell was denied by members of the tribe many years later, see Oscar Handlin and Irving Mark, eds., "Chief Daniel Nimham v. Roger Morris, Beverly Robinson, and Philip Philipse: An Indian Land Case in Colonial New York, 1765–1767," *Ethnohistory* 11 (1964): 193–246.

39. A. W. B. Simpson, *A History of the Common Law of Contract: The Rise of the Action of Assumpsit* (Oxford: Clarendon Press, 1975), 552–57; David J. Silverman, "Conditions for Coexistence, Climates for Collapse: The Challenges of Indian Life on Martha's Vineyard, 1524–1871" (Ph.D. diss., Princeton University, 2000), 222–224.

40. Colin G. Calloway, *New Worlds for All: Indians, Europeans, and the Remaking of Early America* (Baltimore: Johns Hopkins University Press, 1997), 122.

41. CO 5/1269, p. 31, PRO. On the litigation, see Joseph Henry Smith, *Appeals to the Privy Council from the American Plantations* (New York: Columbia University Press, 1950), 422–442; David W. Conroy, "The Defense of Indian Land Rights: William Bollan and the Mohegan Case in 1743," *Proceedings of the American Antiquarian Society* 103 (1993): 395–424; Mark D. Walters, "*Mohegan Indians v. Connecticut* (1705–1773) and the Legal Status of Aboriginal Customary Laws and Government in British North America," *Osgoode Hall Law Journal* 33 (1995): 785–829.

42. Nathaniel Sheidley, "Hunting and the Politics of Masculinity in Cherokee Treaty-Making, 1763–75," in Martin Daunton and Rick Halpern, eds., *Empire and Others: British Encounters with Indigenous Peoples, 1600–1850* (London: UCL Press, 1999), 167–185; "The Importance of Attaching the Indian Tribes to the English Interest" (1760), 23, Ayer MS 403, NL; *PWJ*, 4:661, 691.

43. Kathryn E. Holland Braund, *Deerskins and Duffels: The Creek Indian Trade with Anglo-America, 1685–1815* (Lincoln: University of Nebraska Press, 1993), 150–152.

44. In the proprietary colonies the purchasing entity was technically the proprietor, not the colonial government, but the distinction had little or no relevance to relations between settlers and Indians, so to avoid unnecessary complication I ignore it.

45. *Pennsylvania Archives* (Philadelphia: Joseph Severns, 1852–), 4th series, 2:704.

46. Peter Francis Jr., "The Beads That Did *Not* Buy Manhattan Island," *New York History* 67 (1986): 4–22; Charles Gehring, "Peter Minuit's Purchase of Manhattan Island—New Evidence," *De Halve Maen* 55 (1980): 6–17; O'Callaghan, *Documents*, 1:37. The earliest mention of the twenty-four dollars figure may have been in E. B. O'Callaghan, *History of New Netherland* (Philadelphia: G. S. Appleton, 1846–1848), 1:104. For advice on Dutch money I am grateful to Jeremy Bangs.

47. O'Callaghan, *History of New Netherland*, 1:104; Edwin G. Burrows and Mike Wallace, *Gotham: A History of New York City to 1898* (New York: Oxford University Press, 1999), 23.

48. The conversion from guilders to pounds is derived from John J. McCusker, *Money and Exchange in Europe and America, 1600–1775: A Handbook* (Chapel Hill: University of North Carolina Press, 1978). The adjustment for inflation between 1626 and 2001, resulting in a figure of approximately £596, was performed at http://eh.net/hmit/ppowerbp. On January 1, 2001, £1 was worth roughly $1.49.

49. *Flow of Funds Accounts in the United States: Flows and Outstandings, First Quarter 2001* (Washington: Board of Governors of the Federal Reserve System, 2001), 102ff.

50. *Papers of the Lloyd Family of the Manor of Queens Village* (New York: New-York Historical Society, 1927), 31; Grumet, "Suscaneman and the Matinecock Lands," 127–128.

51. Leonard W. Labaree, et al., eds., *The Papers of Benjamin Franklin* (New Haven: Yale University Press, 1959–), 8:373–374, 5:372–373; George Milligen-Johnston, *A Short Description of the Province of South-Carolina* (London: John Hinton, 1770), 72–73; *PWJ*, 12:73, 192; *An Answer to the Council of Proprietor's Two Publications* (New-York: Catherine Zenger, 1747), 1.

52. Solomon Stoddard, *An Answer to Some Cases of Conscience Respecting the Country* (Boston: B. Green, 1722), 12–13.

53. Ezra Stiles, *The United States Elevated to Glory and Honor* (New-Haven: Thomas and Samuel Green, 1783), 8–9.

54. Locke, *Two Treatises*, 316, 314.

55. *Minutes of the Provincial Council of Pennsylvania* (Harrisburg: Theo. Fenn & Co., 1851–1853), 4:570–572.

56. See, e.g., Arthur Young, *Political Essays Concerning the Present State of the British Empire* (London: W. Strahan and T. Cadell, 1772), 372.

3. From Contract to Treaty

1. Peter Wraxall, "Some Thoughts Upon the British Indian Interest in North America" (1755), CO 5/285, pp. 9–10, PRO; *PWJ*, 9:613.

2. Daniel K. Richter, *Facing East from Indian Country: A Native History of Early America* (Cambridge, Mass.: Harvard University Press, 2001), 182, 184; *PWJ*, 2:737.

3. Wraxall, "Some Thoughts," 10; Wilbur R. Jacobs, ed., *Indians of the Southern Colonial Frontier: The Edmond Atkin Report and Plan of 1755* (Columbia: University of South Carolina Press, 1954), 90; E. B. O'Callaghan, ed., *The Documentary History of the State of New-York* (Albany: White, Parsons and Co., 1849–1851), 2:611; Thomas Pownall, *Proposals for Securing the Friendship of the Five Nations* (New-York: J. Parker and W. Weyman, 1756), 8.

4. Oliver Morton Dickerson, *American Colonial Government 1696–1765* (Cleveland: Arthur H. Clark Company, 1912), 340; O'Callaghan, *Documentary History*, 2:611; Jacobs, *Indians of the Southern Colonial Frontier*, 78.

5. *PWJ*, 2:879, 3:308.

6. Two wartime events, the 1758 Easton conference and a 1761 order of Colonel Henry Bouquet, the commander at Fort Pitt, are sometimes erroneously cited as changes in land policy prefiguring the Proclamation of 1763. Clarence Walworth Alvord, *The Mississippi Valley in British Politics* (1917) (New York: Russell and Russell, 1959), 1:121–122; Thomas Perkins Abernethy, *Western Lands and the American Revolution* (1937) (New York: Russell and Russell, 1964), 11; Jack M. Sosin, *Whitehall and the Wilderness: The Middle West in British Colonial Policy, 1760–1775* (Lincoln: University of Nebraska Press, 1961), 42–43. At Easton, the colonial government of Pennsylvania did not promise the Delawares that it would ban settlement west of the Alleghenies. Rather, Pennsylvania merely returned to the Delawares land west of the Alleghenies that the colony had previously purchased but not yet paid for or settled. Pennsylvania made no commitment to refrain from purchasing land in the future. *Colonial Records of Pennsylvania* (Harrisburg: T. Fenn, 1851–1853), 8:199, 204. In 1761, Bouquet prohibited settlement west of the Alleghenies, but not all settlement—only settlement without the permission of the colony from which the settler had come. As Bouquet's subsequent correspondence made clear, he meant only to exclude settlers who had not purchased the Indians' land. Douglas Brymner, ed., *Report on Canadian Archives 1889* (Ottawa: Brown Chamberlin, 1890), 72–77.

7. *PWJ*, 10:212.

8. *PWJ*, 10:571–572.

9. CO 324/17, pp. 67–68, 82–87, PRO; E. B. O'Callaghan, ed., *Documents Relative to the Colonial History of the State of New-York* (Albany: Weed, Parsons and Co., 1853–1887), 7:472–479.

10. R. A. Humphreys, "Lord Shelburne and the Proclamation of 1763," *English Historical Review* 49 (1934): 252.

11. Verner W. Crane, "Hints Relative to the Division and Government of the Conquered and Newly Acquired Countries in America," *Mississippi Valley Historical Review* 8 (1922): 371; CO 5/65, p. 67, PRO; Adam Shortt and Arthur G. Doughty, eds., *Documents Relating to the Constitutional History of Canada* (Ottawa: J. de L. Taché, 1918), 152, 154.

12. The proclamation is published in several places, including Clarence S. Brigham, ed., *British Royal Proclamations Relating to America, 1603–1783* (1911) (New York: Burt Franklin, 1964), 212–218.

13. Max Farrand, "The Indian Boundary Line," *American Historical Review* 10 (1905): 784.

14. Clarence Edwin Carter, ed., *The Correspondence of General Thomas Gage with the Secretaries of State, 1763–1775* (New Haven: Yale University Press, 1931–1933), 1:278. For a more skeptical view of the imperial government's motivation, see Gregory Evans Dowd, *War Under Heaven: Pontiac, the Indian Nations, and the British Empire* (Baltimore: Johns Hopkins University Press, 2002), 233–236.

15. Leonard W. Labaree et al., eds., *The Papers of Benjamin Franklin* (New Haven: Yale University Press, 1959–), 13:172; CO 5/66, p. 112, PRO; Carter, ed., *Correspondence of General Thomas Gage*, 1:11.

16. CO 323/20, p. 79, PRO.

17. CO 324/17, pp. 204–23, CO 5/65, pp. 350–51, PRO.

18. Louis De Vorsey Jr., *The Indian Boundary Line in the Southern Colonies, 1763–1775* (Chapel Hill: University of North Carolina Press, 1966).

19. *PWJ*, 12:405, 374, 417–18.

20. Michael N. McConnell, *A Country Between: The Upper Ohio Valley and Its Peoples, 1724–1774* (Lincoln: University of Nebraska Press, 1992), 248–253; *PWJ*, 6:483; Colin G. Calloway, *New Worlds for All: Indians, Europeans, and the Remaking of Early America* (Baltimore: Johns Hopkins University Press, 1997), 122; *PWJ*, 7:332, 167.

21. Stephen Aron, "Pigs and Hunters: 'Rights in the Woods' on the Trans-Appalachian Frontier," in Andrew R. L. Cayton and Fredrika J. Teute, eds., *Contact Points: American Frontiers from the Mohawk Valley to the Mississippi, 1750–1830* (Chapel Hill: University of North Carolina Press, 1998), 175–204; *Virginia Gazette* (PD), 1 August 1766, 2:3; Carter, ed., *Correspondence of General Thomas Gage*, 1:142; CO 5/67, p. 61, PRO.

22. K. G. Davies, ed., *Documents of the American Revolution* (Shannon: Irish University Press, 1972–1981), 3:133.

23. Kenneth P. Bailey, ed., *The Ohio Company Papers, 1753–1817* (Arcata, Calif.: n.p., 1947), 250; Davies, *Documents of the American Revolution*, 2:207.

24. John C. Fitzpatrick, ed., *The Writings of George Washington* (Washington: Government Printing Office, 1931–1944), 2:468–470.

25. Philip M. Hamer et al., eds., *The Papers of Henry Laurens* (Columbia: University of South Carolina Press, 1968–), 8:76.

26. Labaree et al., *Papers of Benjamin Franklin*, 20:303–304; Anthony F. C. Wallace, *Jefferson and the Indians: The Tragic Fate of the First Americans* (Cambridge, Mass.: Harvard University Press, 1999), 21–49; Woody Holton, *Forced Founders: Indians, Debtors, Slaves, and the Making of the American Revolution in Virginia* (Chapel Hill: University of North Carolina Press, 1999), 3–38.

27. Sosin, *Whitehall and the Wilderness*, 259–267, 232–233; Labaree et al., *Papers of Benjamin Franklin*, 20:300–302; John C. Fitzpatrick, ed., *The Diaries of George Washington* (Boston: Houghton Mifflin, 1925), 2:95.

28. Alden T. Vaughan et al., eds., *Early American Indian Documents: Treaties and Laws, 1607–1789* (Washington: University Publications of America, 1979–), 5:325; CO 5/66, p. 143, PRO; Carter, *Correspondence of General Thomas Gage*, 1:148; *PWJ*, 12:715, 376.

29. Carter, *Correspondence of General Thomas Gage*, 2:98, 105.

30. Dorothy V. Jones, *License for Empire: Colonialism by Treaty in Early America* (Chicago: University of Chicago Press, 1982).

31. Eugene M. Del Papa, "The Royal Proclamation of 1763: Its Effect upon Virginia Land Companies," *Virginia Magazine of History and Biography* 83 (1975): 406–411; *PWJ*, 8:152–153.

32. Henry Moore to William Johnson, 23 May 1766, HM 8228, American Indian File, HL; Davies, *Documents of the American Revolution*, 3:24, 6:153–154.

33. Shaw Livermore, *Early American Land Companies* (1939) (New York: Octagon Books, 1968), 74–132; Clarence Edwin Carter, *Great Britain and the Illinois Country, 1763–1774* (1910) (Freeport, N.Y.: Books for Libraries Press, 1971), 103–144.

34. Kenneth P. Bailey, *The Ohio Company of Virginia and the Westward Movement, 1748–1792* (Glendale, Calif.: Arthur H. Clark Co., 1939), 36; George E. Lewis, *The Indiana Company 1763–1798: A Study in Eighteenth Century Frontier Land Speculation and Business Venture* (Glendale, Calif.: Arthur H. Clark Co., 1941), 46.

35. Davies, *Documents of the American Revolution*, 6:154.

36. Julian P. Boyd et al., eds., *The Papers of Thomas Jefferson* (Princeton: Princeton University Press, 1950–), 6:656.

4. A Revolution in Land Policy

1. *RC*, 284 (emphasis in original).

2. Walter H. Mohr, *Federal Indian Relations, 1774–1788* (Philadelphia: University of Pennsylvania Press, 1933), 38–39; *JCC*, 2:182; Jeremy Adelman and Stephen Aron, "From Borderlands to Borders: Empires, Nation-States, and the Peoples in Between in North American History," *American Historical Review* 104 (1999): 814–841.

3. James Muldoon, "Discovery, Grant, Charter, Conquest, or Purchase: John Adams on the Legal Basis for English Possession of North America," in Christopher L. Tomlins and Bruce H. Mann, eds., *The Many Legalities of Early America* (Chapel Hill: University of North Carolina Press, 2001), 25–46; John Phillip Reid, *Constitutional History of the American Revolution: The Authority of Rights* (Madison: University of Wisconsin Press, 1986), 127–131.

4. John Adams, *Novanglus* (1774), in Charles Francis Adams, ed., *The Works of John*

Adams (Boston: Little, Brown, 1850–1856), 4:124–125, 149. For the view among lawyers that statutes passed by Parliament were automatically in force in newly discovered, uninhabited lands, see *Blankard v. Galdy*, 90 Eng. Rep. 1089 (K.B. 1693); William Blackstone, *Commentaries on the Laws of England* (1765–1769), 9th ed. (London: W. Strahan, 1783), 1:107–108.

5. Leonard W. Labaree et al., eds., *The Papers of Benjamin Franklin* (New Haven: Yale University Press, 1959–), 17:385, 16:291–292, 20:119.

6. Labaree et al., *Papers of Benjamin Franklin*, 22:150–151.

7. Julian P. Boyd et al., eds., *The Papers of Thomas Jefferson* (Princeton: Princeton University Press, 1950–), 2:67; *Pennsylvania Gazette*, 15 August 1781. See also Samuel Wharton, *Plain Facts: Being an Examination Into the Rights of the Indian Nations of America, to Their Respective Countries* (Philadelphia: R. Aitken, 1781), 10–11, 17.

8. Boyd et al., *Papers of Thomas Jefferson*, 1:352, 383; William F. Swindler, ed., *Sources and Documents of United States Constitutions* (Dobbs Ferry, N.Y.: Oceana Publications, 1982–), 7:407, 178; *JCC*, 7:166; *Papers of the Continental Congress* (Washington: National Archives and Records Service, 1959), reel 72, 2:347.

9. H. R. McIlwaine et al., eds., *Journals of the Council of the State of Virginia* (Richmond: Virginia State Library, 1931–), 3:193.

10. Zachry Johnson to Richard Law, 30 May 1781, Ayer MS 459, NL; Peter S. Onuf, *The Origins of the Federal Republic: Jurisdictional Controversies in the United States 1775–1787* (Philadelphia: University of Pennsylvania Press, 1983); *JCC*, 15:1249, 9:823–824.

11. Francis Paul Prucha, *The Great Father: The United States Government and the American Indians* (Lincoln: University of Nebraska Press, 1984), 37; Merrill Jensen, ed., *The Documentary History of the Ratification of the Constitution* (Madison: State Historical Society of Wisconsin, 1976–) 1:81; *JCC*, 9:919; Jack Campisi, "From Stanwix to Canandaigua: National Policy, States' Rights and Indian Land," in Christopher Vecsey and William A. Starna, eds., *Iroquois Land Claims* (Syracuse: Syracuse University Press, 1988), 49–65.

12. *JCC*, 25:602; Jensen, *Documentary History*, 1:151.

13. *JCC*, 24:503, 28:119; Gayle Thornbrough, ed., *Outpost on the Wabash, 1787–1791: Letters of Brigadier General Josiah Harmar and Major John Francis Hamtramck* (Indianapolis: Indiana Historical Society, 1957), 36–37.

14. Robert Scigliano, ed., *The Federalist* (New York: Modern Library, 2000), 16.

15. Max M. Mintz, *Seeds of Empire: The American Revolutionary Conquest of the Iroquois* (New York: New York University Press, 1999); Edward J. Cashin, "'But Brothers, It Is Our Land We Are Talking About': Winners and Losers in the Georgia Backcountry," in Ronald W. Hoffman, Thad W. Tate, and Peter J. Albert, eds., *An Uncivil War: The Southern Backcountry during the American Revolution* (Charlottesville: University Press of Virginia, 1985), 240–275; Colin G. Calloway, *The American Revolution in Indian Country: Crisis and Diversity in Native American Communities* (Cambridge: Cambridge University Press, 1995); *JCC*, 9:942.

16. *RC*, 218, 251.

17. Philip M. Hamer et al., eds., *The Papers of Henry Laurens* (Columbia: University of South Carolina Press, 1968–), 14:169, 484.

18. Richard B. Morris et al., eds., *John Jay: The Making of a Revolutionary* (New York: Harper and Row, 1975), 659; *JCC*, 25:683; Edmund C. Burnett, ed., *Letters of Members of the Continental Congress* (Washington: Carnegie Institution, 1921–1936), 7:308.

19. *RC*, 317, 323–324.

20. Colin G. Calloway, *Crown and Calumet: British–Indian Relations, 1783–1815* (Norman: University of Oklahoma Press, 1987), 5–12; K. G. Davies, ed., *Documents of the American Revolution* (Shannon: Irish University Press, 1972–1981), 21:170–171.

21. Wallace Brown, *The Good Americans: The Loyalists in the American Revolution* (New York: William Morrow, 1969), 126–146.

22. W. W. Abbot et al., eds., *The Papers of George Washington* (Charlottesville: University Press of Virginia, 1983–), Confederation Series, 2:119–120.

23. Robert H. White, ed., *Messages of the Governors of Tennessee* (Nashville: Tennessee Historical Commission, 1952–1990), 1:320.

24. Charles R. King, ed., *The Life and Correspondence of Rufus King* (New York: G. P. Putnam's Sons, 1894–1900), 1:106–107; *Letters of Benjamin Hawkins, 1796–1806* (Savannah: Georgia Historical Society, 1916), 102.

25. Joel W. Martin, "Cultural Contact and Crises in the Early Republic: Native American Religious Renewal, Resistance, and Accommodation," in Frederick E. Hoxie, Ronald Hoffman, and Peter J. Albert, eds., *Native Americans and the Early Republic* (Charlottesville: University Press of Virginia, 1999), 244–246; William S. Coker and Thomas D. Watson, *Indian Traders of the Southeastern Spanish Borderlands: Panton, Leslie & Company and John Forbes & Company, 1783–1847* (Pensacola: University of West Florida Press, 1986), 227–272.

26. *JCC*, 25:682; Daniel K. Richter, "Onas, the Long Knife: Pennsylvanians and Indians, 1783–1794," in Hoxie, Hoffman, and Albert, *Native Americans and the Early Republic*, 133–136.

27. *JCC*, 25:683.

28. Reginald Horsman, *Expansion and American Indian Policy, 1783–1812* (East Lansing: Michigan State University Press, 1967), 19–23.

29. *DHFFC*, 2:137–139; *RC*, 324–325.

30. Consul Wilshire Butterfield, ed., *Journal of Capt. Jonathan Heart* (Albany: Joel Munsell's Sons, 1885), 53; *DHFFC*, 2:140–142.

31. *RC*, 346–347; *DHFFC*, 2:143–144.

32. *JCC*, 28:119.

33. *JCC*, 28:119; *DHFFC*, 2:169–180.

34. *RC*, 504, 507; *JCC*, 34:124.

35. *By the United States in Congress Assembled. October 20, 1786 . . .* (New York, 1786); Boyd et al., *Papers of Thomas Jefferson*, 10:135, 598–599.

36. *RC*, 452–453. Knox's title was Secretary *at* War under the Articles of Confederation; under the Constitution his title would change to Secretary *of* War.

37. John C. Fitzpatrick, ed., *The Writings of George Washington* (Washington: Government Printing Office, 1931–1944), 27:136.

38. *JCC*, 34:125–126.

39. *JCC*, 34:125; *RC*, 528, 522.

40. Jensen, *Documentary History*, 1:173; *DHFFC*, 2:149–150.
41. *DHFFC*, 2:161, 153.
42. Ibid., 5:1006.
43. Harold C. Syrett et al., eds., *The Papers of Alexander Hamilton* (New York: Columbia University Press, 1961–1987), 6:503; Boyd et al., *Papers of Thomas Jefferson*, 10:44, 14:144.
44. *DHFFC*, 13:1066; *Annals of Congress*, 4th Cong., 1st Sess. (1796), 230; *DHFFC*, 9:181.
45. *ASP*, 1:234, 338, 341.
46. William A. Starna, "'The United States Will Protect You': The Iroquois, New York, and the 1790 Nonintercourse Act," *New York History* 83 (2002): 5–33; Barbara Graymont, "New York State Indian Policy after the Revolution," *New York History* 57 (1976): 438–476; Boyd et al., *Papers of Thomas Jefferson*, 16:407; Petition, 17 February 1794, A1823: Petitions, Correspondence and Reports Relating to Indians, 1783–1831, NYA.
47. The most well known (because it reached the Supreme Court) is *County of Oneida v. Oneida Indian Nation*, 470 U.S. 226 (1985).
48. Franklin B. Hough, ed., *Proceedings of the Commissioners of Indian Affairs, Appointed by Law for the Extinguishment of Indian Titles in the State of New York* (Albany: Joel Munsell, 1861), 91; Samuel Kirkland, "Memoir of Negotiations Relative to Indian Lands Within the State of New York" (ca. 1807), HM 2140, American Indian File, HL; *DHFFC*, 6:1596–97; Boyd et al., *Papers of Thomas Jefferson*, 22:114–116.
49. William N. Fenton, ed., "The Journal of James Emlen Kept on a Trip to Canandaigua, New York," *Ethnohistory* 12 (1965): 298; *Message from the President of the United States, Transmitting a Letter and Report from the Agent Appointed to Transact Business with the Indians* (Washington, 1804); Petition to Governor Daniel D. Tompkins, ca. 1810, Ayer MS 650, NL.
50. *ASP*, 1:353–354.
51. *ASP*, 1:356.
52. *The Statistical History of the United States* (New York: Basic Books, 1976), 1106.
53. Syrett et al., *Papers of Alexander Hamilton*, 11:377; Richard C. Knopf, ed., *Anthony Wayne: A Name in Arms* (Pittsburgh: University of Pittsburgh Press, 1959), 397; Andrew R. L. Cayton, "'Noble Actors' upon 'the Theatre of Honour': Power and Civility in the Treaty of Greenville," in Andrew R. L. Cayton and Fredrika J. Teute, eds., *Contact Points: American Frontiers from the Mohawk Valley to the Mississippi, 1750–1830* (Chapel Hill: University of North Carolina Press, 1998), 235–269; Barbara Alice Mann, "The Greenville Treaty of 1795: Pen-and-Ink Witchcraft in the Struggle for the Old Northwest," in Bruce E. Johnsen and Vine Deloria Jr., eds., *Enduring Legacies: Native American Treaties and Contemporary Controversies* (Westport, Conn.: Praeger, 2004), 135–201.
54. Charles M. Snyder, ed., *Red and White on the New York Frontier: A Struggle for Survival; Insights from the Papers of Erastus Granger, Indian Agent, 1807–1819* (Harrison, N.Y.: Harbor Hill Books, 1978), 93; John Ross et al. to James Monroe, 19 Jan. 1824, document TCC035, *SNA*.
55. Joel W. Martin, *Sacred Revolt: The Muskogees' Struggle for a New World* (Boston:

Beacon Press, 1991), 119; Return J. Meigs to Andrew Jackson, 6 July 1816, document THS016, *SNA.*

56. Jacob Lindley, *Jacob Lindley's Account of a Journey to Attend the Indian Treaty, Proposed to be Held at Sandusky, in the Year 1793* (Philadelphia, 1832), 122–124.

57. Gayle Thornbrough, ed., *The Correspondence of John Badollet and Albert Gallatin, 1804–1836* (Indianapolis: Indiana Historical Society, 1963), 151; Robert M. Owens, "Jeffersonian Benevolence on the Ground: The Indian Land Cession Treaties of William Henry Harrison," *Journal of the Early Republic* 22 (2002): 405–435.

58. Claudio Saunt, *A New Order of Things: Property, Power, and the Transformation of the Creek Indians, 1733–1816* (Cambridge: Cambridge University Press, 1999), 215–217; Robert V. Remini, *Andrew Jackson and His Indian Wars* (New York: Viking, 2001), 111, 127, 176; *DHFFC*, 2:249; Florette Henri, *The Southern Indians and Benjamin Hawkins, 1796–1816* (Norman: University of Oklahoma Press, 1986), 175; Laurence M. Hauptman, *Conspiracy of Interests: Iroquois Dispossession and the Rise of New York State* (Syracuse: Syracuse University Press, 1999), 91.

59. Creek delegation to Secretary of War, 16 Dec. 1825, Document TCC009, *SNA.*

60. Logan Esarey, ed., *Messages and Letters of William Henry Harrison* (Indianapolis: Indiana Historical Commission, 1922), 1:71.

61. *RC*, 444; *Annals of Congress*, 3rd Cong., 2nd Sess. (1795), 1400; Clarence Edwin Carter, ed., *The Territorial Papers of the United States* (Washington: Government Printing Office, 1934–1975), 5:323.

62. John Sevier to Captains Sparks and Wade, 17 Feb. 1797, Document GS035; Sevier to Andrew Jackson, 19 Nov. 1797, Document GS044; Sevier to "the Inhabitants and people said to be settled on the Indian Lands," 1 April 1804, Document GS056, *SNA.*

63. *ASP,* 1:88.

64. *Register of Debates,* 19th Cong., 1st Sess. (1826), 733.

65. Royce, 660–725. This figure includes only those treaties that contained land cessions. The total number of ratified Indian treaties between 1801 and 1830 was 131. Francis Paul Prucha, *American Indian Treaties: The History of a Political Anomaly* (Berkeley: University of California Press, 1994), appendix B.

66. *Annals of Congress,* 8th Cong., 2nd Sess. (1804), 13; *ASP,* 2:10.

67. Robert A. Rutland, ed., *The Papers of George Mason, 1725–1792* (Chapel Hill: University of North Carolina Press, 1970), 1258–59.

68. *RC,* 512.

69. Eric Kades, "The Dark Side of Efficiency: *Johnson v. M'Intosh* and the Expropriation of American Indian Lands," *University of Pennsylvania Law Review* 148 (2000): 1065–1190.

5. *From Ownership to Occupancy*

1. *DHFFC*, 5:1005; Harold C. Syrett et al., eds., *The Papers of Alexander Hamilton* (New York: Columbia University Press, 1961–1987), 14:144, 6:503.

2. *Lessee of Plumsted and M'Call v. Rudebagh*, 1 Yeates 502, 504 (Pa. 1795).

3. James Sullivan, *The History of Land Titles in Massachusetts* (Boston: I. Thomas and

E. T. Andrews, 1801), 22–24. Sullivan gave a shorter and slightly more sympathetic account of Indian agriculture in James Sullivan, "The History of the Penobscott Indians," *Collections of the Massachusetts Historical Society*, 1st Series, 9 (1804): 213.

4. Levi Frisbie, *Discourse Before the Society for Propagating the Gospel Among the Indians, and Others, in North America* (Charlestown, Mass.: Samuel Etheridge, 1804), 30; DeWitt Clinton, *Discourse Delivered Before the New-York Historical Society, at Their Anniversary Meeting, 6th December 1811* (New-York: James Eastburn, 1812), 49; "On the Causes of the Depopulation of the American Indians," *Analectic Magazine* 7 (1816): 324; "Reflections on the Institutions of the Cherokee Indians," *Analectic Magazine* 12 (1818): 43; Lydia H. Sigourney, *Traits of the Aborigines of America: A Poem* (Cambridge, Mass.: University Press, 1822), 3; Robert F. Berkhofer Jr., *The White Man's Indian: Images of the American Indian from Columbus to the Present* (New York: Alfred A. Knopf, 1978), 138.

5. Daniel H. Usner Jr., "Iroquois Livelihood and Jeffersonian Agrarianism: Reaching behind the Models and Metaphors," in Frederick E. Hoxie, Ronald Hoffman, and Peter J. Albert, eds., *Native Americans and the Early Republic* (Charlottesville: University Press of Virginia, 1999), 200–225; William T. Hagan, "Justifying Dispossession of the Indian: The Land Utilization Argument," in Christopher Vecsey and Robert W. Venables, eds., *American Indian Environments: Ecological Issues in Native American History* (Syracuse: Syracuse University Press, 1980), 65–80; *Annals of Congress*, 15th Cong., 2nd Sess. (1819), 698.

6. Susannah Willard Johnson, *A Narrative of the Captivity of Mrs. Johnson* (Walpole, N.H.: David Carlisle, Jr., 1796), 143; Jedidiah Morse, *Signs of the Times: A Sermon, Preached to the Society for Propagating the Gospel Among the Indians and Others in North America, at Their Anniversary, Nov. 1, 1810* (Charlestown, Mass.: Samuel T. Armstrong, 1810), 34–35; Elijah Parish, *A Sermon Preached at Boston, November 3, 1814, Before the Society for Propagating the Gospel Among the Indians and Others in North-America* (Boston: S. T. Armstrong, 1814), 33; "An Evangelist," *A Plan for the More Successful Management of Domestic Missions* (Albany: Henry C. Southwick, 1816), 14–15; Gavin Cochrane, "Treatise on the Indians of North America Written in the Year 1764," introduction, Ayer MS 176, NL; Adam Smith, *Lectures on Jurisprudence* (delivered 1760s), ed. R. L. Meek, D. D. Raphael, and P. G. Stein (Oxford: Clarendon Press, 1978), 107; Emer de Vattel, *The Law of Nations* (London, 1758), ed. Edward D. Ingraham (Philadelphia: T. & J. W. Johnson, 1853), 99–100; William Robertson, *The History of America* (London, 1777), in *The Works of Wm. Robertson, D. D.* (Oxford: Talboys and Wheeler, 1825), 6:236, 290; C. F. Volney, *View of the Climate and Soil of the United States of America* (London: J. Johnson, 1804), 432–448.

7. *Memorial of the Religious Society of Friends, in the States of Ohio, Indiana, and Illinois, Praying the Adoption of Measures for the Civilization and Improvement of the Indians* (Washington: E. de Krafft, 1818), 3; John Lathrop, *A Discourse, Before the Society for "Propagating the Gospel Among the Indians, and Others, in North-America"* (Boston: Manning and Loring, 1804), 23; Lemuel Covell, *A Narrative of a Missionary Tour Through the Western Settlements of the State of New-York* (Troy, N.Y.: Moffitt & Lyon, 1804), 37; *A Brief Account of the Proceedings of the Committee, Ap-*

pointed by the Yearly Meeting of Friends, Held in Baltimore, for Promoting the Improvement and Civilization of the Indian Natives (Baltimore: Cole and Hewes, 1805), 25–26; *The Annual Report of the Board of Directors to the Northern Missionary Society of the State of New-York for the Year 1811* (Albany: Websters and Skinners, 1811), 12; *An Address of the Society of Friends, to the Indian Tribes, Residing in the State of New-York* (New-York: Samuel Wood and Sons, 1815), 8.

8. Ezekiel Sanford, *A History of the United States Before the Revolution* (Philadelphia: Anthony Finley, 1819), clxxxvii–cxc; Anne MacVicar Grant, *Memoirs of an American Lady* (1808; New York: Dodd, Mead, 1903), 1:204.

9. William G. McLoughlin, *Cherokee Renascence in the New Republic* (Princeton: Princeton University Press, 1986), 64–67; Benjamin Hawkins, *Letter from the Principal Agent for Indian Affairs, South of the Ohio* (Washington, 1801), 4–5.

10. R. Douglas Hurt, *Indian Agriculture in America: Prehistory to the Present* (Lawrence: University Press of Kansas, 1987), 57–62; Symmes C. Oliver, *Ecology and Cultural Continuity as Contributing Factors in the Social Organization of the Plains Indians* (Berkeley: University of California Press, 1962), 20–46; *Discoveries Made in Exploring the Missouri, Red River and Washita, by Captains Lewis and Clark, Doctor Sibley, and William Dunbar, Esq.* (Natchez: Andrew Marschalk, 1806), 15, 17, 19, 21, 37, 72, 74.

11. Maxine Benson, ed., *From Pittsburgh to the Rocky Mountains: Major Stephen Long's Expedition 1819–1820* (Golden, Colo.: Fulcrum, 1988), 335 (Long's account was first published in 1823); Thomas Nuttall, *A Journal of Travels into the Arkansas Territory During the Year 1819* (Philadelphia, 1821), ed. Savoie Lottinville (Norman: University of Oklahoma Press, 1979), 95; Henry Marie Brackenridge, *Journal of a Voyage Up the River Missouri; Performed in Eighteen Hundred and Eleven*, 2nd ed. (Baltimore: Coale and Maxweld, 1815), 163; John F. Schermerhorn, *Report to the Society for Propagating the Gospel Among the Indians and Others in North America* (Boston, 1814), 11 (on the Chippewas); John Dunn Hunter, *Manners and Customs of Several Indian Tribes Located West of the Mississippi* (1823; Minneapolis: Ross and Haines, 1957), 291 (on the Kansas and Osages); John Bradbury, *Travels in the Interior of America, in the Years 1809, 1810, and 1811* (London, 1819), ed. Reuben Gold Thwaites (Cleveland: Arthur H. Clark Co., 1904), 175; William Wells, "Indian Manners and Customs," *Western Review and Miscellaneous Magazine* 2 (1820): 162.

12. John Quincy Adams, *An Oration, Delivered at Plymouth, December 22, 1802* (Boston: Russell and Cutler, 1802), 22–25.

13. Robert H. White, ed., *Messages of the Governors of Tennessee* (Nashville: Tennessee Historical Commission, 1952–1990), 1:58; *Annals of Congress*, 15th Cong., 1st Sess. (1817), 16.

14. Logan Esarey, ed., *Messages and Letters of William Henry Harrison* (Indianapolis: Indiana Historical Commission, 1922), 1:71; *Message from the President of the United States to the Senate; Transmitting Indian Treaties for Ratification* (Washington: William A. Davis, 1816), 59.

15. William Strickland, *Journal of a Tour in the United States of America 1794–1795*, ed. J. E. Strickland (New York: New-York Historical Society, 1971), 165–168.

16. William Moultrie to the South Carolina House of Representatives, 9 February 1786, Ayer MS 823, NL.

17. *Marshall v. Clark*, 8 Va. 268, 273 (1791); *Weiser's Lessee v. Moody*, 2 Yeates 127 (Pa. 1796); *Glasgow's Lessee v. Smith*, 1 Tenn. 144, 167 (1805).

18. Sam B. Smith and Harriett Chappell Owsley, eds., *The Papers of Andrew Jackson* (Knoxville: University of Tennessee Press, 1980–), 1:54.

19. *Annals of Congress*, 3rd Cong., 2nd Sess. (1795), 1148–59.

20. *Annals of Congress*, 4th Cong., 1st Sess. (1796), 894–904.

21. *Strother v. Cathey*, 5 N.C. 162, 167–168 (1807).

22. *Jackson ex dem. Klock v. Hudson*, 3 Johns. 375, 384–385 (N.Y. Sup. 1808).

23. *Van Gorden v. Jackson*, 5 Johns. 440, 461 (N.Y. 1809).

24. C. Peter Magrath, *Yazoo: Law and Politics in the New Republic: The Case of Fletcher v. Peck* (Providence: Brown University Press, 1966).

25. *Copy of the Record, in the Case, Robert Fletcher vs. John Peck* (Boston: Munroe, Francis and Parker, 1808), 13.

26. *Fletcher v. Peck*, 10 U.S. 87 (1810).

27. *Thompson v. Johnston*, 6 Binn. 68 (Pa. 1813).

28. *Meigs v. M'Clung's Lessee*, 13 U.S. 11, 15 (1815); *Gilman v. Brown*, 10 F. Cas. 392, 399 (C.C.D. Mass. 1817), aff'd, 17 U.S. 255 (1819); *Bleecker v. Bond*, 3 F. Cas. 687, 692 (C.C.E.D. Pa. 1819); *Preston v. Browder*, 14 U.S. 115, 118 (1816); *People v. Godfrey*, 17 Johns. 225, 229 (N.Y. Sup. 1819); *Arnold v. Mundy*, 6 N.J.L. 1, 17–18 (1821).

29. *Jackson ex dem. Gilbert v. Wood*, 7 Johns. 290, 295 (N.Y. Sup. 1810); *Annals of Congress*, 15th Cong., 2nd Sess. (1819), 773.

30. *The Seneca Lands*, 1 Op. Att. Gen. 465, 466–467 (1821).

31. Hugh Montgomery to William Rabun, 3 July 1817, Document TCC453, *SNA;* Jedidiah Morse, *A Report to the Secretary of War of the United States, on Indian Affairs* (New-Haven: S. Converse, 1822), 67; anonymous and untitled review of Morse's 1822 *Report*, in *North American Review* 16 (1823): 32. This review appeared in January 1823, before *Johnson v. M'Intosh*. See also "Rights of the Aborigines of Our Country," *Western Review and Miscellaneous Magazine* 4 (1821): 296.

32. John Heckewelder, *An Account of the History, Manners, and Customs of the Indian Nations, Who Once Inhabited Pennsylvania and the Neighbouring States* (Philadelphia, 1819), ed. William C. Reichel (Philadelphia: Historical Society of Pennsylvania, 1876), 76–81; anonymous and untitled reviews in *North American Review* 9 (1819): 167–178; and *Western Review and Miscellaneous Magazine* 1 (1819): 70–71.

33. My account of the factual background draws on two excellent recent treatments of *Johnson*, which emphasize different aspects of the case. Lindsay Gordon Robertson, "*Johnson v. M'Intosh*: Land, Law and the Politics of Federalism, 1773–1842" (Ph.D. diss., University of Virginia, 1997); and Eric Kades, "History and Interpretation of the Great Case of *Johnson v. M'Intosh*," *Law and History Review* 19 (2001): 67–116. The case is reported at 21 U.S. 543 (1823).

34. E.g., Howard R. Berman, "The Concept of Aboriginal Rights in the Early Legal History of the United States," *Buffalo Law Review* 27 (1978): 644.

35. Jean Edward Smith, *John Marshall: Definer of a Nation* (New York: Henry Holt, 1996), 74–75; Robertson, "*Johnson v. M'Intosh*," 169–197.

36. *PWJ*, 3:319.

37. Lindsay G. Robertson, "John Marshall as Colonial Historian: Reconsidering the Origins of the Discovery Doctrine," *Journal of Law and Politics* 13 (1997): 759–777; Herbert A. Johnson et al., eds., *The Papers of John Marshall* (Chapel Hill: University of North Carolina Press, 1974–), 9:281.

38. R. Kent Newmyer, *John Marshall and the Heroic Age of the Supreme Court* (Baton Rouge: Louisiana State University Press, 2001), 236–244.

39. James Kent, *Commentaries on American Law*, 2nd ed. (New-York: O. Halsted, 1832), 1:257–258, 3:379–381; Joseph Story, *Commentaries on the Constitution of the United States* (Boston: Hilliard, Gray, 1833), 3–7; "Georgia and the United States," *Niles' Weekly Register* 32 (1827): 90. For discussions of the right of occupancy in the years immediately after *Johnson*, see Joseph Blunt, *A Historical Sketch of the Formation of the Confederacy* (New-York: Geo. and Chas. Carvill, 1825), 11–12; *A Brief View of the Present Relations Between the Government and People of the United States and the Indians Within Our National Limits* (late 1820s), 1; Henry Marie Brackenridge, *Remarks on the Opinion of Judge Randal in the Case of Forbes & Co.* (J. Elliot, 1820s or early 1830s), 2–3.

40. Wirt to James Madison, 5 October 1830, in John P. Kennedy, *Memoirs of the Life of William Wirt* (Philadelphia: Blanchard and Lea, 1852), 2:262; Calvin Colton, *Tour of the American Lakes, and Among the Indians of the North-West Territory, in 1830* (London: F. Westley and A. H. Davis, 1833), 2:35; Little Prince et al. to unidentified federal officials, 11 December 1824, document TCC181, *SNA*.

6. Removal

1. H.R. Doc. No. 147, 25th Cong., 3rd Sess. (1839), 8. Mortality figures are uncertain because of insufficient data and because they are capable of being calculated in more than one way. For a full discussion, see Russell Thornton, "The Demography of the Trail of Tears Period: A New Estimate of Cherokee Population Losses," in William L. Anderson, ed., *Cherokee Removal: Before and After* (Athens: University of Georgia Press, 1991), 75–95. Classic treatments of removal include, from the federal government's point of view, Ronald N. Satz, *American Indian Policy in the Jacksonian Era* (Lincoln: University of Nebraska Press, 1975); and from the Indians' point of view, Grant Foreman, *Indian Removal: The Emigration of the Five Civilized Tribes of Indians* (Norman: University of Oklahoma Press, 1932), and John Ehle, *Trail of Tears: The Rise and Fall of the Cherokee Nation* (New York: Anchor Books, 1988).

2. William Shakespeare, *Macbeth*, ed. Stephen Orgel (New York: Penguin, 2000), 87 (act V, scene 3, line 2); Benjamin Franklin, *Two Tracts; Information to Those Who Would Remove to America. And, Remarks Concerning the Savages of North America* (London: John Stockdale, 1784); Jane Austen, *Emma* (1816), ed. Alistair Duckworth (New York: Palgrave, 2002), 255.

3. *ASP*, 2:125; William H. Crawford to Jared Irwin, 4 Feb. 1809, Document TCC722, *SNA*.

4. C. A. Weslager, *The Delaware Indian Westward Migration* (Wallingford, Penn.: Middle Atlantic Press, 1978).

5. In the Louisiana Purchase, the United States bought *sovereignty*, the right to gov-

ern the area, and *property* in whatever land within the territory had been owned by the French government. The government of the United States did not acquire ownership of land not owned by the government of France. Existing property owners under grants from France and Spain kept their land. Indian tribes within the Louisiana Purchase territory kept their "right of occupancy" as it would be defined in *Johnson v. M'Intosh*. The same rules would apply in the later territorial enlargements of the United States.

6. Bernard W. Sheehan, *Seeds of Extinction: Jeffersonian Philanthropy and the American Indian* (New York: W. W. Norton, 1973), 245–248; Christian B. Keller, "Philanthropy Betrayed: Thomas Jefferson, the Louisiana Purchase, and the Origins of Federal Indian Removal Policy," *Proceedings of the American Philosophical Society* 144 (2000): 39–48; 2 Stat. 283 (1804); *ASP,* 2:124–125.

7. Stanley W. Hoig, *The Cherokees and Their Chiefs: In the Wake of Empire* (Fayetteville: University of Arkansas Press, 1998), 104; Joseph McMinn to Daniel Graham, 11 Dec. 1818, *SNA; ASP,* 2:180–181; S. Doc. No. 616, 26th Cong., 1st Sess. (1840), 3–4.

8. *Annals of Congress,* 16th Cong., 1st Sess. (1820), 1644.

9. *Annals of Congress,* 18th Cong., 1st Sess. (1824), 463.

10. *Register of Debates,* 18th Cong., 2nd Sess. (1825), App. 63.

11. Reginald Horsman, "The Origins of Oneida Removal to Wisconsin, 1815–1822," in Laurence M. Hauptman and L. Gordon McLester III, eds., *The Oneida Indian Journey: From New York to Wisconsin, 1784–1860* (Madison: University of Wisconsin Press, 1999), 53–69; Royce, 700–714.

12. Alexis de Tocqueville, *Democracy in America,* ed. J. P. Mayer, trans. George Lawrence (New York: Perennial Classics, 2000), 325.

13. Michael D. Green, *The Politics of Indian Removal: Creek Government and Society in Crisis* (Lincoln: University of Nebraska Press, 1982), 69–141; 7 Stat. 215 (1821); "Creek Indians," *Niles' Weekly Register* 22 (1824): 223; U.S. Commissioners to Creek Chiefs, 9 Dec. 1824, Document TCC008, *SNA.*

14. Little Prince et al. to U.S. Commissioners, 11 Dec. 1824, Document TCC181, *SNA.*

15. 7 Stat. 237 (1825).

16. Mary Young, "The Exercise of Sovereignty in Cherokee Georgia," *Journal of the Early Republic* 10 (1990): 43–63; *Register of Debates,* 18th Cong., 1st Sess. (1825), App. 61.

17. David M. Wishart, "Evidence of Surplus Production in the Cherokee Nation Prior to Removal," *Journal of Economic History* 55 (1995): 120–138; Douglas C. Wilms, "Cherokee Indian Land Use in Georgia, 1800–1838" (Ph.D. diss., University of Georgia, 1973).

18. *ASP,* 2:467–470, 473–474.

19. Ga. Acts 1826, 207, 234.

20. Ga. Acts 1826, 68; Ga. Acts 1827, 99, 236; Ga. Acts 1828, 87, 88; Ga. Acts 1830, 154, 127, 114, 118.

21. Jackson to Monroe, 4 March 1817, in Sam B. Smith and Harriett Chappell Owsley, eds., *The Papers of Andrew Jackson* (Knoxville: University of Tennessee Press, 1980–), 4:95.

22. Monroe to Jackson, 5 Oct. 1817, in Smith and Owsley, *Papers of Andrew Jackson*, 4:147; Stanislaus Murray Hamilton, ed., *The Writings of James Monroe* (New York: G. P. Putnam's Sons, 1898–1903), 6:38–40.

23. "Removal of the Indians," *North American Review* 31 (1830): 402.

24. Georgia delegation to James Monroe, 10 March 1824, Document TCC032, *SNA;* H.R. Doc. No. 102, 20th Cong., 1st Sess. (1828), 9; "Georgia Controversy," *Southern Review* 2 (1828): 541–582.

25. Jeremiah Evarts, *Cherokee Removal: The "William Penn" Essays and Other Writings*, ed. Francis Paul Prucha (Knoxville: University of Tennessee Press, 1981), 58; "Memorial of the Cherokee Indians," *Niles' Weekly Register* 38 (1830): 53–54.

26. *ASP*, 2:123–24; *Annals of Congress*, 12th Cong., 2nd Sess. (1812), 195; *Register of Debates*, 19th Cong., 1st Sess. (1826), 347–48; *Speech of Mr. Wilde, of Georgia, on the Bill for Removing the Indians from the East to the West Side of the Mississippi* (Washington: Gales and Seaton, 1830), 12.

27. H.R. Doc. No. 79, 21st Cong., 1st Sess. (1830), 1; *Register of Debates*, 18th Cong., 2nd Sess. (1825), 639–643.

28. Isaac McCoy, *Remarks on the Practicability of Indian Reform, Embracing Their Colonization* (Boston: Lincoln and Edmands, 1827), 25; *Register of Debates*, 19th Cong., 1st Sess. (1826), App. 40.

29. *AIUS*, 9–10.

30. *Niles' Weekly Register* 31 (1826): 155; Isaac McCoy, *To Philanthropists in the United States, Generally, and to Christians in Particular, on the Condition and Prospects of the American Indians* (1831?), 2; John Jolly, *An Examination of the Indian Question* (1832?), 16; Lewis Cass, "Removal of the Indians," *North American Review* 30 (1830): 107; *Documents and Proceedings Relating to the Formation of a Board in the City of New York, for the Emigration, Preservation, and Improvement of the Aborigines of North America* (New York: Vanderpool and Cole, 1829), 37–38; H.R. Rep. No. 233, 21st Cong., 1st Sess. (1830), 2.

31. *American Baptist Magazine* 10 (1830): 54–55; "Indian Stations," *American Baptist Magazine* 10 (1830): 215; H.R. Rep. Nos. 59 and 253, 21st Cong., 1st Sess. (1830); "Roger Williams," "Removal of the Indians," *American Baptist Magazine* 10 (1830): 364; *The First Annual Report of the American Society for Promoting the Civilization and General Improvement of the Indian Tribes in the United States* (New Haven: S. Converse, 1824), 69; "Removal of the Indians," *Evangelical Magazine and Gospel Advocate* 1 (1830): 205–206.

32. John A. Andrew III, *From Revivals to Removal: Jeremiah Evarts, the Cherokee Nation, and the Search for the Soul of America* (Athens: University of Georgia Press, 1992); Heman Humphrey, *Indian Rights and Our Duties* (n.p.: Association for Diffusing Information on the Subject of Indian Rights, 1831), 9.

33. "Indians of North America," *North American Review* 22 (1826): 117; "Proposed Residence of the Indians," *Religious Intelligencer* 14 (1830): 793.

34. *Register of Debates*, 21st Cong., 1st Sess. (1830), 1074; H.R. Rep. No. 245, 21st Cong., 1st Sess. (1830), 5.

35. *Niles' Weekly Register* 32 (1827): 228; H.R. Doc. No. 74, 21st Cong., 1st Sess. (1830), 3; *Cherokee Phoenix*, 13 March 1828, 3:2.

36. "The Indians," *The Berean* 1 (1824): 379–380; "Georgia and the Cherokees," *Re-*

ligious Intelligencer 13 (1828): 458; "Removal of the Indians," *Religious Monitor and Evangelical Repository* 6 (1829): 568–569; "An Article in the North American Review on the Removal of the Indians," *American Monthly Magazine* 1 (1829): 701–718; "Indian Controversy," *Christian Examiner* 9 (1830): 107–160; "Review of an Article in the North American Review," *Spirit of the Pilgrims* 3 (1830): 141–161; H.R. Doc. No. 246, 21st Cong., 1st Sess. (1830); "Indian Affairs," *Biblical Repertory and Princeton Review* 10 (1838): 513–535; "The Cherokees," *Religious Intelligencer* 13 (1829): 597–598; Jack Frederick Kilpatrick and Anna Gritts Kilpatrick, eds., *New Echota Letters: Contributions of Samuel A. Worcester to the Cherokee Phoenix* (Dallas: Southern Methodist University Press, 1968), 84–90.

37. Herman J. Viola, *Thomas L. McKenney: Architect of America's Early Indian Policy: 1816–1830* (Chicago: Sage Books, 1974).

38. *AIUS*, 11; H.R. Rep. No. 227, 21st Cong., 1st Sess. (1830), 23–24; S. Rep. No. 61, 21st Cong., 1st Sess. (1830), 3; Claudio Saunt, "Taking Account of Property: Stratification among the Creek Indians in the Early Nineteenth Century," *William and Mary Quarterly* 57 (2000): 733–760; Theda Purdue, "The Conflict Within: Cherokees and Removal," in Anderson, *Cherokee Removal*, 55–74; *Register of Debates*, 19th Cong., 2nd Sess. (1827), 71–75.

39. *Speeches on the Passage of the Bill for the Removal of the Indians* (Boston: Perkins and Marvin, 1830), 150; H.R. Doc. No. 53, 21st Cong., 1st Sess. (1830), 4.

40. S. Doc. No. 98, 21st Cong., 1st Sess. (1830).

41. For a summary of the literature depicting Jackson as an Indian-hater, see Ronald N. Satz, "Rhetoric Versus Reality: The Indian Policy of Andrew Jackson," in Anderson, *Cherokee Removal*, 31–32. Jackson is defended in Robert V. Remini, *Andrew Jackson and His Indian Wars* (New York: Viking, 2001). A short, balanced account is Anthony F. C. Wallace, *The Long, Bitter Trail: Andrew Jackson and the Indians* (New York: Hill and Wang, 1993).

42. *Niles' Weekly Register* 36 (1829): 259.

43. *Examination of the Relations Between the Cherokees and the Government of the United States* (New-York, 1829), 15; *Speeches on the Passage of the Bill for the Removal of the Indians*, 231.

44. *Register of Debates*, 20th Cong., 1st Sess. (1827–1828), 819–822, 1540–92; H.R. Rep. No. 56, 20th Cong., 1st Sess. (1828); Donna L. Akers, "Removing the Heart of the Choctaw People: Indian Removal from a Native Perspective," *American Indian Culture and Research Journal* 23 (1999): 63; McKenney to James Barbour, 4 Jan. 1828, in H.R. Doc. No. 44, 20th Cong., 1st Sess. (1828), 5–6; 4 Stat. 411–412 (1830).

45. H.R. Rep. Nos. 263 and 264, 21st Cong., 1st Sess. (1830); S. Rep. No. 66, 21st Cong., 1st Sess. (1830), 1. Women played a large role in the opposition to removal. Mary Hershberger, "Mobilizing Women, Anticipating Abolition: The Struggle against Indian Removal in the 1830s," *Journal of American History* 86 (1999): 15–40.

46. *Letters from John Pintard to His Daughter* (New York: New-York Historical Society, 1940–1941), 3:156.

47. Wilson Lumpkin, *The Removal of the Cherokee Indians from Georgia* (New York: Dodd, Mead, 1907), 1:47.

48. *State v. Tassels*, 1 Ga. Ann. 478 (Dud. 229) (Ga. Super. 1830). On George Tassels's actual name, and other aspects of the case, see Tim Alan Garrison, *The Legal Ideology of Removal: The Southern Judiciary and the Sovereignty of Native American Nations* (Athens: University of Georgia Press, 2002), 119–122, 264–266 n15.

49. Wirt to Judge Carr, 21 June 1830, in John P. Kennedy, *Memoirs of the Life of William Wirt* (Philadelphia: Blanchard and Lea, 1852), 2:256.

50. *Cherokee Nation v. Georgia*, 30 U.S. 1, 17 (1831).

51. *Worcester v. Georgia*, 31 U.S. 515 (1832).

52. E.g., Jill Norgren, *The Cherokee Cases: The Confrontation of Law and Politics* (New York: McGraw-Hill, 1996), 122–130.

53. Gerald N. Rosenberg, *The Hollow Hope: Can Courts Bring About Social Change?* (Chicago: University of Chicago Press, 1991).

54. *Cherokee Nation v. Georgia*, 30 U.S. at 20; Joseph C. Burke, "The Cherokee Cases: A Study in Law, Politics, and Morality," *Stanford Law Review* 21 (1969): 500–531.

55. Walter H. Conser Jr., "John Ross and the Cherokee Resistance Campaign, 1833–1838," *Journal of Southern History* 44 (1978): 191–212; Ross et al. to Andrew Jackson, 28 March 1834, and Ross to Joaquin Maria del Castilla y Lanzas, 22 March 1835, in Gary Moulton, ed., *The Papers of Chief John Ross* (Norman: University of Oklahoma Press, 1985), 1:283, 1:334.

56. Thurman Wilkins, *Cherokee Tragedy: The Story of the Ridge Family and the Decimation of a People* (New York: Macmillan, 1970); Theda Purdue, ed., *Cherokee Editor: The Writings of Elias Boudinot* (Knoxville: University of Tennessee Press, 1983), 225.

57. Gary E. Moulton, *John Ross: Cherokee Chief* (Athens: University of Georgia Press, 1978), 87–106; Francis Paul Prucha, *The Great Father: The United States Government and the American Indians* (Lincoln: University of Nebraska Press, 1984), 1:214–269; Laurence M. Hauptman, *Conspiracy of Interests: Iroquois Dispossession and the Rise of New York State* (Syracuse: Syracuse University Press, 1999), 176; *Report on the Memorials of the Seneca Indians and Others* (Boston: Dutton and Wentworth, 1840), 25.

58. *Army and Navy Chronicle* 3 (1836): 72; Thomas McKenney to Hugh Montgomery, 28 July 1828, in H.R. Doc. No. 95, 20th Cong., 2nd Sess. (1829), 7; *Niles' Weekly Register* 51 (1836): 34; "The Emigrating Indians," *The Friend* 10 (1836): 163; "Frauds Upon the Indians," *Boston Weekly Magazine* 3 (1841): 230.

59. S. Doc. No. 616, 26th Cong., 1st Sess. (1840), 4–5; Royce, maps following page 997.

60. Jack Campisi, "The Emergence of the Mashantucket Pequot Tribe, 1637–1975," in Laurence M. Hauptman and James D. Wherry, eds., *The Pequots in Southern New England: The Fall and Rise of an American Indian Nation* (Norman: University of Oklahoma Press, 1990), 117–140; John R. Finger, *The Eastern Band of Cherokees 1819–1900* (Knoxville: University of Tennessee Press, 1984); *Annual Report of the Commissioner of Indian Affairs . . . 1855* (Washington: A. O. P. Nicholson, 1856), 255–256.

61. "Life of Black Hawk," *North American Review* 40 (1835): 75. For contemporaneous statements of the same point, see Job R. Tyson, *Discourse on the Surviving*

Remnant of the Indian Race in the United States (Philadelphia: A. Waldie, 1836), 24–25; "Harrison's *Historical Discourse*," *North American Review* 51 (1840): 68.

7. Reservations

1. Dee Brown, *Bury My Heart at Wounded Knee: An Indian History of the American West* (New York: Holt, Rinehart and Winston, 1971).
2. Yasu Kawashima, "Legal Origins of the Indian Reservation in Colonial Massachusetts," *American Journal of Legal History* 13 (1969): 42–56; Jill St. Germain, *Indian Treaty-Making Policy in the United States and Canada, 1867–1877* (Lincoln: University of Nebraska Press, 2001), 80; Heather Goodall, *Invasion to Embassy: Land in Aboriginal Politics in New South Wales, 1770–1992* (St. Leonards, NSW: Allen and Unwin, 1996), 44–56.
3. Sam B. Hilliard, "Indian Land Cessions West of the Mississippi," *Journal of the West* 10 (1971): 497.
4. "Our Indian Policy," *United States Magazine and Democratic Review* 14 (1844): 184; H.R. Rep. No. 133, 33rd Cong., 1st Sess. (1854), 2.
5. H.R. Exec. Doc. No. 1, 30th Cong., 2nd Sess. (1848), 388; S. Exec. Doc. No. 1, 31st Cong., 1st Sess. (1849), 942, 946; S. Exec. Doc. No. 1, 32nd Cong., 1st Sess. (1851), 268; S. Exec. Doc. No. 1, 33rd Cong., 1st Sess. (1853), 251–252.
6. Paul Stuart, *The Indian Office: Growth and Development of an American Institution, 1865–1900* (Ann Arbor: UMI Research Press, 1979), 13; Edmund Jefferson Danziger, *Indians and Bureaucrats: Administering the Reservation Policy during the Civil War* (Urbana: University of Illinois Press, 1974), 201; *New York Times*, 22 Nov. 1869, p. 4, col. 4; S. Exec. Doc. No. 1, 32nd Cong., 1st Sess. (1852), 293.
7. Francis Paul Prucha, "American Indian Policy in the 1840s: Visions of Reform," in Francis Paul Prucha, *Indian Policy in the United States: Historical Essays* (Lincoln: University of Nebraska Press, 1981), 153–179.
8. S. Exec. Doc. No. 1, 31st Cong., 2nd Sess. (1850), 39; S. Exec. Doc. No. 5, 34th Cong., 3rd Sess. (1856), 574.
9. Kah-ge-ga-gah-bouh, "The American Indians," *American Whig Review* 9 (1849): 632; H.R. Exec. Doc. No. 1, 34th Cong., 1st Sess. (1855), 337; H.R. Exec. Doc. No. 2, 35th Cong., 2nd Sess. (1858), 354.
10. John Walton Caughey, ed., *The Indians of Southern California in 1852: The B. D. Wilson Report and a Selection of Contemporary Comment* (Lincoln: University of Nebraska Press, 1995), 55–57; William Welsh, "Concluding Appeal," in *Taopi and His Friends, or the Indians' Wrongs and Rights* (Philadelphia: Claxton, Remsen and Haffelfinger, 1869), 86.
11. Robert A. Trennert Jr., *Alternative to Extinction: Federal Indian Policy and the Beginnings of the Reservation System, 1846–51* (Philadelphia: Temple University Press, 1975); George Harwood Phillips, *Indians and Indian Agents: The Origins of the Reservation System in California, 1849–1852* (Norman: University of Oklahoma Press, 1997).
12. Mark David Spence, *Possessing the Wilderness: Indian Removal and the Making of the National Parks* (New York: Oxford University Press, 1999); Royce, plates 43 (Nevada) and 9 (Colorado).

13. *Annual Report of the Commissioner of Indian Affairs to the Secretary of the Interior for the Year 1882* (Washington: Government Printing Office, 1882), xxi; Robert Weil, *The Legal Status of the Indian* (New York, 1888), 58.

14. *Mitchel v. United States*, 34 U.S. 711, 745–746 (1835); *Leavenworth, Lawrence, & Galveston R.R. Co. v. United States*, 92 U.S. 733, 742–743, 755 (1875).

15. *Marsh v. Brooks*, 49 U.S. 223, 232 (1850); *Fellows v. Blacksmith*, 60 U.S. 366, 370–372 (1856); *New York ex rel. Cutler v. Dibble*, 62 U.S. 366, 371 (1858).

16. John M. Carroll, ed., *The Sand Creek Massacre: A Documentary History* (New York: Sol Lewis, 1973), 5–6.

17. William Haas Moore, *Chiefs, Agents and Soldiers: Conflict on the Navajo Frontier, 1868–1882* (Albuquerque: University of New Mexico Press, 1994), 1–31; Armstrong quoted in Frederick E. Hoxie, *Parading through History: The Making of the Crow Nation in America, 1805–1935* (Cambridge: Cambridge University Press, 1995), 20.

18. Edward Lazarus, *Black Hills, White Justice: The Sioux Nation versus the United States, 1775 to the Present* (New York: HarperCollins, 1991), 71–95.

19. Albert L. Hurtado, *Indian Survival on the California Frontier* (New Haven: Yale University Press, 1988), 125–148; *Report of Colonel Robert J. Stevens, Special Commissioner to Make an Investigation and Report Upon Indian Affairs in California* (Washington: Government Printing Office, 1868), 30.

20. William Welsh, *Report of a Visit to the Sioux and Ponka Indians on the Missouri River* (Philadelphia: M'Calla and Stavely, 1872), 31–32.

21. William T. Hagan, *United States–Comanche Relations: The Reservation Years* (1976; Norman: University of Oklahoma Press, 1990), 124.

22. Alvin M. Josephy Jr., *The Nez Perce Indians and the Opening of the Northwest*, abridged ed. (Lincoln: University of Nebraska Press, 1979), 516–557; John H. Monnett, *Tell Them We Are Going Home: The Odyssey of the Northern Cheyennes* (Norman: University of Oklahoma Press, 2001); Valerie Sherer Mathes and Richard Lowitt, *The Standing Bear Controversy: Prelude to Indian Reform* (Urbana: University of Illinois Press, 2003); James T. King, "'A Better Way': General George Crook and the Ponca Indians," in Richard N. Ellis, ed., *The Western American Indian: Case Studies in Tribal History* (Lincoln: University of Nebraska Press, 1972), 76–87; *United States ex rel. Standing Bear v. Crook*, 25 F. Cas. 695, 700 (C.C.D. Neb. 1879); "The Indian in Court," *Harper's Weekly*, 16 August 1879, 642–643; Thomas Henry Tibbles, *The Ponca Chiefs: An Indian's Attempt to Appeal from the Tomahawk to the Courts* (Boston: Lockwood, Brooks, 1880); Valerie Sherer Mathes, ed., *The Indian Reform Letters of Helen Hunt Jackson, 1879–1885* (Norman: University of Oklahoma Press, 1998), 24–29.

23. Jane F. Lancaster, *Removal Aftershock: The Seminoles' Struggles to Survive in the West, 1836–1866* (Knoxville: University of Tennessee Press, 1994), 28; William G. McLoughlin, *After the Trail of Tears: The Cherokees' Struggle for Sovereignty, 1839–1880* (Chapel Hill: University of North Carolina Press, 1993), 258–260; H.R. Misc. Doc. No. 35, 30th Cong., 2nd Sess. (1849).

24. Vine Deloria Jr. and Raymond DeMallie, eds., *Proceedings of the Great Peace Commission of 1867–1868* (Washington: Institute for the Development of Indian Law, 1975), 121–122; F. Todd Smith, *The Caddos, the Wichitas, and the United States, 1846–1901* (College Station: Texas A&M University Press, 1996), 117–141.

25. Robinson quoted in Alban W. Hoopes, *Indian Affairs and Their Administration with Special Reference to the Far West 1849–1860* (Philadelphia: University of Pennsylvania Press, 1932), 226; Shelley Bowen Hatfield, *Chasing Shadows: Indians along the United States–Mexico Border 1876–1911* (Albuquerque: University of New Mexico Press, 1998), 56.

26. American Indian Aid Association, *Petition to Congress for the Preservation and Elevation of American Indians* (New York: Varey's Steam Print, 1857).

27. *Punchinello* 1 (1870): 136.

28. Robert H. Keller Jr., *American Protestantism and United States Indian Policy, 1869–82* (Lincoln: University of Nebraska Press, 1983); John G. Whittier, "Introduction," in Stanley Pumphrey, *Indian Civilization: A Lecture* (Philadelphia: Bible and Tract Distributing Society, 1877), 6; C. C. Painter, *The Condition of Affairs in Indian Territory and California* (Philadelphia: Indian Rights Association, 1888), 13–14; *New York Times*, 5 June 1882, p. 4, cols. 4–5; Helen Jackson, *A Century of Dishonor: A Sketch of the United States Government's Dealings with Some of the Indian Tribes* (1881) (Norman: University of Oklahoma Press, 1995).

29. *The Cherokee Tobacco*, 78 U.S. 616 (1870); *Missouri, Kansas and Texas Railway Co. v. Roberts*, 152 U.S. 114 (1894); *Spalding v. Chandler*, 160 U.S. 394 (1896); *Lone Wolf v. Hitchcock*, 187 U.S. 553, 566–568 (1903).

30. Blue Clark, *Lone Wolf v. Hitchcock: Treaty Rights and Indian Law at the End of the Nineteenth Century* (Lincoln: University of Nebraska Press, 1994); Tim Alan Garrison, "The Nadir of Native American Sovereignty," *Reviews in American History* 24 (1996): 265; *Taylor v. Morton*, 23 F. Cas. 784 (C.C.D. Mass. 1855) (Curtis, J.); *In re Clinton Bridge*, 5 F. Cas. 1060 (C.C.D. Iowa 1867) (Miller, J.); *Edye v. Robertson*, 112 U.S. 580 (1884); *Whitney v. Robertson*, 124 U.S. 190 (1888); *Horner v. United States*, 143 U.S. 570 (1892).

31. Philip P. Frickey, "Doctrine, Context, Institutional Relationships, and Commentary: The Malaise of Federal Indian Law through the Lens of *Lone Wolf*," *Tulsa Law Review* 38 (2002): 13–14.

32. E.g., *Buttz v. Northern Pacific Railroad*, 119 U.S. 55 (1886); *Holden v. Joy*, 84 U.S. 211 (1872).

33. Vine Deloria Jr. and Raymond J. DeMallie, *Documents of American Indian Diplomacy* (Norman: University of Oklahoma Press, 1999), 233–248; Francis Paul Prucha, *American Indian Treaties: The History of a Political Anomaly* (Berkeley: University of California Press, 1994), 289–310; John R. Wunder, "No More Treaties: The Resolution of 1871 and the Alteration of Indian Rights to Their Homelands," in John R. Wunder, ed., *Working the Range: Essays on the History of Western Land Management and the Environment* (Westport, Conn.: Greenwood Press, 1985), 39–56.

34. *Report of the Commissioner of Indian Affairs for the Year 1862* (Washington: Government Printing Office, 1863), 7; H.R. Exec. Doc. No. 1, 41st Cong., 2nd Sess. (1869), 448; *Congressional Globe*, 41st Cong., 3rd Sess. (1871), 765.

35. D.C. Poole, *Among the Sioux of Dakota: Eighteen Months Experience as an Indian Agent* (New York: D. Van Nostrand, 1881), 39; George Armstrong Custer, *My Life on the Plains; or, Personal Experiences with Indians* (1874; Norman: University of Oklahoma Press, 1962), 13; *Harper's Weekly*, 23 July 1870, 466.

36. *Congressional Globe*, 41st Cong., 3rd Sess. (1871), 764–765.

37. *Report of the Commissioner of Indian Affairs, Made to the Secretary of the Interior, for the Year 1869* (Washington: Government Printing Office, 1870), 50; Henry B. Whipple, "The Indian System," *North American Review* 99 (1864): 450–451; T. S. Williamson, "The Indian Tribes, and the Duty of Government to Them," *American Presbyterian and Theological Review* 2 (1864): 597.

38. 16 Stat. 566 (1871).

39. *Report of the Commissioner of Indian Affairs to the Secretary of the Interior for the Year 1872* (Washington: Government Printing Office, 1872), 82–83.

40. Charles F. Wilkinson, *American Indians, Time, and the Law: Native Societies in a Modern Constitutional Democracy* (New Haven: Yale University Press, 1987), 8.

41. Theodora R. Jenness, "The Indian Territory," *Atlantic Monthly* 43 (1879): 444–452; Henry B. Carrington, *The Indian Question* (1884; New York: Sol Lewis, 1973), 12–13.

42. *Fourth Annual Report of the Board of Indian Commissioners to the President of the United States* (Washington: Government Printing Office, 1872), 11.

43. Sometimes the government was not careful in setting the external boundaries of reservations either. "More than one fifth of the Navajo tribe live on [land in the] public domain," one tribe member observed in the 1920s, because "when the reservation was made, for some reason, somebody placed an imaginary line through the Indian country leaving these Indians off the reservation." Minutes of the Navajo Tribal Council, 7 July 1926, Thomas H. Dodge collection, box 3, folder 1, ASU.

44. J. B. Harrison, *The Latest Studies on Indian Reservations* (Philadelphia: Indian Rights Association, 1887), 164.

45. Leonard A. Carlson, *Indians, Bureaucrats, and Land: The Dawes Act and the Decline of Indian Farming* (Westport, Conn.: Greenwood Press, 1981), 79–132; David Sloan Wilson, "Hunting, Sharing, and Multilevel Selection: The Tolerated-Theft Model Revisited," *Current Anthropology* 39 (1998): 73–86.

46. "The Condition and Needs of the Indian Tribes," *North American Review* 90 (1860): 69; *Third Annual Report of the Board of Indian Commissioners to the President of the United States* (Washington: Government Printing Office, 1872), 8; Lydia Maria Child, *An Appeal for the Indians* (New York: Wm. P. Tomlinson, 1868), 24; George W. Manypenny, *Our Indian Wards* (Cincinnati: R. Clarke, 1880), xxiv.

47. Edward D. Neill, *Effort and Failure to Civilize the Aborigines: Letter to N. G. Taylor, Commissioner of Indian Affairs* (Washington: Government Printing Office, 1868), 10; Henry S. Pancoast, *Impressions of the Sioux Tribes in 1882* (Philadelphia: Allen, Lane and Scott's Printing House, 1883), 10; Jefferson Davis (yes, that Jefferson Davis), "The Indian Policy of the United States," *North American Review* 143 (1886): 443.

48. *Proceedings of the Third Annual Meeting of the Lake Mohonk Conference* (1885), excerpted in Francis Paul Prucha, ed., *Americanizing the American Indians: Writings by the "Friends of the Indian" 1880–1900* (Cambridge, Mass.: Harvard University Press, 1973), 34; Elaine Goodale, "Plain Words on the Indian Question," *New England Magazine* 8 (1890): 146; Eugene V. Smalley, "A New Solution of the Indian Question," *Century* 30 (1885): 813.

49. Francis A. Walker, "The Indian Question," *North American Review* 116 (1873): 329–388; Francis A. Walker, "Indian Citizenship," *International Review* 1 (1874): 305–326; "Indian Citizenship," *Every Saturday* 3 (1871): 627; Lyman Abbott, "Our Indian Problem," *North American Review* 167 (1898): 726.

8. Allotment

1. Frederick E. Hoxie, *A Final Promise: The Campaign to Assimilate the Indians, 1880–1920* (Cambridge: Cambridge University Press, 1989).
2. Janet A. McDonnell, *The Dispossession of the American Indian 1887–1934* (Bloomington: Indiana University Press, 1991), 121; Leonard A. Carlson, *Indians, Bureaucrats, and Land: The Dawes Act and the Decline of Indian Farming* (Westport, Conn.: Greenwood Press, 1981), 133–162.
3. J. A. Yelling, *Common Field and Enclosure in England, 1450–1850* (London: Macmillan, 1977).
4. Donald N. McCloskey, "The Economics of Enclosure: A Market Analysis," in William N. Parker and Eric L. Jones, eds., *European Peasants and Their Markets: Essays in Agrarian History* (Princeton: Princeton University Press, 1975), 123; J. M. Neeson, *Commoners: Common Right, Enclosure and Social Change in England, 1700–1820* (Cambridge: Cambridge University Press, 1993); Stuart Banner, "Transitions between Property Regimes," *Journal of Legal Studies* 31 (2002): S359–S371.
5. Jeremy Burchardt, *The Allotment Movement in England, 1793–1873* (Woodbridge, UK: Boydell Press, 2002); Denis M. Moran, *The Allotment Movement in Britain* (New York: Peter Lang, 1990), 9–39.
6. John C. Weaver, *The Great Land Rush and the Making of the Modern World, 1650–1900* (Montreal: McGill-Queen's University Press, 2003); E. P. Thompson, *Customs in Common: Studies in Traditional Popular Culture* (New York: New Press, 1993), 164–175; Lilikalā Kame'eleihiwa, *Native Land and Foreign Desires* (Honolulu: Bishop Museum Press, 1992); David V. Williams, *"Te Kooti Tango Whenua": The Native Land Court 1864–1909* (Wellington: Huia, 1999); Peter France, *The Charter of the Land: Custom and Colonization in Fiji* (Melbourne: Oxford University Press, 1969), 129–164.
7. *Laws of the Colonial and State Governments, Relating to Indians and Indian Affairs* (Washington: Thompson and Homans, 1832), 9; Jean M. O'Brien, *Dispossession by Degrees: Indian Land and Identity in Natick, Massachusetts, 1650–1790* (Cambridge: Cambridge University Press, 1997); Jeremy Belknap and Jedidiah Morse, *Report on the Oneida, Stockbridge and Brotherton Indians, 1796* (New York: Museum of the American Indian, 1955), 29.
8. Archibald Loudon, *A Selection, of Some of the Most Interesting Narratives, of Outrages Committed by the Indians, in Their Wars, with the White People* (1808–1811; New York: Arno Press, 1971), 1:241; *DHFFC*, 5:1120; Benjamin Lincoln, "Observations on the Indians of North-America," *Collections of the Massachusetts Historical Society*, 1st series, 5 (1798): 9; *Annals of Congress*, 14th Cong., 2nd Sess. (1816), 14; S. Doc. No. 1, 25th Cong., 3rd Sess. (1838), 454.
9. *AIUS*, 1234.

10. *AIUS*, 93; Paul W. Gates, "Indian Allotments Preceding the Dawes Act," in John G. Clark, ed., *The Frontier Challenge: Responses to the Trans-Mississippi West* (Lawrence: University Press of Kansas, 1971), 141–170; Royce, 645–647.

11. *Smith v. Stevens*, 77 U.S. 321, 326 (1870).

12. Charles W. Shelton, "Is the Indian Dying Out?", *American Missionary* 40 (1886): 66–68; J. Worden Pope, "The North American Indian—The Disappearance of the Race a Popular Fallacy," *Arena* 16 (1896): 945–959; Brian W. Dippie, *The Vanishing American: White Attitudes and U.S. Indian Policy* (Middletown, Conn.: Wesleyan University Press, 1982), 124–129.

13. *New York Times*, 7 July 1873, p. 4, col. 6; *Annual Report of the Commissioner of Indian Affairs to the Secretary of the Interior for the Year 1873* (Washington: Government Printing Office, 1874), 4. Smith's successors made the same point. *AIUS*, 335–336 (Hiram Price's 1882 report), 356–357 (John Atkins's 1885 report).

14. *AIUS*, 219, 1849.

15. Tom Holm, "Indian Lobbyists: Cherokee Opposition to the Allotment of Tribal Lands," *American Indian Quarterly* 5 (1979): 115–134; *Congressional Record*, 45th Cong., 2nd Sess. (1878), 351; *Indian Titles* (n.p., ca. 1882), 25–26; Bushyhead et al. to Henry Dawes et al., 28 Oct. 1897, from the *Indian Chieftain*, 11 Nov. 1897, Dennis W. Bushyhead collection, box 3, file 158, OU.

16. Kenneth H. Bobroff, "Retelling Allotment: Indian Property Rights and the Myth of Common Ownership," *Vanderbilt Law Review* 54 (2001): 1559–1623; Isparhecher to Creek Council, n.d., reported in the *Indian Chieftain*, 14 Oct. 1897, Isparhecher collection, file 21, OU; H.R. Exec. Doc. No. 83, 47th Cong., 1st Sess. (1882), 2; Message, 9 Oct. 1890, Wilson N. Jones collection, file 1, OU.

17. *AIUS*, 1764.

18. Henry King, "The Indian Country," *Century* 30 (1885): 605; Charles F. Meserve, *The Dawes Commission and the Five Civilized Tribes of Indian Territory* (Philadelphia: Indian Rights Association, 1896), 11–15; *AIUS*, 404; H.R. Rep. No. 165, 45th Cong., 3rd Sess. (1879), 2.

19. William Justin Harsha, "Law for the Indians," *North American Review* 134 (1882): 291.

20. Elaine Goodale, "How to Americanize the Indian," *New Englander and Yale Review* 52 (1890): 452. See also William Barrows, *The Indian's Side of the Indian Question* (Boston: D. Lathrop, 1887), 6–7; "The Indian Problem," *American Missionary* 42 (1888): 178; James Wickersham, "The Indian as a Citizen," *American Antiquarian and Oriental Journal* 17 (1895): 331.

21. Carl Schurz, "Present Aspects of the Indian Problem," *North American Review* 133 (1881): 17; "How to Treat the Indians," *Scribner's Monthly* 10 (1875): 486–487; *Eighth Annual Report of the Board of Indian Commissioners* (Washington: Government Printing Office, 1877), 4.

22. Message, 3 Nov. 1897, from the *Indian Chieftain*, 11 Nov. 1897, Isparhecher collection, file 22, OU; Resolution of Choctaw Council, 3 Apr. 1894, from the *Muskogee Phoenix*, 12 Apr. 1894, Wilson N. Jones collection, file 24, OU.

23. Julius H. Seelye, "The Indian Problem," *American Missionary* 41 (1887): 8; *AIUS*, 1673; Michael C. Coleman, "Problematic Panacea: Presbyterian Missionaries and the Allotment of Indian Lands in the Late Nineteenth Century," *Pacific Historical Review* 54 (1985): 143–159.

24. *New York Times*, 15 Dec. 1895, 10; *Indian Citizen*, 2 Dec. 1897, Wilson N. Jones collection, file 36, OU; *Annual Report of the Commissioner of Indian Affairs to the Secretary of the Interior for the Year 1887* (Washington: Government Printing Office, 1887), xii; *AIUS*, 537; *Caddo Banner*, 22 June 1894, Wilson N. Jones collection, file 27, OU; Porter to Isparhecher, 13 June 1891, from the *Purcell Register*, 26 June 1891, Pleasant Porter collection, box 1, file 4, OU.

25. Alexandra Harmon, "American Indians and Land Monopolies in the Gilded Age," *Journal of American History* 90 (2003): 106–133.

26. S. Misc. Doc. No. 16, 45th Cong., 2nd Sess. (1878), 1; *AIUS*, 455.

27. *AIUS*, 1761–1762, 1704; *Denial of Indians to Charges of Dawes Commission* (Washington: Gibson Bros., 1894), 3; *Indian Journal*, 16 June 1887, John F. Brown collection, file 6, OU.

28. *Annual Report of the Commissioner of Indian Affairs to the Secretary of the Interior for the Year 1878* (Washington: Government Printing Office, 1878), viii.

29. *Annual Report of the Commissioner of Indian Affairs to the Secretary of the Interior for the Year 1883* (Washington: Government Printing Office, 1883), xvi; *AIUS*, 392.

30. *Congressional Record*, 45th Cong., 2nd Sess. (1878), 2711.

31. H.R. Misc. Doc. No. 18, 47th Cong., 2nd Sess. (1883), 1.

32. Ibid., 26.

33. *AIUS*, 313–314; H.R. Exec. Doc. No. 21, 49th Cong., 1st Sess. (1886), 8; *Annual Report of the Commissioner of Indian Affairs to the Secretary of the Interior for the Year 1880* (Washington: Government Printing Office, 1880), xvii; Merrill Edwards Gates, *Land and Law as Agents in Educating the Indians* (n.p., 1885), 5.

34. 24 Stat. 388 (1887); *Cherokee Nation v. Hitchcock*, 187 U.S. 294, 307–308 (1902); *Lone Wolf v. Hitchcock*, 187 U.S. 553, 568 (1903). For the contrary view, that a lawyer of the era would have found the compelled distribution of a corporation's assets unconstitutional (and thus that the Supreme Court was exhibiting a bias against Indians), see Joseph William Singer, "*Lone Wolf*, or How to Take Property by Calling It a 'Mere Change in the Form of Investment,'" *Tulsa Law Review* 38 (2002): 43–45.

35. 26 Stat. 794 (1891).

36. 27 Stat. 645 (1893); 30 Stat. 497 (1898); Kent Carter, *The Dawes Commission and the Allotment of the Five Civilized Tribes, 1893–1914* (Orem, Utah: Ancestry.com, 1999).

37. James B. Thayer, "The Dawes Bill and the Indians," *Atlantic Monthly* 61 (1888): 318.

38. Thomas J. Morgan, *The Present Phase of the Indian Question* (Boston: Frank Wood, 1891), 7; *The Fifth Annual Report of the Executive Committee of the Indian Rights Association* (Philadelphia: Indian Rights Association, 1888), 4; Charles C. Painter, *The Dawes Land in Severalty Bill and Indian Emancipation* (Philadelphia: Indian Rights Association, 1887), 1.

39. *AIUS*, 484; Carlson, *Indians, Bureaucrats, and Land*, 74, 204.

40. Alexandra Harmon, *Indians in the Making: Ethnic Relations and Indian Identities around Puget Sound* (Berkeley: University of California Press, 1998), 137–144; E. Jane Gay, *With the Nez Perces: Alice Fletcher in the Field, 1889–92*, ed. Frederick E. Hoxie and Joan T. Mark (Lincoln: University of Nebraska Press, 1981), 54–58;

Emily Greenwald, *Reconfiguring the Reservation: The Nez Perces, Jicarilla Apaches, and the Dawes Act* (Albuquerque: University of New Mexico Press, 2002), 60–67.

41. Barbara Leibhardt, "Allotment Policy in an Incongruous Legal System: The Yakima Indian Nation as a Case Study, 1887–1934," *Agricultural History* 65 (1991): 88; Greenwald, *Reconfiguring the Reservation*, 147–149; David Rich Lewis, *Neither Wolf nor Dog: American Indians, Environment, and Agrarian Change* (New York: Oxford University Press, 1994).

42. Gregory S. Camp, "Working Out Their Own Salvation: The Allotment of Land in Severalty and the Turtle Mountain Chippewa Band, 1870–1920," *American Indian Culture and Research Journal* 14:2 (1990): 29; McDonnell, *The Dispossession of the American Indian*, 20–21; *Davis Weekly News*, 10 Oct. 1901, in Pleasant Porter collection, box 2, file 84, OU; *Dustin Dispatch*, 3 June 1905, in Mrs. Alfred Mitchell collection, box 2, file 36, OU; *Indian Journal*, 24 April 1908, in Mrs. Alfred Mitchell collection, box 1, file 8, OU.

43. The controversy runs through Montezuma's papers. See especially Montezuma to R. A. Ballinger, 30 Jan. 1911, box 3, file 3; C. F. Hauke to Montezuma, 11 March 1911, box 3, file 3; Montezuma to Hauke, 31 March 1911, box 3, file 3; George Dickens to Montezuma, 14 May 1917, box 4, file 3; and Montezuma to Mike Burns, 24 March 1921, box 5, folder 2; all in the Carlos Montezuma collection, ASU. See also Peter Iverson, *Carlos Montezuma and the Changing World of American Indians* (Albuquerque: University of New Mexico Press, 1982), 121–146.

44. 26 Stat. 795 (1891); 28 Stat. 305 (1894); D. S. Otis, *The Dawes Act and the Allotment of Indian Lands* (1934), ed. Francis Paul Prucha (Norman: University of Oklahoma Press, 1973), 99–123.

45. *AIUS*, 701; Benson Tong, "Allotment, Alcohol, and the Omahas," *Great Plains Quarterly* 17 (1997): 21–22; John D. McDermott Jr., "Allotment and the Sissetons: Experiments in Cultural Change, 1866–1905," *South Dakota History* 21 (1991): 67.

46. 32 Stat. 275 (1902).

47. *Okemah Independent*, 14 Oct. 1904, in the Pleasant Porter collection, box 4, file 224, OU; Sean J. Flynn, "Western Assimilationist: Charles H. Burke and the Burke Act," *Midwest Review* 11 (1989): 1–15; *Report of the Thirty-first Annual Lake Mohonk Conference* (Lake Mohonk, N.Y.: Lake Mohonk Conference of Friends of the Indian and Other Dependent Peoples, 1913), 50–51.

48. 34 Stat. 182 (1906); 34 Stat. 1018 (1907).

49. Carlson, *Indians, Bureaucrats, and Land*, 185–186; Office of Indian Affairs, *Indian Land Tenure, Economic Status, and Population Trends: Part X of the Supplementary Report of the Land Planning Committee to the National Resources Board* (Washington: Government Printing Office, 1935), 6.

50. *AIUS*, 890, 814; *Report of the Thirtieth Annual Lake Mohonk Conference of Friends of the Indian and Other Dependent Peoples* (Lake Mohonk, N.Y.: Lake Mohonk Conference of Friends of the Indian and Other Dependent Peoples, 1912), 43; Laurence F. Schmeckebier, *The Office of Indian Affairs: Its History, Activities and Organization* (Baltimore: Johns Hopkins Press, 1927), 150–163.

51. Francis E. Leupp, "The Indian Land Troubles and How to Solve Them," *Amer-*

ican Review of Reviews 42 (1910): 470; Melissa L. Meyer, *The White Earth Tragedy: Ethnicity and Dispossession at a Minnesota Anishinaabe Reservation, 1889–1920* (Lincoln: University of Nebraska Press, 1994), 137–172. Sales of allotments in Minnesota and the Indian Territory were governed by different statutes than the ones discussed above, but policy with respect to the sale of allotments was almost identical and changed at approximately the same time in all parts of the country, so for present purposes we can ignore regional distinctions.

52. *Chicago Chronicle*, n.d., in the Palmer S. Mosely collection, file 9, OU; H. Craig Miner, *The Corporation and the Indian: Tribal Sovereignty and Industrial Civilization in Indian Territory, 1865–1907* (Norman: University of Oklahoma Press, 1989), 192–197.

53. *Collinsville News*, 5 Nov. 1903, in the Pleasant Porter collection, box 4, file 236, OU; Richard Martin to Charles Curtis, n.d., Richard L. Martin collection, file 2, OU.

54. Office of Indian Affairs, *Indian Land Tenure*, 6.

55. Office of Indian Affairs, *Indian Land Tenure*, 8–11; *Hodel v. Irving*, 481 U.S. 704, 713 (1987).

56. Carlson, *Indians, Bureaucrats, and Land*, 146–160.

57. Charles L. Thompson, "The Indian as a Man," *Report of the Thirty-second Annual Lake Mohonk Conference on the Indian and Other Dependent Peoples* (Lake Mohonk, N.Y.: Lake Mohonk Conference on the Indian and Other Dependent Peoples, 1914), 104; G. E. E. Lindquist, *The Red Man in the United States: An Intimate Study of the Social, Economic, and Religious Life of the American Indian* (New York: George H. Doran Co., 1923), 36.

58. Hoxie, *A Final Promise*, 186–187.

59. 48 Stat. 984 (1934).

60. Institute for Government Research, *The Problem of Indian Administration* (Baltimore: Johns Hopkins Press, 1928), 7, 460, 39–40.

61. My account draws on Vine Deloria Jr., ed., *The Indian Reorganization Act: Congresses and Bills* (Norman: University of Oklahoma Press, 2002); Elmer R. Rusco, *A Fateful Time: The Background and Legislative History of the Indian Reorganization Act* (Reno: University of Nevada Press, 2000); Lawrence C. Kelly, *The Assault on Assimilation: John Collier and the Origins of Indian Policy Reform* (Albuquerque: University of New Mexico Press, 1983); Graham D. Taylor, *The New Deal and American Indian Tribalism: The Administration of the Indian Reorganization Act, 1934–45* (Lincoln: University of Nebraska Press, 1980), 1–38; and Kenneth R. Philp, *John Collier's Crusade for Indian Reform 1920–1954* (Tucson: University of Arizona Press, 1977). Felix Cohen, Margold's assistant solicitor of the interior, who drafted much of the Indian Reorganization Act and who spent the rest of his career as an advocate for the Indians, had no experience in Indian affairs before joining the Interior Department.

62. *AIUS*, 1960, 1959; Joseph C. Harsch, "Star of Self-Rule for American Indian Rises," *Christian Science Monitor*, 11 April 1934, weekly magazine section, p. 7. The rise and fall of eastern white humanitarian support for allotment better explains events, in my view, than the effects of allotment and its subsequent abolition on the BIA's budget, the hypothesis advanced in Fred S. McChesney,

"Government as Definer of Property Rights: Indian Lands, Ethnic Externalities, and Bureaucratic Budgets," in Terry L. Anderson, ed., *Property Rights and Indian Economies* (Lanham, Md.: Rowman and Littlefield, 1992), 109–146.

63. Charles H. Berry to Commissioner of Indian Affairs, 5 March 1934, RG 75, entry 1011, box 1, folder 1, NA.

Epilogue

1. Office of Indian Affairs, *Indian Land Tenure, Economic Status, and Population Trends: Part X of the Supplementary Report of the Land Planning Committee to the National Resources Board* (Washington: Government Printing Office, 1935), 7; Klaus Frantz, *Indian Reservations in the United States: Territory, Sovereignty, and Socioeconomic Change* (Chicago: University of Chicago Press, 1999), 44; U.S. Department of the Interior, *Annual Departmental Report on Accountability: Fiscal Year 2001* (Washington: U.S. Department of the Interior, 2002), 46. The figures discussed in these sources are incomplete, because they include only land on reservations owned by tribes or held by the government in trust for allottees. They exclude land owned in fee simple by individual Indians, whether on or off reservations, a figure for which no data appear to exist. The overall trend toward the slowing or even reversal of land loss nevertheless seems clear, as individual Indians almost certainly own much more land today, especially off reservations, than they did in the early twentieth century.

2. H. D. Rosenthal, *Their Day in Court: A History of the Indian Claims Commission* (New York: Garland, 1990); *Cayuga Indian Nation of New York v. Pataki*, 165 F. Supp. 2nd 266 (N.D.N.Y. 2001). As of September 2004 an appeal was pending.

3. Stephen Cornell, *The Return of the Native: American Indian Political Resurgence* (New York: Oxford University Press, 1988).

ACKNOWLEDGMENTS

I am grateful for the assistance of the librarians and archivists at the Public Record Office, the National Archives, the Library of Congress, the Newberry Library, the Huntington Library, the New York State Library and Archives, the University of Oklahoma, Arizona State University, Washington University, and UCLA. Thanks especially to Laura Godfrey, Cindy Cretan, and Mike Campion, my research assistants.

I am also thankful for the helpful suggestions I have received from the many people who read the manuscript or who heard me present parts of it, including Jeremy Bangs, Carole Goldberg, Kent McNeil, Anthony Pagden, Dan Richter, Carol Rose, Rick Sander, and participants at workshops at Washington University, UCLA, USC, Columbia, the University of Michigan, Chicago-Kent Law School, and the University of San Diego, and at the annual meetings of the American Society for Legal History and the Australia and New Zealand Law and History Society. I am very lucky to have had the advice of Joyce Seltzer, Camille Smith, and Wendy Nelson at Harvard University Press.

For financial support, I thank the John Simon Guggenheim Memorial Foundation, the UCLA Center for American Politics and Public Policy, and three deans at two law schools: Joel Seligman at Washington University, and Jon Varat and Norm Abrams at UCLA. Pictures are courtesy of the Library of Congress.

INDEX